HISPANO BASTION

HISPANO BASTION

New Mexican Power in the Age of Manifest Destiny, 1837–1860

Michael J. Alarid

University of New Mexico Press | Albuquerque

© 2022 by the University of New Mexico Press
All rights reserved. Published 2022
Printed in the United States of America

First paperback printing 2024

ISBN 978-0-8263-6432-6 (cloth)
ISBN 978-0-8263-6625-2 (paper)
ISBN 978-0-8263-6433-3 (electronic)
Library of Congress Control Number: 2022944803

Founded in 1889, the University of New Mexico sits on the traditional homelands of the Pueblo of Sandia. The original peoples of New Mexico—Pueblo, Navajo, and Apache—since time immemorial have deep connections to the land and have made significant contributions to the broader community statewide. We honor the land itself and those who remain stewards of this land throughout the generations and also acknowledge our committed relationship to Indigenous peoples. We gratefully recognize our history.

Cover design by Mindy Basinger Hill
Interior text design by Isaac Morris
Display font: Composed in Adobe Caslon 10 | 12

DEDICATION

To Michael Jr. and Thomas, that they may never forget who they are and from whence they came.

And for my ancestors and the other families of New Mexico, who found themselves in the path of an empire.

CONTENTS

List of Illustrations	ix
Preface	xiii
Acknowledgments	xvii
Introduction	1
CHAPTER ONE The Rise of the Patrónes and the Burden of the *Vecinos*	15
CHAPTER TWO *Vecino* Larceny and the Process of Territorialization	45
CHAPTER THREE Between a Rock and a Gun: *Vecino* and White Homicide	79
CHAPTER FOUR 1856	109
CHAPTER FIVE At the Wrong End of the Lash	136
Epilogue	169
Appendix	175
Notes	179
References	219
Index	229

ILLUSTRATIONS

Figures

9   Figure I.1. Approximate divide between the Rio Arriba and Rio Abajo, 1854

57 Figure 2.1. Santa Fe County real estate owned, 1850 vs. 1860

58 Figure 2.2. Anglo property owned by occupation in 1850

58 Figure 2.3. Hispano property owned by occupation in 1850

60 Figure 2.4. Distribution of real estate among Hispanos by age

60 Figure 2.5. Distribution of real estate among Hispanos by gender in 1850

63 Figure 2.6. Ages of Hispanic adult males in Santa Fe County in 1850

63 Figure 2.7. Ages of Anglo adult males in Santa Fe County in 1850

64 Figure 2.8. Composition of the US Army in Santa Fe County, 1850

68 Figure 2.9. Types of *vecino* larceny, 1847–1860

69 Figure 2.10. Cases adjudicated by Anglo judges in Santa Fe County, by percentage, 1847–1854

73 Figure 2.11. Hispano and white larceny rates compared, adults 16 and older, per 100,000, 1838–1863

73 Figure 2.12. Types of white larceny, 1847–1860

77 Figure 2.13. List of thirty-five people in the Santa Fe County jail in 1850

83 Figure 3.1. Homicide in commercial and agricultural centers in California, 1850–1865, compared to Santa Fe County, 1847–1853

84 Figure 3.2. Estimated Mexicano population in the Southwest, by percentage, 1848

84 Figure 3.3. 1850 vs. 1860, Hispano, Anglo, and Native American populations in Santa Fe County, by percentage

88 Figure 3.4. New Mexican Council members ethnicity, by percentage, 1847, 1851–1860

88 Figure 3.5. New Mexico House of Representatives members by ethnicity, by percentage, 1847, 1851–1860

ILLUSTRATIONS

88   Figure 3.6. Santa Fe County representatives in the House of Representatives, by percentage, 1847, 1851–1860

100 Figure 3.7. An artist's portrayal of a traditional fandango as would occur in the Mexican countryside

107 Figure 3.8. Homicide rates per year among Hispanos and Anglos in Santa Fe County, adults 16 and older, per 100,000

112 Figure 4.1. Hispano assault and homicide rates in Santa Fe, New Mexico, 1847–1860 per 100,000 per persons per year

112 Figure 4.2. Hispano violent crime rates, including assault and homicide, by year, 1847–1860

112 Figure 4.3. Hispano and white homicide rates grouped, per persons per 100,000, 1847–1860

112 Figure 4.4. Hispano and white assault rates grouped, per persons per 100,000, 1847–1860

112 Figure 4.5. Hispano and white violent crime rates compared, per persons per 100,000, 1847–1860

117 Figure 4.6. Distribution of total wealth, males over 15, Santa Fe County, 1860

138 Figure 5.1. Known punishments by ethnicity, by percentage, Santa Fe County, 1846–1854

149 Figure 5.2. Total *vecino* known trial conviction rates in Santa Fe County, by Percentage 1846–1860

150 Figure 5.3. *Vecino* trial conviction percentages for homicide, larceny, assault, and other crimes, by period, 1846–1860

150 Figure 5.4. White trial conviction percentages for homicide, larceny, assault, and other crimes, by period, 1846–1860

150 Figure 5.5. Conviction by percentage, *vecinos* in Santa Fe County vs. Chatham County, GA (black only), Greene County, GA (black only), South Carolina (black only), and the slave courts in Virginia and Colonial Jamaica

159 Figure 5.6. *Vecino* and white punishments (without larceny), 1846–1860

165 Figure 5.7. Known homicide verdicts, 1846–1860, *vecino* and white

Photographs follow page 78

TABLES

21 Table 1.1. Occupational Structure of Santa Fe County, 1790, 1827, and 1850

22 Table 1.2. Occupational Structure in Santa Fe County, Including Large Landholders, 1850

22 Table 1.3. Large Landholders in Santa Fe County, Including Those without a Profession, Males Over 20 Years of Age Only, 1850

62 Table 2.1. Land Distribution among Males Only in 1850, Santa Fe County

66 Table 2.2. Hispano and White Larceny in Santa Fe County, by Perpetrator Ethnicity and Crime, Adults 16 and older, per 100,000

80 Table 3.1. Homicide Rates per Year among Hispanos and Anglos in Santa Fe County, Adults over 16 and older, per 100,000

81 Table 3.2. Western Homicide Rates per Year, Per 100,000, Persons Ages 16 and Older

85 Table 3.3. 1850 vs. 1860 Census Data, Santa Fe County

90 Table 3.4. Homicide Rates per Year among Californios and Non-Mexicano Whites in California, Adults 16 and Older, per 100,000 vs. Homicide Rates among Hispanos and Non-Mexicano Whites in Santa Fe County, Adults 16 and Older, per 100,000

91 Table 3.5. Known Homicide Rates and Known Manslaughter Rates per Year among Hispanos and Anglos (Non-Mexican Whites) in Santa Fe County, Adults 16 and older, per 100,000

110 Table 4.1. Homicide Rates among Hispanos and Anglos in Santa Fe County, Adults over 16 and older, per persons per 100,000

115 Table 4.2 Changes in Hispano Male Population by Age and Land Distribution by Age Group, 1850-1860

125 Table 4.3. Western Homicide Rates, Per Persons per 100,000, Ages 16 and Over

PREFACE

My friend and I had just taken our lunch in Albuquerque, a meal of carne adovada stuffed sopapillas, when he asked if I'd like to take a drive to the National Hispanic Cultural Center. The structure was still new, and I had not yet seen the final product. As he drove, my friend shared his version of the story of Adela Martinez and her family, which went something like this: The concept of the center originated in the community, but as the project progressed, "elites and Hispano-philes" shouldered their way in and ultimately took control. They used the courts to buy out and remove residents of the old barrio, but the Martinez family refused to, in his words, "sell their heritage." Adela Martinez then beat them at their own game: she too used the courts, traditionally a tool of those in power, to thwart their plans. The developers were forced to alter designs and build the center around the Martinez homestead. Now every visitor is confronted with the Martinez lot, juxtaposed with the dramatic background of the center's campus, with its "Santa Fake" facades and "Disney-like architectural interpretations" of Nuevomexicano culture. As my friend talked to one Martinez family member at the house that day, it was clear they were both amused by the contrast between the neo-Pueblo temple and the simple Barelas style yard-scape. The Martinez lot was, to use his words, "The actual heritage site." As our visit ended, Martinez pointed out the biggest perk of the arrangement: free twenty-four-hour security. He quipped, "The neighborhood has never been safer!"[1]

The story of Adela Martinez and her resistance against the National Hispanic Cultural Center is well known in New Mexico, and there are many versions of it, but I tell this specific one to highlight the power struggle it came to represent for many everyday Nuevomexicanos. On one side were those with power and influence, and on the other were everyday Nuevomexicanos. Similar chasms separate Latino communities across the nation, and these class differences often supersede ethnic ties in the borderlands.

Resistance, however, is not static, and it can manifest in many ways. What began as Adela's direct resistance to power was transformed into something akin to the phenomena in Sarajevo known as Inat Kuća, or a "Spite House."[2] With a Spite House, the home remains, is maintained, and even presented in a manner meant to disrupt the vision of those who seek to wipe the memory of a place or people from a landscape. It's still a type of resistance, but one enacted after a battle for space is complete. It's a way for those without power to thumb their nose at the ones who have it. Others view the Martinez home differently. A recent article portrays the end product as a peaceful resolution and claims that continuity and harmony were ultimately achieved through incorporation.[3] But the massive walls and trees they placed around the Martinez property suggest that the Martinez home remains a bulwark of the past against the reimagined landscape of New Mexico, and for some perhaps an inconvenient reminder of the old barrio.

New Mexico has other Spite Houses, and they extend beyond Albuquerque. In Santa Fe, for example, by the year 2000 there was only one Alarid left in the wealthy neighborhoods near the plaza. I encountered this elderly man while on a drive with the late Waldo Alarid, who was the longtime keeper of our family history. As Waldo explained, this Alarid was the last holdout in our family, a man who simply refused to let the droves of white tourists turn his ancestral house into a vacation home. As we drove up, we could hear the echo of a heavy hammer striking against his roof. "Oh, he's on the roof again," Waldo laughed. "He's always up there hammering. He drives his neighbors nuts!" We pulled up alongside the house, and there on the roof of the old single story adobe home was a man in excess of eighty years, wearing jeans, a blue button-up shirt, and a stained and well-used straw cowboy hat. "Hola, Alarid!" yelled Waldo from the car window. "I NO SELL!" shouted the *viejito*, shaking his fist in resistance. "Oh, he doesn't recognize me," said Waldo with a laugh. "He can't see like he used to. People are always trying to buy him out. We better leave him alone." As we drove away, he hammered just a little bit harder than before, which his neighbors no doubt appreciated.

Resistance. Spite Houses. Those of us with Latino roots in the old borderlands know many stories like this. But even after the strikes of a hammer grow silent, our history remains. Somewhere, beneath the concrete shroud of American colonialism that blankets the Plaza in Santa Fe, deep beneath the landscaping, is the ground that our ancestors traversed. The window on the southern face of the Palace of the Governors offers a glimpse of the old structure. The peoples of the Pueblo and Navajo nations remind us of our tradition as merchants and traders. On the other side of the palace doors are artifacts of our people, most of which belonged to our ancestors. True, high-end shops, hotels of faux adobe, and wealthy *extranjeros* overshadow the scene for most of the year. But during events like the New Mexico LowRider Art and Cultural Exhibit, Nuevomexicanos again dominate the Plaza, and in those moments we reclaim our space.

If families are trees, the Alarid family roots lie beneath the foundation of what is now Hotel La Fonda on the Plaza. For generations we owned and operated the first boarding place on that land. It was simply known as Alarid House, and through the eighteenth century we held title to the land from the modern Hotel La Fonda to what is now Water Street. Most in our family were soldiers of the Presidio during that period, and it is well-documented that we actively supported the American Revolution. My ancestor, Jose Ignacio Alarid, is said to have served with distinction in the effort to raise funds for the American colonists. By 1833, our family had divested from Alarid House, which was subsumed by the Exchange Hotel, a structure that features prominently in the pages that follow.[4]

My ancestors knew no other home but Santa Fe until 1846, when the Americans colonized our homeland. That year my great-great grandfather, Matias Alarid, was forced to resettle our family in the small mountain town of Rowe, New Mexico. We know that the Americans compelled Matias to swear an oath of loyalty to the United States before he departed. The historical record isn't clear on the reason, but it is the understanding in our family that he, like most Nuevomexicanos, disliked outsiders. Moreover, the timing of his oath suggests he may have been part of an early plot to expel the Americans, but we will get to that later.

In Rowe, Matias Alarid became a blacksmith and there my great grandfather, Antonio Jose De La Cruz Alarid, was born in 1857. Jose Cruz Alarid (Cruzito), for whom my father was named, was five years old when the Americans encroached on our family again. In March of 1862 the Confederates pursued Union forces to Pigeon's Ranch, thirteen miles north of Rowe. Always the soldiers, our greater family supported the Union. They funded "Alarid's Independent Company," and joined the ranks for the Battle of Glorieta Pass, where the Confederates were turned back.

Cruzito grew up and became a blacksmith in Rowe, like his father before him. My grandfather, Jose Magdaleno Alarid, was born in 1889 and was raised in the shadows of the Sangre de Cristo Mountains. Like his father and grandfather before him, Magdaleno had an affinity for horses. Or, as the writer in the *St. John's Herald and Apache News* put it, of my grandfather and two others, "These gentlemen were suspected of having disappeared some time ago with a number of horses to which their title was not entirely clear."[5] The sheriff and his posse gave "a hot chase" to my grandfather and his friends, but they escaped into the brush and trees of the Zuni Mountains. I have little doubt that my grandfather led this escape, for they fled to Bernalillo, a known safe haven for Nuevomexicanos and outlaws alike.[6]

The law finally caught up with grandpa in Bernalillo, and he was arrested and subsequently transported back to Holbrook, Arizona. There, in the old Nuevomexicano tradition, my grandfather admitted his guilt, after which he was sentenced to prison. Ever the soldier, Magdeleno then followed another family tradition when he volunteered to fight in World War II, this time against the Nazis. He was relegated to logistical support for the army, but the sounds of war haunted him the rest of his days. By 1943, at the age of fifty-four, my grandfather left his first family in Colorado and went to California. There he met my grandmother, who was much younger than he. They had two children, my father and my aunt, but the trauma of his service drove him to drinking.

When my father was five, Magdaleno returned to New Mexico and started a third family. With little memory of his father or knowledge of our family heritage, my father went to work in the fields of northern California to help make the ends meet. After he graduated high school he began a job at a department store, but when the Vietnam War escalated, he was drafted and unwittingly became yet another Alarid to fight on behalf of the very empire that colonized our homeland. Before he left for the war he married my mother, Mary Carmen Saldivar, a member of the old Saldivar and Flores families from Bexar, Texas.[7] He returned from Vietnam long ago, but the memories of war have made sleep difficult for him to find.[8]

Beyond these facts, I cannot begin to explain the unlikely set of circumstances that brought me to this moment. Four generations removed from the US-Mexican War and one from the cotton field, I am a history professor at University of Nevada, Las Vegas, and I have spent the past decade building what I hope is a worthy contribution to the historiography of my homeland. This is certainly not the book I thought I would write. Originally, I believed I was going to tell the story of an epic and united Hispano resistance to American authority. A story of a people who fought for their land but who were compelled by numbers and resources to accept the framework of their new reality. A people who still trend toward resistance, but within the context of the new nation-state. New Mexico seemed to be the place to do such a study, but the more I processed the documents and data from this period of New Mexico's past, the clearer it became that it simply didn't happen that way.

What follows is an attempt to reconstruct the history of New Mexico in a moment of transformation, one in which the old bonds, social relations, and inequality of the Mexican period gave way to new forms of opportunism and created the foundations for the extreme inequality and disjointed social relations we see today.

Michael J. Alarid
Las Vegas, NV

ACKNOWLEDGMENTS

I am indebted from the start to Randolph Roth for his training and support during my career at Ohio State University. He influenced my intellectual development, trained me in quantitative methods, and taught me what it meant to be a historian. In addition, I benefited from the mentorship of Kenneth Andrien, who supported me personally and professionally during my many years at Ohio State. Without his friendship and support, this project would not have been possible. I am also indebted to the late John F. Guilmartin, a fellow southwesterner, a true American hero, and one of the great gentlemen of the profession. His intellect and humor are missed by all who knew him. I must also thank Alan R. Millett, the folklorist Patrick Mullen, and the great William B. Taylor for their early support. Additionally, I must thank David J. Weber, who took time during his cancer treatment to offer his feedback and his encouragement. His work inspired many who study the Southwest, including myself, and in this way his legacy has only begun to unfold.

    I am grateful to the State of New Mexico and all of my friends in Santa Fe and Albuquerque. To Samuel Sisneros, for his guidance in the archives and for our long discussions about what it means to be Nuevomexicano. To Tomas Jeahn of the Fray Angélico Chávez Library and now the Zimmerman Library, a master of the archives in New Mexico and a dear friend. His knowledge is reflected in these pages. To Estevan Rael Galvez, who was a major source of intellectual and personal support in my early career. A special thanks to my editor at the University of New Mexico Press, Sonia Dickey, who always believed in this project and worked tirelessly to see it through. I was supported by funding from the Graduate School and the Department of History at Ohio State University; the History Department, College of Liberal Arts, and the Honors College at the University of Nevada, Las Vegas; and the American Folklore Society.

    I am tremendously indebted to Susan Lee Johnson, the Harry Reid Endowed Chair of Intermountain West History, whose arrival to UNLV came not a moment too soon. Her contributions to this project are immeasurable. In addition to her comments and critiques, in her capacity as an endowed chair, she organized and facilitated a workshop that proved transformative for this book. I am tremendously thankful for the support of those who participated in that workshop, including Maria E. Montoya and Omar Valerio-Jimenez, who took time out of their busy schedules to act as my primary outside readers. I am also grateful to Raquel Casas for acting as my primary inside reader, as well as all of my UNLV colleagues who participated and shared their feedback: William

ACKNOWLEDGMENTS

Bauer, Gregory S. Brown, Carlos Dimas, Michael Green, Andrew Kirk, Mark Padoongpatt, David S. Tanenhaus, and Tessa Ong Winkleman. I am blessed to call them all friends. I greatly benefited from the support of Annette Amdel, who makes the wheels turn in our department, as well as so many others at UNLV.

I am still more fortunate than all that. I am thankful to Steven L. Hyland, an old colleague from graduate school, a reader of many of my articles and final chapters, and the best left tackle in the game. Carlos Dimas also served an important role in the last push to complete the manuscript, as did Jeffrey Schauer: both suggested final cuts and edits even when they had no time to do so. I am fortunate to have them both as colleagues, and I count them among my closest friends. Among my other friends, I have benefited from the longtime support of Kyle Sisk, Quentyn Daniels, Carson Dye, Jessie Eck, Jake and Andrea Fray, David Hudson, Robert Martz, Mike Mitchell, Kurt Mueller, Matthew Peters, Paul Rogers, and Jason Seaman.

My family was central and they supported me throughout this process. In fact, they helped shape who I am as a person and scholar. I am thankful for my parents, Joseph and Mary; my sisters, Jeanette and Joetta, and their partners Rodney and Louis; and my brother Joseph and his partner Alicia. I am eternally grateful for my nieces and nephews for all their love and support: to Christopher, Joelle, Nicolas, Jessica, Jocelyn, Joey, Louie, Lauren, and Taylor. I have also been blessed with the best in-laws one could ask for: To Russell and Francis Bock, who have made my life so much better, and to my sister-in-law Tamara and her family. Finally, I am blessed by my neighbor-in-law, Amy Ayoub, who makes our family life here in Las Vegas better every day.

More than anyone in the world, I am thankful for my wife, Sheila Bock, and the life and family we have built together. It's impossible to convey how supportive my wife was throughout the entirety of this project. Even when work nights ended at sunrise, she held our family together, especially as I made my final big push. She and our two boys are the true lights of my life, and there are no words to express my love for them. I must also include our dog, Harley, who has been by my side from the first page to this final moment. I close with a direct message to my two sons. To Michael Joseph Alarid Jr. (age seven) and Thomas Michael Alarid (age four), thank you for patiently waiting on me to shed the cloak of professor each day and to emerge as both the silly monster who chases you about the house and the father who holds your hands and doesn't leave the room till you're fast asleep. May this book make you both proud.

Introduction

Mustering his servants and gathering several wagonloads of cedar pickets, Manuel Chaves ordered the construction of a fence to block the Catholic Church from claiming the western boundary of his vast property. Chaves was never one to be intimidated, even when confronted by ecclesiastical authorities. When the priest from Guadalupe Chapel in Santa Fe, New Mexico, encroached upon his land, Chaves took action. He constructed a large, purposefully unsightly barrier as close to the chapel as possible. The frustrated cleric admonished Chaves and complained to his superior, Bishop Jean Baptiste Lamy, who summoned Chaves and threatened excommunication if the obstruction was not immediately dismantled:

> "You have encroached upon lands of the church," thundered the bishop.
> "I have fenced what is legally mine," retorted Manuel.
> "You will remove the offending barrier."
> "I will not!"
> "You will comply under pain of excommunication."
> And a final burst from Manuel, "The fence remains, and you will not excommunicate me. It would break my poor wife's heart." And he stalked from the interview.[1]

Lamy was determined to make an example of Chaves, so he completed orders for the landowner's excommunication and had them delivered to the Guadalupe Chapel for pronouncement. Rumors of the confrontation circulated before the Sunday sermon, which began peacefully enough but was interrupted when Chaves, a friend, and two of his men entered the chapel. Armed with rifles, the members of the Chaves faction followed him down the center aisle and seated themselves in the Chaves family pew. Each sat attentively. Their rifles rested across their laps as they waited for the pronouncement. But when the priest unfurled his orders, the sound of Manuel Chaves cocking the hammer of his rifle echoed past the podium, a warning that discouraged the ecclesiastic from performing his duty and ended the threat of excommunication.[2]

This memory of resistance survived 110 years through oral tradition before it found its way into publication in 1973, when historian Marc Simmons—who learned it from Consuelo Chaves Summers—shared it in his book *The Little Lion of the Southwest*.[3] It reads like a story from the Mexican period, when one might expect a prominent large landholding Nuevomexicano and his henchmen

INTRODUCTION

to brandish their firearms and intimidate a local cleric. That Chaves and his men defied Lamy in 1858—after more than a decade of American suzerainty in Santa Fe, New Mexico—might seem more unexpected. To boot, this story is far from an anomaly. New Mexican history abounds with many stories of Chaves-like Nuevomexicanos seemingly pushing back against the forces of colonization. Indeed, the closer one looks at the New Mexican landholders, their social structure, their caudillo-like behavior, and how their decisions affected the lives of everyday people, the more one sees that stories like this provide windows into how large landholders projected power in New Mexico territory.

Simmons dealt with this incident by situating Chaves within the context of a heroic tale of resistance to foreign colonization; indeed, the story of Manuel Chaves bringing his guns into the church seems to dovetail nicely with romantic ideas of Hispano resistance to American authority.[4] Fray Angélico Chávez recounted the dispute to illustrate the abuses of power that accompanied what he astutely termed the *ecclesiastical colonialism* of New Mexico.[5] But the retellings of both Chávez and Simmons only tell part of what is a story that offers a window into the far more complex reality of the dynamic history of New Mexico. To truly understand this story, it is important to also understand the context within which it took place.

The story of Manuel Chaves had many meanings: It was certainly in part a flagrant act of resistance, but it was also an indicator of the powerful position that Manuel Chaves and other Nuevomexicano landholders occupied in New Mexican society during the early years of American consolidation. Additionally, it was indicative of the unity that arose between *patrónes* like Chaves and their Nuevomexicano allies when they felt threatened by outside forces during the first ten years of American dominion. Importantly, it was not an isolated occurrence: it exemplified the bold actions that Nuevomexicanos were willing to take against outsiders, and it demonstrates the willingness of many poorer Nuevomexicanos to both support these bold actions and—in some cases—even mimic them. The majority of landholding Hispanos did not care that the flag had changed in the plaza. Many were in fact pleased at the opportunities they thought American capitalism might bring.[6] But whenever outsiders infringed on their autonomy they rallied their allies and took to their horses. Invariably, violence, intimidation, and unrest followed.

This book is the story of many cultures caught within the maelstrom of colonization, of complex peoples with their own power structures who occupied a space in the path of a burgeoning empire. More specifically, this is the tale of how ethnically distinct, religiously different, and politically and economically keen Nuevomexicanos together endured the imposition of new formal institutions that accompanied the process of both Mexican and American colonization, only later to be fractured by the draws of capitalism. My focus is 1837 to 1860, and I examine the relationship between large landholding Hispanos,[7] poor

Nuevomexicanos, and incoming immigrants, first from Mexico and later from the United States and abroad.[8] During the Mexican period, I focus on the relationships between Hispanos, Mexican officials, and newly arrived white traders. During the American period, I focus on the relationships between large landholding Hispanos, increasingly poorer Nuevomexicanos, old white settlers, and new white immigrants who sought to utilize political, economic, and military coercion to carve out a space for themselves in the newly acquired territory.

My overarching thesis is that large landholding Hispanos maintained a great deal of political, economic, and social autonomy in the age of Manifest Destiny; I argue that with its sixty thousand residents, New Mexico itself constituted a *Hispano Bastion* in a greater Southwest awash in a deluge of violent white settlers and soldiers in search of the spoils of war. I argue that the key to the Nuevomexicano transition under the American regime was that the large landholding patrónes embraced American capitalism, which offered all the class advantages they enjoyed under Mexican rule but with none of the responsibilities of caring for people in need.[9] I show that the large landholding Nuevomexicanos benefited financially from the American territorial government during this period of study. Ultimately, I contend that these large landholders abandoned their traditional responsibilities as patrónes to the poor and working peoples. And yet, as the story of Manuel Chaves shows, there was still plenty of room for Nuevomexicano landholders to use violence and intimidation to achieve their ends within this new American political structure. This was the backdrop for everyday life in Santa Fe County.

Reconstructing *Vecino* Actors

In New Mexico, the economic florescence that straddled 1800 began to produce a class of economically and politically connected landowners, and these are the people I label the patrónes in this book. It is not that such distinctions did not exist earlier, but there was so much less wealth and power they had control over that the material and experiential consequences for others—vecinos, Indios de los pueblos, *genízaros*, unfree people—are much less discernible in the kinds of records from before the mid-nineteenth century to which we have access.[10] So I do not use the Spanish term "vecino" as an all-encompassing word for citizens, but instead to describe the poor and working populations in New Mexico, as opposed to the patrónes who governed their lives.[11] I do so in recognition of the increased class differences that arose in nineteenth-century New Mexico, which widened the gap between patrónes and vecinos. I do not, however, include Indigenous peoples in this category, because most were captives who were treated far more harshly within Santa Fe County and did not have the same rights as vecinos.[12]

In my quest to reconstruct the vecino experience in nineteenth-century New Mexico, I focused my analysis on two sources of data: the Mexican and US censuses and criminal court records from both the Mexican and American periods. I first used the census to understand changes in demographics, occupation, class divisions, and distribution of wealth over time. For the purpose of this study, I categorized anyone with less than one hundred dollars in wealth into the vecino population, because statistically there was a great divide along that line when I analyzed the US Census data. I next used the census in concert with crime data in order to create a quantitative picture of violence and crime in New Mexico during these moments of extreme sociopolitical and economic change. To complete that analysis, I relied heavily on the collection, transcription, organization, and analysis of both census data and the criminal court records in the Mexican and US periods of rule. This allowed me to create data that spanned more than three decades, so that I could track change over time. With these data I constructed probability tables to assess risk of homicide, which was my initial point of enquiry.[13] Simply put, what was the risk of being murdered in Santa Fe County in the early years of American territorialization? How quantitatively dangerous was New Mexico for vecinos, but also for patrónes and white settlers, and how did these numbers fluctuate over time? To answer this initial question, I needed to calculate risk over time in Santa Fe County.

Homicide rates and risk are vital indicators of both community stability and safety, but their importance extends far beyond that. Criminologist Gary Lafree and historian Randolph Roth show that homicide had a strong correlation with two different variables. The first was the percentage of people who trusted their government, which correlated with homicide rates over time. They demonstrate that when trust was high, homicide was correspondingly low, but that when trust was low, homicide increased. The second variable was the percentage of people who believed government officials are crooked; when the percentage of people who distrust government increased, homicide rates also increased.[14] Further, Roth postulates that the confidence that people have in their government—including their legal and judicial institutions—to work on their behalf to provide redress against those who have wronged them is strongly correlated to homicide.[15] He notes, "If no government can establish uncontested authority and impose law and order, if political elites are deeply divided and there is no continuity of power or orderly succession, men can lose all faith in the effectiveness or impartiality of political, legal, and judicial institutions." In these situations, "They may take up arms on behalf of particular political factions or racial groups and kill without restraint."[16] These theories of homicide are among the central theoretical frameworks of this book, and I use them to explain the ebbs and flows of vecino and white homicide in New Mexico.

To construct the necessary data, I used the formula for homicide rates, which is homicide rate = (number of homicides/population at risk) x 100,000/ number of years the data encompass.[17] Once I had the risk for Santa Fe County, I explored the rise and fall of these rates over time. I next linked these data to homicide rates in other parts of the borderlands, as well as North America more broadly. This allowed me to contextualize homicide in New Mexico, to get a better idea of how homicidal Nuevomexicanos and newly arrived settlers in Santa Fe County truly were in relation to other parts of the borderlands and beyond.[18] This, however, was only the starting point.

In the course of my research, I also calculated rates for other crimes of record, which included larceny, assault, and commerce violations. As a result, I found myself able to answer questions about the vecino community that went far beyond homicide risk. For example, I was able to calculate the chances of being arrested, convicted, and punished for a specific crime based on a person's ethnic or socioeconomic class identity. I was also able to calculate larceny rates and increases and decreases in larceny over time, by both ethnicity and gender, which allowed me to focus in on periods when larceny was higher and on years when it precipitously fell.[19] I was able to compare these crimes by ethnicity, which allowed me to determine which groups were more given to criminal activity in a given period. Although no great theories yet exist regarding larceny, assault, and commerce violations, I found that assault in Santa Fe County correlated with homicide, a possible indicator that similar patterns may exist between assault and people's faith in their government, as they do with homicide. For larceny and commerce violations, I offer new hypotheses that I hope will inspire further research and a more widespread exploration of their cause and importance.[20]

I relied heavily on my spreadsheets to explore all manner of questions that arose over the course of this study, but my central mission was to understand how the vecino community experienced the transition of New Mexico from a Mexican department into an American territory. Through these data, I was able to track vecino crime over time to understand how they reacted to the imposition of both American authority and to the changes in their relationship with the patrónes. This is the methodological framework with which my study was constructed, and these data showed that the patrónes and the vecinos had vastly different, and primarily class-based, experiences and responses with and to the process of territorialization.

INTRODUCTION

The Increasing Power and Wealth of the Patrónes

While numbers can be used for close analysis of crime in the vecino community, the vecinos still lived within the political and economic realities of Spain, Mexico, and the United States respectively, but the one constant in their community was the local patrónes. Early on, Spanish efforts to centralize power and collect taxes were a point of emphasis in Mexico during the Bourbon Reforms, but Mexican independence removed the specter of Spanish intervention and allowed local patrónes to emerge throughout the diverse expanses of the Mexican Republic.[21] New Mexico's large landholders, which included families such as the Armijos, Archuletas, Ortizes, and their lot, emerged as legitimate power brokers in New Mexico. They did so organically and as representatives of all vecinos. They filled the power vacuum left by Mexican independence, and in their new roles they began to accumulate a greater proportion of land wealth, which ultimately changed the social fabric of the vecino community in New Mexico.[22] In short, they became typical Latin American caudillos.[23] Over time, their land ownership and influence became increasingly hereditary, especially after the Americans invaded, and the class differences between patrónes and vecinos were exacerbated to a point that ultimately fractured the community.

The patrónes' authority was predicated on the confidence and support they received from the larger vecino community during the Mexican period. For their part, the vecinos remained loyal because they believed that the local patrónes provided them with their best chance for stability. They tolerated the recurring factionalism that erupted between centralist-minded conservative and liberal-leaning patrónes, so long as the patrónes preserved local stability.[24] The vecinos and patrónes lived symbiotically—if unequally—alongside one another for generations. Specifically, poorer vecinos depended on the patrónes both for subsistence and to organize defense against Apache, Comanche, Navajo, Pueblo attacks, while the patrónes depended on the vecinos for labor and to fill the ranks of their militias when threats to New Mexico arose.[25] The patrónes profited greatly from this arrangement, while the vecinos were plunged deeper into poverty and merely subsisted. Vecinos suffered an increasing classism at the hands of the patrónes, and the situation worsened after 1846. Once the Americans arrived, vecinos also endured racism and violence from both American state institutions and newly arrived settlers. Rather then protect the vecinos from these new threats, the patrónes ultimately betrayed their traditional responsibilities to everyday vecinos.

Still, the vecinos were never altogether powerless. As I will show, when life proved too difficult and opportunities too scant in the 1850s, disaffected vecinos turned violent, then ultimately left Santa Fe County. Even before the community fractured, the increase in those accused of larceny, assault, homicide, and other crimes represented a surge in the frustrations felt by the vecino community. The criminal court data reveal that vecinos were aggravated as a whole, but of course not everyone who experienced that frustration broke the law. Those that broke the law or took the law into their own hands were merely the ones who acted on their frustrations. Accused criminals thus are a good point of access to the reactions of the vecino community to change over time, because they represented the level of frustration within the vecino community as a whole. Accused criminals were but the tip of the iceberg, a small representation of the mountain of frustration beneath the surface.

There remained many vecinos who supported the patrónes, as is evidenced by the fact that so many vecinos continued to turn out and vote for the old patrónes family members during American territorialization. As a result, emerging political positions within the American territorial government were filled by a combination of patrónes and their old white trading partners, many of whom had either married into the landholding families or had participated in joint ventures with them.[26] Often both. As a result, the patrónes dominated the territorial legislature, which implemented policies that demonstrated the continued power of the patrónes in New Mexico. Still, during the Mexican territorial period, the caudillos dominated the political landscape, with the Ortiz, Chávez, Otero, and Armijo clans dictating the direction of local affairs in concert.[27]

In addition, many of the priests, who were themselves from large landholding families, actively participated in politics. This was especially true after New Mexico was removed from the Archdiocese of Durango and resituated into the Archdiocese of Baltimore in 1850.[28] The new Archdiocese appointed Jean Baptiste Lamy as archbishop of New Mexico, and from his new position of power he famously disenfranchised the Nuevomexicano padres. When that happened, many turned to politics in order to have a voice in local affairs. These Hispanos proved popular and held elected positions, while longtime white residents controlled the appointed positions. The Hispanos continued to dominate elected positions through 1860, even as longtime white residents lost their positions to federal appointees. As for the new white settlers, they did not fare well in elections, because for the vecinos it was better to vote for patrónes than for extranjeros, that is, strangers or newcomers.

Militarily, the local patrónes remained actively involved in the fight against the Navajo, Apache, and Ute peoples, who were prone to raiding throughout northern Mexico.[29] During the Mexican period, the Nuevomexicanos forged treaties with the Comanche, and the Pueblos followed, but for the most part the Nuevomexicanos remained at war with the Navajo, Apache, and Ute.[30] In New

Mexico the patrónes complained to Mexico City of "Indian depredations," but Indigenous reprisals were hardly unprovoked. The large landholders and vecinos had monopolized precious resources, such as water, food, and the weapons necessary for protection in this politically tense period.[31] The addition of Nuevomexicano colonizers challenged New Mexico's carrying capacity, and the land simply did not have the resources to support both the Indigenous and the newly arrived and entrepreneurial Nuevomexicanos, who had established their settlements on lands traditionally utilized by the Pueblo, Apache, and Navajo peoples.[32] When the Hispanos came, the Indigenous armed themselves and commenced raids against the Hispano settlements. Natives then traded stolen goods for food, supplies, and firearms to be used in future raids.[33]

Economically, Nuevomexicanos actively sought ways to translate their landholdings into various forms of wealth, including household wares, liquid capital, and luxury goods. Initially, landholders developed their ranches and produced goods that were intended for trade. These Hispanos proved enterprising, forging paths to markets in California, Chihuahua, and Missouri. Nuevomexicano merchants formed trade partnerships with newly arrived white immigrants, who began settling in Santa Fe as early as the 1820s, and these early partnerships ultimately provided inroads into the American market.[34]

While vecinos hauled nuts, hides, and small goods down the royal road to Chihuahua, the local patrónes used vecino labor to move massive herds of sheep, consigned goods, and other items they had received from American traders.[35] As Susan Boyle notes, the sheep-trading families dominated the sale of all foreign merchandise: "Five families (Armijo, Chávez, Otero, Perea, and Yrizarri) owned 81.68 percent (148,248 pesos) of the 181,492 pesos worth of foreign goods listed in the guías."[36] Most of the New Mexican landholders involved in the sheep trade lived in the Rio Abajo, and they proved most enterprising. With their profits the New Mexican patrónes often expanded their operations by purchasing more land, hiring more vecinos and enslaving more captives, breeding more sheep, and eventually expanding their trade connections. Ultimately, many of the large landholders of southern New Mexico became great sheep barons.[37]

New Mexican landholders continued their entrepreneurialism well into the American territorial period, and benefited greatly from their relationships with early white immigrants. Maurillo Vigil writes, "In 1850 there were approximately 380,000 head of sheep; thirty years later the number was about four million." He notes that 3 million of these sheep were owned by a mere twenty families, of which roughly 2.5 million belonged to Hispanos in 1880.[38] As Susan Boyle showed, the New Mexican patrónes benefited from commerce on the Santa Fe Trail. But the wealth they accumulated during the American territorial period rarely permeated to the vecinos, especially in Santa Fe County.

Socially, Hispanos kept relying on their family connections for partnerships and support in times of need. Interrelations among large landholding Mexican families in the borderlands were intricate, and when challenges arose they looked to family first.³⁹ Kinship networks protected caudillo family members, and they stuck by one another even when their kin went awry of the law. This remained true during the American period as well, and if white immigrants wanted access to New Mexican markets, it behooved them to cooperate and respect these kinship networks. Social relations thus first grew through family, and this was the basis of the New Mexican social hierarchy. Importantly, these connections then grew by extension through family friends and their associates, which became the basis of the trade relationships that increased the patrónes' economic position.⁴⁰

In these ways, the New Mexican patrónes were politically, militarily, economically, and socially entrenched when Americans arrived in 1846, and they remained so throughout the American territorial period. Within this context, the 1858 story of Manuel Chaves and his intimidation tactics is more understandable: Chaves could threaten a local cleric because he was a patrón, a respected and connected member of New Mexico's landholding class who was protected by his kinship network and supported by his vecino followers; Lamy was just some extranjero *gringo* from France who had threatened Chaves's land boundary.

The Americans were confronted by this powerful social structure, and Brig. Gen. Stephen Watts Kearny recognized the importance of catering to the local patrónes. When Kearny commissioned his men to write legal code, he stressed the importance of continuity. He wanted to facilitate a peaceful transition and he hoped the military government would be accepted by the local power structure.⁴¹ As a result, the Kearny Code was partially drawn from local Mexican legal custom. Still, even if the American military challenged the legal, political, and social structure in New Mexico, as Lynch notes, "A caudillo could rule with or without

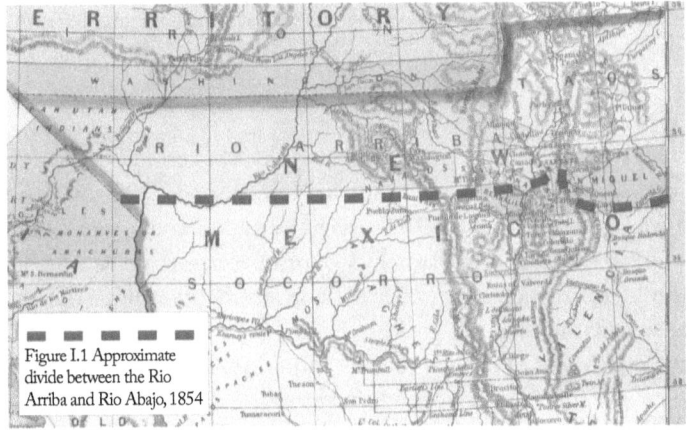

Figure I.1 Approximate divide between the Rio Arriba and Rio Abajo, 1854

a constitution; his authority and legitimacy were personal and did not depend on formal institutions."[42] Thus the New Mexican patrónes continued to dominate the region without fearing repercussions, much as they had for the majority of the Mexican period. The patrónes continued to prosper, American authorities cashed in, and the vecinos continued to be impoverished.

The Importance of Santa Fe County

I have chosen to focus on Santa Fe County because it served as the political center, economic hub, and a microcosm of the vecino experience in New Mexico. Santa Fe is situated between what has long been recognized as the two distinct regions of New Mexico: the Rio Arriba in the north and the Rio Abajo in the south.[43] The boundary between the Rio Arriba and Rio Abajo is La Bajada Mesa (the Descent), a treacherous geographical obstacle for early settlers (map I.1). The Rio Arriba was north of La Bajada and home to small farmers, merchants, vecinos, and numerous settlements of Christianized Indigenous.[44] During the Mexican period, white traders were allowed to settle in the Rio Arriba because Hispanos hoped a white presence would serve as a buffer zone between the United States and New Mexico; Hispanos also hoped that the white traders would become targets for Apache, Comanche, and Ute and provide a buffer between Hispanos in the south and the Indigenous Peoples of the north. Meanwhile, the Rio Abajo was generally south of La Bajada and was dominated by the patrónes, who used vecinos both as laborers and servants to cultivate crops and raise sheep, which they then traded for valuable goods and monies.[45] The landholding ranchers of the Rio Abajo tapped into the extensive trade networks to the south and west more so than did those of the Rio Arriba; they traded goods as far as Chihuahua in the south and California in the west.[46] Santa Fe served as the seat of government and contained a mixture of people from both the Rio Arriba and Rio Abajo, and because people from both regions lived in Santa Fe, studying it provides us with access points into the cultures of both major regions of New Mexico.

Another reason for choosing Santa Fe is that the records for Santa Fe County are the most intact of any region in New Mexico, especially for the period of Mexican rule.[47] Of the 160 surviving criminal court cases from the Mexican period, 127 are from Santa Fe County. Because these data are intact in both the Mexican and American eras, these records allow us to test one of the major hypotheses of this project: that the New Mexico district courts disproportionately victimized the vecinos during American territorialization. From the county court documents we find extensive data that reveal the daily trials and tensions that existed among vecinos, the patrónes, and white settlers across the imagined boundary of regime change. For example, since whites had settled in Santa Fe during the Mexican period, we are better equipped to track white immigrant crime in Santa Fe County than in any other part of New Mexico. These records indicate that though Santa Fe was home to a few white immigrants in the Mexican period, it was not until after their numbers increased during American territorialization that white settlers became aggressive. More specifically, it was not until the entitled white Americans came to Santa Fe that violence and homicide became commonplace among whites.

One major problem, however, remained: the voices of women and the Indigenous seldom appeared in criminal court documents. On top of this, when women do show up, it was most often in the role of the victim, rather than as the central movers and shakers that they were in Santa Fe County. The fact has always been that women simply do not commit crime—especially violent crime—at a rate that even remotely approaches that of men.[48] Of the 398 crimes committed in Santa Fe County between 1821 and 1860, 38 were committed by women, and nearly all of the charges were for larceny. In that same period, women appeared as victims in 58 cases: 22 women were victims of assault, 5 were victims of homicide, and 1 was a victim of rape (clearly there were more, but they were never reported). Women are only represented as actors in 9.5 percent of the documents, while they were represented as victims in 14.6 percent of the documents used in my quantitative study of crime.[49]

Women were far more represented in the census data, and it is in those records that their power and influence come through. For example, when I examined land distribution in 1850, I found that many of the wealthiest landholders were in fact women, widowed matriarchs who are listed as heads of households. Widowed women were not always listed as heads of households. In most instances, they appeared at the bottom of the household list. But in the case of the Doñas, they were always listed above their eldest children, and the value of the estate was in line with their information. The matriarchs passed on by the time of the 1860 census, and only then was their wealth broken up among their heirs.

The census revealed many other important aspects of New Mexican society. First, it revealed the demographic makeup of Santa Fe County in 1850 and 1860 and showed that by 1860 the number of newly arrived white settlers declined precipitously. In addition, sorting the census revealed the types of occupations held by large landholders, vecinos, white Americans, and white Europeans. Through these occupations, the social stratification of New Mexican society was revealed at the intersection of both class and ethnicity. Thus, comparing the occupations of these ethnic groups provides insight into the livelihoods of both Hispanos and newly arrived American immigrants in Santa Fe County.[50]

The historical testimonies I have gathered for this project come from a wide array of sources, including the Santa Fe County court records, personal

INTRODUCTION

journals, newspapers, oral history interviews conducted by earlier historians, and anecdotes contained in the works of other historians. All stories were read through a critical lens that is mindful of the motives of the storyteller and their purpose in recounting it, as well as that of the historian and their purpose. In engaging these materials, I was primarily concerned with understanding the context of each narrative and how it situated within my quantitative understanding of New Mexico. In order to test my hypotheses, I actively sought narratives that contradicted my data, but I found I was able to reconcile the discrepancies between my work and the surviving documents, oral traditions, and stories shared by previous scholars.

Outline of Chapters and Conclusions

The structure of this book is simultaneously chronological and thematic. In chapter 1, I argue that the Spanish colonial legacy of New Mexico allowed regional patrónes to use kinship networks and wealth to dictate policy, to provide protection, and to exploit and intimidate the vecino population in order to maintain their authority. More specifically, this chapter highlights how the hierarchical social structure in New Mexico developed during the Mexican period and documents how the Hispanos first solidified this structure during the Chimayo Rebellion of 1837 and later defended it during the Taos Rebellion of 1847. Titled "The Rise of the Patrónes and the Burden of the *Vecinos*," this chapter argues that power in New Mexico during the latter part of the Mexican period rested in the large landholding patrónes, who sought autonomy from any and all centralist forces.

Chapters 2 and 3 are dedicated to the experiences of the vecino community as New Mexico transitioned into an American territory. They highlight the cooperation between the landholding Hispanos and the American authorities to show how the compromises they made affected the vecinos in their everyday lives. Chapter 2 demonstrates that wealth inequality surged during the first thirteen years of American rule, which I hypothesize led to an increase in vecino larceny. I argue that the vecinos were affected by the process of territorialization on multiple fronts: it changed their lives legally, spiritually, and economically.

In chapter 3, titled "Between a Rock and a Gun," I show that while vecinos often used rocks in their violent acts, white settlers almost always used their guns. I utilize data from the criminal court records at the New Mexico State Records Center and Archives from 1837 to 1860 to illuminate the stability of the early Hispano community, as well as the instability brought by recently arrived gun-toting American immigrants. I contend that these new white immigrants were vying for wealth, but the New Mexican landholders and local white officials walled them out. I conclude that because recently arrived white settlers did not feel represented by the local authorities, they responded with violence and acts of open civil disobedience.

Chapter 4 illustrates how 1856–1857 were the pivotal years in the development of Santa Fe County and New Mexico more broadly during my period of study; therein I elucidate the factors that caused the Hispano community to become more violent after 1855 and exponentially more homicidal in the years 1856 and 1857. Titled simply "1856," the chapter shows that this was the watershed moment, the breaking point between poor and working-class Nuevomexicano vecinos and the large landholding patrónes, and it marked the end of a long period of symbiotic—if highly unequal—coexistence.

In chapter 5 I argue that the New Mexican patrónes used their power in the legislature to exercise indirect control of the legal system; at the same time, they allowed American-appointed judges and territorial juries to mete out justice along ethnic lines. Together, the local patrónes and the courts applied justice in manner indicative of a colonial society. Entitled "At the Wrong End of the Lash," this chapter illuminates how the new judicial apparatus and jury system resulted in both higher conviction rates and harsher punishments for the vecinos than it did for their white counterparts.

It is impossible to think of people like Manuel Chaves—who risked excommunication and threatened to shoot a priest over but a sliver of his land—and his fellow patrónes allowing American authorities to pilfer land from them. It is equally a folly to believe that the patrónes in New Mexico allowed the public lands that belonged to the vecinos to be claimed by white immigrants without securing the lion's share for themselves. As this study will demonstrate, the New Mexican caudillos were economically and politically savvy people; the vecinos were pragmatic ones. The New Mexican patrónes were seasoned veterans of a generations-old conflict with the Pueblo, Navajo, Apache, and Ute, and they had horses, guns, and more vecino support than any American authority could muster. When the Americans tried to control New Mexico, they even had support from the Puebloans. Likewise, the vecinos supported the patrónes when the caudillo system was threatened. When the local patrónes fomented unrest, the vecinos took up arms, and the power these Hispanos wielded together made New Mexico a veritable Hispano bastion.

Santa Fe County remained decidedly Hispano after the Americans arrived: The Hispano population increased during the first thirteen years of territorialization, while the white population dwindled. In 1850 the Hispano population in Santa Fe County was 6,683, and by 1860 that number increased to 7,384. At the same time, the white population declined by 36 percent, from 803 in 1850 to 511 in 1860. The Hispanos gave birth to 2,282 children between 1850 and 1860, while whites gave birth to 48. The Hispanos were settled and rooted, while most whites that came to Santa Fe soon drifted away. In short, Americans did not have the power to do what many historians have contended they did.[51]

After 1847, the New Mexican patrónes, who had maneuvered their way into power in 1837, now worked alongside older white immigrants to acquire property and increase their influence. They forged relationships with new white settlers when it suited them and ignored them when it did not. Thus it should not be surprising that while the number of small landholding New Mexicans was declining during the early years of territorial consolidation, the aggregate amount of property held by Hispanos was actually increasing. As this study will demonstrate, what was happening in New Mexico in regards to property was not a byproduct of ethnic domination, but was instead a consequence of a society undergoing a further concentration of wealth.

Throughout these processes, vecinos remained the basis of the New Mexican patrónes' power. Because of this, my study remains centered on vecinos in relation to the New Mexican patrónes and the assortment of recently arrived American and European settlers. In doing so, my goal is to avoid constructing a history that is too heavily focused on elites, empires, flags, politicians, and soldiers. Many of the new characters I introduce are in fact convicted criminals. Most are everyday people who—as a result of either pressure, frustration, or desperation—committed an act that runs contrary to societal norms. The most common crime was larceny, and crimes like larceny often happen when society leaves some of its members desperate or in need, just as in assaults and homicides. To be more succinct, when a society fails its people, the people either break the law or take the law into their own hands.[52]

By foregrounding vecinos in relation to the patrónes power system, I hope to contribute to the existing scholarship on New Mexico and the borderlands, spaces where class and ethnicity are interwoven in an intricate braid. To that end, this project introduces data that highlight the social dynamics of New Mexico through a combination of quantitative and qualitative analysis. My goal is to resurrect the New Mexican vecinos and return to all Nuevomexicanos the agency that is rightfully part of our history. As my study will show, the Nuevomexicanos controlled New Mexico when they could, adapted when it was necessary, and continued to redefine themselves in whatever manner that was needed to preserve and extend their holdings. Above all else the Hispanos, both the patrónes and vecinos, did what they judged to be in their best interests, something their American partners could easily understand.[53]

CHAPTER ONE

THE RISE OF THE PATRÓNES AND THE BURDEN OF THE *VECINOS*

In 1843 Father Antonio José Martinez stood at the great *portale* of the Palacio Nacional in Santa Fe anxiously awaiting an election that was sure to name him New Mexico's representative for the Mexican congress. Vicar Juan Felipe Ortiz presided over the departmental assembly and—having just completed his own term as New Mexico's representative—publicly endorsed Martinez as his replacement.[1] As voting began, an aggravated governor Manuel Armijo appeared before the congregation, twirling his trademark baton of office and flanked by armed soldiers on both sides.[2] Armijo was angry at Martinez for challenging the former's land grants to American traders and their Nuevomexicano business partners, and he was concerned that Martinez might take his challenge to Mexico City.[3]

Armijo commanded Vicar Ortiz and the other delegates to elect Diego Archuleta instead.[4] Well-known in New Mexico, Archuleta was the son of Juan Andres Archuleta, one of the wealthiest patrónes in the Rio Arriba and a valuable ally to Armijo.[5] "And since the noise of arms silences the rights and even the laws themselves," as an early biographer of Padre Martinez has noted, "Archuleta was elected."[6] Like the priest of San Miguel Chapel, who some fifteen years later wilted in the presence of Manuel Chaves, the gentle Vicar Ortiz and his assembly bowed to the intimidation tactics of Manuel Armijo.[7] With that, Governor Armijo thwarted Padre Martinez and ensured that Martinez would not bring Armijo unwanted attention from the Mexican congress.[8]

By the time this incident occurred late in 1843, Manuel Armijo and the other large landholders had secured power in New Mexico. Spanish efforts to centralize that power and collect taxes had defined the era of the Bourbon Reforms, but Mexican independence removed the specter of Spanish intervention and allowed the patrónes to emerge across the Mexican Republic.[9] This was especially true in New Mexico, where the opening of the Santa Fe Trail from Missouri to New Mexico in the late 1820s stimulated the local economy and buoyed local merchants and producers.[10] Mexico fueled regionalism by failing to fund local governments, causing Mexicans to drift from the Mexican central government. Like New Mexico, the departments of Mexico were forced to deal with justifiably frustrated Indigenous peoples without support from the central government. Like the Nuevomexicanos, vecinos throughout Mexico turned to emerging local patrónes—essentially regional caudillos—for protection. In this way the Mexican federal government's failure to fund local governments and provide military aid strengthened the bond between Nuevomexicano patrónes and vecinos. It was a bond that held for many years after the Americans invaded, in spite of gross and ever-increasing wealth inequality in New Mexico.

Patrónes such as Manuel Armijo, Juan Andres Archuleta, and his son Diego Archuleta emerged within the fluidity of the New Mexican borderlands and the limits of the Mexican state. These Nuevomexicano landholders derived their authority from the land and resources that their ancestors had first monopolized during the era of the Bourbon Reforms and then expanded after Mexican independence.[11] Larger landholders benefited from a series of Bourbon decrees issued between 1805 and 1820 that were intended to allow poorer Nuevomexicanos access to land, something meant to help them establish economic security. Ironically, as Thomas Hall notes, "Large tracts of land were sold throughout the region, but the prices were such that the landless could not buy, and the wealthy saw the prices as 'ridiculously cheap.'"[12] As a result, wealthier Nuevomexicano landholders entered the era of independence with vast amounts of land, which positioned them to benefit from the opening of the Santa Fe Trail.[13] The confluence of Mexican regionalism and the Bourbon Reforms allowed Nuevomexicano patrónes to emerge as brokers within the power vacuum created by Mexican independence. Once in power, these patrónes used their control of local resources and foreign goods to manipulate everyday vecinos.

This chapter examines the world in which the vecinos lived, documents the rapid occupational shift from farmers to laborers, and ultimately identifies a pattern in how Nuevomexicanos—both patrónes and vecinos—resisted when their power was jeopardized in New Mexico. Specifically, patrónes resorted to rebellion when their autonomy was threatened, while vecinos rebelled when their subsistence was imperiled. The first part of the chapter examines New Mexico within the context of the Spanish empire and the Mexican Republic and contends that the devolution of power in Mexico paved the way for the rise of powerful local landholders. It demonstrates how the legacy of Spanish mercantilism fueled regionalism and empowered local landholders during the early years of Mexican independence.[14] Although Spain attempted to stimulate New Mexican manufacturing, its broader economic policies in New Mexico made Nuevomexicanos dependent on trade with Chihuahua.[15] The Nuevomexicano need for excess agricultural goods, New Mexico's chief export, meant that farmers and sheep herders needed to produce at higher levels. In the process, small vecino farmers and families were transformed into day laborers, who became directly dependent on the large landholding patrónes for survival.

The second part of this chapter focuses on the Chimayo Rebellion of 1837, which I argue was largely initiated by the patrónes in response to the Mexican federal effort to centralize power. That it was not simply a rebellion among the people.[16] In 1835 the Mexican government appointed a centralist from Mexico City as governor of New Mexico. By 1837 the New Mexican patrónes tired of the centralist policies and fomented a rebellion against the centralist governor. The patrónes used propaganda to push the already agitated vecino and Pueblo populations into rebellion, but once the governor was dead the movement took on a life of its own and established its own government. When the patrónes from the Rio Abajo saw this, they again acted to secure their autonomy, deposing the rebel government and declaring themselves defenders of liberty. The patrónes spun their action as a victory for the centralist government, when it was in fact just another triumph for local autonomy.

This was the moment when the emerging patrónes and vecinos cemented their social contract. By necessity, the vecinos were bound and subjugated to the large landholders for the rest of the Mexican period.[17] The patrónes were too powerful to be deposed in the wake of the Chimayo Rebellion, and in a region marked by scarcity, being bound to the local patrónes was the vecinos' best chance for survival. The Mexican government lauded Manuel Armijo for his supposed heroics against the Chimayosas, and four years later they rewarded him and his fellow patrónes again for their service during the Texas Incursion of 1841. The Mexican government granted the local patrónes their autonomy and legitimized them as the rightful rulers of New Mexico.

In 1846 the United States conquered New Mexico. The patrónes resisted the appointment of Charles Bent—a trader and merchant from the Rio Arriba—to the governorship. As before, they fomented a rebellion among the vecinos and the Pueblos, and yet another governor lost his head. This time their plot was uncovered before the rebellion could commence, but by then the propaganda they promoted had already done its job. The vecinos languished in poverty in the wake of the Chimayo Rebellion, but they still believed that the patrónes were key to their survival, likely because they believed the nativism promulgated by the local patrónes. Together, struggling vecinos and opportunistic patrónes secured, maintained, and bolstered their power in what became New Mexico territory.[18]

Toward Patronismo

There was nothing exceptional or different about the rise of patrónes in New Mexico during the era of independence; caudillos seized power throughout the vast expanses of the independent Mexican Republic once they had the opportunity to do so. These so-called "strongmen" became determinedly autonomous. When Spanish officials, loyalists, and local clergymen either absconded or joined the independence movement, local rule was cemented in the distant regions of Mexico. In New Mexico, the key change that accompanied independence was the removal of the strict trade embargoes that Spain placed on the entire empire, embargoes that in New Mexico specifically banned trade with Americans.[19] The influx of trade goods from Missouri meant Nuevomexicanos were no longer exclusively dependent on Chihuahua for trade, and this broke Chihuahua's long-held monopoly. The opening of trade with the United States reoriented the New Mexican economy and triggered a shift from independent small farming to dependent day labor for everyday Nuevomexicanos.[20]

Nuevomexicano landholders needed to secure a labor force to capitalize on the emerging trade opportunities. Large landholders compelled vecinos to become laborers, but they also benefited from the unpredictable nature of agriculture in New Mexico. Their overall intent was to entrap small farmers, to make them indebted.[21] The loss of farms plunged vecinos into day labor, which meant their work exclusively benefited Nuevomexicano landholders. In this way, the patrónes increased their holdings and their political positions, and they were determined to maintain this newfound autonomy.[22] They often behaved badly, especially toward poorer vecinos: they demanded labor, they pulled vecinos into debt when their crops failed, and they ultimately forced many vecinos into indebted peonage. They extended credit to poor farmers, and when a vecino could not pay, they even took poorer vecino children as servants in lieu of payment.[23]

The Nuevomexicano patrónes were profiting, and they wanted stability and economic support from the central government in order to continue their success, but they also coveted their local autonomy. They wanted the capitalist dream, which is to rule and to benefit from the system, but without paying their fair share. Far from being interested in independence, the Nuevomexicano patrónes sought both protection and resources from the central government.[24] New Mexico remained distant from the centers of power, and they long decried their tenuous existence in the expanses of the empire. Mexican federal officials, however, stressed that the preservation of distant settlements was beyond their responsibility.[25] Indigenous unrest, like other sources of instability, had to be dealt with locally because the Mexican economy was still in shambles.[26] The central government simply could not afford to defend its departments.[27]

Gov. Manuel Armijo became a central figure in the struggle for autonomy, but in reality he represented the interests of his fellow large landholding patrónes. Manuel Armijo initially served as governor in 1827 but was forced to retire amidst accusations of corruption in 1828.[28] Although he returned to Albuquerque and profited from the trade of sheep and other goods, Armijo resented Mexican attempts to centralize power in 1835. Aggravated by the appointment of Gov. Albino Pérez in 1836, Armijo capitalized on discontent within his class and seized the governorship in 1837 with the support of other patrónes from the Rio Abajo.

Armijo adopted land policies that benefited his peers, and he granted large tracts of land to local patrónes and their white business partners under the pretense of economic development, likely because they had supported his coup

THE RISE OF THE PATRÓNES AND THE BURDEN OF THE VECINOS

and formed his power base.[29] Armijo derived his authority from informal relationships with local elites, rather than from his political office. Families and their vast kinship networks, which were constructed over several generations through business partnerships, marriages, and alliances, continued to dominate New Mexico after Mexican independence. Cementing these alliances, and through them his legitimacy, allowed Armijo to govern New Mexico effectively.

Although Armijo's authority was not absolute, that did not stop him from abusing his power as governor; he physically abused vecinos, intimidated American merchants, and even threatened fellow patrónes and their family members on occasion.[30] Armijo's power had limitations, however, and his actions did not go unchecked. When Armijo crossed members of his own class, as he did on more than one occasion, he was often forced to back down by other powerful patrónes.[31] Armijo seemed acutely aware of his limitations in 1841 after he caught a young Rafael Chacón—the son of the powerful Albino Chacón—crossing his property and overreacted. Armijo and Albino Chacón were close friends who frequently defended one another's interests. In his autobiography, Rafael Chacón wrote, "The general was the owner of a field.... I was in the habit of going to school through this field in order to shorten the distance when, all of a sudden, the general caught me and struck me with his cane."[32] Chacón explains that through his fright and the pain from Armijo's numerous strikes, he begged forgiveness until the caudillo finally asked who he was. Upon hearing that this was the son of Albino Chacón, Armijo stopped the thrashing and released young Rafael. "Well, so you are the son of my compadre," Armijo said.[33] Armijo quickly reversed his position, granted Rafael Chacón free access to his fields, and awarded him a piece of candy. Armijo continued to do so whenever they crossed paths.

The rise of patrónes in New Mexico stemmed from Spain's economic approach to New Spain. Spanish officials advanced mercantilist policies during their period of rule, judging their success by how much wealth they exported to Spain, specifically in the form of gold, silver, tobacco, and other materials. Over time, Spain's policies fostered competition between different regions of New Spain, and rivalries developed between places like New Mexico and Chihuahua.[34] Early Nuevomexicano patrónes—especially in the Rio Abajo—organized vecino labor and exported unrefined resources to trade for refined goods. Patrónes cornered local markets with varying degrees of success, but they generally realized there was more to gain from exports than from cultivating local trade relationships. They learned that opportunities to profit from both local and intrastate trade were short-lived; in most of New Spain officials either outlawed or taxed internal trade items, and this discouraged merchants from diversifying. The message was clear: to prosper in New Spain one first needed to export.[35]

Spain enacted the Bourbon Reforms (1750–1788) when profits from the Spanish colonies declined in the mid-eighteenth century, but early reforms were geared toward the mining and trade sectors of New Spain.[36] As part of the reforms, peninsular Spaniards replaced local criollos in positions of authority and instituted taxes throughout the empire. More specifically, the system of *corregimientos* (the older system in which rural colonies were ruled by appointees) was abolished and was replaced by the intendancy system (a more centralized system). Thomas Hall described this process as "an attempt to restore order and integrity to colonial government." To criollos, however, these reforms were an attempt by *peninsulares* to usurp their privileges and wealth.[37] In fact, Spanish officials enacted these reforms because they suspected that criollos were lining their pockets with profits intended for Spain. They appointed new officials to end local corruption and maximize profits from New Spain. To this end, the new intendants legislated to favor peninsular merchants, degrading manufacturing, commerce, and urban development in New Spain, and regulating to quash potential threats to their bottom line.[38]

Although Spanish intendants restricted manufacturing in New Spain during the Bourbon Reforms, the Spanish approached New Mexico differently because they valued New Mexico as a foothold in the far north. More specifically, the Spanish hoped New Mexico would protect their silver mines in the northern provinces of Nueva Galicia, Nueva Vizcaya, and Nuevo León. As Ramón Gutiérrez noted, "New Mexico's defense became an acute preoccupation for the Spanish crown in the eighteenth century because the silver-producing provinces of New Spain were at risk."[39] Spanish officials intended New Mexico to be a valuable buffer between the silver mines and both frustrated Indigenous peoples and the fast approaching American empire. To prop up New Mexico, Spanish officials freed New Mexican merchants from both trade and travel restrictions, made New Mexican products tax-exempt, and sent agricultural specialists, veterinarians, and master weavers to New Mexico to upgrade their livestock, crops, and textiles.[40] In spite of these concessions, Spanish officials still refused to allow the New Mexicans to trade with the Americans. They hoped that by making New Mexico economically viable they would solidify their northern outpost and strengthen their position in North America. Spanish officials also encouraged emigration to New Mexico from central Mexico, and they granted land to new migrants in order to increase production of sheep, wool, and agricultural goods, which they believed would solidify the New Mexican economy.[41]

One of the key Spanish moves—the advent of the Commandancy General of the Interior Provinces of the North in 1776—ultimately bore fruit in their efforts to strengthen New Mexico; it spurred greater peace between Nuevomexicanos, Apaches, Comanche, and Utes, and that meant wealthy Nuevomexicanos had more time to focus their energies on the production of goods.[42] This period of relative peace resulted in increased reproduction among Nuevomexicanos, expanding the available workforce.[43] Large landholders and merchants in New

Profession	1790		1827		1850	
	No.	Pct.	No.	Pct.	No.	Pct.
Farmers	350	85%	467	55%	662	38%
Craftsmen/Artisans	28	7%	101	12%	312	18%
Merchants	1	0%	12	1%	312	18%
Laborer/Servants	34	8%	256	31%	757	43%

Table 1.1. Occupational Structure of Santa Fe County, 1790, 1827, and 1850

Mexico took full advantage of both the benefits and autonomy that came with the Bourbon Reforms, and as poorer farmers struggled and became indebted, large landholders seized ownership of their property. This led to major changes in the social fabric of New Mexico, as independent landholders increasingly became laborers, compelled to tend livestock and gather exports in exchange for their survival. Landholders traded these exports for finished goods in an effort to grow their wealth and power.[44]

The Bourbon Reforms also refocused production in New Mexico, expanded trade to Chihuahua in the short term, and increased the amount of liquid currency available for New Mexicans.[45] The volume of goods traveling from New Mexico increased due to the Spanish incentives, but the New Mexicans lacked equipment, and the goods that they produced remained low in quality.[46] Better goods were available in Chihuahua at lower price points, and Nuevomexicanos could not compete with that market. In fact, New Mexico ran a massive trade deficit with Chihuahua and required external funding to balance its shortfall. In his 1812 account of New Mexico–Chihuahua trade, Pedro Bautista Pino, New Mexico's representative to the Spanish Cortes, "claimed that the annual trade with Chihuahua involved purchases of 112,000 pesos and sales of 60,000 pesos, for a net deficit of 52,000 pesos."[47] Using this leverage, Chihuahua merchants swindled New Mexicans at every opportunity by undervaluing New Mexican exports. Ultimately, New Mexicans abandoned unviable manufacturing and turned instead to agricultural exports, including crops and sheep.[48]

The growing number of large landholding farmers and the decreasing viability of small farms led to the rise of local patrónes in New Mexico (table 1.1).[49] Although the actual number of farmers increased from 1790 to 1850, the proportion of New Mexicans in Santa Fe County who owned farms declined from 85 percent in 1790 to 55 percent in 1827 and finally to 38 percent in 1850. Over the same sixty-year span, the percentage of craftsmen/artisans increased from 7 percent in 1790 to 12 percent in 1827 to 18 percent in 1850. The population of laborers/servants increased more dramatically: from 8 percent in 1790 to 31 percent in 1827 to 43 percent in 1850. In 1790 craftsmen/artisans and laborers/servants made up 15 percent of the population, but by 1850 they made up 61 percent of the population in Santa Fe County. In essence, the rise in land and wealth for the Nuevomexicano landholders resulted in the displacement of small farmers and transformed them into craftsmen/artisans, laborers, and even servants if they were indebted.

In 1850 the actual proportion of large landholders to vecinos was even higher than indicated in table 1.1. Of the 662 remaining farmers in Santa Fe County, 329 were nonexporting small farmers (table 1.2). Only 333 farmers possessed more than $100 in property, which means the other 329 nonexporting farmers were vecinos. These vecino farmers usually did not own the rights to the land they worked and the fields they used for grazing; they increasingly leased their rights from the large landholding patrónes in Santa Fe County. Thus in 1850 only 19 percent (333) were large landholding farmers, while 81 percent (1,398) were small farmers, craftsmen/artisans, and laborers/servants.

Alas, the data from tables 1.1 and 1.2 are incomplete because these tables do not account for persons listed in the census who were without occupation; when they are accounted for the percentage of large landholding farmers becomes even smaller. The data from 1790 and 1827 was drawn from Ramón Gutiérrez, and he only accounted for individuals in the census who had a declared occupation. Therefore, missing data skews the percentages in tables 1.1 and 1.2. In 1790, 22 percent of males over the age of twenty had no occupation: there were 527 total males over twenty, of whom 114 were listed as not having an occupation.[50] By 1850 only 15 percent of males over twenty had no occupation: there were 2,043 males over the age of twenty, of whom 307 were listed as not having an occupation (table 1.3).

Profession	1850	
	No.	Pct.
Large Farmers	333	19%
Small Farmers	329	19%
Craftsmen	312	18%
Merchants	7	1%
Laborers/Servants	757	43%

Source: 1850 Federal Census, Santa Fe County, New Mexico Territory. These numbers include only Hispanos living in Santa Fe County.

Table 1.2. Occupational Structure in Santa Fe County, Including Large Landholders, 1850

Profession	1850	
	No.	Pct.
Large Farmers	333	16%
Small Farmers	329	16%
Craftsmen	312	15%
Merchants	7	1%
Laborers/Servants	757	37%
None	307	15%

Table 1.3. Large Landholders in Santa Fe County, Including Those Without a Profession, Males Over 20 Years of Age Only, 1850

These dramatic changes were the local consequences of Spain's mercantilist policies in New Mexico. By the time the Americans arrived there was already a gross level of land inequality in Santa Fe County, the result of empowered large landowners and impoverished vecinos.[51]

Vecinos' ties with another source of stability and authority and New Mexico were also undermined because of the way the Bourbon Reforms targeted the church.[52] The church's mission to save souls cut into profitability, both by protecting Native populations from emerging patrónes and by collecting those profits to maintain their mission. As Spain's profits from New Spain waned, officials decided it was time to take power back from the church.

To pursue this end, officials withdrew royal stipends from the priests, leaving the latter increasingly dependent on clerical fees that were imposed on the laity. In 1781 the Franciscans in New Mexico lost their rights to collect labor and goods from the Pueblo people, making them dependent on the fees they collected from Nuevomexicanos. At the same time, the Bourbon Reforms eroded the viability of small farms and weakened vecinos' relationships with the church, while enriching and empowering large landowners. Although vecinos in New Mexico were dedicated Catholics, they had fewer assets and simply couldn't afford the new fees. Nuevomexicanos complained that the priests charged exorbitant fees for simple services, which included marriage and burial services. The Franciscans resented what they viewed as the vecinos' unwillingness to pay and denounced their flocks as an uncivilized rabble.[53]

The tensions that emerged between parishioners and priests in New Mexico mirrored those that William B. Taylor describes as defining this period in Mexico more broadly.[54] By making priests dependent on direct fees, the Bourbon Reforms drove a wedge between the vecinos and the New Mexican priests. And that was precisely the intent. In truth, the padres had to charge for services to survive, but by doing so they sowed the seeds for their own downfall in New Mexico. It damaged their relationships with the people on one hand. On the other, it enabled Lamy and Machebeuf to later cite those very fees as proof of the padres' corruption, and they ultimately used that accusation to depose the padres from their parishes.[55] As a result, the number of priests in New Mexico declined dramatically: in 1692 New Mexico hosted seventy Franciscan missionaries but by 1792 only sixteen Franciscans remained.[56]

Spanish policies, however, also devastated the Mexican infrastructure, and this too affected New Mexico's relationship with Mexico more broadly. By Mexican independence, travelers faced roads that were ruined, unsecured, and undersupplied. After independence the Mexican government was hindered by the extractive mercantile economy and as a result Mexican officials did not have the resources to fund local governments and protect their settlements from Native American incursions. As a result, new national leaders faced extensive infrastructure problems and were left without the means to safeguard the Mexican people. Patrónes filled this role, guarding and controlling vecino populations in power vacuums.

In practice, the Mexican economy operated much as it had during Spanish rule, but Mexican officials struggled to collect proceeds from the system. Under Spanish rule merchants in towns like Chihuahua pooled goods from smaller settlements like Santa Fe and supplied miners in the northern provinces with necessities; the miners then funneled silver to the coastal regions, where the crown collected it and shipped it back to Spain.[57] After Mexican independence, silver still made up 70 percent of all Mexican exports.[58] Mexican officials recognized that the Spanish system worked and they tried to use it to raise money for the central government. Instead, wealthy merchants and local patrónes from the more distant regions increasingly pocketed the profits. In this way the Mexican system disproportionately favored large settlements over small ones. Local patrónes continued as before: they identified valuable exports, used vecino labor to collect or cultivate them, and traded them to regional trading centers. Largely untaxed, regional patrónes were empowered against the Mexican central government in a dance of resistance and rebellion that came to define the Mexican nation.

During the Spanish period the structural limits on New Mexico profits, compared to larger settlements like Chihuahua, induced Nuevomexicanos to seek out trade with the Americans. Regionalism made fair trade nonexistent at every step along the Camino Real: New Mexican patrónes took advantage of poor vecinos and Indigenous while being cheated by Chihuahua and Durango merchants, who were in turn taxed at a high rate and fleeced by miners from Zacatecas, who were being swindled by foreign merchants and taxes.[59] New Mexican patrónes decided that their only recourse was to seek out new trade partners in the north.

Another incentive for New Mexicans to seek trade with American merchants was the poor condition and dangerous nature of Mexico's roads. Mexican roads were often impassable, either because they had fallen into disrepair or because they were never intended to transport goods by beasts of burden.[60] The bad roads in Mexico stretched across long distances and impeded internal transportation to and from New Mexico. From New Mexico, the Camino Real was rough in many places and traversed high mountains and vast deserts. "The seventeen hundred miles separating Santa Fe from Mexico City were not as formidable an obstacle as the hardships of the trip," noted Susan Boyle. "The terrain was rugged, the Indian threat was always present, and scarce water was found most often in 'fetid springs or pools . . . only rendered tolerable by necessity.'"[61] During both the Spanish and Mexican periods New Mexican merchants were forced to travel in armed caravans when they departed for Chihuahua, which further reduced their profit margins.

The journey to Chihuahua therefore proved far more perilous than the route north to Independence, Missouri. This reality hastened New Mexican cooperation with American traders. To the south was the infamous Journey of the Dead Man—or Jornada del Muerto—a barren expanse of land populated by hostile Indigenous populations.[62] Apache and Comanche controlled much of the route to Independence, Missouri, as well, but traveling north was still safer because it was less arid. In addition, New Mexican merchants traded on better terms with Americans than they did in Chihuahua. Missourians in particular sought inroads into Mexico through Santa Fe, and this made them more enthusiastic trade partners. Once independence from Spain opened the door to American traders, New Mexican landholders charged into the merchant business, developed partnerships, and utilized these slightly safer northern routes to build trade networks into the United States.[63]

These relationships broke Chihuahua's monopoly from the Spanish period and empowered Nuevomexicanos to make demands when they traded in Chihuahua.[64] Location was everything, and for Americans Santa Fe was the gateway first to Mexico and later to California. Suddenly the Nuevomexicano merchants had the power to purchase more than they needed from American merchants, travel down the Royal Road to Chihuahua, and to ultimately profit from the venture. In this manner, they secured and increased their position of power in New Mexico.[65]

The New Mexican patrónes forged partnerships with the American traders, which was a fundamental departure from the policies during both the Spanish colonial and Mexican Republic periods. As a result, they faced resistance from Mexican officials, who argued that the government needed to protect the Mexican markets from American traders. Mexican officials declared numerous items from the American market to be contraband in order to stymie New Mexican trade with the Americans. The list of contraband items grew annually in both size and absurdity. For example, by August 1843 President Antonio Lopez de Santa Anna passed a decree that forbade the importation of more than two hundred items from the American market, many of them oddly specific, all of them aimed at preventing trade with Texas. The list included all coaches and carriages, saddles, furniture, pianos, hats, and any type of toy, especially dolls. It was illegal to import all products made of either precious metal or that had metal plating, along with any steel or iron goods. Also forbidden were holy water fonts, soap, cookware, torch stands, hair curlers, keys for clocks, and anything that could be used to create a santo. If the church needed candlesnuffers, wafer boxes, and any manner of cross or amulet, it had to be made in Mexico. Should a trader from Missouri travel the twelve hundred miles from Independence to Santa Fe with a water fountain in his wagon—a scenario difficult to envision—his cargo was to be refused. Cheap jewelry was illegal to import, as were tongs for smoking, dog collars, gravy dishes, finger rings, soup plates, and, of course, all manner of chocolate makers and urns. Ironically—in a city desperately in need of a jail—padlocks, door springs, and iron bars were considered contraband.[66]

Unsurprisingly, local New Mexican officials felt they owed little to the Mexican government and they increasingly ignored Mexican regulations. Instead, they allowed illegal imports into their market in order to improve both prices and the quality of goods available to their fellow Nuevomexicano landholders.[67] New Mexican officials decided it was not in their best interests to heed Mexican regulations, and contraband-related cases seldom appeared in courts.[68] As David Weber noted, "New Mexico lacked factories and manufactured goods, and if manufactures could not be imported from the Americans, New Mexico would once again fall under the monopolistic control of Chihuahua and Durango merchants."[69] Feeling little responsibility to obey federal authorities, New Mexican officials simply ignored these laws and developed their own rules for dealing with contraband.

Quite cleverly, New Mexican patrónes in fact profited from the selective enforcement of Mexican trade regulations; they used them to leverage American traders for a cut of their profits. Local patrónes conducted secret meetings with American traders and took possession of American contraband. They pretended to help American traders avoid Mexican taxes, but this was a ruse. The patrónes did not fear retaliation from the local government because in the wake of Mexican independence they and their kin controlled New Mexico. The patrónes pretended to follow Mexican law, but in practice their personal interests superseded Mexican law. When local patrónes were reported to the New Mexican authorities the courts held obligatory hearings, but in the end patrónes were not punished.

American merchants were aware of these schemes, which had been a problem for them since the opening of the Santa Fe Trail, and they complained that New Mexican officials in the government and at the customs houses were corrupt and self-serving. The American trader Josiah Gregg bemoaned of the officials, "An 'arrangement'—a compromise, is expected, in which the officers are sure in the least to provide for themselves." As he so often did, Gregg accused the local officials of corruption, writing, "At some ports, a custom has been said to prevail, of dividing the legal duties into three equal parts: one for the officers—a second for the merchants—the other for the government"[70] Although it is certain that New Mexican officials kept some of what they collected, Gregg overestimated how organized the process was by which he and his fellow traders were fleeced. Duties were divided on a case-by-case basis and not systematically; the patrónes had to share with one another, but the arrangement was informal and there was no blueprint to be followed.

Nuevomexicanos monitored Anglo traders closely and made them pay dearly when they tried to hide their illegal imports without the aid of local merchants. These patrónes and their followers stalked white American traders who avoided partnerships, and then either stole their goods or reported the contraband to officials. Nuevomexicano officials then seized these goods and rewarded the informant with a portion of the merchandise. Nuevomexicano Customs House officials were compelled to distribute seized property more widely when the value of the contraband was exceedingly high. In those instances, officials confiscated the smuggled goods and the surplus was then divided between the treasury, the denouncer, the apprehender, the local alcalde, and several other officials.[71] Administrators shared these profits, but Nuevomexicano patrónes benefited too because by allowing contraband into the market the local patrónes introduced better quality items in New Mexico and this further reduced their dependence on imports from Chihuahua and Durango.

For some white American traders, Gov. Manuel Armijo was the embodiment of the troubles with trade in New Mexico. Richard L. Wilson amplified the views of other traders when he expressed his belief that Armijo changed laws to favor Hispano merchants and seized white Americans' goods on numerous occasions. Wilson wrote that he wanted to avoid paying a tax levied by Armijo because, "It was exclusively a revenue tariff for the sole use and benefit of his obesity, the Governor."[72] Though Wilson exaggerated the extent of Armijo's personal benefits, there is strong evidence that Armijo used his office for profit, but this was no different than the other New Mexican patrónes who held office.[73] This was how things worked at the end of the Santa Fe Trail.

Manuel Armijo's status allowed him to pressure American merchants for tribute on a whim. On one occasion Armijo made himself unpopular by taxing American and European merchants by the wagon instead of by the item. This decision affected New Mexico in two ways: it allowed for direct taxation to the government and it veiled contraband from being noticed on the books.[74] In essence, New Mexican officials collected some of the duties that other patrónes had informally collected. The $500 per wagon charge saved Americans money because they no longer had to divide their profits with their Nuevomexicano business partners, but white Americans resented that Hispano merchants were granted exemptions from these importation duties.[75] Traders like James Josiah Webb were even more incensed later when Armijo's brief replacement, Mariano Martínez de Lejarza, raised the tax to $750 per wagon.[76] Regardless, white American merchants blamed Armijo for the trade levies in New Mexico, and he became the face for corruption in American writings.

In 1832 Manuel Armijo was indicted for smuggling and he appeared before the court to answer charges made against him for illegally importing American goods. Armijo brazenly admitted that he had indeed unlawfully introduced foreign merchandise into the Mexican market on behalf of an American merchant.[77] Armijo's frankness to the court reveals that he—like the other patrónes—did not fear reprisals for his actions. Like Armijo, the other patrónes smuggled American goods without the fear of consequences. Even when local patrónes were indicted and admitted guilt, like Armijo they invariably went unpunished.

Patrónes like Armijo also did not shrink from punishing uncooperative American traders for violating Mexican law. For example, during his first term as governor in 1827, Manuel Armijo used his power to confiscate pelts from an Anglo trapper who had illegally hunted in Mexico, going so far as to level cannons at one trapper on the wrong side of the law.[78] An American named Ewing Young and his partners illegally trapped in Texas and Sonora before Armijo took office. James Baird, a former American who was now a newly naturalized Mexican citizen, reported Young to the New Mexican authorities shortly before Armijo assumed office. From his home in El Paso in the year 1826, Baird warned Governor Narbona:

> I have learned that with scandal and contempt for the Mexican Republic a hundred odd Anglo-Americans have introduced themselves in a body to hunt beaver in the possessions of this state and that of Sonora ... that they have openly said that in spite of the Mexicans, they will hunt beaver wherever they please.... I beg that your Excellency may make such provisions as you may deem proper, to the end that the national laws may be respected and that foreigners may be confined to the limits which the same laws permit them, and that we Mexicans [!] may peacefully profit by the goods with which the merciful God has been pleased to enrich our soil.[79]

Baird alerted Governor Narbona out of self-interest, and by doing so he provided the Nuevomexicano patrónes with a valuable target they were ultimately able to profit from. Baird presented himself as a Mexican citizen who wanted his trapping rights protected, but in fact Baird had only been a citizen for one year. Baird qualified for Mexican citizenship because he met the one year in residence requirement, which he exceeded only because he had spent so much time in the Santa Fe jail for illegal trapping himself. Manuel Armijo was made aware of the accusations against Ewing Young when he assumed the governorship. In a manner that would have made Santa Anna proud, Armijo declared that it was his responsibility to protect Mexico and announced that it was his duty to crack down on illegal trapping for the good of the nation.

Ewing Young and his partners had been away since 1826, and when they returned in 1827 they were alerted about Governor Armijo's intentions. Despite that warning, they proved unable to keep their goods from the new governor. This wasn't for lack of effort: Young heeded the warnings he received from friends and secretly moved his twenty thousand dollars' worth of pelts from their company building to a private house outside of town. Unfortunately for Young and his associates, an unknown informant tipped off Armijo. When Armijo heard the pelts had been moved, he must have supposed that Young and his associates planned to abscond with the goods, because he quickly mustered a squad and ordered his men to seize the pelts.[80] Armijo's men stormed the safe house and killed the owner, who they claimed resisted their entry. Afterward, the soldiers confiscated the pelts and brought them to Santa Fe.[81]

The trappers filed several lawsuits to protest Armijo's actions, but their goods were never returned.[82] The closest Young came to his pelts was when Armijo granted Young permission to clear the pelts of dust and moths. While Young and his partners cleaned the pelts, one of them absconded to Taos with two bundles, and Young followed close behind. Armijo was furious, and he tracked down Young and his partner, Big Milton Sublette, at a home in Taos that they had barricaded. Armijo implemented what might be termed patrón diplomacy in order to end the siege: he ordered his men to load the cannon and aim it at the domicile, which frightened the trappers and forced their surrender. Young never saw the twenty thousand dollars' worth of pelts again; a portion went to the treasury, while the rest were divided between Governor Armijo, Baird, and the soldiers who recovered them.

In spite of the relative autonomy they enjoyed, Nuevomexicanos chafed under central government regulations. In 1829 Juan María Alarid condemned a protective tariff that prohibited the importation of various woolen and cotton goods, nails, locks, and other necessities. Alarid, who was kin to local patrónes, complained that the law might be "beneficial and necessary for more populous and industrious states . . . but very prejudicial for the poor and ignorant inhabitants of this territory."[83] In New Mexico high tariffs and trade restrictions hurt everyone, Alarid concluded, especially the poor vecinos.

In spite of the Mexican government's efforts to use regulations and contraband lists to control New Mexico, Nuevomexicanos continued to act in their own interests. The local patrónes claimed to be patriots and celebrated their Mexican citizenship in letters and speeches, but in practice they showed little regard for the laws issued from Mexico City. Ironically, the Mexican government's promulgation of stricter regulations made it easier for the local patrónes to secure both their profits and their positions of power. Nuevomexicano officials—drawn from the large landholders and their families—pocketed money with one hand and decried intervention by outside forces with the other. Early in the Mexican period they successfully cast themselves to vecinos as the only ones who had the best interests of the people at heart; the more that distant governments tried to tighten their grip on Santa Fe, the more the vecinos slipped through their fingers and into the arms of the large landholders.

CHAPTER ONE

ALBINO PEREZ AND THE CENTRALIST THREAT

In 1835 President Antonio López de Santa Anna and his allies in Mexico City backed a centralist movement they hoped would strengthen the Mexican Republic, but the movement failed because regional Mexican patrónes refused to relinquish their power to the central government. The centralists in Mexico City argued that the power of the Mexican Republic was being weakened by the legacy of the Spanish economic system; regional interests superseded national agendas and made Mexico vulnerable to foreign threats. Mexican officials grasped the need to address what Spain had failed to accomplish; to assert authority in places like New Mexico, they needed to supplant local officials with appointees who were loyal to the central government. In short, the centralists believed that local patrónes were too selfish and could not be trusted with liberty as defined in Mexico City. As part of these reforms, Santa Anna appointed Albino Pérez as governor of New Mexico. Pérez was a respected colonel in the Mexican army and Santa Anna believed Pérez's military experience would serve him well in the unstable north. But instead of having to defend himself from the Comanche and Apache, Albino Pérez discovered that he was surrounded by patrónes who were more concerned with their own interests than the good of the nation.[84] The centralists had hoped that replacing local officials would allow them to reel in peripheral states like New Mexico, but they soon discovered that the regional patrónes were too entrenched in local politics, ranching, and trade to be dislodged.

From Mexico City, Santa Anna led a charge to reassert Mexican central authority over the loose collection of states that made up the Mexican Republic.[85] During his past terms as president Santa Anna had represented himself as an advocate of democracy, but by 1835 he was disenchanted with the regionalism and social unrest that plagued Mexico in the wake of independence.[86] In addition, Armijo and many others in Mexico City were tired of the economic problems that plagued the Mexican government.[87] As a result of these frustrations Santa Anna and the centralists devised the departmental plan, which was intended to reorganize Mexico into departments and centralize power with the goal of securing revenue for the federal government.[88] The new plan was simultaneously intended to curb the power of regional patrónes and force them to abide by central authority.

In 1835 Santa Anna used his office to abolish the constitution of 1824; by doing so he cleared the way for the constitution of 1836—the Siete Leyes—to be ratified. His actions sparked a series of rebellions throughout Mexico, among them the Chimayo Rebellion of 1837.[89] Local patrónes and the people they represented responded to the new laws in a variety of ways, most of them violent.

Some ignored the laws or found ways around them, but many ultimately resorted to open rebellion. Unrest swept through the countryside. As David Weber noted, the imposition of the conservative, centralist regime in Mexico sparked the series of revolts in the 1830s.[90] The patrónes and their people resisted centralization. California, New Mexico, and Texas all revolted against the centralist movement, and rebellions also erupted in the Mexican interior states, including Zacatecas in 1835 and the Yucatan in 1840. Intermittent rebellions occurred in Sonora, Tamaulipas, and Sinaloa.

The Texas rebellion was driven by white settlers, who rallied against the centralists' attempts to end immigration from the United States altogether. Whites immigrated to Texas both legally and illegally, pouring in from the United States until they outnumbered the Tejano population.[91] They forged partnerships with wealthy Tejanos and together they dominated both the local economy and local politics. When Santa Anna proposed to end American immigration and outlawed slavery in Texas, the white settlers and their Tejano allies rebelled.[92]

This played out differently in New Mexico, because the number of both American and European immigrants remained low, even if the members of the small community were influential.[93] With their numeric advantage, the patrónes in New Mexico had far more leverage over their American and European partners than did their counterparts in Texas. Still, they cooperated with American merchants because they wanted to develop and exploit their new commercial connections. The Nuevomexicano merchants proved successful. They introduced American goods into the Mexican marketplace, which created competition for Mexican manufacturers and traders in Chihuahua.[94] As a result, Santa Anna resolved to protect Mexican manufacturers and merchants from American goods. To this end, Santa Anna appointed Albino Pérez to the governorship. Pérez was charged with regulating the New Mexican economy, reeling in the upstart patrónes, and securing the northern border. In response, the local patrónes incited an already agitated population of vecinos and Puebloans in the Rio Arriba.

When the Texas revolt erupted Santa Anna undertook the now infamous Texas expedition of 1836. The campaign was a disaster for Santa Anna, who was ultimately defeated at the Battle of San Jacinto.[95] Santa Anna was captured, and during his confinement he received a message from Joel Poinsett, a US government official in Mexico who for many years had argued that Santa Anna was Mexico's only hope for stability. Poinsett was disgusted with Santa Anna's newfound conservatism and told Santa Anna that he no longer believed him to be a champion of democracy. "Say to General Santa Anna that when I remember how ardent an advocate he was of liberty ten years ago, I have no sympathy for him now, that he has gotten what he deserves." To this, Santa Anna retorted:

> Say to Mr. Poinsett that it is very true that I threw up my cap for liberty with great ardor, and perfect sincerity, but very soon found the folly of it. A hundred years to come my people will not be fit for liberty. They do not know what it is, unenlightened as they are, and under the influence of a Catholic clergy, a despotism is the proper government for them, but there is no reason why it should not be a wise and virtuous one.[96]

Santa Anna's words captured both the centralist and patrónes mindsets: simply put, upper-class Mexicans believed that the people needed to be controlled. On the regional level patrónes believed they were entitled to rule over vecinos because they were descendants of the old ruling families. Long before social Darwinism became popular, New Mexican landholders believed that their rule was justified by their station in life, their skills, and of course their hereditary superiority to the vecinos, whom they considered inferior in every way. Many believed they were nobles and that marriage to vecinos polluted their bloodlines. The local patrónes even forced local priests to marry them to their cousins instead of to vecinos, in order to keep their supposed *Spanish* bloodlines pure.[97]

Santa Anna, however, did not differentiate between regional patrónes and vecinos in seeking to transform rural Mexico. To the centralists, the local patrónes were self-interested thugs who needed to be brought to heel. The centralist Mexican perspective was not spoken as much in words as it was in action, and centralist policies situated regional patrónes—or so-called elites—within the same category as poor vecinos, which offended patrónes. Not surprisingly, the patrónes in most of the peripheral regions of Mexico grew to resent the centralists, and this was the root cause of the rebellions that took place throughout the Mexican borderlands.

As in many other parts of Mexico the patrónes in New Mexico openly opposed the departmental plan because it curbed their power. Those in the Rio Abajo resented Santa Anna's plan most of all.[98] As Lecompte wrote, the Rio Abajo "was the home of most of the *ricos*, the rich and educated men, the ruling class. They lived in many-roomed adobe houses, or walled plazas along with their peons, who tended their houses, fields, orchards, and sheep, and were tied in debt to their masters."[99] The new centralist governor challenged their authority when he displaced them from the highest political offices and appointed his allies to these positions.[100] New Mexican patrónes in the Rio Abajo who resented the centralist governor and Jefe Politico y Militar, Col. Albino Pérez, immediately began undermining Pérez's legitimacy among their peers.[101] Patrónes were convinced that a Nuevomexicano should be governor and were angered at the suggestion that federal interests should supersede local agendas. They were right to be concerned. Under the Pérez administration the New Mexican patrónes faced a loss of sovereignty, new trade regulations, and, worst of all, federal taxes, things all Nuevomexicanos adamantly opposed.[102] To combat this threat, the local patrónes plotted against Pérez, and their schemes ultimately blossomed into a full-blown rebellion.[103]

Pérez did little to improve his popularity among the patrónes after he took office in 1835. In fact, he appeared out of touch with the Nuevomexicano community. First, rather than appointing patrónes, Pérez appointed local residents who shared his belief in Santa Anna and the new centralist government.[104] As a result, the New Mexican patrónes in both the Rio Arriba and Rio Abajo disdained Pérez's appointees, especially Don Ramón Abréu and Francisco Sarracino.[105] Many of the patrónes, including Manuel Armijo, believed they were better qualified for these offices because of their "wealth, respectability, and prestige."[106] Donaciano Vigil recalled in his 1846 speech to the legislative assembly that Pérez was undercut because "In the nomination of his employees he entirely neglected to consider influential men of wealth, who lacked the knowledge he thought indispensable for the undertaking, and considering themselves spurned, they soon tried to impair the reputation of Señor Pérez."[107] Vigil's allusions were to, among others, Judge Juan Estevan Pino, postmaster Juan Bautista Vigil y Alarid, and former governor Manuel Armijo.[108]

The centralist government exacerbated the situation when it passed the Decree of 1837, which expanded Pérez's powers to include supervision of the treasury. This ignited more anticentralist sentiment and led to open conflict between Pérez and the local patrónes. The powerful judge Juan Estevan Pino openly criticized the appointment of Santiago Abreu, Pérez's closest political ally, and publicly accused *subcomisario* Francisco Sarracino of embezzlement.[109] Pino found willing allies in postmaster Juan Bautista Vigil y Alarid and interim subcomisario Manuel Armijo, both of whom resented the centralists, and the case went to trial.[110] Earlier Manuel Armijo had helped Vigil y Alarid fend off charges of mismanagement that were filed by Sarracino and Miguel Sena, another Pérez devotee; in return, Pino and Vigil y Alarid maneuvered to attain the appointment of subcomisario for Manuel Armijo. Somehow Judge Pino ended up presiding over the case against Sarracino and found him guilty. Sarracino and his allies, including Governor Pérez, however, refused to abide by the judge's ruling.[111]

If Pérez angered Manuel Armijo and his allies when he disregarded Judge Pino's ruling, he made things all the worse when he reinstated Sarracino in his position as subcomisario. Pérez had pushed Armijo out of that position, so to be replaced by Sarracino was a personal affront. Publicly, Armijo claimed that he surrendered his post due to failing health, but in truth he resigned to avoid the disgrace of being removed.¹¹² Janet Lecompte contends that Armijo's health problems were real and that they affected his ability to serve as subcomisario.¹¹³ It is clear, however, that Armijo and his supporters resented Pérez's decision to reinstate Sarracino and replace Armijo. Armijo was also accustomed to his salary of 4,000 pesos per year, all for minimal work. Politically, Pérez's decision to disregard Judge Pino's ruling amounted to classic confrontation between a federal authority and a regional figure, and it left Armijo's resentment of Perez smoldering.¹¹⁴

THE CHIMAYO REBELLION OF 1837

In 1837 the Chimayo Rebellion erupted in the Rio Arriba and overthrew the Pérez administration. Then and since, the vecinos and Puebloans have been exclusively blamed for this uprising. If we revisit and critically engage the original documents, however, it becomes clear that the patrónes also played an important part in this rebellion. Specifically, they utilized propaganda to incite an already nervous populace against the centralist government. The traditional chronology of the rebellion is straightforward: the rebellion formally began when a local judge in Santa Cruz de la Cañada was jailed because he refused to obey the Pérez administration. It turned violent when Pérez tried to subdue the rebellion and was murdered; and it concluded when Manuel Armijo and the patrónes from the Rio Abajo defeated the rebels and executed their leaders. But as we will see, long before the vecinos and Puebloans revolted, the patrónes circulated rumors among the vecinos and convinced them that the centralist government was a threat to both their rights and future prospects.¹¹⁵

Manuel Armijo and the Rio Abajo patrónes have been portrayed as heroic figures who brought order to New Mexico, but in reality they spread rumors that Pérez's excessive taxes and wayward policies threatened the vecinos' very survival.¹¹⁶ After he helped set the initial rebellion in motion, Manuel Armijo secretly attended the *canton* at Santa Cruz de la Cañada, where he expected to be named governor in the wake of the rebellion.¹¹⁷ As we will see, however, the vecinos surprised Armijo when they did not choose him as governor, and in doing so they transformed the rebellion into a broader political movement. An angry Armijo returned to the Rio Abajo, where he rallied the patrónes against the rebels.¹¹⁸ Armijo later portrayed himself as the hero who defeated the uprising, and the centralists in Mexico City named him governor once more.¹¹⁹ Thanks to the vecinos' political maneuver, the patrónes solidified their autonomy by way of this supposed counterrevolution. Instead of freedom, the vecinos unwittingly strengthened their bond—indeed their social contract—with the patrónes.

THE RISE OF THE PATRÓNES AND THE BURDEN OF THE VECINOS

The uprising in La Cañada signaled the onset of the Chimayo Rebellion, but the course for rebellion was first charted when Governor Pérez clashed with the local patrónes in the Rio Abajo. As noted, Governor Pérez angered the local patrónes when he selected the unpopular Don Ramón Abréu and Francisco Sarracino for government positions, instead of selecting Juan Estevan Pino, Manuel Armijo, and Juan Bautista Vigil y Alarid.[120] This move pitted Pérez against three of the stoutest power brokers in New Mexico, well-connected patrónes by virtue of kinship networks and old friendships. These appointments and the passage of new tax laws made New Mexico ripe for rebellion.[121]

When Governor Pérez also passed tax reforms targeting local patrónes, those power brokers responded by disseminating rumors that Pérez intended to drain *both* local landholders and vecinos of their holdings with outlandish taxes.[122] In reality, Governor Pérez targeted trade items that affected the wealthy patrónes and their American business partners rather than the poor vecinos or the Puebloans. Taxes targeted imported vehicles and animals, lumber, livestock, dances and other performances, and immigrants. Violations of the new laws were to be met by fines.[123] The patrónes in the Rio Abajo profited from agricultural exports and those in the Rio Arriba profited from trade, meaning that patrónes in both regions were affected by these taxes. Armijo and the other patrónes banded together and condemned the new taxes. They also launched a public campaign to inaccurately describe the new tax code to the vecinos. Even though Governor Pérez's policies had little to no effect on the vecinos, they soon resented his taxes as well.

The Chimayo Rebellion was ultimately ignited from the bottom up, but in the time leading up to the rebellion the invisible hand of the local patrónes—who objected to the centralist movement—agitated the vecinos and Puebloans through rumor and innuendo. Armijo was a major part of that effort, and he spoke for his fellow landholders when he publicly denounced the power that Mexico City had given to the Jefe Politico in Santa Fe.[124] Together the patrónes circulated specific rumors that vastly overstated the new tax laws. They claimed that the vecinos and Pueblo peoples would lose half their property, that shepherds would be taxed for moving sheep. They said that the governor's proposed taxes would include water, food, land, and even their wives and children. Patrónes went so far as to tell vecinos that they would be taxed each time they lay with their wives.[125] The Puebloans were easy to incite because they were already primed for rebellion; for very good reasons they distrusted foreigners, and they were already accustomed to their vecino neighbors. As Donaciano Vigil recounted in an 1847 speech, "As soon as the people were brought to a certain level of discontent, distrust, and exaltation by this means, the tenacious enemies of Señor Pérez planned a revolution that had for its ostensible object only the jobs of the present favorites of Señor Pérez."[126] Vigil chose not to name those involved during his oratory—they were present while he spoke!—but he clearly established that the motive for the rebellion was not the spontaneous passions of vecinos and Puebloans. Instead, Armijo and his coconspirators had created a toxic environment in which one small spark could ignite a rebellion.

It didn't help that Governor Pérez was a young aristocrat who publicly flaunted his wealth and position.[127] The patrónes cited his lavish spending and extravagant tastes to turn the vecinos against him. When Governor Pérez arrived in New Mexico he went on a spending spree. He borrowed money from local patrónes and purchased expensive silks, new furniture for the Palacio Nacional, and other fine goods. The patrónes circulated rumors that Governor Pérez and his administration had used treasury money to fund all manner of extravagances, rather than spend on defense, and that by doing so he endangered all Nuevomexicanos.[128] This of course further primed the vecinos for rebellion.

These are the reasons that in December of 1836, a simple court case in Santa Cruz de La Cañada exploded into a battle between centralist and local authorities. The conflict began when the unpopular prefect Ramón Abréu ordered the popular alcalde Juan José Esquibel to administer justice against two landholders from the Rio Arriba. The alcalde refused.[129] Governor Pérez resolved to demonstrate his authority. He dissolved the municipal council of Santa Cruz de la Cañada on the grounds that most of the seven members were related.[130] Ramón Abréu ordered Esquibel imprisoned after he disobeyed the order to dissolve, but numerous unnamed citizens freed Esquibel. Next, Esquibel and his allies, including members of his family, formed a canton and composed this proclamation:

> Long live God and the Nation and the faith of Jesus Christ, for the most important issues that they stand for are as follows:
> - To be with God and the Nation and the faith of Jesus Christ.
> - To defend our country until the last drop of blood is shed to achieve the desired victory
> - Not to allow the Departmental Plan.
> - Not to allow any taxes.
> - Not to permit the excesses of those who attempt to carry this out.
>
> God and the Nation, Santa Cruz de la Cañada, August 1, 1837, in camp.[131]

The canton denounced Gov. Albino Pérez, his administration, and his policies in this proclamation and they vowed violent resistance against the centralists.

The authors of the proclamation were clearly educated; they penned a coherent agenda that demonstrated their understanding of the core conflict between the Nuevomexicano patrónes and the centralists. They understood that the conflict with Governor Pérez was rooted in the departmental plan, which was the centralist attempt to reorganize Mexico and assert authority over its semiautonomous regions, and they denounced both taxation and those who implemented taxes.[132]

The vecinos and Pueblo dissidents joined the northern patrónes in rebellion. It's unclear if Governor Pérez realized how few allies he really had in New Mexico, but he was determined to quash the rebellion, and so he launched an offensive against them. He called on the local patrónes in the Rio Abajo to support him and attempted to gather an army to subdue the rebels. But Pérez found little support despite his best efforts. The patrónes of the Rio Abajo gave many excuses for why they could not come to the governor's aid. Mostly, they claimed they were too busy with local matters. Governor Pérez stubbornly mustered a small militia and rode north anyway. In the battle that ensued he was betrayed by his Pueblo militiamen and forced to retreat.[133] Albino Chacón recalled that "The governor traveled toward the Rio Abajo until he encountered a force of militiamen commanded by the insurrectionist Don A. Antonito Chávez who refused the governor all protection, which is why, while returning from there toward Santa Fe, he was killed by two Indians in the suburbs, and his head carried to the camp and scoffed at by the naturalized villains."[134]

A number of other notable figures—Ramon Abréu, Miguel Sena, and Jesus Maria Alarid—were also killed by rebels. Four years later the German immigrant Charles Blumner remembered the details of the massacre in a letter to his mother:

> All these gentlemen, after governor Don Albino Pérez lost his battle with the revolutionary party, were caught escaping and all of them were murdered! Several of them in a very gruesome manner! The governor, for instance, they cut off his head from the rump before he was dead and they left his mutilated body in the street! Another one, a very powerful and most hated person, Don Santiago Abreu, they cut his tongue out of his throat while he was still alive! He was such an eloquent speaker![135]

Benjamin Read postulated that Manuel Armijo orchestrated the uprising.[136] The evidence from memoirs, proclamations, and later speeches substantiates the idea that—at least in part—Armijo did in fact agitate and instigate the vecinos into a rebellious state. Armijo also had motive, means, and a personal grudge against Governor Pérez. Those who accused Armijo included American traders and

CHAPTER ONE

Nuevomexicanos who lived beyond Armijo's reach. Many incriminating documents, however, are missing because—as Donaciano Vigil later told the historian William G. Ritch—once Armijo claimed the governorship, "All documents and papers relating to the revolution and opposition to Pérez were gathered together, as he knew from personal knowledge, and it was well understood that they were destroyed by Armijo."[137]

In 1909 historian L. B. Prince interviewed Aniceito Abeytia, who was a young boy during the rebellion and was then advanced in age. Abeytia claimed that Manuel Armijo cautioned the revolutionaries at the commission in Santa Fe, which met shortly after Pérez was murdered. Armijo advised the rebels to be vigilant when dealing with Mexico City; Armijo recommended that they send a report to Mexico City that outlined the incident in a favorable light and then await guidance. According to Abeytia, Armijo contended that the local forces could not hope to survive an assault by the Mexican army, and that if they wanted to survive, they needed to be cautious. Abeytia's account contained great detail, and the savvy advice he attributed to Armijo is convincing.[138] Additionally, numerous American accounts accused Armijo and contended that he had designs on regaining the governorship, the position he was forced to abdicate in 1828 in the midst of scandal. According to Abeytia—and he is very clear on this subject—Manuel Armijo traveled north after rebels murdered Pérez because he anticipated being named governor by the rebels.[139]

Armijo and the Rio Abajo patrónes were dissatisfied when the rebels failed to elect Armijo as governor. The rebels commissioned Armijo to organize the Rio Abajo and he hastily departed for his home in Albuquerque.[140] The rebels elected as governor Jose Angel Gonzales, a buffalo hunter and son of a Pueblo mother and genízaro father, said to be unable to pen his own name. And so, Armijo brought word to the Rio Abajo that the rebels elected an illiterate genízaro. The New Mexican patrónes viewed Gonzales's governorship as even more illegitimate than Albino Pérez's. According to Abeytia the opportunistic Armijo used his kinship network and rallied patrón support against the rebels.[141] The patrónes who were close to Armijo responded to his call, and he used their endorsement to lead a counterrevolution against the rebels who failed to appoint him.

In contrast to Abeytia's account, a literalist reading of the surviving nineteenth-century Mexican records tells a story of heroism and gallantry: Manuel Armijo and the so-called elites from the Rio Abajo rode north to quell a rebellion. Empowered by the hyperbolic Plan de Tomé, Armijo and his men supposedly saved New Mexico from dissident vecinos and the Pueblo people:

Pronouncement at Tome on the 8th day of September 1837 by the citizens—lovers of their country in favor of the Constitution and laws; and they are those hereto subscribed.

In the town of Tome on the 8th day in the year 1837, the neighbors of said point, and those of Santa Maria of Belen, being assembled, with their respective alcaldes, the parish priest of Tome, the lieutenant of the active militia, the honored citizen Don Manuel Armijo, from the jurisdiction of Albuquerque, fearing the disorders resulting from the anarchy, in which the Territory of New Mexico was plunged, by the deaths inflicted on the persons of the iniquitous measures which the so called "Canton of La Canada" is taking for the destruction of peace, harmony and good order of the citizens, and we being desirous to submit ourselves to the laws, and to keep within bounds the insults with which at every step we are threatened with as well as protecting our properties, and to make the supreme government know the good disposition and obedience which the District of Albuquerque professes it, they have agreed on the following articles:

- Until the supreme government determines to execute what it may see fit in this Territory, no other authority is recognized but that of the Prefect of the District of Albuquerque, the only legal one remaining.
- No one shall be attacked in his property or rights.
- An armed force will be placed under the command of the citizen Manuel Armijo, whom we have generally proclaimed as commandant, and as his second, the citizen Mariano Chavez, neighbor of Los Padillas, and his secretary, the citizen Vicente Sanchez Vergara.
- If, after all the forces are assembled, it is desired by the commanding officer to appoint another his will shall be obeyed in everything the same as it now is being done.
- It being fit that the pueblos remain tranquil and not meddle in the difficulties of the Mexican citizens, they will be informed, that the war not being against them nor directed against them nor directed against any of them, not to take part in favor of either party, and that, until the supreme government appoints a governor, they may not flow from themselves.
- That the preceding article may have effect, it has been made known to three native Indians, that were present from the Pueblo of Isleta, all the just causes that exist, and which they must manifest to their comrades.

CHAPTER ONE

- This pronouncement does not recognize the authority which the appointed Canton placed.
- The liberating forces being once assembled, the commander shall take the measures which to him may seem convenient for the necessary expenses which may incur, and if he should seize any private property, it will be reintegrated, a thing that will be done religiously.
- An extraordinary envoy shall be at once sent for the purpose of giving notice to the General Commandant at Chihuahua, and to the supreme government.
- Anything that may have been contributed by the natives in the shape of pension for the commissioners that had been appointed in Santa Fe shall be returned to them.
- In witness whereof we have signed this on said day.

Tome, September 8, 1837.

Manuel Armijo	(Seal)
Jose Salazar	(Seal)
Pablo Salazar	(Seal)
J. Franco Montoya	(Seal)
Miguel Olona	(Seal)
Manuel Madariaga	(Seal)[142]

The proclamation was shrewdly composed. It distanced the Rio Abajo patrónes from the uprising and simultaneously defined them as the lone legitimate Mexican entity remaining in New Mexico. In fact, it followed the exact advice that Aniceito Abeytia claimed Manuel Armijo gave the rebels in suggesting that they proactively take control of the narrative of events and send their version to Mexico City.[143] Mailed to Mexico City, the Plan de Tomé declared the Rio Arriba in the state of rebellion and singled out patrónes Manuel Armijo and the Rio Abajo as representative of the "good disposition and obedience" of the people in the District of Albuquerque to the "supreme government."[144] "The Honored Citizen Don Manuel Armijo" was the only individual mentioned in the preamble, a reference that further distanced him from the rebels.[145]

Through this proclamation the counterrevolutionaries decided that Manuel Armijo and Mariano Chavez (indeed, Manuel Chaves's uncle) would lead a "liberating force" into Santa Fe to depose the rebel governor, Jose Gonzales.[146] At the meeting at Tomé, Mariano nominated Manuel Armijo to lead the assault; in turn Manuel named Mariano Chavez as his second in command. Armijo lamented that the command was thrust upon him, and that he accepted only because it was his duty. It is doubtful that he faced competition, because most of the landholders avoided signing the pronouncement.[147] As John Baxter notes, "The sheep traders remained unconcerned . . . and refused to let politics interfere with business."[148] At best the other landholders ignored Armijo's efforts because they were busy; at worst they distanced themselves from Armijo's ambition for fear of the Mexican army.

On September 9, Manuel Armijo and Commandant Jose Caballero entered Santa Fe and publicly denounced the canton of Santa Cruz de La Cañada. Their counterrevolution marked the end of Mexico's centralization efforts in New Mexico. As Thomas D. Hall writes, "This local episode, lasting only a few months, presents in a New Mexican microcosm all the features of the general state of affairs in Mexico: a local caudillo taking action against a group of anti-centralist rebels in the name of order, but also in his own personal and class interest."[149] Carrying the Plan de Tomé, Armijo asserted his authority in a manner characteristic of a caudillo: he seized power, used violence against all who resisted, and furthered the interests of those who constituted his power base.

When Gov. Jose Gonzales heard about the Plan de Tomé he agreed to transfer power to Armijo peacefully, but the rebels remained discontented in early 1838. A rebel named Antonio Vigil denounced Armijo in a circular he distributed in Santa Fe. In it, Vigil argued that Armijo was not the legitimate governor and that Armijo needed to release the four rebel prisoners who had surrendered and been handed over to Armijo by Pablo Montoya, a rebel patrón from Rio Arriba, in exchange for the latter's immunity.[150] Vigil called Armijo's rule illegal and illegitimate and maintained that Jose Gonzales was the rightful governor.[151] The circular infuriated Armijo, and he responded by ordering the rebels to disband. When they refused, he had the four rebel leaders decapitated.[152] Armijo and his army attacked the rebels and routed them in the mountains. Padre Martinez himself gave Gonzales his last rites before Manuel Armijo had the revolutionary governor executed.

Like Santa Anna after a foreign war, Armijo glorified himself after the rebellion was quelled. Control over the narrative of rebellion "soon won him confirmation as governor and supreme commander of military forces."[153] Others celebrated the counterrevolution, including Albino Chacón, who attributed the Plan de Tomé to "The virtues, patriotism, and talents actively displayed by the gentlemen who signed it."[154] Chacón sincerely believed in the counterrevolution, but it is doubtful he understood how the rebellion had unfolded. In 1846 Donaciano Vigil also celebrated Armijo. "Don Manuel Armijo, present governor and commanding general of this department who took command of the lovers of order and of the constitutional government, had the honor of putting down the revolutionary hydra in 1837 and of reestablishing order and peace among us," Vigil proclaimed to the Departmental Assembly.[155] Vigil's speech at the assembly, however, was influenced by Manuel Armijo's presence; as we have seen, Armijo was not afraid to bring his guns to bear against public officials who crossed him. Additionally, Armijo and Vigil were friends, which is evidenced by the numerous letters Vigil wrote to Armijo during the American period.[156] Finally, Donaciano Vigil wasn't in position to criticize those who were complicit in the rebellion, given that he served as secretary for the canton, so it was wise not to bring too much attention to himself.[157]

Armijo sent an account of the counterrevolution to Mexico City and Chihuahua that painted him in a favorable light, a move that solidified his authority as Jefe Politico y Militar. Santa Anna read the report of Armijo's exploits and patriotism and recognized Manuel Armijo as the new governor. In the years that followed Armijo pushed his weight around New Mexico. He brutalized vecinos, bullied fellow patrónes, and squeezed American merchants for money. As governor, Armijo granted more than 16.5 million acres of land to his allies, far more than any other governor in New Mexican history. His actions allowed the regional patrónes to avoid taxes and regain control of local affairs, while the vecinos returned to their labors.

Conclusion

Manuel Armijo may have ordered the documents pertaining to the Chimayo Rebellion destroyed, but between Donaciano Vigil's public oratory and Aniceto Abeytia's interview, it is reasonable to conclude that Armijo and his fellow landholders fomented unrest in a rebellion that ultimately claimed Gov. Albino Pérez's life.[158] The contention that the vecinos and Puebloans were solely responsible for the rebellion is also undermined by a reading of the surviving historical data in the territory's social and political context. The Chimayo Rebellion was just one of many rebellions that occurred in response to the centralist movement in greater Mexico. Throughout Mexico, caudillos rebelled against Santa Anna's centralist movement and many rebuffed the federal authorities. By securing local autonomy, rebels also weakened the Mexican nation and its infrastructure, ripening Mexico for American conquest.

In 1846 the American military marched into Santa Fe unopposed; Manuel Armijo promised to defend New Mexico, but instead fled south to Chihuahua. The ever-savvy Armijo realized what many patriotic Mexicans did not: that open warfare was bad for business. The postmaster Juan Bautista Vigil y Alarid—indeed Armijo's old ally—assumed the governorship, while Manuel Armijo fled south to Chihuahua. Vigil y Alarid read the following proclamation to Gen. Stephen Watts Kearny and his men in front of the Palacio Nacional:

> General:—The address which you have just delivered, in which you announce that you have taken possession of this great country in the name of the United States of America, gives us some idea of the wonderful future that awaits us. It is not for us to determine the boundaries of nations. The cabinets of Mexico and Washington will arrange these differences. It is for us to obey and respect the established authorities, no matter what may be our private opinions.
>
> The inhabitants of this Department humbly and honorably present their loyalty and allegiance to the government of North America. No one in this world can successfully resist the power of him who is stronger.
>
> Do not find it strange if there has been no manifestation of joy and enthusiasm in seeing this city occupied by your military forces. To us the power of the Mexican Republic is dead. No matter what her condition, she was our mother. What child will not shed abundant tears at the tomb of his parents? I might indicate some of the causes for her misfortunes, but domestic troubles should not be made public. It is sufficient to say that civil war is the cursed source of that deadly poison which has spread over one of the grandest and greatest countries that has ever been created. To-day we belong to a great and powerful nation. Its flag, with its stars and stripes, covers the horizon of New Mexico, and its brilliant light shall grow like good seed well cultivated. We are cognizant of your kindness, of your courtesy and that of your accommodating officers and of the strict discipline of your troops; we know that we belong to the Republic that owes its origin to the immortal Washington, whom all civilized nations admire and respect. How different would be our situation had we been invaded by European nations! We are aware of the unfortunate condition of the Poles.
>
> In the name, then, of the entire Department, I swear obedience to the Northern Republic and I tender my respect to its laws and authority.[159]

The Chimayo Rebellion should be remembered for what it was: a popular political coup instigated if not performed by Manuel Armijo and the emerging patrónes in the Rio Abajo. Like so many coups before and since, it was fueled by the rumors and misinformation that the ruling class disseminated. Noting Armijo's subsequent prorogation of the legislative assembly and centralization of power in the governorship, historians have characterized Armijo as a "trader, judge, lawmaker, and soldier," who used others to obtain power and discarded them when they were no longer useful.[160] By all counts, Manuel Armijo was the *caudillo supremo*[161] or *superpatrón* in New Mexico, a wealthy leader among many patrónes who used his station as governor to intimidate his enemies and promote the interests of his fellow Nuevomexicano landholders. Shortly after the US-Mexican War, Armijo returned to Albuquerque, where he remained until his death. With his departure from public life, a new power vacuum formed, and other patrónes rose to political power and filled the void left by his retirement.

CHAPTER TWO

VECINO LARCENY AND THE PROCESS OF TERRITORIALIZATION

On Christmas Eve of 1865, Bishop Jean Baptiste Lamy was fast asleep in his bed in Santa Fe, New Mexico, when a drunken man entered his apartment, walked through his living room, and pointed a gun at him.[1] Lamy awoke to the glint of a revolver, a scowl, and the words, "Give me fifty dollars or I will kill you."[2] Lamy consented and when his assistant rushed into the room, Lamy ordered, "Take him out and give him fifty dollars."[3] Lamy's assistant showed the assailant to the door, but then ejected him without paying and locked the door behind him. Thwarted but not deterred, the man broke into a different apartment on the church grounds, where two other priests slumbered. Once inside and out of the cold, the intoxicated assailant reasoned that he would like to warm himself by a fire. So he built one. His body now warm, the intruder drew his gun and woke both priests with yet another demand, "If you don't give me something to eat, I will kill you!"[4] But this time, in his drunken haze, he indiscriminately opened fire, striking one priest in the neck and the other in the head and the leg. Miraculously, both men survived the attack. Sister Catherine, who tended the wounded and nursed them back to health at St. Vincent Hospital, later recalled that it was the worst Christmas Eve of her life.[5]

Social histories, especially of the Mexican North and US West, are ripe with fantastic stories like this one, but both scholars and readers have tended to focus exclusively on the violent aspects of these crimes. Murder is interesting, as is the notion of lawlessness, and when someone is shot, stabbed, or clubbed, readers want to know more. The Christmas Eve attack on Lamy is particularly entertaining for its imagery: a desperate rogue threatening an actual bishop before shooting two priests, and on Christmas Eve no less. For scholars looking to attract readers, this is archival gold, and indeed we will discuss violence in the next chapter. At its core, though, this incident is the story of an attempted armed robbery gone wrong. It is not only about a bishop and his clergy being victimized; it is also the story of a man who was so cold, hungry, drunk, and desperate that he was willing to risk a date with the hangman's noose for $50 or a meal.

In fact, Bishop Jean Baptiste Lamy was mugged at least four times during his first thirteen years in Santa Fe. In one week during December 1852 alone, Lamy was mugged no fewer than three times. Records exist for two of them: on December 15 he was mugged by Juan Lucero, who relieved him of $10 in coin, and on December 20 Lamy was mugged by Antonio Lucero, who stole an unknown amount of money from his person.[6] These crimes go unmentioned, even by Lamy's award-winning biographer, who only recounted what happened on Christmas Eve. Considered together, however, these four larcenies can tell us more than just one suspense-filled story of lawlessness; they have the potential to illuminate the larger trends of growing inequality, social change, and, ultimately, poor Hispano resistance to both the changes taking place and the increasingly unequal system of power that emerged in the power vacuum of New Mexico.[7]

Scholars and others debate whether larceny can be a legitimate form of resistance used by the poor in the power struggle against the wealthy. Frederick Douglass proposed that a slave stealing from a master was both legitimate and justified. More recently, literary scholar Lovalerie King has shown how African American writers have justified African American theft as a legitimate form of resistance and a response to a history of extreme inequality.[8] Less conclusively, in his study of Malaysia, James Scott notes that poor villagers almost exclusively targeted wealthier landholders when they committed petty larcenies. Citing a paucity of evidence, however, Scott stopped short of declaring it resistance, noting, "This pattern is not itself proof that such thefts are conceived by the poor as a means of resistance or some form of 'social banditry.'"[9] Sociologist Gary Lafree attributes the twentieth-century rise in street crime (including homicide, rape, assault, and property crimes) to the decline of social institutions in post–World War II America.[10] He argues, "Historical and social changes in America created a crisis in institutional legitimacy that produced a postwar crime wave." For LaFree, legitimacy is key, and he defines it as "the ease or difficulty with which institutions are able to get societal members to follow these rules, laws, and norms."[11]

A handful of legal scholars have tracked the evolution of larceny laws over time from the perspective of lawmakers.[12] Michael E. Tigar illuminates the relationship between the emergence of a capitalist ruling class in the English and American legal traditions and the upsurge in larceny laws, demonstrating that the ruling class changed definitions of theft at particular historical moments to fortify their dominant social position and extend their power to enforce order through law. Tigar contends that larceny law was created to legitimize the idea of ownership, specifically for the ruling class. Tigar notes, "If we survey the law in historical context, we will see deliberate manipulations of the legal definition of theft, as well as patterns of prosecutorial and police discretion designed to achieve these goals."[13] Elites have redefined traditional modes of lower-class subsistence as theft by transforming that which was communal (hunting and access to raw materials on communal lands) into private property. Through these laws, the ruling class stripped the poor of their independence and bound them to the labor force.[14]

This chapter examines how territorialization affected the vecinos in Santa Fe County and argues that the new government, which favored local patrónes and their longtime American business partners, spurred high larceny rates in Santa Fe County. By territorialization, I mean the process by which New

Mexico was incorporated into a US federal territory. I argue that vecinos were pushed into petty larceny by the legal, spiritual, and economic pressures that accompanied territorialization. The first section examines the origin of the territorial system and its laws. I argue that after the Taos campaigns of 1847, the local patrónes moved their fight into the political arena, where they wrangled for their private interests.[15] Local patrónes and their American allies walled out new Anglo settlers and limited their political and economic prospects in Santa Fe County. The patrónes and their allies used the new system to increase their property.

The second part of this chapter uncovers how the wealth inequality that resulted from the new system caused larceny to spike in Santa Fe County. The data suggest that vecinos resorted to petty larceny because they needed food, clothing, and shelter. In contrast, new Anglo settlers either stole firearms or committed grand larceny. Ultimately, this chapter shows that the partnership between the local patrónes and Americans ensured that their interests would continue to be protected at the expense of both vecinos and new Anglo settlers. The vecinos became desperate, the Anglo settlers became angry, and ultimately larceny in Santa Fe County skyrocketed.

Territorialization as Process

The process of territorialization changed the lives of Nuevomexicano vecinos on multiple fronts: legally, spiritually, and economically. Legally, the vecinos faced laws that mirrored the code they were accustomed to, but larceny laws were strengthened and the judicial apparatus was modified in ways that put vecinos at the mercy of the courts. Spiritually, the vecinos watched as a foreign authority seized the New Mexican pulpits; the Diocese of Durango was replaced by the Diocese of Baltimore, and French clergymen displaced Hispano spiritual leaders. Economically, vecinos lost access to public lands, which were seized by the US military and ultimately sold off to patrónes and their business partners. The patrónes transitioned away from their responsibilities to the vecinos; instead, they increasingly became their employers. They left the vecinos to fend for themselves against the courts, the church, and the threat of starvation.

In 1846, the vecinos also faced the legal changes that accompanied the American invasion. General Kearny appointed many of the Anglo immigrants who were already settled in New Mexico to the new territorial government.[16] In 1846 these early Anglo immigrants—many of whom had married into the local landholding families—brokered negotiations between the New Mexican patrónes and the United States Army.[17] The Nuevomexicanos prepared to fight, but there was little chance of victory. To avoid open warfare, General Kearny took advantage of old Anglo settlers' relationships with the New Mexican patrónes. Kearny appealed to the business interests of New Mexican landholders, and through friendly channels he guaranteed the patrónes that their properties would be secured.[18]

General Kearny hoped for peace and stability in New Mexico, and he sought to create laws that facilitated a smooth transition. To that end, he instructed Col. Alexander William Doniphan to create a legal code for New Mexico. The result was a complex legal system that incorporated, in Doniphan's estimation, the best aspects of Spanish, Mexican, and English law, as well as elements of Texas Law, Louisiana's Livingston Code, and Missouri's Organic Acts.[19] Doniphan was aided by Charles Bent, who advised the committee on how local law worked in New Mexico.[20] The result was a hybrid code that dictated harsh punishments for vecinos and newly arrived settlers, especially for the crime of larceny.[21]

The Kearny Code undergirded a power structure that both the patrónes and the American military understood; it was a set of laws that prescribed force to empower rulers and subjugate followers. The patrónes and the ruling Americans believed in rule by force because both groups were positioned at the top of the socioeconomic and ethnic hierarchies. The Nuevomexicano patrónes increasingly viewed themselves in terms of class after the Americans arrived. They considered themselves better than the vecinos, primarily because of their wealth, but also because of their supposedly pure Spanish heritage. Meanwhile, most Americans viewed Nuevomexicanos through their preconceived construct of race. They categorized the New Mexican patrónes as European Spanish elites, but at the same time they wrongly discriminated against the vecinos, whom they viewed as barbaric peoples incapable of civilization because they had mixed their blood with that of the Indigenous. These ruling groups believed their interests were more important than those of the poorer vecinos and newly arrived white settlers. They also believed that the lower classes in New Mexico needed to be ruled with a firm hand. For example, the section of the new legal code that designated corporal punishment for larceny fit with New Mexican patrónes' informal behavior over several generations toward vecinos.[22] Who would rule was one matter, but the New Mexican patrónes and the American authorities were never far apart in their beliefs about how the people in New Mexico should be compelled to follow law.

Although the legal codes remained similar, there were significant changes in the judicial structure. Kearny named new judges to the criminal courts, and the Kearny Code introduced the jury system to New Mexico.[23] Mexican alcaldes continued to serve as arbitrators in civil cases, but new judges were appointed to deal with criminal cases. Kearny appointed white settlers who had been in Santa Fe for more than twenty years to the judgeships, the very white men who helped facilitate the surrender of New Mexico. These new judges lacked formal legal training, but the military government assumed that their long-standing relationships with patrónes made them the best candidates. Territorial authorities depended on these judges and hoped that their extensive knowledge of the local community—along with their familiarity with the Spanish language—compensated for their lack of formal training.

The first white judges whom Kearny appointed believed that New Mexico was a lawless land where criminals ran free; they condemned the Hispano alcaldes and vowed to bring justice to New Mexico. Foremost among the new justices was Chief Justice Joab Houghton, who sought to organize the judicial system in New Mexico.[24] Houghton divided New Mexico into three districts: the First District in Santa Fe, the Second District in the Rio Abajo, and the Third District in the Rio Arriba.[25] Houghton hoped to consolidate and centralize legal authority in New Mexico, but the residents outside of Santa Fe County often resisted.[26] From 1846 to 1854, Judges Rufus Beach, Hugh N. Smith, Edward Hoffman of Maryland, and Joseph Johnston of Virginia all served as judges of the Santa Fe County First Judicial District.[27] Tomás Ortiz was the lone Nuevomexicano judge in Santa Fe County, but he was a probate judge.[28] Elsewhere Kearny appointed Antonio José Otero to the Second District, which encompassed Bernalillo and Valencia, and the Taos merchant Charles Beaubien to the Third District, which included Taos and Rio Arriba.[29]

The white judges believed that the Nuevomexicano alcaldes were lax and that criminals in New Mexico went unpunished, but this perception demonstrated how little they knew about New Mexico's justice system. This misnomer was fueled by longtime white residents, journalists, chroniclers, and scholars, who all rebuked New Mexican justice during the Mexican period. They argued that the alcaldes were lazy and that as a result sentences were soft and murderers escaped punishment. But the court records from the Mexican period indicate that the alcaldes thoroughly examined crimes and meticulously documented them, especially in homicide cases.[30] As historian Jill Mocho writes, "Although justices in New Mexico had no formal legal education, they apparently did have access to laws and procedures. . . . It appears from trial records that they made every attempt to follow accepted judicial methods in handling criminal cases."[31] The fact is that the alcaldes worked hard during the Mexican period and produced far more detailed records than the American-run courts did during the years of territorialization.[32] The Mexican alcaldes left paper trails that included the process of investigation (*summaria*), the initial proceedings (*auto de cabeza*), and the examination of the body (*reconocimiento de heridas*). The New Mexican courts even transcribed witness testimonies in meticulous detail and had witnesses for both the defense and prosecution sign them.

The Mexican alcaldes went to great efforts to curb local crime and uphold social order in Santa Fe County, but what stands out is the degree to which the local vecinos cooperated and displayed considerable honesty during these processes.

Normally vecinos and the Indigenous confessed to their crime and explained why, if there was a reason, they broke the law.[33] Vecino defendants rarely denied their guilt, but when they did, both sides presented their arguments in a scenario called a *plenario*. The alcaldes did not let defendants off easy when they denied their guilt. Instead, the alcalde detained the accused in jail for many months, and sometimes years, while the long and difficult trial played out.[34] More often the offender confessed his crime, was punished, and returned to society.[35]

For the alcaldes, the Mexican legal system functioned to maintain order within the community and not to mete out punitive punishments, but Americans mistook this for leniency.[36] For Americans, it was difficult to comprehend a judicial system that prioritized redemption. After 1820, alcaldes did not give overly punitive sentences: there were no lengthy prison terms, and a royal decree abolished corporal punishment.[37] As Charles Cutter noted, one legacy of the Spanish era was the belief that punishment should repair the damage a criminal did to society; at the same time, it should deter potential criminals from repeating the crime.[38] American judges mistook the alcalde's thoughtful punishments for weakness, and they resolved to reform the vecinos with hard punishments.

The American judges may have been equally meticulous in their investigations, but few written records remain that document either their investigations or deliberations.[39] This was especially true in the first six years of American rule. In the early years sheriffs wrote up simple form-letter-style statements that did little more than name the accused and the crime they supposedly committed. American territorial judges did no better. They also utilized form letters that recorded the names of the accused and the victim, a summary of the crime or assault, and sometimes the harm that was done. These judges seldom recorded important details like witness testimonies, motive for the crime, and whether the perpetrator felt remorse.[40] Overall, the territorial judges did a poor job of keeping records when compared to the Mexican alcaldes.

The criminal courts represent the only space in which patrónes lost their autonomy in Santa Fe County during the process of territorialization. They relinquished this power willingly, however. The patrónes were consumed with their business interests and did not care about the criminal courts. American judges adjudicated criminal court cases against both the vecinos and the new American settlers; they did not prosecute the local patrónes.[41] Although the laws remained aligned with Mexican law, in Santa Fe County the patrónes conceded direct control of the legal apparatus in exchange for federal money.[42] After 1853, the *politicos* in the legislature took steps to assert their authority over the courts. They were angry because the federal government appointed judges from outside of New Mexico, so they passed legislation that affected court procedures. Even then, the patrónes endorsed the punishments in the Kearny Code and left the vecinos at the mercy of American judges and their punitive court system.

Overall, the Kearny Code enabled patrónes to keep their power in New Mexico, but Kearny alienated the patrónes in the Rio Abajo when he appointed Charles Bent as governor.[43] Kearny intended to change little in New Mexico: he announced that the officials that had served the Mexican government were permitted to remain in office if they signed an oath of allegiance. Among the many who swore the oath was the ever-opportunistic Donaciano Vigil. Vigil had served the centralist governor Albino Pérez before the Chimayo Rebellion of 1837; he also agreed to act as secretary for the rebel government after Governor Pérez was murdered, and he was a known Amerophile. When the rebels failed, he claimed that he had only served the rebels under duress and he was next allowed to serve Manuel Armijo.[44] When Armijo fled south and the Americans assumed power, Vigil switched allegiance again and became an American citizen.

Donaciano Vigil benefited most when Kearny appointed Bent as governor, though not by his design; when Bent was murdered, Vigil became interim governor because he was the highest-ranking official below him.[45] From his new position, Vigil appealed to his fellow landholders to use their good sense and end their efforts to re-establish independence. Vigil condemned Pablo Montoya, and what he labeled a rebellion, in a proclamation titled "Triumph of Principles Over Turpitude."[46] He denounced the 1847 Taos Rebellion as a rabble composed of scoundrels and desperados, and proclaimed that no sensible person would join their ranks. He appealed to their economic savvy in a separate proclamation:

> Whether this country has to belong to the government of the United States or return to its native Mexico, is it not a gross absurdity to foment rancorous feelings toward people with whom we are either to compose one family or to continue our commercial relations? Unquestionably, it is.[47]

By July 1847, the efforts to re-establish independence ended, and in December Donaciano Vigil was named governor of New Mexico; later that month, Vigil and the local landholders organized the territorial legislature. The local patrónes wanted to end military rule, so they formed alliances with influential Americans in Santa Fe.[48] When the legislature met, it became clear that local rulers and the military shared similar ideas of how to rule, but a rift seemed to develop over distribution of profits under the new regime. The representatives faced a great question: Should New Mexico become a state or a territory? The participants in the first legislature could not decide, but they accomplished their goal of taking the initial steps toward establishing a civilian-controlled government.[49]

In 1848, Governor Vigil called for a second convention, and the goal of this assembly was to ask Congress to make New Mexico a civilian-run territory.[50] The list of the attendees at this convention was a roll call of some of the best-known Nuevomexicano landholders: Donaciano Vigil, Santiago Archuleta, Francisco Sarracino, Manuel A. Otero, Gregorio Vigil, Juan Perea, Ramon Luna, and Padre Antonio Jose Martinez—who had served in the last convention and was kin to patrónes in the Rio Abajo—all attended. Anglos attended as well, including longtime resident Charles Beaubien of the Rio Arriba, Elias P. West, and James Quinn.[51]

The patrónes who participated in the second legislature were divided in their interests, and rifts developed between those from the Rio Arriba and Rio Abajo, but in the end they were united by their determination to maintain home rule. During the first convention, members argued the virtues of forming a territory versus establishing New Mexico as a state; by 1848, that discussion was moot, as the national controversy over slavery made statehood untenable. Hispanos aligned themselves by region, but whites like the wealthy merchant Charles Beaubien allied themselves with their business partners. Their personal interests came first, so some sided with the Rio Arriba and others the Rio Abajo. In reality, Anglos and Nuevomexicanos on both sides were more interested in personal gain than they were in policy differences.[52] The members proved that their loyalty was fluid: when the territorialists sensed that their position was becoming unpopular, they suddenly espoused the virtue of home rule.[53] The meeting dragged on, but things changed when the representatives started to suspect that the military government was conspiring with Texans. In 1849, the rivals from Rio Arriba and Rio Abajo were united by this threat, and together they rallied public support. They campaigned and called for a vote among all Nuevomexicanos, who voted 6,371 to 39 to adopt a state constitution and expel the military government.[54] As this incident shows, when home rule was threatened, the feud between factions had its limitations.

What mattered most to the Nuevomexicano patrónes was that the government and the legal system protected the interests of the local landholders: military and caudillo law dovetailed seamlessly, and the vecinos suffered under the new system. The Kearny Code codified important elements of the evolving Mexican social structure into territorial law—a good portion of it drawn directly from local Mexican law—and this encouraged patrónes to cooperate with the American authorities.[55] In the moments when Nuevomexicano landholding interests clashed with the laws, local patrónes fell back to the established practice of *obedezco pero no cumplo* ("I obey but do not comply") and did what they deemed appropriate.[56] Later they used their influence in the legislature to dictate laws and support their interests. The Kearny Code proved beneficial to the patrónes, who had the power to defy the law, but it caused great harm to the vecinos, many of whom fled north to escape poverty and punishment.

If vecinos faced the punitive Kearny Code in the legal realm, they confronted what Fray Angélico Chávez astutely labeled the ecclesiastical colonization of New Mexico in the spiritual realm. Vecinos lost their closest allies when new church authorities displaced the Nuevomexicano padres. The padres occupied a middle ground in New Mexican society: Although many were from the landholding families, they were also connected to the vecinos by spiritual bonds. The padres provided the vecinos with religious guidance and an outlet for their grievances, and the vecinos brought their complaints to the padres, who tried to resolve them peacefully. In 1850, the Catholic Church compromised that bond when they removed New Mexico from the Archdiocese of Durango and resituated it within the Archdiocese of Baltimore. That same year, the Archdiocese of Baltimore appointed Jean Baptiste Lamy as bishop of Santa Fe, and once he arrived he used his office to systematically dislodge the Hispano padres from their churches. The vecinos lost their closest allies because of Lamy's actions, which were guided by a combination of ignorance, racism, and bad information.[57]

Soon after his arrival in Santa Fe in 1850, Lamy encountered resistance from the padres, the vecinos, and the local patrónes. Local padres maintained they were still under the Archdiocese of Durango. To end the confusion, Lamy traveled south to Durango, where the bishop of Durango endorsed him as the new bishop of Santa Fe. Although Lamy had legitimated his authority, Hispanos still viewed him as an outsider. This was especially true after 1852, when upon settling in Santa Fe, Lamy immediately changed the clerical hierarchy. Over the next twenty years Lamy used his office to push the local clergy from their pulpits and replace them with non-Hispano priests. In the process, Lamy alienated many of the vecinos and became widely resented by Nuevomexicanos. Local landholders were angered when Lamy dislodged several respected padres, men who were related to the patrónes, which explains in part why Manuel Chaves quarreled with Lamy in 1858.[58]

Lamy and his fellow immigrant clergymen faced mounting resentment in Santa Fe. Lamy hoped his new community would embrace him, and on his first Sunday Lamy preached, "In my absence, the greatest joy I could have would be to hear that my parishioners, my children, are walking in truth, walking in the way of virtue."[59] Some scholars write of the deep affection between the New Mexican people and the newly arrived clergy.[60] In reality Lamy's relationship with the Hispano population was troubled. Certainly respect and affection had not inspired Manuel Chaves to threaten a priest at San Miguel Chapel. And indeed, as we saw, Bishop Lamy was mugged on two or three separate occasions during his first year in Santa Fe, which might betray a type of dependence on the bishop, but certainly not respect.[61]

Lamy earned every bit of the resentment he received. After only one year in Santa Fe he slandered respected priests and forced them to leave the clergy. Lamy's longtime friend Joseph P. Machebeuf replaced Vicar Juan Felipe Ortiz, and together they plotted to remove the remainder of the native padres.[62] Lamy allied himself with Anglo merchants and believed the rumors they spread about excesses among the padres.[63] He was convinced that the local padres were "for the most part incapable and unworthy."[64] Most of the padres they targeted were from the landholding families, particularly Juan Felipe Ortiz and Padre Antonio José Martínez of Taos, who had trained many of the padres serving in New Mexico.[65]

Lamy and Machebeuf particularly despised Padre Juan Felipe Ortiz—and targeted him for removal despite his distinguished record as a cleric—because in 1850 Ortiz insisted that New Mexico was still part of the Archdiocese of Durango. After they came to power, Lamy and Machebeuf maligned Ortiz for his portliness and claimed his weight was evidence of his indolence.[66] In truth, Padre Ortiz was an active cleric. He journeyed to Mexico City in 1837 as the deputy to the Mexican congress, where he represented New Mexico and lobbied for funds. In 1851 he was elected president of the second session of the New Mexico Legislative Council under the new United States territorial government; Padre Martínez served as the president of the first session. The Archdiocese of Durango recognized Padre Ortiz for his hard work as a priest in New Mexico and bestowed upon him the title *cura propio*, or irremovable priest.[67] These factors, far from representing indolence, suggest that Ortiz was both devout and hard working. In March of 1853, Lamy and Machebeuf contended that Ortiz's status as an irremovable priest did not apply in the United States of America, and they removed him from his parishioners. Ortiz begged Lamy, from the moment of his removal, to return him to his church in Santa Fe. He pleaded for grace till January 1858, when he died a pariah from the church he had served so devoutly.

Next to Ortiz, Lamy and Machebeuf viewed Padre Martínez as the biggest threat to their authority because he was both popular and unbending. Lamy and Padre Martínez initially liked one another, but because Lamy and Machebeuf systematically displaced Nuevomexicanos from the clergy, they quickly became enemies. Padre Martínez had educated eighteen padres in New Mexico, including Padre José Manuel Gallegos, and he was protective of his students. When Lamy suspended Gallegos, Padre Martínez defended him and disparaged Machebeuf.[68] Padre Martínez felt a special disdain for Machebeuf, who he believed was responsible for problems that plagued Nuevomexicano padres, and this strained his relationship with Lamy.[69]

Moreover, Lamy and Machebeuf reinstituted tithing and threatened to withhold sacraments from parishioners who did not pay. This angered Padre Martínez, who had abolished tithing twenty years earlier because he knew that the vecinos simply could not afford to pay the padres.[70] In 1856, Lamy formally suspended Padre Martínez, but Padre Martínez refused to abide by Lamy's suspension. Padre Martínez wrote a letter to Lamy and told him that he had overreached his authority. "I do not consider myself suspended, nor am I so."[71] Padre Martínez ignored Lamy and continued to preach in Taos, although he did so in a private church.[72] For Lamy, it became clear that Martínez was the true ecclesiastical authority in Taos.

Other padres resisted Lamy as well. Padre Jose Francisco Leyva y Rosas argued that New Mexico was still a Mexican department and rejected Lamy's appointment as bishop. In a letter dated June 9, 1850, Padre Leyva declined an invitation to serve on the departmental assembly in New Mexico. Padre Leyva explained that he could not serve New Mexico for three reasons: first, he believed that a padre should not be political; second, he planned to depart for Mexico; and finally, he contended that his loyalties to Mexico made him a extranjero (stranger). By 1850, however, Padre Leyva y Rosas was seventy years old, and he never left New Mexico. He finally accepted a political appointment, but in 1852 he transferred to San Miguel del Bado. That year, Lamy accused Leyva of "drunkneness" and suspended him until 1853, when he died.[73]

Lamy's systematic expulsion of Hispano priests furthered the ecclesiastical colonization of New Mexico. In the process, Lamy deprived the vecinos of their spiritual leaders and added to their economic burden. It is therefore unsurprising that Lamy was mugged numerous times by vecinos in the streets of Santa Fe. In 1853, the editors of the *Santa Fe Weekly Gazette* warned the bishop directly in their column, "No Respect for Persons." They cautioned Lamy to beware of the indiscriminate criminals of Santa Fe, who cared little about the character of their victims.[74] The vecinos who robbed Lamy may have had respect for other persons, but they did not respect Lamy. The vecinos still attended church, regardless of the increased fees and the displaced padres; although many resented Lamy, they never ceased caring about their salvation.

Economic changes impacted vecinos more than any other aspect of territorialization. Mercantile capitalism destroyed the land-tenure system in New Mexico, and over time vecinos were transformed from independent subsistence farmers into cheap laborers.[75] Since the Spanish colonial period, small farmers had participated in the local subsistence economy, but large landholders changed that system when they began exporting agricultural commodities. The New Mexican market was infused with goods brought in by the large landholders, and the small farmers increasingly used credit to attain goods they could not afford. In the process, vecinos became indebted to the large landholders. The small farmers were forced to utilize the *partido* system, which was essentially sharecropping but with sheep instead of crops.[76]

The small farmers borrowed sheep from the local patrónes, cared for the sheep, and worked to increase the herd. Invariably, sheep died from heat and drought caused crops to fail, and the small farmers could not meet their debts. Once the small farmers were indebted, they moved from being independent to being one drought away from losing their land. Even before the Americans arrived, the small farmers were displaced by the rising patrónes, and the ranks of the vecinos continued to swell. By 1850, vecinos made up 79 percent of the Hispano population in Santa Fe County (table 1.3). In short, small farmers were displaced and transformed into craftsmen/artisans, vecino laborers, and servants.[77]

Vecinos survived in New Mexico in part on community lands; for vecinos, land was a resource to be shared, rather than a commodity. Vecinos shared the water supply, the pastoral land for grazing, and the parcels of land for homesteads. They also became indebted to landholders in times of struggle, and when vecinos defaulted they paid with labor or servitude.[78] Vecinos started to lose access to communal lands after the Americans invaded New Mexico. For Americans, the concept of community land was foreign, especially when that community was made up of people of color. Land was a commodity, and if no one fenced the land it belonged to the government. But Americans ultimately recognized land that was held by the local patrónes, as dictated by Article VII of the Treaty of Guadalupe Hidalgo.[79]

The problem for vecinos was that they depended on public lands, and the Americans decided that public land belonged to the government. To be clear, this had nothing to do with personal land grants made by Spain. The vecinos did not technically own the community land, and as a result they lost access to pasturage.[80] For the vecinos this was disastrous, and they were left with two options: either participate in the partido system or become day laborers. Both choices compelled them to take on debt, and many were eventually either bound into servitude or dispossessed of their children or their homesteads. For this reason, many ultimately left Santa Fe County.

The patrónes were positioned to profit from communal land because they participated in the new government. The communal lands were seized by the US military and ultimately sold to patrónes and their business partners. Just as during the late Spanish period, the patrónes were the only Nuevomexicanos who could afford the newly available land. They transitioned away from being patrónes to the vecinos, and increasingly became their employers during American territorialization. Although the patrónes understood how important the communal lands were to the vecinos, it seems they cared more about increasing their wealth. Their concern shifted from caring for the vecinos to protecting their property from them, and in this way the Nuevomexicano landholders increased their wealth while the vecinos plunged deeper into poverty, representing two components of the transition into capitalism.[81]

It's impossible to see this transformation in New Mexico unless it is examined through the lens of refined census data, which means I must turn to quantitative methods to demonstrate these statistical transformations. First I will write up the data summary. Then I will provide a visual representation of the data. The same data are represented in both the statistical and the visual representations below, but I do so in an effort to make these data accessible for both numerical and more visual thinkers. As I move forward in this narrative, I will continue to use this dual presentation method, with the hope that it makes this information accessible to all readers.

The local patrónes expanded their holdings in the first thirteen years of American territorialization, a reality that debunks the narrative that crafty American settlers dispossessed Hispanos of their land in New Mexico and that is borne out by census data.[82] Statistically, Nuevomexicanos owned 16 percent more land after thirteen years of American rule (figures 2.1a and 2.1b): real Hispano property ownership increased from 36 percent of Santa Fe County property in 1850 to 52 percent in 1860.[83] Hubert Howe Bancroft noted, "Horses and mules increased during the decade, from 13,733 to 21,357; cattle from 32,977 to 88,729; and sheep from 377,271 to 830,116."[84] During this same decade American-born settlers witnessed a 20 percent decline in their real property holdings in Santa Fe County. New Mexican patrónes absorbed 15 percent, while European-born Anglos (who had immigrated to New Mexico via the United States) acquired the remaining 5 percent of what the white settlers lost.

By 1850, American-born Anglos held 56 percent of the real estate in Santa Fe County, which seems to suggest a rapid dispossession, but the government claimed much of this land, and it is included in these numbers.[85] To be precise, 27 percent of the property held by American-born Anglos (figure 2.2) belonged to the military. Additionally, legal officials owned another 9 percent of this real estate, which means that the territorial government owned a combined 36 percent of Anglo property.[86] In total, $173,750 of the $482,186 owned by American-born Anglos was federal property, most of which was communal property that the American authorities seized from the vecinos. Anglos without occupations, most of whom were advanced in age and had lived in Santa Fe for many years, owned an additional 18 percent of this property, worth $86,218. Merchants and farmers constituted another 12 percent—or $60,750 to be exact—and the majority of these lived in New Mexico before the American

a.

6%	Anglo European Property	11%
36%	New Mexican Property	52%
2%	Mexican Born Property	1%
56%	Anglo American Property	36%

b.

Figure 2.1a. 1850 Santa Fe County real estate owned. Source: 1850 Federal Census, Santa Fe County, New Mexico Territory.

Figure 2.1b. 1860 Santa Fe County real estate owned. Source: 1860 Federal Census, Santa Fe County, New Mexico Territory.

CHAPTER TWO

invasion as well. Thus, at least 67 percent of the American-born Anglo property in New Mexico—meaning $320,718 of the $482,186—belonged either to established residents or was acquired via military conquest.[87]

By comparison, 88 percent of the real estate in Santa Fe County that was owned by Hispanos (figure 2.3) belonged to permanently settled farmers, retired landowners, and merchants. In other words, Nuevomexicano patrónes owned most of this property. The local patrónes possessed real and established wealth, while the landholding Anglo settlers relied on their work in law, carpentry, blacksmithing, medical services, food services, and other services as their leading nonmilitary sources of ownership.[88] This reflected the transient nature of Anglo wealth in Santa Fe County, which in 1850 depended on an Anglo's skilled labor rather than New Mexico's natural resources.

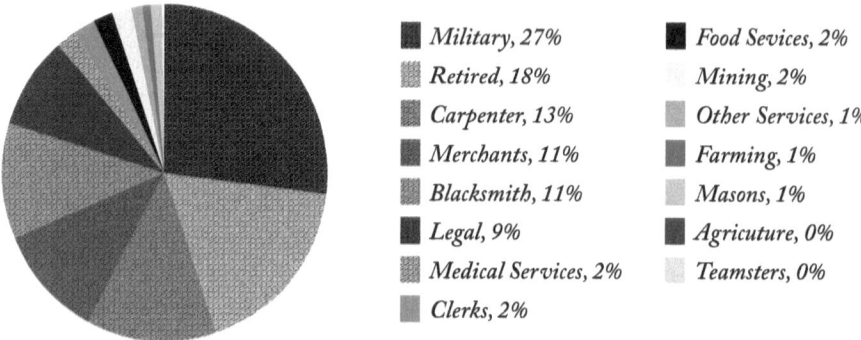

Figure 2.2. Anglo property, as owned by occupational group in 1850. Source: 1850 Federal Census, Santa Fe County, New Mexico Territory.

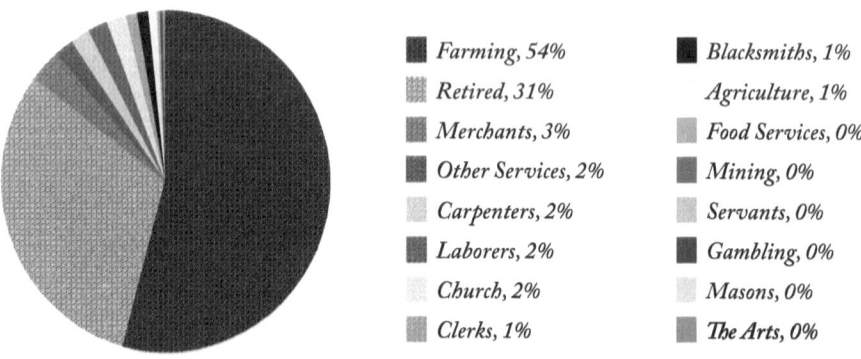

Figure 2.3. Hispano property, as Owned by Occupational Group in 1850. Source: 1850 Federal Census, Santa Fe County, New Mexico Territory.

Among Hispanos, farmers owned $167,243 worth of real estate, retired landholders owned $96,004 worth of real estate, and merchants owned $8,300 worth of real estate, for a combined $271,547 of the total of $308,110.[89] Many who identified themselves as farmers—including Manuel Chaves, Donaciano Vigil, and Gaspar Ortiz—were politically, socially, and militarily active in New Mexico. These notable patrónes are indicative of the larger roles that landholders played in New Mexican society. Meanwhile, many of the statistically wealthy retirees were widowed matriarchs, among them the three wealthiest Hispanos in Santa Fe County: Ana Baca del Pino ($20,000), Gertrudis Pino de Ortiz ($10,000), and Manuela Baca y Sena ($8,000). The list of elderly women as heads of households and with significant wealth in Santa Fe County is extensive and is an indicator of the important role elders played in household, regardless of gender.

Among Santa Fe County Hispanos, a disproportionate 58 percent of real estate (figure 2.4), with a real dollar amount of $132,153, belonged to individuals over the age of fifty. The majority in this demographic were either listed as farmers or without occupation, which suggests they were either widowed or they had retired. These older landholders represented the patriarchs and matriarchs of the old Nuevomexicano families, wealthy Hispanos whose ancestors acquired vast amounts of land during the Spanish colonial and Mexican eras.

By tradition the children of these *patrones* and *matrones* inherited this land when the older generation passed on, but in the meantime the younger generation was responsible for protecting the family holdings from outside threats. In New Mexico, issues of gender did not deny women their rightful place as heads of extended families; when a husband passed away the wife took control of the family holdings. This explains why the wealthiest individual Hispanos in Santa Fe County were not men. At some point before 1850, the patrónes Pino, Ortiz, and Baca y Sena passed on, leaving Ana Baca del Pino, Gertrudis Pino de Ortiz, and Manuela Baca y Sena with massive sums of wealth. Distribution of land between both men and women in Santa Fe County was similar (figure 2.5), although the disproportionate increase among women over fifty—and the fact that they are listed as heads of household—suggests that widows possessed the bulk of female-owned land.

Older residents held a disproportionate amount of land in Santa Fe County, and within this demographic, real estate was heavily concentrated in the hands of the few. The numbers betray a stunning disparity between those who had land and those who did not: 62 percent of Hispano males in Santa Fe County had absolutely no property. Even among the 38 percent of Hispano males who actually held property, wealth was heavily concentrated in the hands of the few. For example, 71 percent of Hispanos (table 2.1) between the ages of twenty-six and thirty had no property; the average amount owned by individuals within this age group was only $52. Comparatively, 31 percent of those between forty-one and fifty held no property, with an average property value among this age group at $179.

Thirty-eight percent of Hispano males over fifteen owned all the Hispano property, and of those who owned land, more than half qualified as vecinos. Among the entire male population over twenty years of age, 79 percent were vecinos, meaning they possessed less than one hundred dollars worth of land (table 2.2). The vecinos pulled down property ownership in every demographic, but young Hispanos owned little property even among the large landholding families. When broken down by age group, the low level of property owned by young Hispanos is striking. Among all Hispanos between twenty-one and twenty-five, 72 percent had no property; this disparity pulled the average property owned down to a meager $24 for this demographic. Only 6 percent of Hispanos between fifteen and twenty years of age held property, but many in this demographic still lived with their families. The more significant demographic is age twenty-six to thirty-one: 71 percent of this age group had no property. While many between twenty-one and thirty-one years of age lived with their families, it is significant that this demographic experienced low ownership rates, low values per household, and a low overall proportion of real estate. Moreover, Hispano males age twenty-one to thirty-one made up the largest proportion of the Santa Fe County population in 1850 (figure 2.6).

We recall that in 1850, 15 percent of all males over twenty had no occupation (307) and that only 21 percent of the adult male population was made up of large landholders; the other 79 percent was made up of vecinos. Nuevomexicanos aged twenty-one to thirty-one struggled most: 28 percent were day laborers, 10

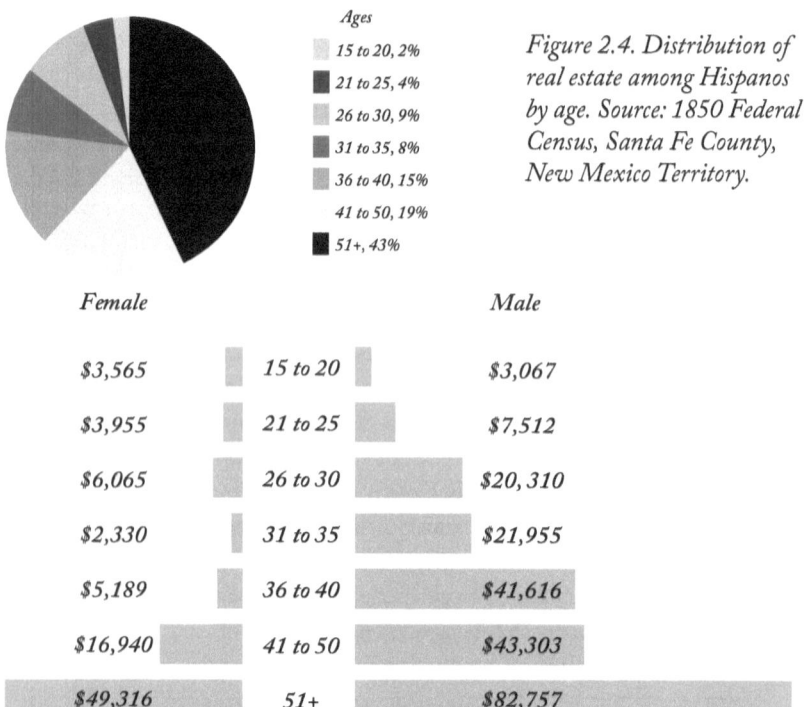

Figure 2.4. Distribution of real estate among Hispanos by age. Source: 1850 Federal Census, Santa Fe County, New Mexico Territory.

Figure 2.5. Distribution of real estate among Hispanos by gender, 1850. Source: 1850 Federal Census, Santa Fe County, New Mexico Territory.

percent were indentured servants, and 18 percent were listed as without occupation. Combined, these factors meant that a large population of young Hispano males were without property and their best chance of acquiring property was to inherit it, but few were so fortunate.

Among young white foreign settlers, the situation was significantly worse. Only 8 percent of foreign-born whites aged twenty-one to twenty-five and 15 percent aged twenty-six to thirty-one held property in Santa Fe County (table 2.1). Meanwhile, only 14 percent of foreign-born whites aged fifteen to twenty held property; unlike the young Nuevomexicano population, however, whites aged fifteen to thirty-one had no family to live with, and neither cultural nor community ties to Santa Fe County. In short, not only were whites in this demographic worse off than Hispanos, but they also lacked the support of family and community to aid them. Additionally, whites aged twenty to thirty, like the Hispano youth, made up the majority of new Anglo settlers in Santa Fe County (figure 2.7).

Number and Age Group		Persons with Land	Percent with Land	Range		Mean
Ages 15–20	427 Hispanos	only 24 have land	6	0	$1,000	$16
	28 Anglos	only 4 have land	14	0	$4,000	$199
Ages 21 to 25	320 Hispanos	only 64 have land	28	0	$800	$24
	220 Anglos	only 18 have land	8	0	$50,000	$306
Ages 26 to 30	393 Hispanos	only 154 have land	29	0	$1,080	$52
	199 Anglos	only 29 have land	14	0	$31,000	$232
Ages 31 to 35	153 Hispanos	only 72 have land	47	0	$6,000	$144
	82 Anglos	only 14 have land	17	0	$32,500	$446
Ages 36 to 40	215 Hispanos	only 111 have land	52	0	$4,000	$194
	38 Anglos	only 9 have land	24	0	$9,000	$377
Ages 41 to 50	242 Hispanos	only 168 have land	69	0	$2,800	$179
	24 Anglos	only 12 have land	50	0	$40,000	$1,923
Ages 51+	253 Hispanos	only 166 have land	66	0	$6,000	$327
	10 Anglos	only 4 have land	40	0	$9,000	$1,126

Note: In 1850, only 430 males were among the so-called elites, meaning they possessed more than $100 worth of land in Santa Fe County. By profession, 333 were farmers, 64 were craftsmen, 21 were laborers, and 12 had no occupation.

Source: 1850 Federal Census, Santa Fe County, New Mexico Territory

Table 2.1. Land Distribution among Males Only in 1850, Santa Fe County

CHAPTER TWO

In Santa Fe County, foreign-born whites were not a monolithic group, but rather a collection of diverse peoples from the United States and Europe. They included first-generation European-born soldiers, American-born soldiers, laborers, teamsters, gamblers, and prospecting merchants.[90] However, many of the young whites who came to Santa Fe County were soldiers who were either active duty or retired veterans of the US-Mexican War. The United States Army was a model of European diversity in the mid-nineteenth century (figure 2.8); in 1850, 67 percent of regular soldiers and 36 percent of army officials stationed in Santa Fe County were European-born.

These soldiers were influenced by the residual propaganda from the US-Mexican War. They believed that Mexicans were uncivilized people that were ethnically inferior.[91] They also believed that the US-Mexican War was a war of conquest, and they came to Santa Fe County expecting their share.[92] Former soldiers turned settlers were frustrated by the US-Mexican War, which had not resulted in the plunder they anticipated, and many arrived in Santa Fe County determined to carve wealth from the holdings of locals whom they viewed as a conquered people.[93]

Foreign-born white Americans tried in many ways to interject themselves into the local economy, but the data show they had little success. Some whites hoped to become merchants, while others tried to enter the political arena; some sought success through the service industry and worked as carpenters and blacksmiths. Very few were interested in hard labor: while 29 percent of the New Mexican population identified themselves as laborers, only 7 percent of American-born whites and 5 percent of European-born whites identified themselves as laborers in 1850. Although they were without property, they refused to do hard labor. Instead they wrangled with established whites and Nuevomexicanos for access to resources.

To their surprise, the patrónes and their American allies walled them out and limited their political, economic, and even social access. These newly arrived foreign-born whites found that property in Santa Fe County was either claimed by the government or held by older settlers who wanted nothing to do with them. Legally, the territorial government treated young soldiers in a similar manner as they treated vecinos: they indicted, prosecuted, and punished—although far less severely—foreign-born whites for their transgressions.[94] Anglo soldiers came to Santa Fe determined to make their fortunes, but instead found themselves without political access, property, or family. Many left, while others became angry and turned to violent crime.

For their part, the majority of Nuevomexicanos were vecinos, and many of them also turned to crime in their poverty and desperation, but they were less likely to commit violent acts between 1847 and 1853. As we have seen previously, in their case they were made desperate by territorialization, which

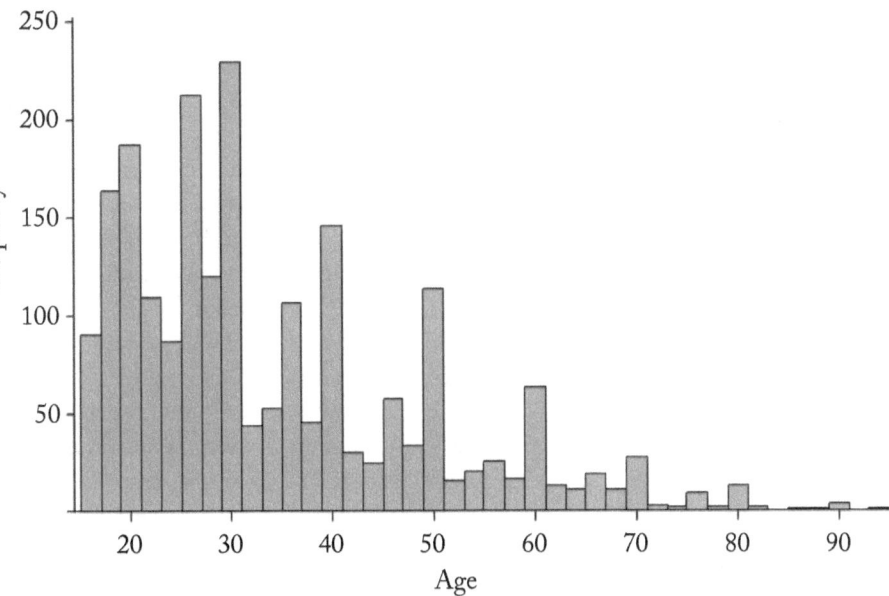

Figure 2.6. Ages of Hispanic adult males in Santa Fe County in 1850. Source: 1850 Federal Census, Santa Fe County, New Mexico Territory.

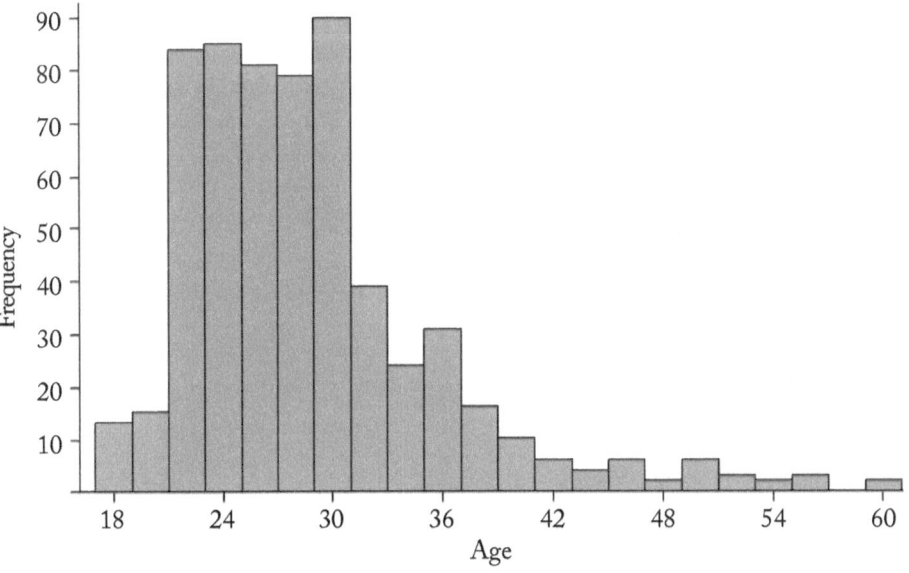

Figure 2.7. Ages of Anglo adult males in Santa Fe County in 1850. Source: 1850 Federal Census, Santa Fe County, New Mexico Territory.

impacted them legally, spiritually, and economically. The vecinos lost their redemptive legal system, their spiritual leaders, and their public lands, and they were betrayed by their patrónes, who left them to fend for themselves against the courts, the church, and the threat of starvation. The damage done when American authorities seized all lands they perceived as unclaimed cannot be overstated; as we have noted, this meant that many poor New Mexicans lost both their own land and their access to communal lands.[95] That process was already underway in New Mexico before the Americans arrived, but claiming communal lands as property and criminalizing alternative uses of those lands guaranteed the dispossession of many vecinos.[96] As Tigar noted in discussing similar attempts by eighteenth-century English elites to force the poor into the labor market, "The law of theft sometimes did more than mirror class interest. It was used as a cudgel for enforcing that interest."[97] While this may not have been the intention of the American authorities, it was certainly the effect. The vecinos became increasingly desperate. When some among them turned to crime between 1847 and 1853, however, they did not become violent. Instead they turned to petty larceny and often stole subsistence items they could no longer afford.

THE LARCENY PROBLEM

Nuevomexicano patrónes pulled away from their traditional obligations as patrónes to the vecinos. The US military was now in charge of the defense of the territory, and they no longer relied on vecinos when threats arose. As a result, wealthy Nuevomexicanos no longer needed vecino allegiances, and thus they ceased activities designed to maintain vecino loyalty. For example, Nuevomexicano patrónes hosted annual fandangos for vecinos to demonstrate that community transcended class barriers and to foster loyalty during the Mexican period. At these events, wealthy Nuevomexicanas waltzed with poor farmers, Indigenous Peoples with Nuevomexicanas, and wealthy elites with poor vecinos.[98] With the

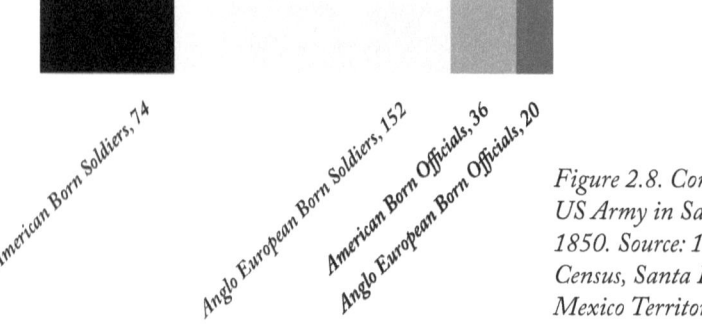

Figure 2.8. Composition of the US Army in Santa Fe County, 1850. Source: 1850 Federal Census, Santa Fe County, New Mexico Territory.

arrival of the American military, traditional fandangos faded. As we will see in chapter 3, opportunistic vecinos became the stewards of the fandango, and they transformed them into entertainment packages for American soldiers.[99] Furthermore, Hispanos-turned-politicos no longer counted on the Mexican style of social control, which was predicated on cultivating loyalty in order to maintain order among the people. Instead—as we will see in chapter 4—they embraced the draconian punishments of the Americans, which included lengthy jail terms, hard labor, lashings, and even indentured servitude. Finally, vecinos were left to depend on the American government for help that traditionally came from the large landholders in times of need.[100] As the nineteenth-century American government was not known for its charity toward those in need—especially people of color—many poorer Nuevomexicanos increasingly resorted to petty larceny.[101] Sometimes they stole opportunistically, filching small items they could easily liquidate. In the end, the data reveal that many vecinos resorted to petty larceny with the ultimate goal of providing themselves food, clothing, and shelter.

Within this context, between 1847 and 1854 vecinos became 5.5 times as likely to commit larceny than during the Mexican era in Santa Fe County (table 2.3). From 1838 to 1845, the vecinos committed larceny at the rate of 91 per 100,000, but that skyrocketed to 495 per 100,000 in the first three years of American territorialization. From 1851 to 1853, vecino larceny continued to climb and reached 568 per 100,000, an increase of 73 per 100,000 (table 2.3).[102] From 1854 to 1860, vecino larceny dipped back to 481 per 100,000, meaning larceny from 1847 to 1860 remained consistently high. Clearly, many vecinos were unable to sustain themselves and their families after they lost both their own farms and access to the communal lands, and in the American period this made larceny a necessity for numerous poor Nuevomexicanos.

Other vecinos simply chose to leave Santa Fe County—as we will see in chapter 5—in an effort to escape inequality or to put distance between themselves and the American regime. The 1860 federal census reveals that thirty-two families abandoned Santa Fe County, leaving their homes designated as "unoccupied" by the census taker.[103] In no way, however, do these thirty-two families tell the complete story. Between 1850 and 1860, 2,280 Hispano children were born, yet the Hispano population only increased by 701. This leaves 1,581 of the Santa Fe County Hispanos unaccounted for, meaning that roughly one-fifth of the population somehow departed the county. Certainly a portion of these Nuevomexicanos died, but the vast majority can be found dotting census pages from the outer reaches of New Mexico territory to California, where they sought better opportunities.[104]

Perpetrator Ethnicity and Crime	1838–1845 Rates (8 Yrs)	1847–1850 Rates (4 Yrs)	1851–1853 Rates (3 Yrs)	1854–1860 Rates (7 Yrs)
H Larceny	91	495	568	481
W Larceny	NA	712	819	489

H = Hispano; W = White

Note: Although all Hispanos and whites are considered when calculating rates, the names of wealthier segments of the population do not appear in the criminal court records. Not surprisingly, this is proof that arrests for larceny occurred exclusively among vecinos and poor white settlers. Source: New Mexico State Records Center and Archives, "Records of the United States Territorial and New Mexico District Courts for Santa Fe County 1847–1951," box 1–3 (hereafter TRNMSF); New Mexico State Records Center and Archives, Mexican Archives of New Mexico, 1821–1846 (Santa Fe: New Mexico State Records Center and Archives, 1969) (hereafter MANM); aggregate data combed from these archives are rates per 100,000 and include only crimes with known perpetrators. In keeping, only criminal court documents that identify perpetrators with Hispanic surnames have been calculated from both the MANM and TRNMSF.

Table 2.2. Hispano and White Larceny in Santa Fe County, by Perpetrator Ethnicity and Crime, Adults 16 and older, per 100,000

For many who stayed, petty larceny became a necessity, and a survey of these larcenies reveals numerous trends. For example, despite dramatic inequality, vecinos seldom targeted the large landholding patrónes in these early years, though on occasion it did happen. In March of 1848, the vecinos Jose Seguro and Jose Francoso—whom we will discuss more in depth later—stole a blanket and a pair of pants from Don Albino Chacón.[105] Seguro and Francoso paid the price for their crime: they were caught burglarizing the home of an elite, and they were publicly lashed thirty-nine times each for their crime.[106] Meanwhile, a vecino named Ortiz stole two wheels from the powerful Manuel Chaves, but the verdict and punishment were not recorded.[107] Vecinos also stole from Judge Tomas Ortiz and Manuel Ortiz, but the value stolen was small and the perpetrators appear to have escaped Santa Fe County without punishment.[108] Outside of these exceptions, the vecinos more often targeted Nuevomexicano craftsmen and merchants, small Nuevomexicano farmers, and especially whites.

Vecino larceny often took place under the cover of night, in homes left unattended, in fields filled with sheep, and in unguarded camps. More than one-third of the time, vecinos stole subsistence items that included blankets, coats, and pants, which suggests the level of need many Hispanos experienced. The majority who stole such items likely did so because it was a low-risk crime that helped augment their everyday needs. Whether they kept these items for themselves, sold them, or traded them away, the logic for committing petty larceny was consistent: it helped make the ends meet in one way or another. For example, in July of 1848, Calistro Garcia was arrested after he stole a blanket that belonged to a white settler named George Peacock.[109] Garcia was convicted and sentenced to one year in prison and a $10 fine. In another incident, Joseph Smith accused three vecinos of stealing blankets, a coat, pants, and shirts.[110] Francisco Griego, Manuel Salvador, and Justo Sandoval were ultimately found guilty of this crime and sentenced to ten lashes each.[111]

Vecinos committed petty larcenies more than any other type, but at times they also committed grand larceny and stole firearms. Seventy-one percent of vecino larcenies were petty, 21 percent qualified as grand, and 8 percent involved stealing guns (figure 2.9).[112]

The laws in New Mexico, however, viewed the value of stolen items as secondary; the general dividing line for punishment was based on whether or not one committed burglary. As it happened, vecino burglaries, meaning break-ins, most frequently resulted in vecino grand larceny. These usually targeted businessmen, involved breaking and entering, and ended with large sums of money disappearing. For example, the vecinos Jesus Garcia, Justo Gonzalez, and Manuel Pena broke in and stole $609 from Jose Arce.[113] They were convicted and sentenced to twenty-nine lashes and twenty days jail and hard labor.[114] Meanwhile, vecinos targeted whites when they sought firearms; they committed twelve of their fourteen firearm larcenies against whites between 1847 and 1860. Jesus Francoso stole a pistol from Thomas Briggs, while Felipe Santiago stole a shotgun, two pistols, a cloak, and a vest from William Z. Angney, who was a US-Mexican War veteran and a prominent lawyer.[115] Among vecinos, however, petty larceny remained the most common, and grand larceny and gun larceny were exceptions to the rule (Figure 2.10).

When poor vecinos stole from Hispanos the crimes were less personal. They targeted items one might find in a field, including a single sheep, a mule, or a collection of tools that included items such as harvesting scythes. Jose Tenorio stole a mule valued at $50 from Benito Lerragota, while Eugenio Ortiz took two wagon wheels that Manuel Chaves's workers had left unattended.[116] Larcenies against Anglos were more invasive. Jose Maria Sanchez broke into George Wells's house and was caught stealing numerous blankets and a couple pairs of pants.[117] When he was convicted, he was sentenced to six months in jail and thirty-nine lashes.

From 1847 to 1853 armed robbery by vecinos was rare, but on five different occasions a vecino stood accused of this crime; three occurred in 1849 and the last occurred in 1850. In February of 1850 the vecinos Jose Francoso and Jose Montoya robbed the soon-to-be-famous John Jones at gunpoint. Francoso and

CHAPTER TWO

Montoya could not have chosen their victim more poorly, as only one year later Jones was named marshal of Santa Fe County.[118] Before Jones took office, Jose Montoya committed another larceny, and he was convicted and sentenced to five years in jail.

But Marshal Jones was not completely deprived of his chance for revenge, because Jose Francoso continued his career as a criminal, as did another vecino named Jose Sena. We do not know much about the life of Jose Francoso. Indeed he, Jose Sena, and so many others would be lost to us were it not for their criminal escapades.[119] What we do know is that Jose Francoso was born in Santa Fe, New Mexico, in 1814, and the 1850 census listed his residence only as the county jail.[120] Between 1848 and 1853, Francoso was arrested a total of six times for larceny. Indeed, Francoso's career was long and distinguished, and his victims were a who's who in Santa Fe County. As previously mentioned, Francoso began his life of crime in March of 1848, when he stole from a well-known landholder named Don Albino Chacón. Francoso and his partner were each lashed thirty-nine times.[121] After this incident, Francoso only targeted whites. As ever more proof that the lash is an ineffective tool of reform, however, Jose Francoso was arrested again one year later. On this occasion Francoso was accused of stealing twenty-two yards of velvet from Andrew S. Bealty, a white trader.[122] If Francoso was punished, it didn't include incarceration, because only six months later he was back in court again, this time for stealing a silver watch from one Christian Mueller.[123]

At this point, Francoso committed his first and only armed robbery; he and Jose Montoya allegedly stole $550 from John Jones. Without a history of violence, it is likely Francoso got mixed up in a crime bigger than his intentions. Still, the fortunate Francoso was exonerated because—it seems—there was not enough evidence to convict.[124] But the news was not all positive: John Jones became Marshal John Jones, and he never forgot Francoso.

Most people would have counted their blessings at that point, but not Jose Francoso. He must have really needed a watch, for three weeks later he was arrested for the second time for stealing one, along with various other tools. This time, Francoso was sentenced to a year in jail, where he languished when

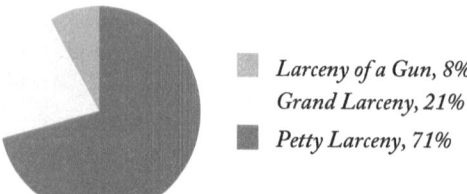

Figure 2.9. Types of vecino *larceny, 1847–1860. Source: New Mexico State Records Center and Archives, "Records of the United States Territorial and New Mexico District Courts for Santa Fe County 1847–1860," Boxes 1–3.*

Larceny of a Gun, 8%
Grand Larceny, 21%
Petty Larceny, 71%

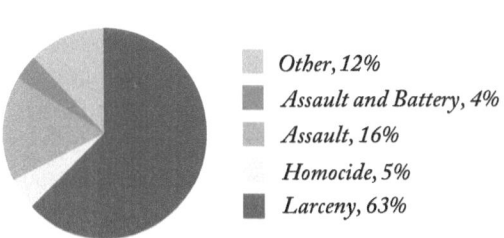

Figure 2.10. Cases adjudicated by Anglo judges in Santa Fe County, by percentage, 1847–1854. Source: New Mexico State Records Center and Archives, "Records of the United States Territorial and New Mexico District Courts for Santa Fe County 1847–1854," Boxes 1–2.

- Other, 12%
- Assault and Battery, 4%
- Assault, 16%
- Homocide, 5%
- Larceny, 63%

the 1850 census was taken. In 1852, Marshal John Jones made one last run at Francoso when he arrested him for larceny, but those charges were dismissed. In what may have been a final relapse, Francoso was arrested one final time in 1856 for stealing a box and a lancet (a total value of $3.25) during a visit to Dr. Kavanaugh. He paid his $3 fine and vanished from the criminal court records.[125]

While Francoso is unique as a career criminal in Santa Fe County, he represented the type of criminals most common among the poorer Nuevomexicanos. Francoso, like most Nuevomexicanos who turned to larceny, was a poverty-stricken laborer who couldn't get ahead. He made the mistake of robbing a patrón once, and then targeted only white settlers, whose notorious drunkenness made them easy targets. His rap sheet does not encompass all the crimes he committed. He likely stole a sheep or two, perhaps pilfered some food from the market on occasion, and certainly did his share of hard labor in between crimes. When it was cold and he needed a jacket, he stole one, when the weather turned, he likely sold it. When he wanted to make a quick dollar, he likely turned pickpocket and sought items that could be easily liquidated, like watches. He likely felt justified stealing from whites; after all, it was their seizure of the public lands and their partnerships with the old patrónes that made subsistence so difficult for poor New Mexicans like himself. Why Francoso and those like him resorted to crime is not difficult to discern; the reason Francoso continued to get caught so frequently is another matter.

Jose Francoso was not the only career criminal in New Mexico, and he certainly was not the only vecino to find himself at the wrong end of the lash. Jose Sena also committed multiple crimes, but he ultimately discovered that the lash was not the worst punishment he could receive in New Mexico, as he was sold into indentured servitude in 1853. Jose Sena was an eighteen-year-old laborer when the Americans arrived in New Mexico.[126] In March of 1847, he broke into the residence of Phillip McGuire and stole several items, including two guns, one lance, and $150 worth of goods.[127] That Sena stole two guns and a lance makes this case interesting, because Sena became one of thirteen Nuevomexicanos indicted for stealing firearms in this early period, as previously noted. It is possible that Sena wanted a gun for self-defense or that he intended to sell it, but it is equally likely that he was preparing for a life of violent crime. On this occasion, his sentence was similar to Jose Francoso's: Sena received thirty-nine lashes and was sentenced to three months in the county jail.

The politicos and their white allies were convinced that corporal punishment was the only sure way to control people like Sena and Francoso, along with the many other vecinos, genízaros, and Puebloans, and the laws they passed in the territorial legislature demonstrate this.[128] Their relationships with the poorer Nuevomexicanos deteriorated after the Americans arrived, and violence seemed to them the only way to dissuade the poor from committing larceny, which was by far New Mexico's number one crime.[129] In 1846, the Americans instituted corporal punishment against robbers, burglars, and those who committed perjury in New Mexico; Jose Sena was only one of the twenty-six vecinos sentenced to lashes in the Santa Fe County between 1847 and 1860.[130] The law dictated that lashing was reserved for individuals convicted of burglary and stealing livestock, but the large landholders did not complain when white judges sentenced vecinos to lashes for petty larceny.[131] In 1857 the politicos, meaning the territorial representatives from the large landholding class, increased the number of lashes from thirty-nine to fifty and raised mandatory jail sentences from two years to five.[132] They also officially legalized lashes for petty larceny and grand larceny; they decreed fifteen lashes for petty larceny and thirty to sixty lashes for grand larceny (plus one to two years in jail).[133] In many ways, these laws from the 1857–1858 session represented the formal end to the large landholder's status as patrónes to the poor. Their position was clear: Instead of relying on traditional Mexican-style loyalty and instead of believing in redemption for the criminal, they now embraced the misguided American belief that state violence was the best deterrent to crime.

Of course, Jose Sena proved this belief wrong—like so many before and after—because the thirty-nine lashes he received in 1847 did not permanently dissuade him from his life of crime. Sena had sought an honest living for almost six years, but on January 6, 1853, he backslid and robbed Pablo Delgado of $1,000 in cash.[134] Delgado started as a clerk in Santa Fe, but he soon became a merchant. By 1860, Delgado was listed as owning real estate valued at $1,000, along with $4,000 in goods and coin.[135] It's possible Jose Sena knew

Delgado—perhaps he even worked for him at some point—because a warrant was issued for Sena's arrest without delay. What is clear is that Jose Sena was extremely desperate, because twelve days later he was fleeing south through Bernalillo County when he threatened to kill twenty-eight-year-old Maria Martin and Maria Cepreana, her five-year-old child.[136] When authorities captured Jose Sena they found the missing $1,000 in his possession.[137]

The judge was merciless when passed sentence against Jose Sena this time. Not only had he stolen a large sum of money, but he had threatened a woman and her child. As punishment, Jose Sena was sentenced to a fine of $1,000, an amount equal to what he had stolen. Certainly no vecino could be expected to satisfy an amount that high, and it seems that was Judge Grafton Baker's intention. In lieu of payment, Baker ordered Jose Sena sold into indentured servitude.

The Kearny Code made the punishment of indentured servitude possible, if not specifically legal, but it was uncommon and only used in particular instances. Jose Sena was the first person sentenced under that law, while most of the rest who were singled out for this punishment were of varying Indigenous descents.[138] At least two other vecinos received the same sentence in 1853, and three wealthy Nuevomexicano landholders seized the opportunity to purchase new household servants.[139] The large landholders already held 242 servants in bondage in Santa Fe County in 1850: 28 were born in Mexico, 20 were Native American, and the other 194 were New Mexican–born vecinos.[140] Their ownership of servants was nothing new in New Mexico, but the purchase of criminals certainly was.

In theory, Jose Sena was to spend the next five years in the service of Miguel E. Pino; in reality, Sena escaped bondage only six months into that term. In June of 1853 Jose Sena stole a double-barrel shotgun from a white settler named Thomas Muffin and disappeared into history.[141] But Jose Sena was not the only person sold into servitude in Santa Fe County. Over the next five years, Marshal John Jones sold eight more vecinos into servitude as punishment, all of them for the crime of larceny.[142] During the next thirteen years the politicos passed numerous laws that reinforced both sentencing prisoners to servitude and the right to keep servants indebted. The bond between patrón and vecino severed, only the whip, the jail, and the threat of servitude remained as tools in their attempt to stem the tide of larceny.

In some ways, recently arrived whites faced similar challenges to those experienced by poorer New Mexicans, but how they committed larceny, and their reasons for doing so, could not have been more different. Many were veterans of the US-Mexican War and they expected to profit from the regime change, but they assumed incorrectly that the territorial government would favor them over the Nuevomexicanos.[143] Santa Fe County remained 89 percent Hispano, and the

Nuevomexicano landholders were too numerous and formidable to be displaced by the traditional nineteenth-century white methods used elsewhere in the West. They had men, horses, and guns, and they knew how to use them.[144] It soon became clear that recently arrived white soldiers and settlers would not directly profit from the American conquest, and white frustration with being both economically and socially walled out of Santa Fe County drove them to commit crime at higher rates than vecinos in every category.[145] As David Lavender noted, soldiers "[ignored] the perfunctory harangues of their officers concerning discipline ... continued with their drunkenness, swaggering, bullying, and petty arrogance to rub raw a New Mexican pride."[146] Still, no matter the level at which recently arrived white soldiers and settlers committed crimes—and no matter how frustrated and disrespectful they became—newly arrived foreign-born whites failed to make inroads in Santa Fe County.

The foreign-born white criminal committed larceny in a different manner than did the vecino. He targeted more valuable items, such as trunks of money, trunks of weapons, barrels of whiskey, and, of course, horses (figure 2.11). There were fewer repeat criminals among the white settler population because they tended to be transient and often resided in Santa Fe County for only a short time. Like the vecinos, whites who resorted to larceny primarily targeted very specific, albeit different types of victims: other white merchants, soldiers, lawyers, and politicians. The whites did not target the local patrónes in Santa Fe County. Of the forty-one larcenies committed by white settlers, twenty-five cases listed victims, of which one targeted a Nuevomexicano landholder, but he was not a patrón. In May of 1849, Charles Robbinsdean stole a sheep from Vicar Juan Felipe Ortiz.[147] Padre Ortiz was a wealthy man, and in the 1850 census he was listed as having $5,000 worth of property in Santa Fe.[148] The sheep that Robbinsdean stole was valued at $2. No other Nuevomexicano landholder was robbed.

In general, recently arrived Anglo settlers felt betrayed by the established local Anglo officials, who cooperated with the local patrónes and rebuffed fellow Anglos. There was a measurable lack of opportunity for white settlers, and this can be seen in the census data. There is little doubt they were frustrated by this lack of opportunity, but they simply could not compete with Nuevomexicanos in the theater of honest labor and ingenuity.[149] As a result, Anglo settlers resorted to theft, violence, and homicide. Larceny was the most frequent crime among whites, as it was among poor vecinos, but whites in Santa Fe County committed larceny at significantly higher rates than did vecinos: white settlers were 1.3 times as likely to commit larceny than vecinos in Santa Fe County from 1847 to 1853 (figure 2.11), and that number only fell after 1853, when the number of foreign-born whites declined (figure 2.1).

During the Mexican period there were too few criminal court cases against foreign-born whites to be calculated, which made it impossible to determine white larceny rates before 1847. Most white settlers in Santa Fe County were merchants and traders, so it is extremely unlikely that they committed larceny. White traders were violent, but most of them had goods and did not need petty items. These whites were businessmen, which means they were arrested for commerce violations rather than larceny. In fact, when whites appeared in the Mexican records for other crimes, they often took the role of victim.[150]

Additionally, the Anglo soldiers were not yet present in Santa Fe during the Mexican period, but Mexican soldiers were, and there were many similarities between them. The Mexican soldiers were poorly paid single males who were frustrated by their inability to succeed in Santa Fe. They proved to be a rowdy lot; they looted, assaulted, and murdered at higher rates than did Nuevomexicanos. The Mexican records indicate that Mexican soldiers committed roughly one-fifth of the crimes in Santa Fe County during the Mexican period.[151] The records for Hispano crime in the villa of Santa Fe are intact. Of the 161 court cases in the Mexican Archives of New Mexico, the 126 from Santa Fe make up the overwhelming majority of this collection.[152] The remaining 34 are sporadically dispersed across some twenty different villas in New Mexico; fourteen of these villas have but one case remaining to represent crime in their town. The Mexican records are incomplete—and indeed there are no doubt missing files—but the sampling from Santa Fe provides data that can

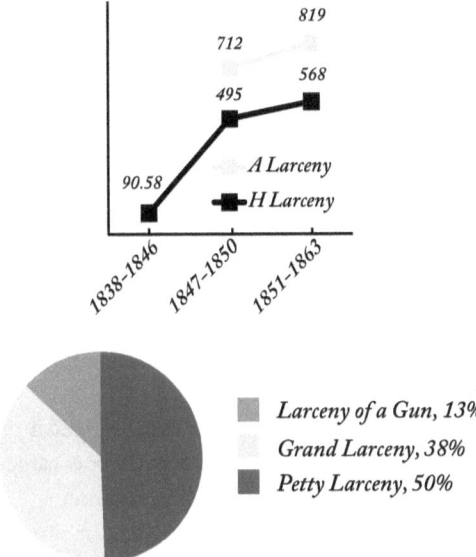

Figure 2.11. Hispano and white larceny rates compared, adults 16 and older, per 100,000, 1838–1863.

Figure 2.12. Types of white larceny, 1847–1860. Source: New Mexico State Records Center and Archives, "Records of the United States Territorial and New Mexico District Courts for Santa Fe County 1847–1860," Boxes 1–3.

be reliably compared with the territorial data. Even still, there was not enough white crime to register in Santa Fe County, where whites were still very much guests.[153] For Nuevomexicanos, these documents reveal a pre-American Santa Fe County that was far less crime ridden than it became in just the first seven years of American suzerainty.[154] They also reveal that the arrival of soldiers increased crime in Santa Fe County during both the Mexican and American territorial periods.[155]

The new Anglo settlers, including many soldiers and veterans, were driven to steal by different factors than the vecinos. Like the Mexican soldiers, many white soldiers and settlers were poorly paid single males whose only inroads into the economy were as consumers. Their proclivity for larger heists meant that 37 percent of white larcenies—along with a good portion of the 13 percent of white larceny of guns—were grand larcenies (figure 2.12). For example, in February of 1850 Henry Potter and Samuel Rino attempted to steal a trunk of money from Henry Martin, Manuel Woods, and William Raymond.[156] Henry Potter was twenty-seven while Samuel Rino was thirty-one, and both were laborers from Missouri.[157] No doubt they came to Santa Fe in search of their fortune, but found only frustration. Potter and Rino broke into the Martin, Woods, and Raymond Company store and stole said trunk. Both Potter and Rino were captured, and each was sentenced to thirty-nine lashes and a year in prison, which was the only time a nonmilitary white was lashed in Santa Fe County.[158] Still smarting from their chastisement, Potter and Rino shared a cell with career criminal Jose Francoso—in jail for stealing a watch—when Charles Blumner marked down their names in the 1850 census.

In another case, Heinrich Boze was looking for a quick score when he stole a cask of brandy and a barrel of whiskey from Charles Higgins.[159] Boze committed another crime around that time, but there is no record to reveal the details. The court may have concluded that Boze either perjured himself or attempted to sell the alcohol, because his sentence was abnormally long.[160] The judge sentenced him to eight years in prison, though within months Boze was no longer in Santa Fe County. Either he was pardoned because the jail was too full, or he escaped. Regardless, he was definitely not in his cell when the census was taken in 1850.[161] Similarly, John Cline sought a big score when he stole $305 in gold and silver, but unlike Boze, Cline escaped the territory before the local authorities could nab him and put him through the judicial process.[162]

In 1850, William Goodfellow pulled off the biggest heist that involved a white settler when he robbed his white employers in Santa Fe. Goodfellow came to New Mexico as a teamster and is listed in the 1850 census as a carpenter working for the military.[163] Goodfellow was not long in Santa Fe when he was indicted for stealing $377 in gold, $600 in clothing, and a butcher's knife from

John Rowe and Sylvester C. Florence of Ohio, a fellow carpenter who owned $300 worth of land in 1850.[164] It is likely that Goodfellow was a part-time employee of Rowe and Florence and it is also likely that he was guilty. There is no record of a decision, and while it is possible Goodfellow was acquitted, it is more likely that he absconded from Santa Fe County before he could be arrested.

Anglo settlers came and went, stealing what they could and fleeing before they faced the consequences. They avoided the powerful patrónes and stole from their fellow Anglo settlers whenever they saw the opportunity for gain. As noted, they were at least 1.3 times as likely to commit larceny than the vecinos were. Ironically, Anglo travelers from this period disparaged Hispanos and claimed that they committed larceny without restraint. In reality, the data show that the Anglo settlers and soldiers stole more frequently. Charles Blumner counted thirty-one people in the Santa Fe County jail in 1850. He counted thirteen Hispano laborers, six Anglo laborers, four U.S. soldiers, two teamsters, two Anglo sailors, one Anglo gunsmith, one Mexican laborer, one Anglo merchant, and a single Mexican-born actor (figure 2.13). Of the thirty-one prisoners, fifteen were Hispano and sixteen were Anglo, meaning more than half of those in jail were Anglo, and the majority of them had committed larceny.[165]

Horses and mules were of great value in the West, and white settlers often targeted these animals when it was time to leave town. For example, William Guiser was either incredibly bold or incredibly foolish, because in 1849 he stole a horse from the U.S. military. The penalty for his crime would have been severe, but Guiser was smart enough to leave the territory.[166] Thomas Stone was just as bold, but clearly not as smart, because he stole a mule valued at $50 from the U.S. military and decided to linger in the county. He was arrested, convicted, and sentenced to two years and seven months in jail, with hard labor owed to the military.[167] Levon Ward snatched his horse from John Watts, and it must have happened while Watts was traveling, because the horse still had its saddle and bridle.[168] He escaped arrest, despite the court's issuing numerous warrants against him. In 1850, Louis Peters made off with a horse valued at $50 that belonged to Charles Jackson, and he too escaped arrest.[169] The lesson seems clear: it was better to steal a horse and leave the territory quickly, and it was unwise to flee either on or with a mule.

In summary, both Anglo and Euro Americans were unable to gain a foothold in New Mexico. The ones who succeeded did so because of their willingness to adapt to Nuevo Mexicano culture. The newly arrived whites who found success most often held federal posts. White immigrants who came to New Mexico for easy money, however, met stiff resistance. Many anticipated that they would become politically relevant landholders and producers, but ultimately most left the territory with only their frustrations and, on occasion, a stolen horse.[170]

CHAPTER TWO

Conclusion

Between 1850 and 1860 vecinos confronted the dramatic legal, spiritual, and economic upheaval that accompanied territorialization. Vecinos faced Anglo judges who scorned them and meted out draconian punishments. They saw their beloved padres, who had protected them from the excesses of the patrónes, displaced. And they lost the communal lands they relied on for subsistence. Most of all, they were betrayed and abandoned by the local patrónes, who forsook their previous responsibilities.

While vecinos struggled to survive, immigrant white Americans and Europeans battled to carve out what they perceived to be their fair share of conquered lands. In reality, whites discovered that they had come to the wrong place and that in Santa Fe County this was a conquest in name only. Local patrónes were too powerful to be displaced, and the Nuevomexicano kinship networks made targeting individual landholders a dangerous venture. In addition, they discovered that the local patrónes were allied with established white settlers and political officials. The foreign-born white settlers became increasingly volatile, and it wasn't long before they turned to violence.

The local patrónes participated in the territorial government and continued to exert influence on political and economic affairs. Both they and their white allies benefited from the process of territorialization. They gained property, expanded their economic interests, and formed new political alliances. The Nuevomexicanos remained determined to control their own destiny, and they utilized both their kinship networks and their political alliances to secure their positions. Only within the court system did Hispanos seem to lose direct autonomy in Santa Fe County, but this seems to have been a calculated loss. Although the territorial laws remained in line with the Mexican laws, in Santa Fe County the local patrónes conceded direct control of the legal apparatus in exchange for political power and profits.[171]

The newly established American legal apparatus remained focused on vecinos and petty larceny, even as more serious crimes like assault and homicide emerged as significant threats to the peace. New Mexican landholders remained indifferent to these changes, for above all they wanted to protect their increasing wealth from thieves. For whites, the impact of poverty was more significant because the overwhelming majority of them had traveled to Santa Fe from places like Texas and Missouri. They had come without families, often brought very little money, and gambled everything in search of their fortunes. While vecinos still had their families and the bonds with their fellow vecinos, whites arrived with nothing to lose. Foreign whites continued to cycle in and out of Santa Fe County. Most arrived determined to strike it rich, and many departed to escape prosecution. Their frustrations drove them to commit violent crime at increasingly higher rates. Overall, crime took a different form among poor vecinos when compared to foreign-born whites from 1847 to 1853. While vecinos turned to petty larceny for survival, whites in their frustration turned to violence.

Many poor Hispanos—along with newly arrived white settlers—were thus compelled to commit larceny by the increasing inequality that accompanied the territory's incorporation into a capitalist system. Indeed, it is no coincidence that criminal trends in New Mexico quickly bore some resemblance to what Gary LaFree documented later in mid-twentieth-century America. The spike in larceny in Santa Fe County was an unmistakable sign that the arrival of the Americans fundamentally undermined the vecinos' ability to subsist in this new capitalist structure, and the relative consistency of the larceny rate proves that

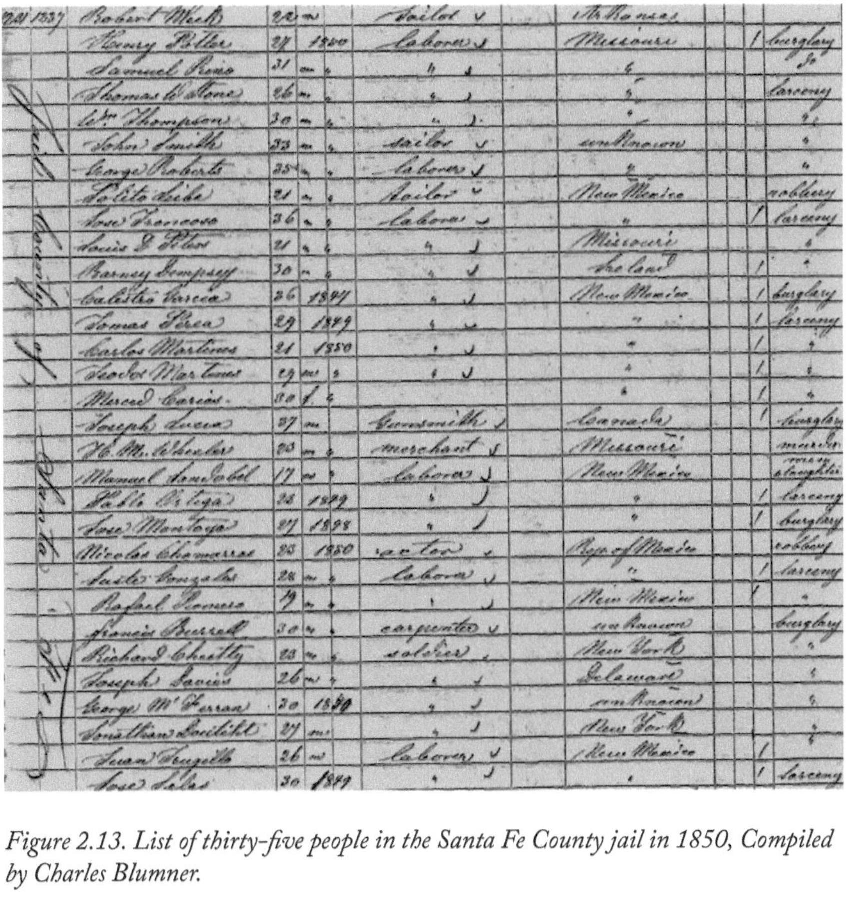

Figure 2.13. List of thirty-five people in the Santa Fe County jail in 1850, Compiled by Charles Blumner.

life did not improve for poor New Mexicans. Indeed, rates only declined when vecinos started to leave Santa Fe County (table 2.3).

As a result of their actions the vecinos became desperate, the foreign-born settlers became angry, and—when compared to the Mexicano period—crime of all types skyrocketed in Santa Fe County.[172] Among those who struggled most, many ultimately stole what they needed in order to survive, and this realization may help us understand why Bishop Lamy and his clergy were repeatedly targeted, even on that notorious Christmas Eve. That unknown man was desperate, so he sought coin; he was cold, so he made a fire; he was hungry, so he demanded food. In the end, he was very much typical of the poor people who resorted to larceny in Santa Fe County, and within this context, his actions seem to have a far more rational purpose.

PHOTOGRAPHS

Group outside the Exchange Hotel, Santa Fe, New Mexico. Once the site of the Alarid House, the Exchange Hotel occupied the Southeast corner of the Plaza in Santa Fe and became the site of numerous assaults and homicide during the American Territorial Period. ca.1890, negative number 039368.

Women walking on La Bajada Hill road near Santa Fe, New Mexico. La Bajada was the generally accepted dividing line between the Rio Arriba and Rio Abajo. The hill was a major geographical obstacle, one that disrupted the flatter landscape of the Rio Abajo. Pictured here are three women standing atop the imposing hill on the road to Santa Fe. Photo by Henry Dorman, ca. 1901–1910, negative number 008228.

San Miguel Church, Santa Fe, New Mexico. Built in 1610, San Miguel Church remains the oldest church in North America. This is the very place where Manuel Chaves and his men brought their guns into the church and frightened the priest who was supposed to excommunicate him. Behind the church is where Chaves built the unsightly fence that nearly got him expelled by Bishop Lamy, but it was long gone by the time this picture was taken in the 1880s. Photo by A.T. & S.F.R.R., ca. 1880–1900, negative number 049154.

Portal of the Palace of the Governors, Santa Fe, New Mexico. The great Portal of the Palace of the Governors, where Manuel Armijo denied Padre Antonio José Martinez the right to represent New Mexico in the Mexican Congress in 1843. To the right is a glimpse of the location where Governor Juan Bautista Vigil y Alarid surrendered New Mexico to the American colonizers. Photo by William Henry Jackson, ca. 1880, negative number 118547.

Mr. Sneider, The Palace Saloon, Santa Fe, New Mexico. The Palace Saloon was once the site of Dona Tules Gambling Hall and Saloon. Once a lavishly decorated space, by the American period the layout was simple and without the character more typical during the Mexican Period. Negative number 150886.

Southwest corner of the Plaza, Santa Fe, New Mexico. The southwest corner of the plaza is pictured here, similar to the way it would have looked when one viewed it from the Palace of the Governors. This was a place of commerce, as opposed the administrative and hospitality focus of the northern and southeastern parts of the plaza respectively. 1866, negative number 038178.

Oxen wagon, Plaza, Santa Fe, New Mexico. A glimpse of the old plaza, as it was before it was transformed into a tourist destination. Pictured center is an unknown Nuevomexicano man being paid for his services by an equally unknown American businessman. Photo by Nicholas Brown, ca. 1869–1871, negative number 011255.

CHAPTER THREE

BETWEEN A ROCK AND A GUN

Vecino and White Homicide

As night fell in the dusty Santa Fe streets on Saturday, November 12, 1853, the plaza was relatively quiet. Families had settled in for the evening, and the working citizens were nestled into local drinking houses. The spirits flowed, producing a casual merriment among the local townsfolk, and some men risked their salaries in the popular games of the day, including Monte, poker, and faro.

The sound of gunfire interrupted the quiet mountain villa and echoed from the Exchange Hotel across the plaza. Two more shots rang out, and the citizens in the back room of the Exchange Hotel, who were eagerly losing their money at Monte, wrestled the perpetrators to the dusty floor. "We're Texans, we can take this town," the prisoners repeated through their drunkenness.[1] On the same floor lay Judge Hugh N. Smith, wounded by a projectile that passed through his lungs and lodged in his shoulder. Somehow Judge Smith survived, though no one imagined he would when hours later a crowd gathered near the plaza and looked on as one of the Texans swayed from a sturdy tree, the light escaping his eyes.

Men like Judge Hugh N. Smith and Gillion Scallion (the lynched Texan) were victims in a rash of violence that swept through the Southwest in the aftermath of the US-Mexican War. The United States occupied New Mexico and California, and white settlers from the north and south flooded into the Mexican towns of the Southwest. These foreign-born white settlers were determined to make their fortunes, but most of them ultimately failed. In their frustration they gambled, drank, caroused, fought, and murdered in the streets and bars in towns across the Southwest. Many were soldiers during the war and most were racist against Nuevomexicanos, Native Americans, Chinese, Latin Americans, free blacks, and anyone else they perceived as different.[2] They transformed the towns of the Southwest into dangerous places in both New Mexico and California. White Americans carried the banner of Manifest Destiny into the Southwest, and from every direction they brought violence with them.

In Santa Fe County this was also true. White settlers were responsible for nine of the sixteen known homicides committed from 1847 to 1853, even though they made up only 10 percent of the population of Santa Fe County.[3] For Nuevomexicanos, both the rate and manner of their homicides remained consistent from 1838 to 1853. Statistically this means that white American and European immigrant settlers were seven times as likely to commit homicide than were Nuevomexicanos in Santa Fe County between 1847 and 1853 (table 3.1).[4]

Regardless, white settlers drove cumulative homicide rates up in Santa Fe

CHAPTER THREE

County and made risk there comparable to what was seen in the most dangerous corners of the West.[5] Between 1847 and 1853, the cumulative homicide rate was 42 per 100,000 in Santa Fe County (Table 3.2).[6] More practically, this meant that roughly one of every twenty-three hundred people in Santa Fe County would be murdered each year they spent in Santa Fe County.[7]

Crime	1838–1845	1847–1850 Rates (4 Yrs)	1851–1853 Rates (3 Yrs)
Hispano Homicide	23	29	23
Anglo Homicide	NA	162	173

Table 3.1. Homicide Rates per Year among Hispanos and Anglos in Santa Fe County, Adults 16 and older, per 100,000

For context, risk in Santa Fe County was similar to other commercial and agricultural counties in California during the Gold Rush years, which was an era of extreme strife (figure 3.2).[8] Although San Francisco was lower at 31 per 100,000 (1850–1865), San Joaquin (61 per 100,000, 1850–1865) and Sacramento (47 per 100,000 1850–1865) were almost identical to Santa Fe County. In contrast to places like San Joaquin (20 percent Californio, 1850–1860), however, Santa Fe was 93 percent Hispano by 1860.[9] This meant that, ethnically, Santa Fe County most closely resembled Santa Barbara, California. Yet the homicide rate in Santa Barbara was nearly double that of Santa Fe County. The nature of the relationship that white settlers had to Nuevomexicano and Californio communities was a factor in the level of risk. In Santa Fe, the patrónes worked in concert with their longtime white business partners, many of whom were kin by marriage. Risk was elevated by recently arrived settlers. In contrast, white settlers in Santa Barbara had only recently arrived, and they were determined to push the Californios out rather than to work with them.

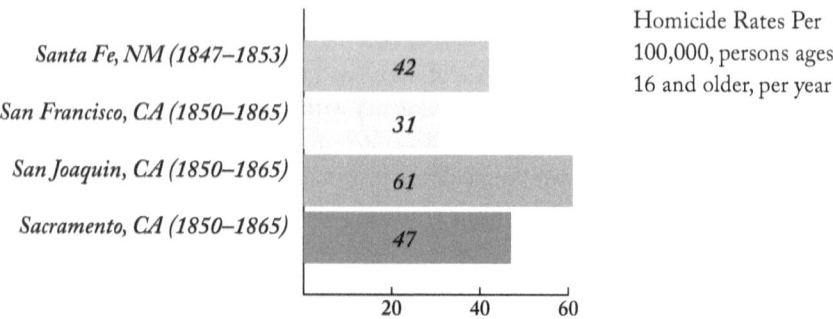

Figure 3.1. Homicide in commercial and agricultural centers in California, 1850–1865, Compared to Santa Fe County, 1847–1853.

Location and Years	Homicides	Ave. annual adult pop.	Adult pop. at risk	Homicide rate
Monterey County, CA, 1855–1857	40	2,189	6,567	609
Nevada County, CA, 1851–1856	98	18,270	109,620	89
Oregon, 1850–1865	114	23,373	373,964	30
British Columbia, 1859–1871	43	13,204	171,653	25
Texas, June 1865–June 1868	1,035	455,000	1,365,000	76
Gila County, AZ, 1880–1900	89	2,580	54,170	164
Pima County, AZ, 1882–1909	106	11,389	182,225	58
Denver, CO, 1859–1865	30	4,058	28,404	106
Las Animas County, CO, 1880–1900	73	10,323	216,777	34
Santa Fe County, NMT, 1847–1853	14	4,707	32,949	42

Table 3.2. Western Homicide Rates per Year, per 100,000, Persons Ages 16 and Older

This chapter focuses on how Nuevomexicano community solidarity and political domination affected the homicide rate—and the manner of killing—among Nuevomexicanos and newly arrived white immigrants from 1847 to 1853.[10] The first section of this chapter, "Politicos and Representation," demonstrates that local patrónes dominated the territorial legislature. This was a period of great transition, as local patrónes took their places in the power structure and began the transition from patrónes to politicos to American-style capitalists. Nuevomexicano political domination had two effects on Santa Fe County. First, it initially held the Nuevomexicano community together and prevented Hispanos from feeling estranged beneath a new flag. Second, it excluded the majority of foreign-born white settlers from the political process.[11] In this chapter I argue that Nuevomexicano patrónes, established white merchants, and vecino solidarity alienated white immigrants in Santa Fe County.[12] The bond between the local patrónes and the vecinos was residual from the Mexican period, and that bond buoyed Nuevomexicano political representation during the early territorial period. Vecinos still believed their government would help them survive—at least for the first seven years of territorialization—and so they committed few homicides, while foreign-born whites first felt entitled, then frustrated, and finally alienated. These feelings fueled their high homicide rate.

The second part of this chapter is focused on eight homicide cases, including one double homicide, that provide examples of how homicide manifested in Santa Fe County. I also highlight four homicide cases from the Mexican period, which show the continuity between homicides across periods. The American territorial cases have been chosen because they are the most heavily documented. They include random acts of unprovoked violence by white immigrants, homicides stemming from drunkenness, domestic homicides, and premeditated execution-style murders. Importantly, they illuminate the different ways that vecinos and white settlers committed homicide from 1847 to 1853.

These homicides are organized into the three different venues in which they occurred in Santa Fe County: *public homicides* that occurred in town over personal or political differences; *community homicides* committed by vecinos and whites within and against the old vecino community; and *social homicides*, which took place at Nuevomexicano socials called fandangos, where both groups came together. Ironically, white settlers, chroniclers, and journalists complained that Nuevomexicanos did not value human lives and that murderers were allowed to go free in Santa Fe County. Examining homicide within these venues illuminates the degree to which foreign-born whites were in fact responsible for the escalating homicide rates in Santa Fe County. Indeed, they were also the murderers who escaped justice.

Politicos and Representation

What distinguished Santa Fe County was that the majority of the population in New Mexico was Hispano, whereas western counties outside of New Mexico were mostly Anglo. In 1848, the Nuevomexicano population in New Mexico made up nearly three-quarters (73 percent) of all Mexicanos in the Southwest; New Mexico was home to 61,547 of an estimated 80,000 Mexicanos in the Southwest (figure 3.2).[13] In California there were only 7,500 Californios (9 percent) and most of them lived in Southern California. There were roughly 14,000 Tejanos in Texas (17 percent), who likewise lived in southern Texas, and in Arizona there were only 1,000 Mexicanos (1 percent).[14] As a result, the Nuevomexicanos were able to dominate New Mexico with their numbers, something Mexicanos in the rest of the Southwest were unable to do.

Santa Fe County, diverse by New Mexican standards, was still overwhelmingly

Hispano. In 1850 there were 6,683 Nuevomexicanos in Santa Fe County, and that number increased to 7,667 by 1860 (figures 3.3a and 3.3b). Nuevomexicanos increased from 87 percent to 93 percent of the population in Santa Fe County, in a decade when Californios were being overrun by immigrants. In contrast, the white population fell from 803 (10 percent) to 511 (6 percent) in Santa Fe County. There were two reasons for this decline. The first was that in 1851 Lt. Col. Edwin V. Sumner moved the U.S. military supply depot one hundred miles east of Santa Fe and briefly relocated the army headquarters to Fort Union, removing many soldiers to Fort Union who were consequently not counted in the 1860 census, although they continued to travel to Santa Fe during their off days and commit crimes there.[15] Second, many white immigrants departed the county during the 1850s. Hispano and white live births demonstrate how few whites actually settled in Santa Fe County from 1850 to 1860: Hispanos gave birth to 2,282 children, while white immigrants gave birth to only 48 children.[16]

By 1848 the Nuevomexicano patrónes in Santa Fe County enjoyed a long tradition of local autonomy, and they maintained that power through at least the first thirteen years of American territorialization. Power increasingly took the form of political representation. New Mexican political participation in the territorial government was entrenched by 1850, and Nuevomexicanos effectively participated in the power sharing system that arose in the territory.[17] Their residual differences from the Mexican period—which in 1847 manifested as Mexicanist versus pro-Americanists—highlighted a conservative versus liberal division that predated the American occupation, and those political divisions remained during the American territorial period.[18]

Above all else, Nuevomexicano patrónes and the vecinos were bound together against newcomers by their symbiotic relationships, which were hardened during their troubled past. These Nuevomexicanos developed an us-versus-them mentality, due in large part to their long history of common struggle. In 1837 they banded together and deposed the centralist governor, an outsider who tried to assert authority over them. In 1841 they united and rebuffed a Texas invasion bound for Santa Fe. In 1847 they rose up against Gov. Charles Bent, whom they labeled a friend of Texas. The bond between patrón and vecino was solidified with each uprising.

Across the Southwest, Mexicanos' different circumstances shaped their reactions toward white immigration. Immigrants overwhelmed the Californios after gold was discovered in California. In 1848 there were 7,500 Californios among 14,000 total residents. By 1852, 250,000 people immigrated to California from all over the world. White immigrants used their superior numbers against the Californios to seize control of most county governments. White miners tried to displace Hispanics and Native Americans from their mines, while white farmers and

CHAPTER THREE

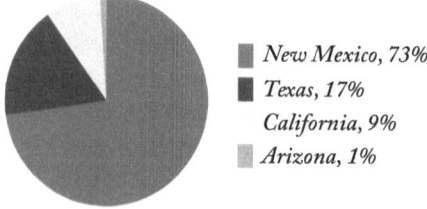

- New Mexico, 73%
- Texas, 17%
- California, 9%
- Arizona, 1%

Figure 3.2. Estimated Mexicano population in the Southwest, by percentage, 1848. Source: Stephen S. Birdsall and John Florin, "Regional Landscapes of the United States: Southwest Border Area," Outline of American Geography, November 1988.

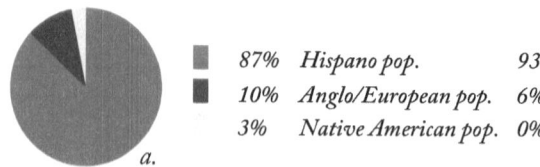 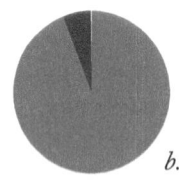

- 87% Hispano pop. 93%
- 10% Anglo/European pop. 6%
- 3% Native American pop. 0%

Figure 3.3a. Hispano, Anglo, and Native American populations in Santa Fe County, by percentage, 1850.

Figure 3.3b. Hispano, Anglo, and Native American populations in Santa Fe County, by percentage, 1860.

ranchers seized land from Californios and Native Americans in other regions so they could dominate the market for provisioning Anglo miners.[19] The Californios fought back against the Anglos, and California became a dangerous place to live.

The white settlers who immigrated to California were aggressive men determined to carve out their fortunes.[20] They responded to competition in the mines, fields, and towns with violence, targeting Hispanics and Native Americans, pushing other communities to the bottom of the social hierarchy.[21] In the 1850s and 1860s whites committed the highest proportion of the total number of homicides in California: they killed their follow immigrants 72 percent of the time, but the remaining 28 percent of their homicides accounted for 55 percent of all Hispanic victims, 56 percent of all Chinese victims, 61 percent of black victims, and 66 percent of Native American victims.[22] Californio homicide rates, however, were significantly higher than white homicide rates. Californios committed homicide at the rate of 161 per 100,000 (1849–1865), which was roughly three times higher than Anglos in California, who committed homicide at the rate of 52 per 100,000 (1849–1865).[23]

In contrast to California, Nuevomexicanos dominated New Mexico and white settlers were the minority, in part because there was no mass migration equivalent to the Gold Rush. Santa Fe County was a true Hispano bastion, a place where the Hispano population both increased and prospered after the first thirteen years of American territorialization (table 3.3). While the Hispano population increased from 87 percent to 93 percent of Santa Fe County, the proportion of Hispano real property owned increased from 36 percent percent to 52 percent percent of Santa Fe County property.[24] White immigrants participated in local politics, and their representation exceeded their population size, but representatives in the New Mexico Territorial Legislature were elected and not appointed.[25] Hubert Howe Bancroft noted that a handful of local families "in connection with the few Anglo residents ... controlled the election of representatives and all other matters of the territorial government, without the slightest interest or action on the part of the masses."[26] Since the Hispanos had the majority of the population, the vote, and much of the power, whites were unable to overrun New Mexico. Longtime white residents and new business associates were sometimes elected to the legislature, but by and large the newest white settlers failed to break through.

Census Year	1850	1860
Population	7713	8213
Hispano Population	6683	7384
Anglo/European Population	803	511
Native American/Mexican Born	227	318
Hispano Child Births Since 1850	NA	2282
Anglo Child Births Since 1850	NA	48

Source: 1850 Federal Census, Santa Fe County, New Mexico Territory; 1860 Federal Census, Santa Fe County, New Mexico Territory.

Table 3.3. 1850 vs. 1860 Census Data, Santa Fe County

Most of the white American settlers who immigrated to New Mexico were attracted to trade and ranching, but they turned violent when they discovered that the local patrónes controlled the land they sought. Interestingly, recently arrived whites did not target the local patrónes. Instead they targeted other whites and vecinos, especially vecinos who could not defend themselves. Most of their victims were fellow white settlers, and they included established whites like Judge Hugh N. Smith and other transient whites who crossed their paths. They attacked the vecinos less often, in part because the vecinos in Santa Fe County shied away from interracial violence during the first seven years of territorialization. Unlike the Californios, the New Mexican vecinos trusted that the local patrónes would save them from taxes and tyranny, just as they had during the 1837 and 1847 rebellions. Unlike California, the white immigrants found themselves on the outside looking in.

Nuevomexicano political power represented a departure from the bond that tied Nuevomexicano patrónes and their vecinos allies, but for vecinos that fact did not become clear until 1855. Hispanos were empowered by the Organic Law of 1850, which established a bicameral legislature consisting of a House of Representatives with twenty-three members and a Council of thirteen members. The local patrónes had the advantage because representatives in the legislature were elected, and the Hispano population was the overwhelming majority in New Mexico. Alvin Sunseri wrote, "The vast majority of legislators in both the House and Council were Mexican-Americans; in 1851, for example, of the ninety-one candidates seeking office all but fourteen were Mexican-American, and in the 1855/1856 sessions there was but one Anglo seated in the house."[27]

Older Nuevomexicanos belonged to the Council, the more powerful body in the territorial legislature. Between 1847 and 1860 Hispanos made up 84 percent of the known council members (figure 3.4). The most powerful families in New Mexico were represented on the Council: the Baca, Chaves, Martínez, Pino, Ortiz, and Otero families.

Padre José Antonio Martínez of Taos, Vicar Juan Felipé Ortiz of Santa Fe, and Padre José Manuel Gallegos of Albuquerque all served in the Council.[28] Both Padre Martínez and Vicar Ortiz served as president of the Council on multiple occasions, while Padre Gallegos became New Mexico's first U.S. Congressman in 1853.[29] Lamy replaced Vicar Juan Felipé Ortiz and removed him from his church in Santa Fe as part of what Fray Angélico Chávez accurately labeled the ecclesiastical colonization of New Mexico.[30] Padre José Manuel Gallegos was expelled on erroneous charges and Padre José Antonio Martínez was suspended for challenging Lamy's authority. In January of 1856 the Hispano-led Territorial Legislature issued a formal address to the pope accusing Lamy and Machebeuf of meddling in politics and of mistreating the Hispano padres. Padre Gallegos authored the address and Padre Martínez was part of the Council that pushed the measure through.[31]

The Hispanos also dominated the twenty-three-member House of Representatives. In 1847 and from 1851 to 1860 the Hispanos made up 89 percent of the House members (figure 3.5). Members of the same Hispano families also dominated the House and among them were Miguel E. Pino, Albino Chacón, and Diego Archuleta, who had masterminded the initial plot to kill Gov. Charles Bent in 1847. They cooperated with the Council in passing a high volume of legislation.

The Hispano majority in the legislature was so overwhelming that proceedings occurred in Spanish. Laws were first written in Spanish and later translated into English.[32] Whites who served in the legislature needed to speak Spanish fluently, which was not a problem because most white settlers who were elected were longtime residents who spoke the local dialect. The white settlers in the legislature were a decided minority with little power. In 1851, white representatives in both houses tried to pass a law to allow judges and justices of the peace to marry private citizens. Alvin Sunseri noted, "Such a proposition was so repugnant to Mexican-Americans that all but one of the Council members disapproved of the bill, and that body adjourned rather than debate the matter."[33] In Santa Fe County only 72 percent of representatives were Hispano, but whites could still not impact policy, and white representatives remained tied to their Hispano allies (figure 3.6).

The Hispano representatives comported themselves well, but they mostly passed legislation that furthered the interests of their fellow patrónes. A white American reporter from the *Missouri Republican* begrudgingly noted, "I have had a sight of the Territorial Legislature, and I am really disappointed in finding so intelligent looking an assembly of Mexicans."[34] The white reporter noted that the Hispanos displayed dignity and decorum while in session, and he conceded that in time they would make a worthy addition to the United States. Hubert Howe Bancroft noted, "In session the members puffed their cigarettes and indulged in other peculiarities of conduct unknown to American assemblies; but the results will I think compare favorably in most respects with those of early legislative efforts in other territories."[35] Only one representative was late to the first legislative session, but he had a legitimate reason for his tardiness: the U.S. Army mistook him for the insurgent Manuel Cortez and arrested him en route to Santa Fe![36]

Although Hispanos were politically divided, many issues transcended their divisions. This was especially true of laws that protected the interests of their families. They passed laws to further economic development, secure their autonomy, and to control violent Anglo settlers. One of their first memorials to the United States

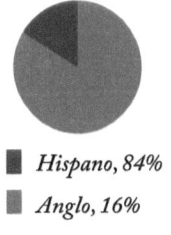
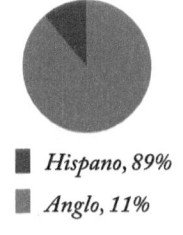
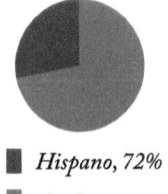

■ *Hispano, 84%*
■ *Anglo, 16%*

■ *Hispano, 89%*
■ *Anglo, 11%*

■ *Hispano, 72%*
■ *Anglo, 28%*

Figure 3.4. New Mexican council members ethnicity, by percentage, 1847, 1851–1860. Source: William G. Ritch, New Mexico Blue Book, 1882 *(Albuquerque: University of New Mexico Press, 1968).*

Figure 3.5. New Mexico House of Representatives members by ethnicity, by percentage, 1847, 1851–1860. Source: William G. Ritch, New Mexico Blue Book, 1882 *(Albuquerque: University of New Mexico Press, 1968).*

Figure 3.6. Santa Fe County representatives in the House of Representatives, by percentage, 1847, 1851–1860. Source: William G. Ritch, New Mexico Blue Book, 1882 *(Albuquerque: University of New Mexico Press, 1968).*

House of Representatives called for funds to repair New Mexico's infrastructure, which had hindered them since the colonial period. They pointed to the geographical peculiarities of New Mexico and formally asked that public highways be built so that the vast expanses between villages might be more easily traversed.[37] Further, they called for Congress to establish routes to California and the Arkansas River.[38] They also requested a mineralogical survey and lamented, "Gold is found in every section of the country, from its extreme northern to its southern limits, but the placers and mines are, as yet, only worked by the poorer class of inhabitants, without capital, skill or enterprise, and in the most rude and primitive manner."[39] Hispano representatives realized that political representation was key to their continued success in New Mexico, and they sought to use their offices to circumvent local whites and appeal to the federal government for resources.

The legislature refused, however, to implement property taxes in New Mexico to pay for the repairs they called for, meaning they refused to tax themselves. American governor after governor tried to convince the legislature to levy taxes on land, but the local patrónes demurred. In 1857 Gov. Abraham Rencher warned that the government was on the brink of collapse, and he pleaded with the politicos to implement property taxes. Local patrónes would not budge. Alvin Sunseri theorized that "Rencher and the other Anglos failed to realize that land taxes were contrary to New Mexican tradition."[40] In actuality, the local patrónes refused to tax themselves because it cut into their profits. They had fought against taxes under Mexico and were determined to avoid them in the American territorial era. The roads needed to be repaired, but someone else was going to have to pay for that.

The legislature also passed laws that declared territorial autonomy. Donaciano Vigil called for the first territorial legislature to meet after the Taos campaigns of 1847, with the primary aim of deposing the American military government in New Mexico. In 1851, Hispanos held their first official meeting, where they decreed that "the military shall at all times be subordinate to the civil authority."[41] They also declared, "No power of suspending laws in this Territory shall be exercised, except by the legislature and its authority" and that "No person prevented by the organic law of the Territory, no officer or soldier in the United States army, and no person included in the term 'camp followers' (teamsters) of the United States army, shall be entitled to vote or hold public office in this Territory."[42] They proclaimed their authority over the military to secure their autonomy and to block white American attempts to influence New Mexican politics, and they denied soldiers—who had a history of illegal voting in New Mexico—the vote. In short, the politicos tried to invest the legislature they dominated with supreme authority.

The politicos targeted white immigrants more directly in the third legislative session. They passed a vagrancy law that applied to people without occupation, drunkards, and those who abandoned their families. Many of the law's details intentionally targeted white soldiers and transients. Vagrants were "Persons in the habit of loitering or sleeping in the grog-shops, beer-shops, out-houses, markets, sheds, stables, granaries, or unoccupied houses, or without any place of habitation, or who cannot give a good account of themselves."[43] The description most likely fit newly arrived Americans who didn't know anyone in the community. The politicos concluded with a special section for these extranjeros:

> Sec. 9. That when any foreigners, who are not residents of this Territory, are found in the county of this Territory for a term of more than ten days, or who have no visible occupation, or mode of maintaining themselves, it is hereby made the duty of the Probate Judge, or Justice of the Peace, to issue his warrant for such persons, and immediately try them as Vagrants under this law.[44]

The politicos also targeted white soldiers and transients when they passed a law that forbade anyone from carrying small arms into settlements and fandangos. The politicos defined small arms as pistols, knives, daggers, and other concealed deadly weapons. In fact, soldiers had a tradition of violent behavior in general. The politicos hoped to discourage whites who behaved badly at fandangos, which was a problem in New Mexico. They mandated a fine of two to ten dollars and a sentence of five to fifteen days for those who violated the law.

THE HOMICIDE PROBLEM

Of the six fully documented Hispano homicides between 1847 and 1853 in Santa Fe County, only two involved a gun, and none of the victims were killed execution-style. Nuevomexicanos attacked with knives, sticks, and occasionally rocks, but in this early territorial period they did not shoot with intent to kill. This represented continuity, as Nuevomexicanos only committed five homicides in the villa of Santa Fe between 1820 and 1846.[45] Even Josiah Gregg, ever critical of New Mexico and its people, conceded the rarity of Nuevomexicano homicide.[46] Risk hinged on stability, and from 1837 to 1853, Hispano homicide rates remained consistent because there were no fundamental changes to the existing system of power. The vecinos were ready to live with inequality in New Mexico, but the patrónes needed to uphold their end of the bargain and protect them from the Americans.

In contrast, recently arrived settlers experienced extreme instability, and they resorted to homicide in Santa Fe County. They were outsiders, or extranjeros, newly arrived whites who found that the Nuevomexicano community was nearly impenetrable. Whereas old white settlers participated in all aspects of New Mexican society, new white settlers were excluded socially, economically, and politically from the community. In this effort, the politicos targeted new white settlers with many of the laws they passed, and white settlers lacked both recourse or representation to push back. The new white settlers—who were a dangerous combination of poor and entitled—were angered by this exclusion and turned violent.

The manner in which new settlers committed homicide betrays their estrangement. All of the eight fully documented white homicide cases involved guns, and six of the eight victims were executed by gunshot to the head.[47] White homicide fell into two basic categories in Santa Fe County: one featured a violent transient with a gun, pitted against his fellow whites; the other featured an ambitious settler with a gun who attacked unsuspecting whites and vecinos. Newly arrived white immigrants expected respect and financial gain in what they viewed as conquered territory, while more ambitious whites sought to settle, buy land, and obtain status. When they failed, they pulled their guns. The shooting of Judge Smith represents the first of these two narrative types, but when drunken whites weren't shooting people with stray bullets, other whites deliberately executed them at close range. The lynching of Gillion Scallion represents something different altogether.

The white experience in Santa Fe County was the opposite of what they experienced in California. As a result, whites committed homicide at a much higher rate in Santa Fe County. While Californios were three times as likely than Anglos to commit homicide in California, whites in Santa Fe County were seven times as likely than Hispanos to commit homicide between 1847 and 1853 (table 3.4).

Ethnicity	California, 1849–1865	Santa Fe County, 1847–1853
Californios/Nuevomexicanos	161	23
Non-Mexican White	52	166

Table 3.4. Homicide Rates per Year among Californios and Non-Mexicano Whites in California, Adults 16 and Older, per 100,000 vs. Homicide Rates among Hispanos and Non-Mexicano Whites in Santa Fe County, Adults 16 and Older, per 100,000

The solidarity that made the Hispano homicide rate low caused the white homicide rate to skyrocket in Santa Fe County, and this is more evident when homicide and manslaughter are differentiated. A homicide is committed with intent, while manslaughter is either accidental or the result of reckless behavior. The Hispano homicide rate was even lower when this standard is applied to homicide in Santa Fe County. Hispanos committed only two willful homicides between 1847 and 1853. When manslaughter is added, the Hispano homicide rate drops to 7 per 100,000, which was lower than the United States homicide rate (10 per 100,000) between 1950 and 1990 (table 3.5).[48] Among Hispanos, the manslaughter rate (13 per 100,000) was higher than the homicide rate in Santa Fe County. In contrast, all but one known white homicide was intentionally committed and there was only a single instance of manslaughter among them.

1847–1853	Ethnicity	Rate
Known Homicide	H	7
Known Homicide	A	129
Known Manslaughter	H	13
Known Manslaughter	A	19

Source: New Mexico State Records Center and Archives, "Records of the United States Territorial and New Mexico District Courts for Santa Fe County 1847–1951."

Table 3.5. Known Homicide Rates and Known Manslaughter Rates per Year among Hispanos and Anglos (Non-Mexicano Whites) in Santa Fe County, Adults over 16 and older, per 100,000

Public Homicides

Public homicides offer insight into how Nuevomexicanos and newly arrived Anglo settlers behaved in public spaces. They are extreme examples that highlight the tension between and among the motley lot that populated Sante Fe. The attempted murder of Judge Hugh N. Smith at the Exchange Hotel is a particularly insightful drunken and disorderly affair, and it did ultimately result in a homicide through the lynching that followed.[49] Although violence of this sort was all but unknown in Santa Fe, recently arrived white settlers or transients were invariably involved when such confrontations occurred. The Texans who attacked Judge Hugh N. Smith were drifters, men who came to Santa Fe to drink, carouse, and make a quick dollar. Typically, foreign-born whites, such as Gillion Scallion and the man known only as Stephenson, would not have remained in town long had it not been for their crime. Both men displayed a sense of entitlement in Santa Fe that was typical of newly arrived whites, who assumed that because they were white men entering a conquered land they would be given whatever they demanded.

More than just being white, Stephenson and Scallion were proud nineteenth-century Texans, which made them absolutely insufferable. They were drinking most of the evening while loudly and proudly proclaiming their Texas heritage to everyone within shouting distance.[50] They knew of the mutual enmity that existed between Texas and New Mexico; the Nuevomexicanos were still angry over the failed invasion of 1841 and the more recent border disputes. For their part, the Texans remained bitter about how their soldiers were treated during 1841 and continued to believe that the boundaries of Texas included nearly everything west of Arkansas.[51]

Later that evening, their binge led them to the Exchange Hotel. The Texans entered, thoroughly inebriated, and approached the bartender. When they heard of the backroom game of Monte that was being played, they demanded a $10 loan from the hotel.[52] When the bartender refused, the intoxicated pair shouted, "We're from Texas, we could take this whole town if we wanted to!"[53] Rebuffed and penniless, the Texans went to the backroom anyway. The Texan named Stephenson overheard that one of the dealers was named Stephens, and he voiced his bet that he could whip anyone in New Mexico territory with that name. Another white resident escalated the argument with his retort, "If you came from Texas, as you keep saying, you will find that at Santa Fe there are men to whom no name or country can communicate terror."[54] Stephenson, whom one eyewitness claimed was more intoxicated, escalated the argument verbally, but before the fighting could break out, the quieter Scallion pulled his Colt revolver and opened fire, shouting, "I'm going to clear this room."[55] The first shot struck Stephenson—his fellow Texas—in the hand. The second hit Judge Smith, and the third missed altogether.

Stephenson was taken to the jailhouse, but some residents cornered Scallion. Across the plaza, word spread that a Texan had gunned down Judge Hugh N. Smith. While the physician cut the bullet from Judge Smith, who surprised everyone by surviving, a mob that sought vengeance gathered outside the Exchange Hotel and milled about the plaza. White settlers led the angry mob. They drew a rogue jury and an eyewitness acted as judge, adjudicating the murder case at the Exchange Hotel.[56] Scallion was reportedly asked how he could fire upon unarmed men. Allegedly, he responded, "I don't care a damn, if you don't like what I have done, help yourselves."[57] The New Mexicans did help themselves: Gillion Scallion was found guilty by the kangaroo court and sentenced to death by hanging. Scallion was marched across the old plaza, that site of so much brutality and public mirth, and lynched.[58]

This homicide was typical of one of the two forms of violent crime among whites: the transient who seemingly killed in a drunken debacle. The manner in which the white citizens dealt with Scallion was typical of the second type: an execution-style murder. This was neither the first nor the last time an individual was lynched in Santa Fe, though the rate of lynching in Santa Fe County would never rival those in other parts of New Mexico territory. Some historians have asserted that lynch mobs saved both time and resources, but these were not the rationales of the lynch mob that murdered Gillion Scallion. The mob took care to create the illusion of justice, but like all executions the sentence didn't fit the crime.

On July 4, 1853, a large group of white Americans were celebrating Independence Day at the Exchange Hotel—which advertised itself as having the best liquor and cigars—when the seemingly inconsequential Ignacio Tapia snuck into the building through the backdoor in search of a little fun and a lot of free booze. Tapia made his way into the ballroom, where the Americans claim he started making trouble and interfering with their celebrations. The American response was characteristically excessive: they assaulted and ejected Tapia, throwing him into the street. It must have seemed like a minor incident to them, so they must have been surprised when Ignacio Tapia returned, led by the powerful, young, and exceptionally violent Nuevomexicano patrón Jesus Maria Sena y Baca, along with a large group of violent men who were loyal to him.[59]

Violence ensued, and in the end a group of Nuevomexicanos stood accused of killing one foreign-born white settler. The white settlers who ran the *Santa Fe Weekly Gazette* were infuriated by the incident: "Our citizens are too discordant to act in concert about anything, not even the celebrating of the fourth of July, an occasion in reference to which, in most other places, secures a union of action."[60] The writer wrote that he hoped all would celebrate July 4th, but instead when the white settlers gathered for a ball at the Exchange Hotel, John Finnegan was shot. The *Gazette* memorialized, nay aggrandized him, as was their custom when white men died:

> Mr. Finnegan was a blacksmith by profession, and by a residence of some five or six years in Santa Fe, had secured many warm friends; he was not only a good mechanic, but a useful, worthy and respectable citizen. He was a native of Cumberland, Maryland, where his mother now resides, to whom but a few days before his death, he enclosed fifty dollars.[61]

Court records indicate that indictments were issued against eleven Nuevomexicanos, but ultimately only Ignacio Tapia, Andres Tapia, and Candido Ortiz were charged with the murder of John Finnegan.[62] For its part, the *Gazette* named Ignacio Tapia as the lone perpetrator.[63] The *Gazette* accused the Nuevomexicanos of starting this fight with the mirthful white settlers, which made it a unique case. On July 16, 1853, the *Gazette* published an article that supposedly detailed what happened that July 4th, and this white account is the only one that survived. The article was written under the pseudonym Fiat Justitia ("Let Justice Be Done"), and the author claimed to have been an American eyewitness. According to this account, a mob of Nuevomexicanos made an all-out assault against a group of innocent and unsuspecting Americans.[64]

CHAPTER THREE

The author claimed that Ignacio Tapia sparked the affray when he entered the celebration with the sole intention of breaking up the gala. Fiat Justitia wrote, "A Mexican *gentlemen (?)*(God save the mark!) who made his way into the ball room ... undertook to interfere with the persons present."[65] The Anglo settlers rebuffed Tapia and ejected him onto the street. Tapia was eager for revenge and returned to his community to "gather a party of *Muchachos*" in order to break up the gathering and to "put down the *Gringos carajos*."[66] Fiat Justitia alleged that the Americans dispersed and started for home, "Some to escort the females out of the reach of danger, and others to procure military assistance."[67] The article then read:

> An organized attack was made upon the Hotel by an armed mob, some of whom broke in the windows of the ball room by throwing stones and other missiles, while others entered the Bar room, armed with pistols, and commenced an indiscriminate fire upon all its occupants, others being engaged in firing (whether at random or not I will not undertake to say) from the street into the ball room. ... By a pistol shot fired through one of these windows Mr. John Finnigan, a man who by his industry, his honesty, and his patriotism, would weigh in the balance as against any number of the cowardly scoundrels who murdered him ... was killed."[68]

Fiat Justitia's account was questionable at best, and he likely exaggerated the scale of the counterattack at the Exchange Hotel. Though it would not have been unrealistic for Jesus Maria Sena y Baca to raise an army and attack the Americans who insulted Ignacio Sena, such an action would certainly have resulted in more documentation. The U.S. Army would have intervened if Nuevomexicanos had actually made an all-out assault on the Exchange Hotel; there were no military records to indicate that the army was involved in the fracas. In addition, there are no records of white settlers indiscriminately retaliating against the Nuevomexicanos—a white tradition in this period and beyond—which would have certainly followed a racially charged uprising of any scale. Instead the Santa Fe County sheriff investigated this singular incident and it ended up in court.

The case files identified Ignacio Tapia, Andres Tapia, and Candido Ortiz as the Nuevomexicanos who made up roughly one fourth of the "mob" that assaulted the party of *patriotic* white settlers.[69] There is little more than that in the file. The judge listened to the charges, the defense filed for a change of venue, and the judge allowed the proceedings to be moved to San Miguel County. He likely did this for one of two reasons: either he feared that the trial in Santa Fe County could lead to a real mob riot or he was worried that Tapia would be lynched, which would start an open battle between the Americans and the powerful and unpredictable Jesus Maria Baca y Sena. The matter seems to have ended at this point. If the *Gazette* published an update, a copy did not survive. What we know for certain is that Ignacio Tapia and his so-called mob were ultimately acquitted of all charges.[70]

Fiat Justitia embellished the details of his article, and the fight at the Exchange Hotel was much smaller than Mr. Justitia and his friends portrayed it to be. It's certain that Jesus Maria Sena y Baca returned with his men and retaliated. As we will see later, such an action is entirely in keeping with his character. It is just as likely, however, that a drunken white settler saw a group of Nuevomexicanos walking toward the Exchange Hotel, pulled out his revolver, and fired at the Nuevomexicanos, who were likely tossing rocks through the windows, and that he accidentally hit John Finnegan with friendly fire.[71] In the end, however, social unrest was bad business, and neither the local white officials nor the Nuevomexicano patrónes wished to have their dealings interrupted by a race war over a bar fight. Ignacio Tapia would have likely met his end as Gillion Scallion did six months later had the writers from the *Gazette* and their Anglo settler allies had their way. But Judge Reed exercised his judicial discretion and moved the case to the heavily Nuevomexicano San Miguel County, and the matter ended there.

Of course questions remain. Had Tapia fired the shot that killed Finnegan? What was Jesus Maria Sena y Baca's part in this affray? Did Mr. Finnegan send money to his mother, and was he the honest and industrious patriot the *Gazette* memorialized? We will never know. What we do know for certain about John Finnegan is that he was a teamster, a civilian who was employed by the army as a blacksmith.[72] We also know that teamsters were violent, usually drunk, committed all manner of crimes, and often ended up in the Santa Fe County jail. Like many teamsters in Santa Fe County, Finnegan may have been violent, but that did not mean he didn't love his mother. Regardless, the Nuevomexicanos and their white allies in Santa Fe continued to do their best to keep the peace, which was in their best interests, and the death of John Finnegan passed into history. But the violence that people like him committed in community spaces was only beginning.

Community Homicides

Community homicides are one gauge of how the Nuevomexicanos experienced the process of territorialization, and the stories that follow suggest that the vecino community by and large remained unshaken by the changes that accompanied American colonization. Murder in the vecino community was seldom premeditated and often involved people who knew each other well. The murder weapons were not guns, but rather whatever happened to be lying close by. The cases against Gallego and Chaves are consistent with what we know about

CHAPTER THREE

homicide among Nuevomexicanos during the territorial period. Hispanos sought to rationalize these actions, which betrayed their belief that sane people don't murder in this fashion.

Of the eight homicide victims who were members of the old community, two were vecinos murdered by a mentally ill vecino farmer, one was a vecino who was accidentally killed by another vecino, and three were vecinos murdered by white settlers. Of the offenders, the three white settlers were the only perpetrators who intended to kill their victims. The juries that deliberated the cases against the white settler defendants were exclusively composed of other white settlers.[73] All three settlers executed their victims with a gunshot to the head, yet all were either acquitted or found not guilty. Meanwhile, Nuevomexicano landholders served as jurors against the vecinos who committed murder; one was declared insane and the other found guilty.

There was a reason that Nuevomexicano jurors dealt with their homicides differently. There was precedent for adjudicating cases of uxoricide from the Mexican period. In those cases, Hispanos wanted to know why their fellow Nuevomexicanos killed their partners, and Nuevomexicano perpetrators had a tradition of telling the truth. Honesty mattered, as we see in 1834, when Manuel Gallego murdered his wife María Espíritu Santo Ruival in the town of Santa Cruz. Ruival's body was found in her home by relatives, and investigators reported that there was still a sinew cord wrapped around her neck. As was custom, Gallego freely confessed his crime to the alcalde, and he explained that he strangled her because she was always arguing with him.[74] Gallego said this to numerous people, including his wife's mother and brother. José Ortega was named prosecutor and he sought to rationalize Gallego's actions when he theorized that Gallego was inherently predisposed to murder. Ortega argued that Gallego was "alienated from all sentiments of humanity" the night he murdered his wife.[75] It was not an insanity plea, but it was certainly akin to one.

In 1846 Juan Antonio Chaves murdered his wife, Maria Angelina Herrera. The murder took place in the woods surrounding Conchita Pueblo, which is about thirty miles southwest of Santa Fe, and both the perpetrator and the victim were Spanish-surnamed Puebloans. Footprints from the crime scene led investigators to the perpetrator, who admitted that he had killed his wife.[76] He told the investigators that he murdered her because they had a heated argument. Investigators noted that while there were no wounds on her body, her face had taken numerous blows; close by was the bloodstained rock Chaves used to bludgeon his wife to death. Chaves was indicted, and the case was moved to Santa Fe for trial.[77] Chaves explained that he came across his wife in the forest and was angry because she had not been home for three days. When Chaves ordered her to return home, she refused, a fight ensued, and Chaves claimed that at this point his wife picked up the rock and began to strike him. Enraged by her actions, Chaves took the rock, bashed her in the face, and was so angry that he could not stop himself from repeating this action until finally she was dead.[78]

While both of these murders were committed with intent, the majority of those committed by Hispanos between 1847 and 1853 were accidental. In 1848 Nuevomexicano landholders were summoned to hear the violent details of a homicide committed by the vecino farmer Pablo Rael. Most homicides committed by vecinos were accidental, but this homicide was intentional. The twenty-four-year-old Rael committed one of the few double homicides on record in the territory, using an axe to kill first his wife Maria and then his sister Rufugia Rael.[79] The jury determined that Rael was guilty of both murders after they interviewed the witnesses and the defendant, but they also found that Rael was mentally ill and that he was incapable of determining right from wrong. To the Nuevomexicano jurors their conclusion was the correct one: a person who murdered his wife and sister must be insane, because the crime was otherwise incomprehensible.

The judge agreed, and—with no options available to assist the mentally ill—Rael was released into the custody of his two brothers, Jose de la Paz and Bartolo Rael, and he lived with them through 1850.[80] Within the Hispano community, this was an isolated incident and one that Nuevomexicanos framed as a tragedy. Pablo Rael would likely have been hanged if an all-white jury had deliberated this case, but Nuevomexicanos came from a different legal tradition. In the Mexican legal tradition, a society did not punish the mentally ill in the way that the American legal system traditionally has. The judge and jury exercised their personal discretion, and their decision no doubt contributed to the white settler belief that Nuevomexicanos did not punish murderers.

In early 1850 Manuel Sandoval, listed as a laborer in the 1850 census, killed Rafael Gonsales when he threw a rock at him. Judge Edward Hoffman adjudicated this case, which was more representative of vecino homicide than the case against Pablo Rael. The prosecution charged the seventeen-year-old Sandoval with murder, explaining that "Being moved and seduced by the instigation of the devil on the first day of November," he had assaulted Rafael Gonsales by throwing a stone at him.[81] Sandoval threw the rock and struck Gonsales in the right temple, which left a gash two inches long and two inches wide on the right side of his head. According to the file, Gonsales remained bedridden, groaning in pain, until Christmas Day, when he finally died. Judge Hoffman and the Hispano jury determined that Sandoval had not intended to murder Gonsales, and Sandoval was convicted of manslaughter and sentenced to six months imprisonment and a one-dollar fine.[82]

In 1847 a white settler named James C. Brady committed a homicide that stands in stark contrast to the one committed by Sandoval. On the night of January 25, 1847, Brady murdered Maria Antonia Lenoia, a member of the vecino community. This was the first of four homicides committed by foreign-born whites against Hispanos, and, like the other three, it was no accident. As in all cases that involved Anglo homicide between 1847 and 1853, a jury was drawn from white settlers to preside over Brady's trial.[83] The primary witness was Sheriff James Powers,[84] who swore under oath to Judge Hugh N. Smith—later shot by Gillion Scallion—that James C. Brady went into Ms. Lenoia's place of residence and murdered her.

The prosecution charged that Brady loaded his pistol, held it to Maria Lenoia's head, and shot her.[85] James Powers was the acting deputy sheriff for Santa Fe County in 1850, and one might think that his testimony would ensure a conviction. Brady, however, was not without resources, and he hired Allen O'Clark as his criminal defense attorney; O'Clark's personal notebook reveals the defense he constructed for Brady. The notes contend that Brady was not guilty because there was not a witness who could describe the details of the assault or how Brady held the pistol as he executed the victim.[86] There was no eyewitness at the moment the gun was discharged, and though Sheriff Powers witnessed Brady entering and exiting the crime scene, and although the sheriff heard the shot fired while Brady was inside, the evidence was circumstantial.[87] The all-white jury returned a not guilty verdict, and no one was punished for the execution-style murder of Maria Antonia Lenoia. Jurors simply weren't willing to convict a white for killing a person of color. After all, many of these men were southerners by birth, so they hardly valued the lives of vecinos. Nothing more is known of Brady, except that by 1850 he was no longer in Santa Fe County.

On November 10, 1850, Oliver P. Anderson was indicted for the murder of a vecino boy named Joseph Garcia, but he too went unpunished.[88] Sunseri noted that Anderson "Fell on an unoffending Hispano boy and mauled him to the point where the boy was senseless. As if that were not enough, Anderson pulled out a pistol, put it to the head of the youth and shot him dead."[89] According to the court records, Anderson assaulted Garcia and then shot him above his right eye, killing him instantly.[90] Anderson murdered Garcia, but through a series of skillfully filed legal petitions, Anderson acquired continuances on two separate occasions.[91] Anderson first petitioned to have the case dismissed on September 4, 1851, but Judge Grafton Baker denied his request and ordered the prisoner remanded until trial.[92] When Anderson was finally tried, an all-white jury acquitted him and—despite clear evidence of his guilt—he departed from the territory a free man. Again, white jurors refused to convict a white man for murdering a vecino.

Social Homicide

Homicides committed at fandangos were a microcosm of how Nuevomexicanos and whites murdered in different ways. Two of these homicides occurred in Santa Fe County, one during the Mexican period and another in the early years of territorialization. The first homicide occurred at a traditional New Mexican fandango; the second occurred at a fandango hosted by a group of German settlers who hired vecinos to throw them a party. A Mexican soldier committed a third homicide outside of Santa Fe County during the Mexican period; the details reveal that Mexican soldiers brought the same sort of violence to New Mexico that white Americans did. All three cases demonstrate consistent patterns with what is known about Hispano and foreign-born white murder.

Fandangos were the most easily commodified resources the vecino community had to offer. The Mexican government sent a permanent garrison of soldiers to Santa Fe in the wake of the 1837 Chimayo Rebellion, and it was stationed there until replaced by Americans in 1847. Santa Fe experienced an unbroken history of military occupation, and since these soldiers were single, paid, and seemingly bored, the fandango became their favorite pastime. The lively fandangos—which traditionally celebrated community and good will—were thus transformed into entertainment packages that incorporated excessive drinking and gambling. Early travelers to New Mexico wrote voluminous accounts of the traditional fandangos they attended, and while their racist opinions of the New Mexican people differed, their reports consistently noted that violence or bad behavior accompanied the presence of soldiers, whiskey, or whites.[93]

Thus, fandangos must be divided into two types: those that were traditional and community-based and those that were commodified for the purpose of eliciting liquid capital from both soldiers and settlers.[94] This is not to suggest that scuffles never occurred during traditional Mexican fandangos, but rather to argue that when conflicts arose at community fandangos they manifested in a distinct fashion. More specifically, violence that occurred at community fandangos, much like violence within the community itself, was rarely intended to cause permanent harm. Of the three homicides at New Mexican fandangos from 1826 to 1853, only one occurred at a traditional community fandango between community members, while the other two involved first a Mexican soldier and years later some American soldiers. In keeping, the records indicate that the one incident of homicide at a traditional fandango was accidental.

The murder of Juan Valdez by his friend Andrés Márquez is similar to the murder of Rafael Gonsales by Manuel Sandoval (the rock-throwing incident), in that it was unintentional.[95] On June 4, 1826, Juan Valdez hosted a fandango for numerous friends and members of the Nuevomexicano community. There is no evidence to suggest there was alcohol present at the celebration. Instead, records indicate that the heat was oppressive, which was amplified by the fact that the partiers were dancing inside.[96] Numerous people blocked the doorway, impeding ventilation, and Valdez, the host, asked them to come into his home or to stand completely outside. Two of the men willingly complied, but Miguel Rodríguez refused to conform, and an argument ensued. The Márquez brothers—José María and Andrés—heard the argument and inserted themselves into the confrontation. As the crowd grew, tempers flared and a scuffle broke out. Witness testimonies confirm that Andrés Márquez charged forward and in the midst of the commotion, full of punching, hair pulling, and slapping, punched Valdez in the stomach. Unexpectedly, Valdez staggered forward, gave a cry, and fell dead on the floor.[97]

Again we see the pattern commonplace in Hispano homicide: an accidental murder committed by a remorseful Nuevomexicano who came forward and admitted his crime. When questioned about the mêlée, the eighteen-year-old Andrés Márquez confessed to having struck Valdez and killed him, though he maintained that the real conflict was between Juan's brother, Francisco Esteban Valdez, and Miguel Rodríguez. Márquez maintained that he had intervened with the sole intention of quelling the situation. According to Márquez, Juan struck him three times in the back, which angered him to such an extent that he simply turned and struck the retreating Juan Valdez. Though no other witnesses could corroborate Márquez's contention that Valdez had struck him, there is

Figure 3.7. An artist's portrayal of a traditional fandango as would occur in the Mexican countryside.

little reason to doubt his honesty, for all testimonies portray the confusion of the moment. Márquez then repeated what many witnesses had stated: there was no pre-existing quarrel, the scuffle was sudden, and all parties involved had been good friends since childhood.[98]

The defensor argued that Márquez had not intended to harm his friend and that he had tried to help. The defensor also noted that there was neither motive nor intent to kill, given no weapon was used in the attack.[99] The defensor insinuated that for such a strike to prove fatal, there must have been some unknown pre-existing condition at work. The prosecution dismissed this reasoning, contending that the act was malicious and that Márquez deserved a stern punishment for his actions. The case was forwarded to Chihuahua for review, and Andrés Márquez waited three years for a reply that never came. The local alcalde realized that judicial help from Chihuahua was not coming, and Andrés Márquez, now twenty-one years old, was released on bail.[100]

Although Chihuahua regularly failed to provide judicial guidance, officials did send soldiers to New Mexico to protect the local population from so-called Indian Depredations, and these Mexican soldiers committed a string of felonies and petty crimes.[101] One of them was responsible for the other homicide committed at a fandango during the Mexican period.[102] Alférez Manuel Garcia de Lara was stationed in San Miguel del Bado as part of a garrison intended to counter peripheral Apache attacks, but like many of the Mexican soldiers he was mostly bored and often drunk. On this night he found himself at a local fandango, and it was there that he murdered a vecino named Antonio Moya.

Witness testimonies revealed that in 1843 the nineteen-year-old Garcia de Lara was single and looking for something to do when he met Antonio Moya, who offered to escort his new acquaintance to a fandango in town.[103] Antonio Moya was a servant of the powerful Antonio José Otero, a wealthy patrón who often provided his servants with money.[104] At the dance, Moya provided Garcia de Lara with a peso so that he might buy a drink for a woman he had danced with.[105] Moya's generosity shamed the Mexican officer, and this indignity was exacerbated when he overheard Moya bragging about the wealth and power of the Otero family. Moya exited the room, then returned and seated himself in a chair that the young Mexican officer was sitting in; Garcia de Lara took this as an affront, a sign that he was indebted to Moya because of the peso he had given him, and he became enraged.[106]

What happened moments later is not entirely clear, largely because the incident took place outside of the house on a dark street. Moya cried out that he had been stabbed through the heart by a large sword, and with his last words he named Garcia de Lara as his attacker. Unlike the homicides that occurred

CHAPTER THREE

within the community, Garcia de Lara did not confess to the murder, but instead maintained that he had left the house in anger and saw nothing. Two witnesses claimed that Garcia de Lara called for Moya to come outside via a message from another soldier, but that other soldier denied all wrongdoings. Indeed, he adhered to the informal military code.

At this point, the case was sent to Gov. Manuel Armijo, who forwarded the case to Commandant Gen. Mariano Martínez, who in turn passed it to Col. Pedro Muñoz, who passed it back to Martínez, who mailed it to Col. don Juan Andrés Archuleta in Taos, who returned it to Capt. Don Damasio Salazar in San Miguel del Bado, who recalled all witnesses in order to hear their testimonies firsthand.[107] During these depositions, eyewitness Francisco Sena confirmed that he had heard Garcia de Lara tell Moya he had embarrassed him and saw him plunge his sword into Moya's heart. At that point, Capt. Don Damasio Salazar in San Miguel del Bado returned the file to Commandant Gen. Mariano Martínez, who complained that Salazar had questioned neither the woman with whom Garcia de Lara had danced nor Felix Montoya.[108] Several months later Salazar located Montoya, who confirmed what he had already sworn to; the woman who danced with Garcia de Lara remained a mystery. Capt. Don Damasio Salazar again returned the file to Commandant Gen. Mariano Martínez, who in turn summoned all witnesses to ratify their statements and, realizing that either Garcia de Lara was lying or all the witnesses were, tried to intimidate all parties involved in the hope that the guilty party would admit to lying.

While this seems like a comedy of errors (and undeniably it was!), that Martínez took such pains to force Garcia de Lara to confess betrays how odd it was that the Garcia de Lara continued to deny his obvious guilt in the murder of Antonio Moya. In New Mexico, the criminal usually confessed; in fact, it was seen as important to the legal process. Only when one confessed could one begin to atone for wrongdoing, which was at the heart of this early Mexican legal system.[109] Garcia de Lara, however, was not a Nuevomexicano from the community. He was a soldier, an extranjero who felt no more ties to the community than did the later white settlers and soldiers in Santa Fe County.

In an effort to force a confession, all witnesses were brought face to face with Garcia de Lara, and all of them, including Garcia de Lara, maintained the veracity of their previous testimonies. When Garcia de Lara was brought forward to confess his crime, he refused and claimed that when Antonio Moya accused him in the throes of death he was both drunk and mistaken. He cursed all the witnesses as liars in his final words.[110] Though the case file now filled some thirty-two folders, there are no pages to indicate how the trial was finally resolved. Clearly Garcia de Lara was guilty, but whom the case was forwarded to next remains a mystery.

What is known is that Garcia de Lara behaved as visiting soldiers in New Mexico often did: he was frustrated by his position as an outsider and in his agitated state violence came easily. It could have been anyone in the community, but as it turned out Antonio Moya became his victim. It's worth noting that this was not a traditional fandango, because soldiers were present and liquor was flowing but not free. Garcia de Lara committed homicide in the Mexican period in the same manner that white soldiers and settlers did during the territorial period. He stabbed Antonio Moya in the heart, deliberately killing him, and refused to confess his crime. Much like James C. Brady some years later, Garcia de Lara was ultimately released and left the territory.

Vecinos transformed the fandango into a full-blown commodity by the time the American soldiers and white settlers arrived in Santa Fe County. Like Mexican soldiers before them, American soldiers and settlers came to New Mexico to make money, and when they did, the vecinos serviced them and collected money in exchange for the entertainment they offered. As American soldiers and settlers came in larger numbers, commodified fandangos became more frequent and more frequently violent. White soldiers and settlers quarreled with other white soldiers and settlers, but incidents of violence between vecinos and Americans remained infrequent. The vecinos had no interest in fighting because they were there to make money. Rather, they provided a service and they entertained at fandangos, while the whites drank and became disorderly.[111] Therefore, it is not surprising that white American soldiers and settlers were involved in the only homicide at a fandango in the first seven years of the American territorial period. At one such fandango, on September 13, 1847, Christian Mild shot and killed United States Army private William H. Bolt.

The trial of Christian Mild for the murder of Private Bolt is particularly interesting because the details of the case resemble those of the Fourth of July shooting that claimed the life of John Finnegan. The murder occurred at a commodified fandango, and the parties involved were not friends. Mild was a recently arrived white settler who hoped to establish himself in Santa Fe County but instead got caught up in a personal quarrel with some party crashers. He did not intend to kill, but his reckless behavior with a firearm left Private Bolt dead. Christian Mild denied his crime and was ultimately released, despite the overwhelming testimony against him.

In fact, Christian Mild's trial resembled the other cases against Anglos: There was an all-white jury, a gun, a murder, many witnesses, no confession, and finally an acquittal. The investigators gathered evidence competently enough in the case against Mild. Sheriff E. L. Vaughn conducted a formal inquest and produced a written record that meticulously provided witness testimonies, physical evidence, and details of the assault for the jury to consider.[112] This was the best-documented homicide in the first seven years of the American period. The records in this case resembled those from the Mexican period, making it stand out among other cases in the American territorial period. Sheriff Vaughn, accompanied by a twelve-member grand jury,[113] arrived at the home of Jesus Romero, where the murder of William Bolt occurred the night before. As the records show, Romero was the host of the commodified fandango, for which he testified that he provided music, dancing, drinking, and women to dance with in exchange for money.[114]

A group of German immigrants and German-born soldiers had commissioned Jesus Romero to host their celebration.[115] According to Romero, a significant number of white American soldiers arrived and were turned away for refusing to pay admission fees to the German hosts, and this sparked the confrontation.[116] Christian Mild was reportedly working the door, so it is likely he personally turned them away. The American soldiers departed but they soon returned with greater numbers, determined to either enter the fandango or break up the celebration.[117] What was agreed upon by all the witnesses is that there was an affray, confusion ensued, and multiple gunshots were fired from inside the house.[118] Outside Jesus Romero's home, the body of Pvt. William H. Bolt lay mortally wounded from a bullet to the heart.[119]

The inquest commenced with an inspection of the body, as the members of the grand jury examined the remains of William H. Bolt. Next they questioned the six vecinos who hosted and worked at the fandango, beginning again with Jesus Romero. The host explained that he had arranged the fandango for the Germans, the Americans had returned and tried to force their way in, he heard gunshots, but he saw nothing and could tell nothing.[120] Elvino Romero claimed to be elsewhere at the time of the murder.[121] Jose Patricio Romero explained that he heard the shots but remembered nothing. Miguel Gonzales's reply was more in depth, but he also claimed he saw nothing.[122] Francisco Martinez claimed he was asleep during the affair and testified that he was awakened by gunshots, though E. L. Vaughn noted that "Witness contradicts himself about guard waking him up."[123] Thomas Alverez concluded the vecino testimonies by explaining that there was a conflict between Americans and Germans at the door, but that he knew nothing.[124] Vecinos regularly testified against parties irrespective of race, but little evidence exists that they did so in homicide cases. If the vecino hosts actually knew anything about this murder, they were unwilling to share it with the sheriff and the grand jury.

A total of ten American whites and Germans—most of them soldiers— testified, and all were far more detailed and accusatory than the vecino accounts. Joseph Donahue and Stephen Huffington claimed they witnessed the murder weapon being passed by Christian Mild into the hands of a vecino woman, who absconded with the evidence, which might partially explain why the vecinos refused to talk.[125] William Price concurred; he testified that he witnessed Mild loading the weapon in the backroom of the house and he identified Alejandra Ortiz as Mild's girlfriend. He claimed she was the woman who allegedly disappeared with the murder weapon.[126] George Morgan, one of the Americans outside the home, verified seeing Mild with the weapon. Although he believed that Christian Mild shot Private Bolt, he confessed that he never actually witnessed the murder.[127] A. J. Mitchell added that he believed the shots fired were not aimed at any particular individuals; rather, Private Bolt was the unfortunate victim of a stray bullet.[128]

The other five soldiers and settlers who gave testimonies did not contribute to the grand jury deliberations. They provided other details, but nothing central to the case. They confirmed that Mild was guarding the door, that the Americans tried to push their way through the door, and that someone restraining the Americans discharged his firearm, which caused Bolt to exclaim that he was wounded.[129] Alejandra Ortiz was the only woman questioned by the grand jury, even though there were many women who danced at the fandango. Ortiz was the woman whom Huffington, Price, and Donahue accused of concealing the murder weapon. Like the vecino males, Ortiz was terse during her testimony. She claimed that she did not know who gave her the weapon and testified, "I had it in my hand, but it was left on the bench and another person took it."[130] The grand jury asked Ortiz if the individual who gave her the gun was Mexican, but Ortiz claimed that she did not know. Ortiz testified that when she heard someone was shot both she and her sister—who also knew nothing of the affair!—departed.

Clearly the vecinos did not cooperate with the grand jury, partially because the vecinos simply did not trust the white settlers who questioned them. Vecinos remained suspicious of white motives; they were part of a parochial culture that viewed whites as outsiders. It is difficult to fault them for their suspicions, given what we know about white soldiers and settlers. The vecinos willingly provided information to the court in cases where Nuevomexicano community members were included in the jury selection, but to them the white jurors in the Mild case were foreigners.[131] The vecinos accepted money from white soldiers and settlers for a service, but beyond that most wanted little to nothing to do with these extranjeros.

But white soldiers and settlers knew the system, so they testified and blamed one another without hesitation. They speculated on what they did not know, divulged rumors, and trusted that their white peers on the jury would not incriminate them. The witnesses were consistent, if nothing else. They accused Christian Mild of firing the shot that killed Pvt. William H. Bolt, and the grand jury charged Mild as the perpetrator. The prosecution presented its case to a different all-white trial jury and proved Mild was guilty of manslaughter. The white jury, however, returned the verdict of not guilty, just as they did in other homicide cases against white soldiers and settlers. Christian Mild left the territory as a free man before the 1850 census was taken, and in this manner the judicial machine that was supposedly failing to punish murders continued to churn.

Conclusion

The patrónes dominated New Mexico economically and politically, and that dominance, together with the numerical superiority they gained through their solidarity with the vecinos, made newly arrived white settlers outsiders in Santa Fe County. Economically, the local patrónes increased their property and denied new white settlers access to land. Politically, they dominated the New Mexico territorial legislature and passed laws that favored their fellow patrónes at the expense of vecinos, though the poorer Nuevomexicanos did not figure that out until 1855. Numerically, they proved too many and too united for recent Anglo immigrants to divide and displace them between 1847 and 1854. This patrón and vecino solidarity alienated new white settlers in Santa Fe County; vecinos were parochial and they committed few homicides, while white settlers remained extranjeros and they turned homicidal (figure 3.9).

White soldiers and settlers tried to make inroads into New Mexican politics, but the local patrónes thwarted them at every turn. In 1851 they tried to impact the election for the New Mexico territorial legislature. In the small town of Anton Chico, south and east of Santa Fe, unregistered white voters and teamsters even voted three and four times, but they failed to impact the election. They tried to do the same in Bernalillo County, which was full of local patrónes. But the local patrónes thwarted their efforts and three men were killed and several wounded. They also tried to corrupt the election at Los Ranchos, which was deep in the Rio Abajo, home to large landholding patrónes. The local patrónes killed two whites in what the *Missouri Republican* erroneously described as a pitched battle.[132] Despite their efforts, only seven whites were elected to the legislature in 1851, and none of them benefited from illegal white voting.[133]

The Nuevomexicanos were a collection of vecinos and patrónes bound together by their postcolonial history, and their political domination of New Mexico further emboldened Nuevomexicano confidence in their autonomy. The relatively low incidence of homicide among Nuevomexicanos was the result of political stability. If the patrónes killed in Santa Fe County, it remains undocumented. When the vecinos killed, it was often accidental. Clare V. McKanna suggests that machismo was a factor in homicide among Mexicanos in California and that honor was a factor when Californios killed. McKanna writes, "In the Hispanic culture a man has two choices; he can be a *chingón* or he can be a *chingada*. The *chingón*, of course, is the *hombre macho* who inflicts pain on the *chingada*, a person who is passive or lacks significant power."[134] It is true that there were patrónes in New Mexico, but poverty did not make vecinos into *chingadas*. The patrónes had power and they bullied vecinos and servants, but there were limits to their power. The patrónes were macho, but that did not make them homicidal. If the vecinos were affected by machismo in any discernible way, it does not come through in the Santa Fe County court documents.

White homicide was directly linked to the white soldiers and recently arrived settlers' lack of faith in the local government, which worked against their interests, making them extranjeros in the insular Nuevomexicano community. McKanna suggests that whites in California might have killed as part of the "Code of the West." According to McKanna, this code had four basic tenets: never shoot an unarmed man; never shoot him in the back; never accept an insult without a fight; and never back away from a fight.[135] McKanna argued that this was a code of honor among whites in the West. The whites in Santa Fe County, however, didn't adhere to any such code, if any whites in the West ever did. White settlers killed at random, out of jealousy, and from ambition. What white settlers in Santa Fe County who killed had in common was their frustration and estrangement.[136] Whites were outsiders and they were alienated politically, economically, and socially in Santa Fe County. They murdered vecino women and children, targeted the helpless, and killed one another in drunken rampages. That they did so and continued to do so through 1860 had nothing to do with honor.

Instead, white settlers who were ambitious and unsuccessful murdered with intent, and they increased risk and made Santa Fe County a dangerous place to

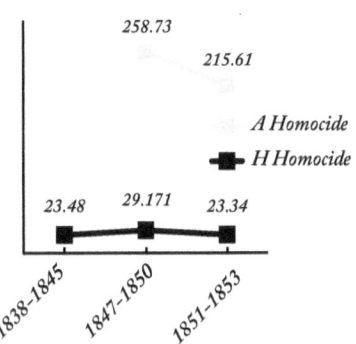

Figure 3.8. Homicide rates per year among Hispanos and Anglos in Santa Fe County, adults 16 and older, per 100,000.

live from 1847 to 1853. Ironically, when white soldiers and settlers voiced their frustrations they focused on the legal system and the inability of the military and legal officials to control Santa Fe County. To them, the argument made sense: They were failing because brown criminals were everywhere in Santa Fe County and because the territorial government could not control the murderous, thieving, barbaric Mexican people.[137] In terms of raw numbers, white were correct that—as Nuevomexicanos made up 87 percent of the population—there were more Nuevomexicanos committing every manner of crime; that did not change the fact that one was in far more danger in the presence of a white settler than a Nuevomexicano in Santa Fe County from 1847 to 1853.

As to Nuevomexicanos, we have seen that while Anglos intentionally executed their victims at close range, vecinos killed without clear intent, and during these first seven years the Nuevomexicano homicide rate remained in check. Vecino frustrations with the new territorial apparatus, however, resulted in major changes both statistically and anecdotally as to how and why Nuevomexicanos killed. As local patrónes increasingly prioritized their accumulation of wealth and progressively shirked their responsibilities to the Nuevomexicano vecinos, poor Nuevomexicanos felt less represented by their old allies. Nowhere was this impact more detrimental to the bond between patrón and vecino than in the judicial system, which Nuevomexicano patrónes all but surrendered to the American government. Frustrated vecinos still attacked with knives, sticks, and occasionally rocks after 1854, but quite suddenly brown bodies began to pile up in the streets of Santa Fe.

CHAPTER FOUR

1856

On the night of October 30th, 1856, Felipe Lovato and Francisco Martin were walking toward the Santa Fe River on a street not far from the plaza in the city of Santa Fe. Both Lovato and Martin were from the vecino class: Lovato was a twenty-year-old servant in the house of the merchant Simon Delgado, while Martin was a drifter from the Rio Abajo.[1] Their night began at a dance near the plaza, where the two were getting along well enough, that is, until a disagreement erupted over a woman, whom they both fancied. Still, both Lovato and Martin remained at the event until 11 p.m., and it seems certain that for his part, Lovato thought the conflict was behind them.[2] How could he have known Francisco Martin's rage was boiling over as they made their way through the quiet streets; how could he have known death was upon him.

They were almost to the river when Martin caught Lovato's attention, and the moment Lovato turned Martin smashed him in the face with a large rock. Francisco Martin fell on Felipe Lovato with all his rage, smashing Felipe again and again, erasing the lines that once defined his countenance.[3] The *Gazette* recounted the incident, and they noted two large rocks, "soaked in blood, skin, and hair."[4] The level of violence inflicted was so great Lovato's mother and younger sister were only able to identify him by his tattered clothes. This homicide was no accident, nor was it an isolated case. Rather, it existed as one part of a sudden surge of intentional homicides within the Nuevomexicano community.[5]

In this chapter, I argue that 1856–1857 marked the end of a long period of symbiotic—even if highly unequal—coexistence between poor and working-class vecinos and the patrónes in Santa Fe County and New Mexico. This rupture is quantitatively evident in three ways. First, there was a large increase in homicide among vecinos during this period. Second, there was a significant increase in wealth inequality between 1850 and 1860, punctuated by land becoming more concentrated in the hands of the few. Third, there was a sudden increase in laws that mandated harsher punishments in the territorial legislature in 1857, a body dominated by the patrónes. My argument here is that 1855 was the calm before the storm and that 1856 marked the moment when many vecinos realized that their patrónes were no longer working to maintain their subsistence. The patrónes instead fully embraced the American style of capitalist rule, which was focused on the aggregation of wealth rather than the welfare of the people in the nation-state. As a result, an increasing percentage of vecinos felt the need to take matters into their own hands, and disputes turned deadly.[6]

The patrónes' avarice made life for the vecinos hard in the American territorial period, and their new laws made it unbearable for many. There may have been other

CHAPTER FOUR

factors that the data do not illuminate, but what is clear is that their social contract was broken.[7] First, the patrónes did little to stop Lamy's purge of clergy, a group that served as advocates and intermediaries for the vecinos, and this isolated them from the patrónes. Second, the patrónes ushered in a decade of land dispossession, which pushed vecinos from small farmers to day laborers and made them more desperate for subsistence. Last, the patrónes consolidated land and capital, which facilitated their movement to full-fledged politicians and created greater distance between them and the vecinos. Once in power, the patrónes passed draconian laws that were aimed to regulate locals, vecinos, and newly arrived settlers. The data suggest that by the mid-1850s vecinos lost faith in their patrónes and the fairness of the political, economic, and legal institutions, and many among them responded by taking the law into their own hands. Others simply left Santa Fe County.

QUANTIFYING THE IMPORTANCE OF 1856

For the first nine years of territorialization, vecino homicide rates were steady in Santa Fe County, but 1855 was riddled with vecino assaults, and what followed in 1856–1857 was an unprecedented surge in vecino homicide rates. A quantitative postmortem of the data reveal how significant the surge was. In the vecino community, there were more homicides in Santa Fe County in 1856 and 1857 than there were in the first nine years of American territorialization, from 1847 to 1855.[8] Nuevomexicanos killed at the rate of 179 per 100,000, which was six times higher than normal. Whereas Hispano homicide between 1847 and 1853 was predominantly accidental, the rise of homicides like the one committed by Francisco Martin against Felipe Lovato became more common. Meanwhile, Anglo homicide was driven by white transients and newly arrived settlers in search of spoils, and they killed at rate of 652.32 per 100,000 from 1858 to 1860 (table 4.1). Taken together, these succeeding waves of homicide left Santa Fe County without reprieve for five consecutive years.[9]

Years	H Homicide	H Rates	A Homicide	A Rates
1847–1850	5	29.17	5	161.71
1851–1855	7	34.16	5	141.24
1856–1857	14	179.03	4	311.53
1858–1860	8	75.44	10	652.32
Total	34		24	

Table 4.1. Homicide Rates per Year among Hispanos and Anglos in Santa Fe County, Adult Males 16 and Older, per 100,000

Assaults in Santa Fe also dramatically increased in the Nuevomexicano community. The big uptick in assault rates began in 1855, one year before the increase in homicide began, and the trajectory of assault rates mirrored that of homicide rates in Santa Fe County (see figure 4.1). As we see, from 1847 to 1860 assault and homicide rates tacked together on nearly identical paths, and they only differed by that single year. Assault was steady from 1847 to 1854 at an average of 122.42 per 100,000, but that rate more than doubled from 1855 to 1857, increasing to 323.96 per 100,000. Interestingly, homicide was a year behind assault *only* during the transition toward the 1856 wave of homicide; in 1858, the number of assaults and homicides similarly dropped by more than 50 percent, assault from thirteen incidents in 1857 to six in 1858 and homicide from seven incidents in 1857 to three in 1858.

When assault and homicide are combined into the single category of "violent crime," a smoother and more gradual trend of increased violence emerges in the Nuevomexicano community (see figure 4.2).[10] As we have seen in Santa Fe County, especially within the Hispano community, homicides prior to 1856 were most often unintentional.[11] By combining these two crimes into one category, however, we temper the distinction between intentional and unintentional homicides. Doing so reveals a far more gradual and steadier rise in violence that culminated in the homicide wave that plagued the Hispano community in 1856–1857.[12]

Of course, Nuevomexicano crime rates paled when compared to the rates at which whites committed violent crime. As estranged as vecinos may have been by 1856, white settlers remained doubly so, for the vast majority were young, male, and away from home, which is the statistical recipe for violent tendencies. The white homicide rate, for example, was significantly higher than the Nuevomexicano homicide rate in every statistical period in this study (see figure 4.3).[13] And while Hispano homicides in the Nuevomexicano community became more ruthless, the gun remained the weapon of choice for white murderers.[14]

Based on these data, it should not be surprising that white settlers and transients were also far more likely to commit assault than their Nuevomexicano counterparts. From 1847 to 1850, the white assault rate was more than double the rates of the Hispano community (see figure 4.4).[15]

When seen comparatively, the category of Hispano vs. white violent crime shows that white violent crime was exceptionally erratic, as opposed to the relatively smooth arc of Nuevomexicano community violent crime (figure 4.5). There are three distinct spikes in white violent crime from 1847 to 1860: the first in 1849–1850, the second in 1852, and the third from 1855 to 1860. It is plausible that these spikes and falls represent the ebbs and flows of white settlers moving in and out of Santa Fe County. Population movement between decades

CHAPTER FOUR

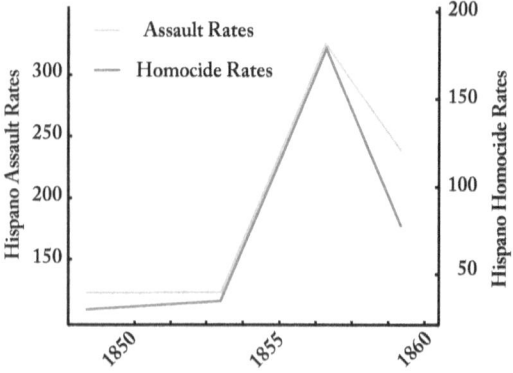

Figure 4.1. Hispano assault and homicide rates in Santa Fe, New Mexico, 1847–1860 per 100,000 per persons per Year.

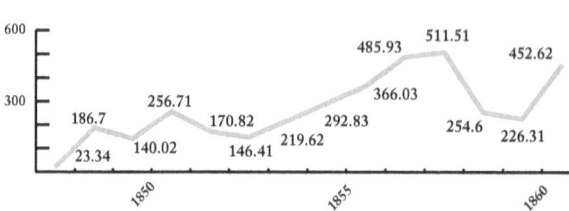

Figure 4.2. Hispano violent crime rates, including assault and homicide, by year, 1847–1860.

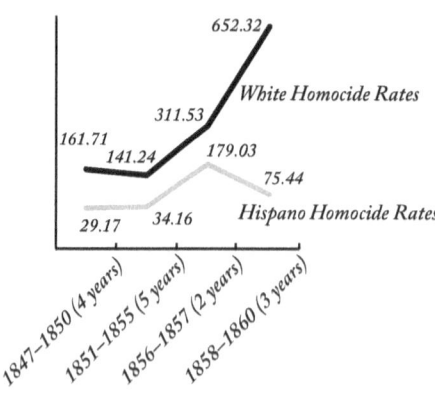

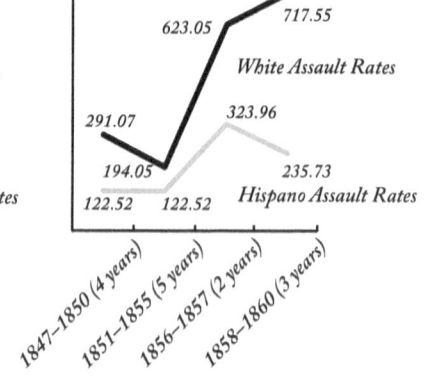

Figure 4.3. Hispano and white homicide rates grouped, per persons per 100,000, 1847–1860.

Figure 4.4. Hispano and white assault rates grouped, per persons per 100,000, 1847–1860.

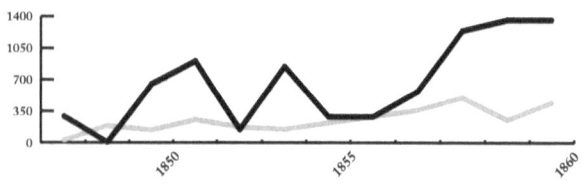

Figure 4.5. Hispano and white violent crime rates compared, per persons per 100,000, 1847–1860.

is something that the US Census is unable to track, but it is telling that most of the white settlers who appear in 1850 are absent from the census in 1860. Regardless, the pattern demonstrates the volatility that white settlers brought to Santa Fe County.[16]

Overall, after 1855 violent crime was on the rise among both groups, reaching rates never before seen in the territory, and the homicide rate of 1856 marked a turning point in the history of territorialization in Santa Fe County and of New Mexico more broadly. The shift was both statistically and anecdotally striking: both whites and Nuevomexicanos increasingly took the law into their own hands at significantly higher rates, and Nuevomexicanos began intentionally murdering members of their own community in both deliberate and exceptionally heinous manners. The strengthening of political, legal, and economic institutions during the late 1850s did nothing to promote feelings of security within both the Nuevomexicano and white communities in Santa Fe County. Instead, these institutions fostered the belief that those in power were failing everyday people.

LAND INEQUALITY, FAILING INSTITUTIONS, AND ESCALATING VIOLENCE

On April 6, 1855, a twenty-one-year-old emerging merchant named Jesus Maria Sena y Baca was confronted by two rival merchants and a couple of their relatives in the city of Santa Fe.[17] Sena y Baca was well known in the territory as the son of don Miguel Sena and doña Manuela Baca (two wealthy Hispanos from powerful families), as the acting clerk for the probate judge Facundo Pino, and as a quick-tempered young man who never shied away from a fight.[18] On this day Sena y Baca ran afoul first of the wealthy Felix Garcia and second of his three sons, Vicente, Juan, and Manuel Garcia.[19] Pablo Delgado joined the Garcia family to round out what the grand jury labeled an "unlawful assembly."[20] Together, they fell upon Sena y Baca and beat him until he was motionless. The group of men started to leave, but Sena y Baca found his feet, pulled his pistol, lurched forward, and fired a single shot at Juan Garcia that missed its mark.[21] Juan Garcia tackled him and stabbed him with his knife, then the rest joined in for a second beating, from which Sena y Baca did not so quickly recover.[22]

It was abnormal for patrónes and their kin to be victims of violence in Santa Fe County, but when it did occur it was usually the result of economic competition with a fellow patrón. The New Mexican economy was booming in the 1850s. The total value of New Mexican property in Santa Fe County increased (from $308,110 to $571,090) between 1850 and 1860, and the amount of both land and assets owned by the patrónes skyrocketed.[23] As a result, rivalries sometimes emerged that pitted patrónes against one another, and this was the case when young Jesus Marie Sena y Baca insulted the elder Felix Garcia with an unspecified slur.[24] Sena y Baca was charged and convicted of assault with intent to kill for the shot he fired at Juan Garcia.[25] They demanded he pay a fine him $50 "for his actions against the Garcias."[26]

This moment represented a larger change, when power legally shifted from being solely based on land, familial ties, and the direct rule of the patrónes to being based on lineage, one's relationship with the territorial apparatus, and indirect rule by the system. More specifically, the formal transition from Mexican direct rule to Pierre Bourdieu's more complex relations of "dominance and dependence" was completed, meaning that an external objective system of power was fully formed, which alleviated the necessity for direct power to be applied by local patrónes.[27] To be clearer, this is why the patrónes no longer needed the loyalty of the poorer Nuevomexicanos to keep the peace and find labor. The new territorial system meant ruling power over the people became indirect. Instead of the direct rule that was the foundation of the old patrónes system, a new structure arose, based on the power of coercive and punitive laws, new ideological norms, and the willingness of law enforcement to impose them both.[28]

Of course kinship networks remained the basis of what Bourdieu labeled "cultural capital" within this new system, and this allowed the so-called dons and doñas to pass down both their wealth and titles to their children, which legitimized them as lawmakers and rulers within this new power structure. But by 1855–1856 Bourdieu's furtive institutionalized mechanisms of domination, intrinsic in the capitalist-centered American territorial system, had taken hold in the territory.[29] This was why poorer Nuevomexicanos no longer had anyone to petition to in times of injustice and need; this new system empowered nameless and faceless institutions over individuals, which allowed the large landholders to divest from their relationships with and responsibilities to the people and thus focus almost exclusively on amassing wealth. To their mind, providing for the poor, resolving disputes, holding fandangos, and continuing to display their generosity in other ways was expensive, time-consuming, and now unnecessary.

This represented a great change for the vecinos. During the Mexican period there were two benefits that made tending to the people worthwhile: first, the pacification of the people, and second, their support and service when defensive and offensive military campaigns against the Navajo, Apache, Comanche, Ute, and Pueblo peoples were desired. The new capitalist reality rendered these benefits superfluous. The courts now resolved disputes, the sheriff and his deputies kept the people in line, their need to survive compelled them to labor, the military fought whatever campaigns were deemed necessary, and maintaining infrastructure was now left to the government. Alas, it no longer benefited them to dance with the poor.

For the first couple of decades this new system was a godsend for the large landholders and by contrast was a cross to bear for poorer vecinos, and nowhere is that clearer than when examining changes in the value and distribution of real estate from 1850 to 1860. These data show a dramatic increase in mean property, property range, and the percent of people with land in New Mexico, which can all be construed as proof that the New Mexican economy was indeed booming for all. But as table 4.2 also shows, nearly 60 percent (754) of the population of landholding aged males aged twenty-one to forty (1295) in 1850 Santa Fe County either emigrated from Santa Fe County or died.[30] As a result, by 1860 there were 146 fewer landholders in Santa Fe County with land, meaning it was far more concentrated than it had been in 1850.[31]

	Number and Age Group (1850/1860)	Persons with Land	% Land	Range		Mean
	Ages 15–20 / 26–30					
1850	427 Hispanos	only 24 have land	6	0	$1,000	$16
1860	361 Hispanos	Only 170 have land	47	0	$15,000	$144
Change	-67	146	41	0	$14,000	$128
	Ages 21–25 / 31–35					
1850	320 Hispanos	only 64 have land	28	0	$800	$24
1860	129 Hispanos	only 76 have land	59	0	$4,000	$161
Change	-191	12	31		$3,200	$137
	Ages 26–30 / 36–40					
1850	393 Hispanos	only 154 have land	29	0	$1,080	$52
1860	202 Hispanos	only 125 have land	61	0	$25,000	$414
Change	-191	-29	41		$23,920	$362
	Ages 31–40 / 41–50					
1850	582 Hispanos	only 294 have land	51	0	$6,000	$109
1860	210 Hispanos	only 150 have land	71	0	$20,000	$726
Change	-372	-144	20		$14,000	$617
	Ages 41–50 / 51–60					
1850	242 Hispanos	only 168 have land	69	0	$2,800	$179
1860	140 Hispanos	only 103 have land	63	0	$3,500	$372
Change	-102	-65	-6		$700	$193
	Ages 51+ / 61+					
1850	253 Hispanos	only 166 have land	66	0	$6,000	$327
1860	129 Hispanos	only 100 have land	78	0	$4,000	$365
Change	-124	-66	13		-$2,000	$38
	Total Pop Loss: 1047	Fewer with land: 146				

Table 4.2. Changes in Hispano Male Population by Age and Land Distribution by Age Group

CHAPTER FOUR

The combination of land value and assets in the 1860 census buttresses the extreme inequality revealed in the data above. It is no exaggeration to state that the distribution of wealth in Santa Fe County in 1860 is comparable to the inequality seen in the United States during its most extreme years, which includes the period before the Great Depression.[32] The top 1 percent in Santa Fe County owned 47 percent of all wealth in Santa Fe County. This means that the richest twenty-eight people owned as much wealth as the bottom 1,811 Nuevomexicanos (figure 4.6).[33]

Jesus Maria Sena y Baca, the elder Felix Garcia, his son Vicente Garcia, and Pablo Delgado were all among the biggest beneficiaries of this system; in fact, all four qualified as members of the top 1 percent of wealth holders, which makes their violent confrontation all the more interesting. For these four members of the 1 percent in Santa Fe County, being indicted was new, but for Sena y Baca in particular it was unimaginable that he, a court clerk, a member of the large landholding class, and one of the wealthiest of his peers, was found guilty of a crime. In fact, he refused to accept the $50 judgment against him and appealed the decision three times over the next year.[34] In mounting his appeal, Sena y Baca's lawyer subpoenaed the Garcias and Pablo Delgado and did an excellent job of spending far more than $50 to waste the time of everyone involved. By March 18, 1856, Sena y Baca seems to have been reasonably pleased with his efforts to defend his honor, because it was at that point that his lawyer came before the court and finally agreed to pay his $50 fine.[35]

Sena y Baca took many lessons from his experiences with the new territorial machine, and it seems he was determined to make sure he never ended up on the wrong side of either a beating or a court judgment again. His most important lesson on how to avoid such legal difficulties likely came courtesy of Sheriff Jesus Maria Baca y Salazar, who was himself the thirteenth wealthiest man in Santa Fe County, a member of the top 1 percent, and a large landholding patrón. In May of 1855 Sheriff Baca y Salazar became angry with the forty-four-year-old Luis Griego, who was the fiftieth wealthiest man in the territory, a member of the top 10 percent, and also a member of the large landholding class. While there is no record of Baca y Salazar's motive, the court documents reveal that he pulled his knife and attacked Luis Griego. The brutality of the attack was shocking: Baca y Salazar stabbed Griego in the face, then used the sharp edge of his knife to repeatedly slice Griego's face in several places.[36] The crime was serious, with Griego being scarred for life in the attack, and Baca y Salazar was ultimately indicted for assault (though, by the precedent established in the Jesus Rael case, he should have been charged with mayhem and assault with intent to maim). The case for simple assault against Baca y Salazar, however, was continued at the initial hearing, and then it inexplicably disappeared from the docket book.[37] No reason was ever given, but what's clear is that Baca y Salazar's office was central in the dismissal.

The case of New Mexico vs. Baca y Salazar gives us insight into why Jesus Baca y Salazar, the thirteenth wealthiest man in the county, would campaign for a position like sheriff of Santa Fe County. It was the allure of privilege and the protection he received from the system when disputes erupted between he and other large landholders. That's what the position of sheriff afforded him. Indeed, the records indicate that the large landholders were increasingly at odds with one another, but by taking the position of sheriff, Baca y Salazar was positioned to intimidate and brutalize his enemies without fear of legal repercussions. In fact, there was one other indictment against Sheriff Baca y Salazar: he was indicted for homicide, specifically for committing manslaughter, but of course nothing whatever came of it.[38] This incident happened two days after his attack on Luis Griego, so it's very likely these events were connected, but Sheriff Baca y Salazar never appeared before a judge on the matter. This was the power of being sheriff of Santa Fe County.

It's not surprising that by December of 1855 Jesus Maria Sena y Baca was deputy sheriff to Baca y Salazar, and when Baca y Salazar retired Sena y Baca was in line to be his replacement.[39] Although an ill-tempered man, Sena y Baca was also shrewd and, no doubt still smarting from the insults he suffered at both the hands of the Garcias and the courts, Sena y Baca understood that being deputy sheriff ensured that his enemies would think twice before they targeted him again. In 1857 Jesus Maria Sena y Baca replaced Jesus Maria Baca y Salazar, and he held onto that position until 1861. Additionally, Marshal Charles P. Clever named Sena y Baca a deputy marshal in 1858. Clever claimed Sena y Baca was the natural choice because he was already deputy sheriff and fluent in both Spanish and English.[40] No doubt it also helped that he was a member of the top 1 percent and the ninth wealthiest man in Santa Fe County. Clever wrote as much in the *Santa Fe Weekly Gazette* (which he operated) when he praised himself in his own paper for having the good sense to select someone with business habits. From these two positions Sena y Baca became significantly more powerful and would thenceforth suffer no beatings at the hands of his rivals.

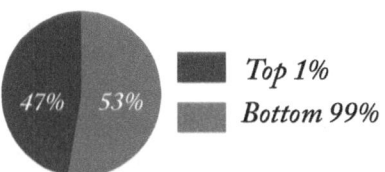

Figure 4.6. Distribution of total wealth, males over 15, Santa Fe County, 1860.

CHAPTER FOUR

As must be clear by now, Nuevomexicano males most often found themselves on the wrong end of these assaults, and no family received (or meted out, for that matter) more beatings than the little-known Tapia brothers. They were Ignacio, Andres, Francisco, and Felix Tapia by name, all dear friends of Sheriff Jesus Maria Sena y Baca, and when a beating needed to be administered, they often backed one another's play. Again, we recall that both Ignacio and Andres were arrested and took the blame for the 4th of July incident in 1853 that claimed the life of John Finnegan. Sena y Baca and the other accomplices were acquitted in Santa Fe County, and thanks to a change of venue both Tapia brothers were ultimately found not guilty.[41] That was not, however, the earliest recorded case of assault involving the Tapia brothers. In March of 1850 Ignacio Tapia had a dispute with Ignacio Sena over some unrecorded issue. Whatever the nature of their quarrel, we know that when Sena turned his back Ignacio Tapia pulled out his knife and with his right hand stabbed Sena on the right side of his back, the knife plunging between two of his ribs.[42] The verdict was not recorded, but whatever it was Ignacio Sena was not satisfied. Sena was fully recovered by November of 1850, and he got his revenge against the Tapia brothers when he stabbed the eldest brother Felix Tapia, who ultimately survived the attack.[43]

The next assault case against one of the Tapia brothers again involved Ignacio Tapia, who this time was indicted in February of 1852 for assaulting Silvario Salas, the very same one who later assaulted Albino Roival. Ignacio Tapia and Dolores Sena were charged for assault with intent to kill, but the case was quickly dismissed.[44] In April of 1853 Jesus Maria Sena y Baca, Felix Tapia, Fernando Sandoval, Pablo Duran, and Jesus Romero were all indicted for assaulting Charles P. Clever, who was later appointed to the position of U.S. marshal for New Mexico. Clever was born in Cologne, Prussia, had moved to Santa Fe in 1850, and was still establishing himself as a trader when he ran afoul of Sena y Baca and his gang. Clever testified that these Nuevomexicanos boldly stormed the room of Joseph D. Ellis (who in 1850 was among the wealthiest merchants in the territory with $10,000 in real estate alone), dragged him out of the house, forced him into another home, and confined him to a room against his will. There was no alleged beating, but given that a gang led by Jesus Maria Sena y Baca, who was a wealthy Nuevomexicano merchant, abducted an aspiring merchant from the home of an elite English merchant, it's reasonable to assume that Sena y Baca was sending a message to a potential new rival. Still, the grand jury zeroed in on the men who did the physical abduction, those being Jesus Romero and Pablo Duran. Both were found guilty, Romero of assault with intent to kill and Duran with simple assault, and both were fined $25.[45] There is no proof that Jesus Maria Sena y Baca stepped in with his vast fortune to tip the scales of justice, but somehow Jesus Romero and Pablo Duran managed to hire a fantastic lawyer. He appealed these verdicts, had their cases transferred to Santa

Anna County (which had a total of eight white people in the entire county in 1850), and saw these verdicts overturned without comment.[46]

The 4th of July homicide, which has been well documented in this book, followed, but the Tapia brothers and their friends were only just beginning. In June of 1853 Ignacio Tapia got into a fight with an unnamed person and was convicted of committing an affray; he was initially fined $25 but after a series of skillful appeals it was reduced to $10.[47] Only one day later, Pablo Duran assaulted Ramon Garcia. He was found guilty but fined only one dollar, which suggests that Garcia may have started that fight.[48] In September of that same year Oliver P. Hovey claimed that Andres Tapia and Jesus Silva attacked him and threatened him with a pistol.[49] This time, however, the jury dismissed the case for lack of evidence.[50]

It wasn't until September of 1855 that the next case involving the Tapia brothers appeared, but this time they were the victims. William Rowan, a drifter who didn't last long in Santa Fe County, became enraged with Francisco and Andres Tapia and attacked them with his knife. He first went after Francisco, who was nimble enough to avoid his blade, then lunged at Andres and stabbed him in the hand.[51] William Rowan was found guilty of assault with intent to kill and sentenced to one year in prison; Rowan did not serve his full sentence, which was unfortunate for him because in August of 1856 he pulled his pistol on Peter Moran, and as the two tussled the gun went off and William Rowan's time in Santa Fe came to an abrupt end.[52]

The next case against Sena y Baca and his men involved the man himself and his fight with the Garcia brothers, but once Sena y Baca became deputy in 1855 and sheriff in 1857 no more cases against him and his men (with one small exception) appeared in the court records until July 25, 1859.[53] On that evening at 9 p.m. the sheriff and his gang seem to have taken things a little too far when a group of more than ten of them made a "noise riot" in the plaza, the streets, and the taverns of downtown Santa Fe. We cannot measure the level of drunkenness in that group, but Gen. Thomas H. Hopkins was especially angry and in the indictment he painted quite a picture: with guns, knives, and a bullwhip the mob shouted their way through the streets firing their guns, brandishing their knives, and cracking their bullwhip as they completed a nineteenth-century version of a pub crawl. Hopkins specifically charged them with "Making a Riot and Tumult; Shooting into a Crowd of Men in a Public Place."[54] Of course the case was immediately thrown out by the grand jury, as Sheriff Sena y Baca was above the law by this point, but not everyone in the group escaped unscathed. Indeed, the case against Jose Gregorio Ribera separated and moved forward. As it turned out, poor Andres Tapia, who had already been beaten twice and stabbed once in the hand, was the victim yet again. This time the twenty-year-old laborer named Jose

Gregorio Ribera (the very man named in the noise riot indictment above) shot Andres Tapia in the right thigh. Ribera and Andres Tapia engaged in a drunken argument, which is likely why the party only lasted a little more than an hour. Ribera was found guilty and fined the maximum $50 for his crime, but Andres Tapia was the only other person who suffered any kind of punishment for the pub crawl of 1859.[55]

Alas, for the Tapia brothers their days of violence proved to be numbered, with the last active case ending in March of 1860. It was an older case that had been continued a few times: on July 6, 1859, Ignacio Tapia pulled his knife one last time and, in what seemed like a final tribute to a violent life well lived, stabbed Eugenio Chaves.[56] For those keeping track, that stabbing marked New Mexico territory's sixth case against Ignacio Tapia for a violent crime; the final count included five for assault with intent to kill and one for homicide. Indeed, there is little doubt that Ignacio was the most prolific violent offender in Santa Fe County during this period, but thanks to his powerful friends, justice never caught up with him. In the end, however, mortality did. Ignacio Tapia died unexpectedly in March of 1860; his dear friends sent the powerful and expensive lawyer Spruce M. Baird to tell the court of his death. Baird moved for the case against Ignacio Tapia to abate, the court agreed, and with that the Tapia brothers vanished from the criminal court records.[57]

A sharp increase in both attacks against women and domestic violence accompanied the rise of assault in Santa Fe County, and this follows with what quantitative scholars know about spousal homicide in the United States more broadly. Randolph Roth demonstrated that there was a sharp increase in marital homicide during the 1840s, which he postulates was tied to the rise in sentiments of romantic love.[58] Lovers increasingly came to believe there was only one person in the world for them, which increased the intensity with which either party might experience rejection.[59] For someone who experienced this new idea of love the stakes were higher, and so they became more likely to lash out if they were rejected.

Americans brought these prejudices to New Mexico, just as they did to California.[60] In New Mexico there was a stark contrast in how these sentiments played out during the periods from 1847 to 1854 and 1855 to 1857. In May of 1857 William Hovey became angry with Apolonia Sanchez and assaulted her with the clear intention of killing her. Indeed, the attack began when Hovey pulled his bayonet and charged Apolonia Sanchez, the blade striking and penetrating the right side of her head, which resulted in what the prosecution described as "One grievous wound."[61] Hovey was not satisfied with the damage from his first assault. He charged her once more, this time with a stick in his right hand, and with that stick he beat her on the right side of her head, where she was already wounded from the bayonet attack. Hovey walked away again, but alas he fell upon her one final time, hitting her first with the stick, but finishing with his fists. Once again, the reason for this cowardly attack is not known (territorial judges didn't care enough to record motives when women were beaten), but given the personal nature of this attack it's likely Hovey was having trouble reckoning some form of rejection with his own frail sense of masculinity.[62]

But Hovey angered some powerful people when he targeted Apolonia Sanchez. Perhaps she was someone important to Sheriff Jesus Maria Sena y Baca, or maybe he was just angry with Hovey for his cravenness, but whatever the reason Hovey's lawyer filed a complaint against both Sheriff Sena y Baca and Justice of the Peace Nicolas Quintana for "depriving him of his liberties."[63] Specifically, Hovey complained that both Sena y Baca and Quintana unlawfully held him for an extended period of time, that they were conspiring to delay his trial for what the defense termed a "supposed assault."[64] When the matter finally went before the judge and jury, William Hovey was found guilty of assault with intent to kill; his punishment was a fine of $50, which was the maximum he could receive.[65]

Although depressing to read, it was not surprising that $50 was the maximum penalty that could be handed down in an attack against a woman. American laws protected white men like Hovey from facing serious repercussions for attacks on women of color. This was certainly the case in New Mexico, where case after case of domestic violence resulted in slap after slap on wrist after wrist. When William Mclaughlin attacked and beat Jesusa Gonzales with his wagon whip in August of 1858, lashing her on her head, back, sides, and breasts, he was also found guilty and fined $50.[66] Even white women were not protected in Santa Fe County during this period, at least not from predatory white men. A man listed only as Private Smith, who served in the American Army, Company B, 7th Infantry (but whose full name was never revealed in the court records), stalked and attacked a white woman named Martha Cutter: he caught her, then he beat her, then he raped her.[67] All indications are that the jury was infuriated by this case, and they found him guilty and ordered that he pay a fine of $338. But Judge Kirby Benedict intervened and changed the fine to the maximum allowed by the law, which was of course the same $50.[68]

Hispano men in Santa Fe County proved just as violent in their treatment of women, and their masculinity afforded them the same privilege enjoyed by white men when they attacked Nuevomexicanas. In October of 1856 Candido Ortiz, who had also participated in the 4th of July attack, became angry with his partner Manuela Baca, and in his rage he pulled his knife and fell upon her. Manuela Baca tried to defend herself, as evidenced by the knife wounds to her wrists, but ultimately Candido Ortiz found his mark and stabbed her in the breast. His attack went all but unpunished, as Ortiz was ordered to pay the a fine of one dollar.[69] In another incident Antonio Rodriguez attacked and beat his partner Juana Maria Lovato because he was angry after Lovato's brother Jesus pummeled him. It is not known why her brother Jesus Lovato, a twenty-six-year-old farmer from Santa Fe, decided to beat Rodriguez. Once home the humiliated Rodriguez grabbed his shovel and began to ruthlessly beat Jesus Lovato's sister, Juana Maria Lovato: he struck her and knocked her to the ground, then beat her with his spade. Rodriguez then put the blade of the shovel against her side and pushed it against her with both hands until the blade of the spade cut into her side. Rodriguez left her writhing on the ground, but his vicious attack was not enough to satisfy his wounded honor, for he returned with his shovel once more and beat her where she lay.[70] This jury was again horrified by the brutality of yet another assault and tried to increase the punishment once more. They found Antonio Rodriguez guilty and sentenced him to a year in prison, but Judge J. J. Davenport amended the sentence and instead Rodriguez was fined $12 for nearly killing his romantic partner.[71]

There was a substantial spike in all white assault and homicide rates in 1857, and the double assaults by Thaddeus M. Rogers encapsulate the period of violence. Rogers was a twenty-three-year-old machinist from Georgia and was extremely wealthy by the standards of the day, with $9,000 in real property and $250 in personal property.[72] He was also—by all counts—one of the most reckless and violent white settlers to enter Santa Fe County, and although he only assaulted these two victims it is certain his real intention was to kill both. In late February Thaddeus Rogers attacked Marcelino Valdez for reasons that are not recorded in the court documents. What we do know is that Rogers walked up to Valdez and shot him in the head. Unlike John Gorman, Rogers's shot was true and penetrated Valdez's skull, making what the indictment described as "a severe wound," but somehow Marcelino Valdez survived.[73] On March 1, only a few days after shooting Valdez, Rogers committed a second assault against Euligio Gonzalez, who may have sought to confront Rogers concerning his assault on Valdez. What we do know is that Rogers knocked Gonzalez to the floor, pulled out his pistol, and shot him in the head at point blank range.[74] Miraculously Gonzalez also survived, so in both cases Rogers was only charged with assault with intent to kill plus the charge of battery. Money was no object to Thaddeus Rogers, so he pled guilty to both charges and agreed to pay his fines, which included $70 for his attempt to execute Marcelino Valdez. But he only paid one dollar for his attempt to execute Euligio Gonzalez, which is why it is likely Gonzalez confronted Rogers and gave him the cover he needed to escape a significant punishment.[75]

As the data reveal, both Nuevomexicano and white assault rates were on the rise from 1855 to 1858, driven by violent men like the Tapia brothers, William Rowan, Thaddeus M. Rogers, and even sheriffs Jesus Maria Baca y Salazar and Jesus Maria Sena y Baca. At both the personal and state levels Santa Fe County was a powder keg of anger and frustration. Domestic violence and violence by men against women more broadly were both part of this increase, but the surge of unrelated assault among men drove assault rates to new levels in 1855. It's not surprising that in these conditions the homicide rate exploded in 1856.

THE HOMICIDE WAVE BREAKS

On December 18, 1855, Benito Borrego, a different off-duty deputy to Sheriff Jesus Maria Baca y Salazar and for the County of Santa Fe, was attending a party at the home of Manuel Baca when a scuffle broke out. Borrego identified Sinaco Garcia as the source of the ruckus and he decided to intervene. In fact, Borrego later claimed that the twenty-five-year-old Garcia had instigated the riot and that as an officer of the law it was his responsibility to first detain and then arrest him. Benito Borrego went into action: he chased Sinaco Garcia, who was now out of the house and casually walking down the street, then grabbed him, stripped him of his cane, and ripped Garcia's gun and holster from his waist. In response Sinaco Garcia grabbed Borrego's coat and tore it at the shoulder; Borrego claimed that Garcia had hold of him and that he feared Garcia was going to unleash a deadly thrashing upon his person. Deputy Benito Borrego drew his gun and fired a single bullet into Sinaco Garcia's left side, the ball traveling eight inches deep into his body and leaving a wound the breadth of three inches. Sinaco Garcia fell to the ground, blood spilling from his wound as his brother Vicente Garcia and friend Pablo Delgado both rushed to his aid. With that, Sinaco Garcia, son of Felix Garcia, brother to Vicente, Juan, and Manuel Garcia, languished for three days before he finally succumbed to his injury and died.[76]

It is somehow fitting that a homicide that involved abuse of power, the implementation of state-sanctioned violence, and quite possibly vengeance was the first in the massive wave of Nuevomexicano and white homicides to come. Six months earlier, Jesus Maria Baca y Salazar used his badge as a shield from justice when he committed a heinous attack that left Luis Griego scarred for life, and this was a further extension of that pattern. It's already clear from the records that the Santa Fe County police force was corrupt. They held grudges and used their badges to brutalize their enemies, as has been been well documented here. It's also not surprising that this particular murder kicked off a wave of homicide, because it happened in concert with the fracture of the relationship between the patrónes and the vecinos, the discriminatory implementation of justice by the legal system, and the ever-increasing inequality of land distribution. Indeed, it was only a matter of time before Nuevomexicanos in Santa Fe County lost faith in both the patrónes and their local government and took the law into their own hands.

CHAPTER FOUR

For his part, Benito Borrego claimed he acted in his capacity as an officer of the state, and thus he was protected much the way Sheriff Baca y Salazar was. His narrative was both simple and familiar: there was a disturbance, it was his responsibility to keep the peace, and it was his intention to quash the tumult by arresting Sinaco Garcia. Deputy Sheriff Borrego claimed that he only wanted to arrest Garcia and take him to jail, that he meant him no harm. According to Borrego once Garcia grabbed him he felt as though his life was in mortal peril. At that point he felt endangered and, in self-defense and in the line of duty, Borrego pulled his gun and shot Garcia. In short, Deputy Sheriff Borrego claimed, as so many officers before him and since, that he killed the unarmed Sinaco Garcia in self-defense and that he did so in his capacity as an agent of law enforcement, for the state, and in the interest of keeping the peace.[77]

The prosecution offered a far different interpretation of the events that took place at Manuel Baca's party. They argued that the twenty-eight-year-old Borrego murdered Garcia in cold blood because of a personal grudge.[78] More specifically, the prosecution contended that Sinaco Garcia had insulted Borrego's forty-three-year-old mother, a widow named Refugio Borrego, and that it was this insult that triggered Benito Borrego.[79] Could some nineteenth-century "yo mamma" style quip have been the last straw in a larger series of conflicts between Borrego and Garcia? The prosecution argued that that was the case and that Borrego stalked Garcia at the party and waited for the moment when Garcia was vulnerable so that he could murder his enemy.[80]

The prosecution remained vague about the larger quarrel that fueled Borrego's grudge, but the influence of Jesus Maria Sena y Baca was likely a factor in the tension between the Garcias and local law enforcement. Still, they noted in their final argument to the jury "That any previous violent conduct, or language on the part of Garcia would not justify Borrego in shooting him."[81] The inclusion of the words "violent conduct" and "language" loom large in this statement. A perusal of the Santa Fe County court records reveals that charges were never filed against Sinaco Garcia for any type of crime, much less for violence. It seems to be a reference to a broader conflict, perhaps the one that involved Sena y Baca, but those specific details were not recorded.[82]

The prosecution focused on the language component of the dispute, but they did not solely base their case on Borrego's motive; instead, they argued that Benito Borrego broke the law when he sought to detain Sinaco Garcia in the first place. "That the fact of Borrego being a constable did not authorize him to take Garcia or commit him to jail, and that he had no more right to do so than anyone else unless he manifested some order or legal process from some judicial, or other, officer."[83] Essentially, the prosecution argued that Borrego unlawfully detained Garcia in the first place, that he certainly had no right to jail him in the second place, and that he illegally initiated the confrontation with Garcia in the third place. Further, they contended, "If at the time that Garcia caught Borrego by the jacket or coat and tore the same neither the life of Borrego was in danger, nor was he in imminent danger of any great bodily harm likely to be perpetuated upon him."[84] They also argued that since Borrego had disarmed Garcia at the start of the confrontation, "Garcia having had a pistol or cane in his possession is no excuse for killing him after these weapons were taken away from him."[85] They concluded with a powerful statement: "The law did not authorize Borrego to shoot him, nor is it an excuse or justification for taking his life."[86] In making this argument, they attacked both Borrego's contention of self-defense and the notion that being an officer of the law gave one the authority to legally kill in the name of the state. The prosecution built a powerful and compelling case, but Benito Borrego was found not guilty and the immunity of the sheriff and his deputies from justice was confirmed yet again.

It wasn't just that homicides were more frequent after 1855. It was that vecino murders became uncharacteristically brutal and callous in nature. To put this level of risk in context, the period of 1856–1857 in Santa Fe County ranked second only to Monterrey County, California, 1855–1857 in the greater American West (table 4.3).[87] Gone were the days of Nuevomexicano manslaughter, of a rock thrown at a distance finding the temple of a young man quite by accident, of a gut punch to a friend resulting in an unexpected fatality.[88] Suddenly, murders like the one committed by Francisco Martin were no longer outliers. Vecinos were angry. In March of 1856, a vecino named Jose Zacharias murdered a fellow vecino, and he did so less than 150 feet from the bustling plaza. Zacharias stabbed Gonzalez in the side with a dagger, then left Gonzalez to die in the street.[89]

Location and Years	Homicides	Ave. annual adult pop.	Adult pop. at risk	Homicide Rate
Monterey County, CA, 1855–1857	40	2,189	6,567	609
Nevada County, CA, 1851–1856	98	18,270	109,620	89
Eight Native American peoples in CA, 1852–1865	289	24,264	339,689	85
Oregon, 1850–1865	114	23,373	373,964	30
British Columbia, 1859–1871	43	13,204	171,653	25
Texas, June 1865–June 1868	1,035	455,000	1,365,000	76
Gila County, AZ, 1880–1900	89	2,580	54,170	164
Pima County, AZ, 1882–1909	106	11,389	182,225	58
Denver, CO, 1859–1865	30	4,058	28,404	106
Las Animas County, CO, 1880–1900	73	10,323	216,777	34
Santa Fe County, NMT, 1847–1853	14	4,915	34,405	41
Santa Fe County, NMT, 1855–1860	36	4,364	21,820	165

Table 4.3. Western Homicide Rates, per Persons per 100,000, Ages 16 and Over

CHAPTER FOUR

Much like the homicide committed by Francisco Martin against Felipe Lovato, Estevan Tenorio had every intention of murdering Ramon Rodriguez. Reports indicate that Tenorio, a twenty-two-year-old servant, issued a severe beating to Rodriguez, who was likely a twenty-four-year-old blacksmith, but that Tenorio was not satisfied with merely embarrassing him.[90] Although the contest was no longer in doubt, Estevan Tenorio pulled his knife and in a thrusting motion plunged his blade into Ramon Rodriguez's head.[91] More specifically, Tenorio stabbed Rodriguez in his left temple with a large blade, which left a wound six inches wide, with the breadth of three inches and the depth of three inches. This was an attempt to execute a fallen foe, and four days after the attack Tenorio's intentions were realized. Although Tenorio was initially charged with assault, the charges were escalated and he was subsequently convicted of murder and sentenced to one year in jail for his actions.[92]

The knife remained the primary weapon used by Nuevomexicanos during the 1856–1857 wave of homicide, and it continued to be throughout this period. For Jose Euligio Sena, the knife was his weapon of choice when he planned to kill Blas Ortiz. Sena was a thirty-two-year-old blacksmith in 1857, which it turned out so was also the age of Blas Ortiz, a laborer from Santa Fe County.[93] This was not the only thing they had in common: both were having intimate relations with Sena's wife, and this was well-known around town. Alas, public secrets are seldom secret for long, and Jose E. Sena learned of her infidelity sometime in December of 1857. Early on the morning of December 12, Sena acted; he pretended to leave his house early in the morning, but instead concealed himself outside of his home.[94] It wasn't long before Blas Ortiz arrived at his residence and entered through the front door. It's unclear how long Sena waited before he entered his home, but it was long enough so that when he opened the door to his bedroom he found Blas Ortiz and his wife unclothed and in the throes of passion. Sena charged forward with his knife in hand and plunged the blade into Ortiz's heart, killing him almost instantly.[95] Although Jose E. Sena faced charges for homicide in 1858, the jury ruled that he was justified in his actions and declared him not guilty.[96] Sena's wife was never identified in the court records and it seems she moved on, for in 1860 Jose E. Sena was listed as living alone with his two young children.[97]

Antonio Padilla also used a knife when he committed a double murder. In 1858 the forty-five-year-old Padilla, who was listed as a servant in 1860, killed two young boys named Bernabel Blea and Valentine Pacheco.[98] Blea was only sixteen years old and Pacheco was seventeen. Both ran afoul of the much older Padilla, who claimed that he was in fact the victim in this conflict. According to Antonio Padilla, Valentine Pacheco attacked him first. He claimed Pacheco charged at him with a knife, and he had no choice but to defend himself with his own blade.[99] Padilla claimed that Bernabel Blea attacked next, that he also charged with a knife, and that he once more defended himself. Antonio Padilla was precise with his knife, for he stabbed Blea in his heart and left a mortal wound two inches wide and six inches deep.[100] Again, this was not an accident and it is clear that Antonio Padilla meant to kill Blea. What is less clear is if the jury believed him, because although they found him guilty of both murders, they only found him guilty of murder in the third degree. But the effect was the same: Antonio Padilla was sentenced to ten years in prison at hard labor.[101] Padilla appealed the verdict, and he argued that Pacheco was well-liked in Santa Fe County and therefore he could not receive a fair hearing. He was granted a change of venue, but was again convicted and given the same sentence, and when the 1860 census was taken he was serving his sentence in the Santa Fe County jail.[102]

The number of Nuevomexicano murders fell by more than forty percent from 1858 to 1860, declining from fourteen to eight, and three of these eight homicide victims were women. In June of 1858 Francisco Quintana, a fifty-three-year-old wealthy farmer from Santa Fe County, murdered Altagracia Tafoya in a most heinous fashion.[103] In June of 1858 Francisco Quintana pulled his knife, raised it over his head, and with extreme force dealt a downward strike so powerful that it penetrated Altagracia Tafoya's left shoulder to the depth of six inches, so deep it likely pierced her heart and killed her instantly.[104] Francisco Quintana was a wealthy farmer from the top 10 percent who owned $1,500 in land in 1860, so this was not a run-of-the-mill homicide. It is telling that Don Gaspar Ortiz y Alarid served on the jury for this case, and as the fifth wealthiest man in the county and one of the most prominent citizens in Santa Fe, his presence demonstrated how serious this crime was taken. Quintana was undeniably guilty, and the jury instructions demonstrate that the judge was determined to see a guilty verdict brought against Quintana. In an anomaly, he was found guilty and sentenced to ten years in the county jail.[105]

Far less is known about the details and outcomes of the other two female victims, Maria Jesus Gonzalez and Theodorita Roybal, other than they were killed in 1859 and 1860 respectively. We also know the details of these murders, as they were laid out in the indictments. We know that Ramon Gonzalez y Moya must have been filled with rage and jealousy when he killed Maria Jesus Gonzalez. He tackled her to the ground, pulled his knife, and stabbed her in both of her breasts; both wounds were close to her nipples and the knife penetrated to the depth of six inches, killing her instantly.[106] These details demonstrate the personal nature of the homicide, yet another murder likely fueled by romantic love. In the case of Theodorita Roybal, we only know that Francisco Trujillo beat her severely on April 15, 1860, that she lingered for six days, and that she finally died from the beating on April 21.[107] The verdicts have not been found for either case, but at least with the sentencing of Francisco Quintana someone was finally punished for domestic violence in Santa Fe County.

CHAPTER FOUR

As we have seen, the vast majority of Nuevomexicanos were intentionally killing their victims during the 1856–1857 wave of homicide, so it harked back to better days when Rafael Rodriguez accidentally killed Jesus Martin in self-defense. Rodriguez testified that he witnessed his father-in-law and Jesus Martin in a serious fight, and that he intervened with the intention of breaking up the two men. Much to Rodriguez's surprise, when he tried to intercede Jesus Martin turned his rage from his father-in-law to him. Jesus Martin charged at him with a stick that was large enough to be considered a deadly weapon, and Rafael Rodriguez reacted as most reasonable people would in that instance: he turned tail and ran. His flight instinct in control, Rodriguez bolted through the dusty streets of Santa Fe with Jesus Martin in hot pursuit. Martin was apparently in better physical shape, because it wasn't long before Martin was at Rodriguez's heels. With the distance between them closing, Rodriguez reached down and picked up a rock from the street, wheeled around, and threw a perfect strike that hit Jesus Martin in his right temple. The rock penetrated Jesus Martin's head to the depth of one inch and left a bloody wound the breadth of three inches. Jesus Martin went down immediately but survived for six more days before succumbing to his injury.[108] Since this homicide was public, there was little debate about the details and everyone seems to have agreed that Rafael Rodriguez killed Jesus Martin in self-defense, so Rodriguez was found not guilty.[109]

The murder committed by Estefanio Prada fit better into this new era of how and why Nuevomexicanos killed, but it was the fascinating arguments that emerged during the trial, specifically dealing with growing class inequality in Santa Fe County, that make this case worthy of closing out Hispano homicide for this period. The case itself was simple enough: Estefanio Prada got into a fight with Jesus Arias and both men faced off with their knives drawn. For whatever reason, Antonio Jose Chaves intervened with the intention of ending the fracas before it became deadly. We don't know exactly how the final moment played out, but we know he epically failed because it ended with Estefanio Prada burying his knife into the right side of the belly of Antonio Jose Chaves. The wound was six inches deep and two inches wide and apparently pierced Chaves's stomach, for three days later Antonio Jose Chaves died.[110]

Estefanio Prada, a forty-nine-year-old day laborer from Santa Fe County, was called before the court and pled not guilty to the charge of murder.[111] Interestingly, his attorney, the well-known Merrill Ashurst of Alabama, told the court that they must consider the circumstances of Estefanio Prada's life: he was an extremely poor man who had suffered in poverty all of his life, who had worked hard to survive, and who deserved leniency in light of his circumstances.[112] Ashurst touched on a core issue when he argued that land and class inequality drove the frustrations that ultimately played a decisive role in Prada's decision to take the law into his own hands, but Judge Kirby Benedict was not at all impressed with this line of argument.¹¹³ Benedict was, however, concerned that Ashurst's argument might resonate with the jury, so he detailed in four dense pages the specifics of the case, why it did not matter that Estefanio Prada had lived a hard life, and the duty of the jury to convict. More specifically, Benedict wrote:

> A man because he is poor has no more right to kill another man than has a rich man and he generally is responsible to the law for his act. The def (defendant) is entitled to the benefit of all reasonable doubts. A reasonable doubt is not such a doubt as a person may imagine or fancy in his own mind but such as necessarily assessed out of the testimony and the laws applicable in this case.¹¹⁴

The irony of Judge Kirby Benedict arguing that a poor man deserved no more privilege than a rich one—especially considering how large landholding Nuevomexicanos were given every privilege politically, socially, economically, and judicially—seems to have been lost on Judge Benedict. And much to his chagrin, Merrill Ashurst's words did not fall on deaf ears, for the jury deliberated late into the night; he was pleased when he finally received the verdict, but opted to keep it sealed until the next day for security reasons.¹¹⁵ Estefanio Prada was found guilty of murder in the fourth degree, and he received the maximum sentence of seven years at hard labor in the county jail, where he sat when the 1860 U.S. Census was taken.¹¹⁶ In this final moment before Judge Benedict, Estefanio Prada was asked, like so many Nuevomexicanos before him, if he had anything to say to the court about the sentence that had been passed and like so many before him and after, Estefanio Prada remained silent.¹¹⁷

White settlers, transients, and adventurers contributed to the high homicide rates from 1856 to 1860, and their murders drove the rate from 1858 to 1860. But even though they weren't the driving force during the first two years of Santa Fe's five-year-long homicide wave, they managed to distinguish themselves with the audacity of their behavior. For example, in March of 1857 George Gruber and a soldier known only as Private Lang were both shopping at a drugstore on the plaza when they suddenly began to quarrel. Whatever the dispute, it escalated quickly and Gruber pulled his gun and shot Private Lang in the chest.¹¹⁸ When Private Lang died days later on Wednesday, March 11, 1857, the American soldiers stationed in the area were furious and they became determined to take the law into their own hands. As the *Gazette* tells us, "The shooting of Lang—who is said to be a favorite in his company—aroused the ire of his comrades to such a pitch that the officers (were) instructed to keep them in their quarters that night in the anticipation of their lynching of Gruber, if allowed to go out, found themselves wholly unable to restrain them."¹¹⁹ But before they could be restrained—if there even was an attempt to do so—the American soldiers grabbed their muskets and left in search of revenge. Thus an armed mob of angry soldiers entered the city of Santa Fe and headed directly for the county jail. At around 9 p.m. they stormed the yard of the jail; the prisoners ran at the sight of the mob and sought shelter in their jail cells. The soldiers commenced their search for George L. Gruber, who along with his wardens apparently anticipated this lynching, because he was nowhere to be found.[120]

Undeterred, the soldiers started breaking into the jail cells and assaulting everyone they came across, resolute that everyone should suffer for the death of Private Lang. Among the prisoners was Matias Ribera, who in July of 1856 dragged one Francisco Prada into the street and callously punched and kicked Prada to death with his fists and boots.[121] Matias Ribera was in jail awaiting trial when his door was kicked in and he was shot and killed.[122] After wounding two other prisoners, the soldiers finally found George Gruber, who was under the protection of two unknown deputies; the soldiers managed to bayonet and shoot Gruber one time, but the jailers grabbed him and made a daring retreat to one of the cells. Both the deputies and Gruber hid behind a large block of wood as the soldiers fired volley after volley into the cell, but the firing ceased when a U.S. Army officer arrived and restored order. As the *Gazette* recounted, "Upon the appearance of the Lieutenant Clitz at the scene of these outrageous proceedings, the men obediently ceased their bloody work, and on his order fell into line and were marched off to their quarters."[123] The *Gazette* reported that in addition to Gruber two other prisoners were gravely wounded in the assault, but only Matias Ribera was killed.

There was much confusion in the wake of the white American soldiers' attack on the Santa Fe County jail, and charges were not filed against any of them until later that month. In total, thirty different soldiers were indicted for their participation in the murder of Matias Ribera.[124] Lesser charges were not filed against any of the soldiers, likely because the case completely overwhelmed the court. The defense called for all thirty men to receive individual jury trials; they contended that three hundred jurors needed to be called in order to accomplish this, one hundred from Santa Fe, San Miguel, and Santa Anna Counties respectively.[125] The court issued orders for three hundred jurors to be gathered, but there is no indication that this was actually done. Instead, eight days later the group was tried together and hastily acquitted by a white jury; even the *Gazette*, which decried the soldiers as cowards and called for swift court-martial hearings, turned a blind eye to this hasty exoneration. Thus, white American soldiers were allowed to march on the county jail, assault the prisoners and guards, and kill one Nuevomexicano prisoner in cold blood, and there were no repercussions for this egregious abuse of military power. Like the sheriff and his deputies, white American soldiers were also above the law in Santa Fe County.

The white homicides that ravaged Santa Fe County from 1858 to

1860—and kept the combined homicide rate in Santa Fe County high—had a new element: quite suddenly there were homicides within the established white community, an indicator that new fissures had developed among established American and European settlers. Why this occurred is difficult to discern, but it's possible that the threat of Civil War and the uncertainty surrounding what would become of New Mexico territory played a role in the increasing number of deadly quarrels among white settlers. That feeling of insecurity may have destabilized whites in Santa Fe County, but whatever the reason, we increasingly saw privileged and established whites move away from reliance on the law and toward the dangerous trend of taking the law into their own hands.

Indeed, the cases of Preston Beck Jr. and John Gorman stand at the forefront of these white community homicides. Preston Beck Jr. was a forty-eight-year-old Missourian who came to New Mexico in 1845, one year before the invasion by the United States. He was both a successful merchant and lawyer by trade who developed friendships in both the Hispano and white communities, and by 1858 Beck was a well-known and respected citizen of Santa Fe County.[126] John Gorman was also a citizen of the county, a thirty-seven-year-old shoemaker by trade from the state of New York, and—as we will later see—a terrible shot with a pistol.[127] Indeed, this was the very same sharp-shooting John Gorman who was indicted for two separate assaults with intent to kill in 1855—during which he fired ten shots and missed with all of them—one of which ended in a ruthless pistol-whipping.[128] By 1858 Gorman was settled and working in the shop of an Irish-born merchant and shop owner named Richard Owens.[129]

According to the *Gazette*, the dispute between Preston Beck Jr. and John Gorman began on March 25, 1858, when John Gorman became jealous over a woman and attacked Francisco Griego, who was one of Preston Beck Jr.'s servants. Gorman heard from friends that she was at a local dance with Francisco Griego and his wife the night before. Unbeknownst to John Gorman, the woman he fancied was actually Francisco Griego's sister-in-law. Gorman confronted Griego and asked if he had taken his girlfriend to a baile, to which the confused Francisco Griego responded that he had. Gorman then asked Griego if he had done so before, but before Griego could answer Gorman started thrashing him with a stick. The *Gazette* recounts a horrific beating, writing that Gorman attacked Griego "and continued beating him until his arms and head and face were a gore of blood."[130] According to the *Gazette*, when Gorman finished his assault, "He then opened the door and threw (him) out into the street, where he was found during the night, and taken home."[131] Francisco Griego survived this senseless assault by John Gorman, but the clash had only just begun.

The next morning Preston Beck Jr. learned that John Gorman had beaten his servant, and he was determined to confront Gorman for his actions. Beck marched down to Richard Owen's shop, where Gorman was employed, flung open

CHAPTER FOUR

the door, and accused Gorman of assault. Gorman called Beck a liar—as those who lie often do—and challenged him to prove his accusations. Once more Preston Beck Jr. implicated Gorman as the perpetrator of the offense, but this time he set to cursing Gorman for his actions. Quick to temper, John Gorman pulled his knife and, according to the *Gazette*, "He threatened to serve him as his servant had been served."[132] It seems that Preston Beck was also quick to temper because he pulled his knife as well, and with weapons drawn they entered the street, where each sought to serve the other. They threatened and cursed one another, swinging their knives at the air in turn, until suddenly Gorman lunged and stabbed Beck in the stomach, near his navel; in the same moment, Beck plunged his knife into Gorman's chest, striking him in the heart. The two separated, and Gorman flailed toward Beck, desperately stabbing at him, but Beck retreated and dodged Gorman's final desperate blows. As Preston Beck Jr. retreated, John Gorman finally stumbled and collapsed onto his back. He rolled over, blood streaming from his body and into the street as his life faded to darkness. According to the *Gazette*, Beck took off his coat, held it to his wound, and immediately sought out the town doctor in order to have his wound dressed. As Dr. Sloan, the local quack, tended Beck's wound he told Beck that he ought to see to his affairs, as he would not be long for this world. Alas, John Gorman's aim with his knife ultimately proved better than his aim with a gun, because two weeks later Preston Beck Jr. died from the knife wound to his stomach that he had sustained in mortal combat.[133]

In another incident, William Henry Elam was indicted for two separate homicides, both of which stemmed from the same incident in 1860. Elam was a twenty-six-year-old stage agent for Santa Fe, was originally from the state of Tennessee, and had settled in Santa Fe County with $1,200 in property by 1860.[134] Elam had taken a room at the El Dorado House and was there with an unnamed woman, who had been acting as his servant. The El Dorado House manager, a man named William Phillips, testified that he saw Henry Elam enter through the lobby on June 7, 1860, and that Elam went straight to his room. It was evening when Elam opened the door to his room. The curtains were drawn, so his room was pitch black. He lit the lantern by the door only to find Thomas McCaren and William Fitzsimmons sitting in his room.[135]

Henry Elam testified that McCaren and Fitzsimmons told him they were there to take away his servant. Elam claimed that both men were armed and that both she and he were endangered, so he pulled his gun and in succession shot both men where they sat. In addition to being a deadly marksman, Henry Elam must have had a large-caliber gun, because his bullets did tremendous damage to both McCaren and Fitzsimmons. Thomas McCaren was shot in the stomach and William Fitzsimmons was shot in the chest. Both wounds measured two inches wide and six inches deep, and reportedly both men died instantly in their chairs.[136] Elam's case went to trial in August, and on the 15th a mixed jury of prominent Hispanos and Anglos heard both cases. They declared that he acted in self-defense and found him not guilty of both murder charges.[137]

You may recall another member of the white community in Santa Fe County by the name of Thaddeus M. Rogers, the wealthy machinist from Georgia with a penchant for shooting people in the head whenever he became angry. On Christmas Day of 1859 Rogers pulled his gun yet again and for the third time shot a Nuevomexicano at point blank range. The homicide began with Thaddeus M. Rogers walking into the store of Joseph Hirsch with his gun drawn, which Jesus Maria Baca y Salazar witnessed.[138] We don't know why Rogers was so angry with Hirsch, who was a thirty-five-year-old merchant from Poland and one of the wealthiest men in the territory, with $60,000 in combined real estate and holdings, but we do know that when he entered Hirsch's store he immediately started challenging Hirsch to a duel.[139] Joseph Hirsch testified that Rogers used violent and abusive language toward him and told Hirsch that he was too cowardly to draw his firearm. Hirsch admitted that Rogers had it right: he was terrified, so instead of pulling his gun he fled from his store, ducked out through an adjoining room, and took refuge in the office of the well-known attorney Merrill Ashurst.[140]

The store was not empty though, because both Matias Dominguez and Felipe Gutierrez testified that they were in the store when Thaddeus M. Rogers made his grand entrance. According to Dominguez, he was positioned where he could both see and hear what transpired between Rogers, Hirsch, and a young shop hand named Marcelino Savalas. Felipe Gutierrez was also present and he corroborated the testimony of Dominguez. Both Gutierrez and Dominguez swore that neither Hirsch nor Savalas had a gun. Most importantly, both witnessed what happened after Joseph Hirsch absconded: Thaddeus M. Rogers charged after Hirsch, but Marcelino Savalas approached Rogers and pleaded with him to put his gun away and "not to kill his master Hirsch."[141] At that point Rogers turned to Savalas, pointed his gun at Savalas's left temple, and shot him in the head. The bullet left a wound the breadth of one half inch and the depth of six inches, and Marcelino Savalas fell to the ground and died instantly.[142]

No matter how intemperate Thaddeus M. Rogers was, he was also wealthy, so there were people who benefited from his affluence, and a few of them testified on Rogers's behalf. Specifically, a forty-one-year-old wealthy merchant from Canada named Joseph Mercure, a thirty-five-year-old aspiring merchant named Salamon Spiegelberg, another merchant named Adolpheus Staab, and a thirty-two-year-old servant named Desiderio Baca all came forward to testify on Thaddeus Rogers's behalf. Spiegelberg and Staab gave the strongest testimony for the defense. They maintained that although they were not in the store they heard a gunshot from within the store before Rogers fired the kill shot at Marcelino Savalas, that Thaddeus Rogers had in fact shot back, and had done so in self-defense.[143]

But an American soldier named Fredrick Burger rebutted Rogers's claim that he had shot Savalas in self-defense. Burger testified that he was near the store when Rogers shot Marcelino Savalas, and that once Rogers had gone he entered the store and found Savalas dead on the floor. Burger claimed that he personally moved the body to examine Savalas, and that there was no firearm on or about Savalas's person. Judge Kirby Benedict reminded the jury of this fact in his instructions, and he placed this information immediately after noting Rogers's claim of self-defense.[144] Both Burger's testimony and Benedict's use of it proved damaging for the defense.

The jury found Thaddeus M. Rogers guilty of first-degree murder and Judge Benedict sentenced him to death by hanging. Of course Rogers had the means to appeal this verdict, and he did so all the way to the Territorial Supreme Court, but the case against Rogers proved too strong to overturn. Rogers got away with shooting two Nuevomexicanos in the head, in part because both men survived, but by shooting Marcelino Savalas—who purportedly fell defending his white "master" and patron—Rogers had finally gone too far. He became the third person in Santa Fe County to receive the death penalty, and he would be the second, after Andrew Jackson Simms, to see his sentence carried out.[145] Alas, violence and homicide between members of the white community in Santa Fe County and beyond was only just beginning.

Conclusion

For Nuevomexicanos in Santa Fe County, the period of 1855–1860 proved to be a breaking point in so many ways: It represented a loss of faith in the political, social, economic, and judicial systems, all of which worked in concert and had made life in the lower classes bearable. Hispanos lost their faith in their old patrónes, who became politicos and used their newfound power to increase their own fortunes and to punish and make day laborers out of the majority of the Nuevomexicano population. Land and wealth inequality reached new heights, and the law was not applied equally, and, taken together, these realities inspired many to leave Santa Fe County in search of better opportunities.

Within this period of 1855–1860, the initial homicide wave of 1856 stands out because to kill so frequently, so cruelly, and so intently was simply not something Nuevomexicanos had done before or something they would do afterwards. We have seen that the homicide rate during the Mexican period, which was a time of instability and upheaval, remained relatively low throughout New Mexico. In many ways, this is because Nuevomexicanos at all levels of society faced the same pressures, and there was at least a sense that they were all in it together. The homicide rates were stable during the early territorial period, from 1847 to 1853, because so little overtly changed in the system of power under which they lived. Yes, there was upheaval and instability again, but once more the community ties held.

From 1856 forward life for poorer Nuevomexicanos only got worse. Their fate was no longer tethered to the community, and the bonds that held them together fell apart. Those vecinos who remained became increasingly violent, taking the law into their own hands instead of looking to their old partners for justice. The large landholders were the primary beneficiaries, at least in the short term. In the midst of their avarice for land, goods, and status, they could never have understood that losing the friendship of the people would ultimately prove to be their undoing. Meanwhile, white settlers complained that murderers were allowed to go free in Santa Fe County, but ironically, and thanks to white judges and jurors, it was the white immigrants who were in fact the murderers who escaped justice.

CHAPTER FIVE

AT THE WRONG END OF THE LASH

On Thursday January 26, 1857, at approximately 10 a.m., the sheriff of Santa Fe County escorted Pedro Sandoval, an elderly Nuevomexicano of nearly seventy years, from his jail cell to the plaza in the city of Santa Fe. Only days before Sandoval pled guilty to stealing both a goat and a woolen cloth from Jesus Garcia's farm. That Thursday was a long day for Sandoval, which was precisely what Judge J. J. Davenport intended. Sandoval admitted his crime, which fit the tradition of the old Spanish and Mexican judicial systems. But there was no leniency for an honest Nuevomexicano in the Santa Fe District Court. Davenport was determined to make an example of the old vecino, who remained stoic during his sentencing. As the judge decreed, Pedro Sandoval was taken to the plaza, tied to the American flag pole, whipped twenty times on his bare back, and left displayed on the pole until 4 p.m. for all to see.[1]

The public lashing and lengthy display of the body of Pedro Sandoval was intended to deter vecinos and Indigenous peoples from committing larceny. In the Western world, corporal punishment was an old practice, one that marked the body to deter crime. But as Foucault wrote, by the mid-nineteenth century attacks against the body were waning. He noted that the practice of punishment as a public spectacle declined widely, and that "It survived only as a new legal or administrative practice."[2] New Mexico was precisely that, a place where a new legal system was created to replace Mexican law. That system was the Kearny Code, which was a textbook deterrence document, and corporal punishment was embedded in that legal code to dissuade property crimes.

The Americans who ran the legal system in Santa Fe County reserved lashes for poor vecinos and the Indigenous, a fact that is quantitatively irrefutable. Vecinos and Indigenous peoples accounted for twenty-six of the twenty-eight prisoners lashed in the plaza, and that was not accidental. Western law, the tradition from which the Kearny Code sprang, is foremost a means for social control rather than a system intended to promote justice. It is meant to legitimize the ruling class and give them a legal means to punish anyone who challenges their right to rule, which is why laws are never applied equally.[3] White American judges and jurors in particular almost exclusively sentenced vecinos convicted of larceny and burglary to be lashed in the plaza; for the same crimes these judges allowed all but two of the seven white American defendants to serve short jail sentences in lieu of lashes.[4] In keeping with that tradition, from 1847 to 1860 American judges and territorial jurors used the legal system as a cudgel to forge a new ethnic and class dominion over poorer Nuevomexicanos in Santa Fe County. Their sentences for vecinos often stretched and even exceeded the law, and they included public lashings, unreasonably long and damaging jail sentences, and even indentured servitude. While poorer Nuevomexicanos were brutalized, white settlers—even poor ones who often committed far more heinous crimes—were only sentenced to fines, served short jail sentences, and were all but spared the lash.

The data are clear on this point. Between 1847 and 1860, white American judges and juries used lashing as a principal punishment against vecinos in Santa Fe County, and the local strongmen passed laws that buttressed their actions. The overwhelming majority of these (24 of 26) were administered during the early period in Santa Fe County, but as Pedro Sandoval—who stole that goat—learned, the lash remained a threat in the years leading up to the Civil War. White American judges gave punishments along racial lines for the duration of this period of study, but the use of lashing was striking from 1846 to 1853: among the *vecinos* with known punishments, 30 percent (31) paid a fine between $1 and $1,000, 42 percent (43) were incarcerated, 24 percent (24) received lashes, and 4 percent (4) were sold into indentured servitude (figures 5.1a and 5.1b).[5] Every vecino who was sentenced to lashes was also jailed for between three months and two years.

Meanwhile, the white American judges selected white American jurors and together they sentenced convicted white Americans to lighter sentences: 58 percent (15) of white Americans received fines ranging from $10 to $50, 34 percent (9) were sentenced to jail, 7 percent (2) received lashes, and 4 percent (1) received the death penalty. In 1850 Henry Potter and Samuel Rino became the only white Americans sentenced to lashes and they received this punishment, but this was an anomaly: Potter and Rino were teamsters in the service of the military who were caught stealing a trunk of money from the store of Raymond, Martin, and Woods, so the white American judges gave them a military punishment rather than a white American civilian one.[6] In reality, white civilians simply were not lashed.

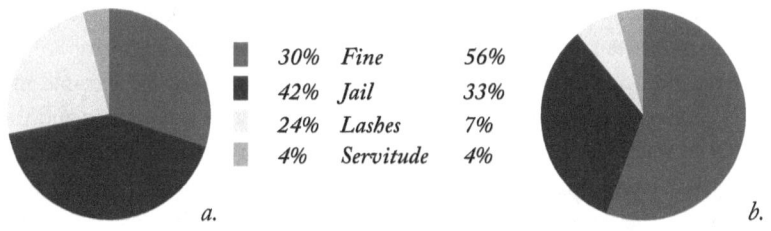

Figures 5.1a and 5.1b. Known punishments by ethnicity, by percentage, Santa Fe County, 1846–1854.

CHAPTER FIVE

This chapter argues that the American judges, territorial jurors, and the patrónes in the legislature used the judicial system as an apparatus of cultural domination in Santa Fe County from 1847 to 1860. The first section, "Politicos and the New Legal System," outlines how many patrónes became politicos through the process of territorialization in New Mexico. In their new roles they prioritized their own interests, and they engaged the legal system when it served their agendas. When they felt the federal government had overextended its reach, they demanded accountability. When vecino and white property crime increased, they passed laws that sanctioned harsher punishments. The politicos cared little for everyday vecinos and their needs, and instead were focused on power and profits.

In the second section, I argue that the overt racism of judges and biased juries ensured guilty verdicts against vecinos and spared white American defendants from guilty verdicts and hard punishments. Together, the judges and juries oversaw a legal system that convicted along racial lines: more than half of Nuevomexicanos were convicted, while only a third of American defendants faced consequences for their crimes. The next section, Racialized Punishment, centers on the forms of punishment that the courts inflicted, including lashing, jail, indentured servitude, and fines. It reveals that Nuevomexicano jurors worked in concert with white American judges and jurors to convict vecinos, while white American jurors worked with white American judges to spare white American criminals from punishment. In the process, the vecino community was further estranged from the patrónes and the new territorial government.

POLITICOS AND THE NEW LEGAL SYSTEM

The Americans came to Santa Fe as colonizers, a fact that can never be forgotten, and they treated New Mexico territory as their colony. In the colonial tradition, they only cooperated with the local "elites" in order to secure a peaceful transfer of power. Had the Americans' final destination been Santa Fe, they would have likely resorted to more direct forms of domination. In this way, Nuevomexicanos were fortunate that New Mexico was but a stop on the road to California. So the Americans created a legal system instead to legitimize their authority over the territory and rule passively over a land that they only needed to be stable and secure. The Americans who came and decided to stay treated the vecinos and the Indigenous in ways that resembled the imperialist nations that colonized African societies, which were similarly founded on war, power, and racial domination.[7] The patrónes, however, remained key to American power, and because it benefited them, they helped the Americans keep their colony secure.

The politicos were not a monolithic group, but still they dominated the political system in New Mexico.[8] Between 1851 and 1855, Hispanos accounted for 83 percent of the Council (52 to 11) and 87 percent of the House (111 to 16) in the New Mexico legislature. As I have noted, they conducted business in Spanish and passed laws in Spanish, then translated them into English. I have also shown that they passed laws that targeted white American criminals, but they also forbade white Americans in the military from voting and walled out white Americans who sought to alter Nuevomexicano traditions.[9] They sent politicos to represent them in the US Congress and wrote memorials to Washington DC that advocated their economic and political interests. Most significantly, it bears repeating that despite their political differences, the politicos refused to pass property taxes against their families in the face of intense pressure from American governors and politicians to do so. All while they prospered. In short, the politicos dominated the legislature by every metric.

The extent to which the patrónes controlled the legislature is accentuated by the election of the aforementioned Diego Archuleta to the territorial legislature in 1850. Archuleta was a patrón, but he fled to Mexico after he was exposed as the architect of the plot to depose their new government in 1847. By 1850 he was back in the Rio Arriba and, as though nothing had happened, he was selected for the legislature. The Americans resented Archuleta, and a group of white Americans and pro-American Hispanos even tried to bar Archuleta from the 1850 Constitutional Convention. Joab Houghton disliked Archuleta, and he threatened to withdraw from the legislature if Archuleta was seated. In the caudillo tradition, Archuleta played the martyr and declared that since he was not wanted, he would not attend.[10] But when Archuleta's enemies voted to exclude him from the convention, the patrónes did what Archuleta hoped they would. The patrónes-turned-politicos made their stand with Archuleta and protested the "undignified expulsion of Archuleta by the American members."[11] The politicos stonewalled the convention, and they refused to relent until finally Archuleta was seated.[12]

The Americans were simply too few to impact the most important policies, so naturally they tried to cheat their way into power.[13] Specifically, the Americans tried to manipulate elections by sending white soldiers to the polls, even though they were forbidden to vote. Soldiers and teamsters were not eligible to vote, but the governor encouraged them to do so. But they were rebuffed by the patrónes at the polls. In Bernalillo County, three white men were killed and several more were wounded when they tried to intimidate the patrónes who controlled the polling station. A different group of Americans tried the same thing at Los Ranchos, and in the pitched battle that followed two more white Americans were killed.[14]

The politicos held the territorial legislature, and by extension the most important power of all: the power to tax. The territorial governors continued their entreaties for property taxes, but the legislature still refused to pass such a law.[15] Even in 1852, when Santa Fe County ran out of money to feed prisoners in the jail, the local patrónes still refused to tax their fellow patrónes. Probate Judge Tomás Ortíz told James S. Calhoun that "without means to feed prisoners . . . the poor 'wretches' must inevitably die or rot in jail."[16] Governor Calhoun was without recourse. He pardoned fourteen prisoners and ordered them to leave the territory. In this way, the New Mexican governors remained at the mercy of the legislature when it came to taxes, even as New Mexico teetered on bankruptcy.

There were divisions among the patrónes, but these were largely residual from the Mexican period.[17] Still, two vague camps emerged in the early days of territorialization. Felipe Gonzales labeled these the American Party and the other as the Mexican Party.[18] Not all Nuevomexicanos, however, fit into these categories. Manuel Chaves and Diego Archuleta were opportunists who were neither pro-Mexican nor pro-Texas, and they cared little about the poor; Padre Manuel Gallegos was neither proslavery nor promilitary, but he did care for the poor; Miguel Otero was proslavery, but he was also anti-Texas; and Padre Martínez was not promilitary, although he cared a great deal for the *pobres*. In many ways, Rio Arriba vs. Rio Abajo interests divided patrónes. Beyond that, these so-called swing politicians gravitated toward whichever party represented their interests in a given moment and commonly along kinship lines.[19]

The issue of slavery in New Mexico illuminates both the fluidity of some politicos and the practicality of others. Prior to 1856 the politicos opposed slavery because they did not want black people in the territory and were against foreigners bringing a labor force to New Mexico that might disadvantage them.[20] They also didn't want Texans migrating to New Mexico. So in 1850, the politicos included the following passage in their constitution:

> Slavery in New Mexico is naturally impracticable, and can never, in reality, exist here; wherever it has existed it has proved a curse and a blight to the State upon which it has been inflicted,—a moral, social, and practical evil. The only manner in which this question now affects us is politically; and on the ground of this character, with its general evil tendencies, we have unanimously agreed to reject it—if forever.[21]

On the surface, this aligned politicos with Republicans. Yet when contextualized it illustrates their pragmatic nature. As Alvin Sunseri notes, "Hispanos were not so much antislavery as they were antiblack," but on this occasion the move to ban slavery was also anticompetition and anti-Texan, for it was designed to prevent white competitors from utilizing unpaid black labor to gain an economic advantage, specifically Texans.[22]

Nine years later the very same politicos passed the Slave Code Act of 1859, which protected blacks as property, and this infuriated Republicans. Here the politicos acted for their own economic interests rather than moral ones. In 1856 Miguel Otero was named New Mexico's representative to Congress. Otero was a politico from a large landholding family, and he proved central in this effort to pass a proslavery clause. Otero represented the business interests of the local patrónes in Washington DC and was a strong advocate of the transcontinental railroad. In Washington, Otero aligned himself with southerners, and in 1857 he married into a southern family. Robert Larson notes, "His marriage to Mary Josephine Blackwood, a Southern belle from Charleston, South Carolina, had brought him close to the Southern political leadership, and he was anxious to have his associates in New Mexico co-operate with the South."[23] Otero sought southern support to build a railroad through New Mexico, which had major economic implications for the merchant prospects of local patrónes.[24]

In 1859, Otero sent a letter to his allies in New Mexico that declared that the territorial legislature needed to pass a slave code to garner favor in Washington, but in reality the code was intended to secure southern support for the railroad. In another letter to his white American ally, the territorial secretary Alexander M. Jackson, Otero wrote, "You will perceive at once the advantage of such a law for our territory, and I expect you will take good care to procure its passage."[25] The editor of the *Watchman and State Journal* argued that southerners were pressuring New Mexicans by threatening to remove the military, but this is doubtful. The editor was more likely correct when he wrote that Otero was assured that slavery would not be introduced to the territory; the slave code was needed to protect the slave owners while they transported their slaves *through* New Mexico.[26] Otero and the other patrónes wanted the railroad to pass through New Mexico, and white southerners wanted their property protected on the way to California. Again, the Nuevomexicano patrónes made a business decision, but the radical Republicans in Washington DC condemned them on moral grounds. On January 29, 1861, Thaddeus Stevens railed against the Hispanos from the House floor:

> They (Southerners) offer to admit as a State about two hundred and fifty thousand square miles of volcanic desert, with less than a thousand white American-Saxon inhabitants, some forty or fifty thousand Indians, Mustees, and Mexicans, who do not ask for admission, and who have shown their capacity for self government by the infamous slave code which they have passed, which establishes the most cruel kind of black and white slavery.[27]

Stevens was correct to condemn the Slave Code of 1859; the politicos passed a cruel and morally reprehensible code, but for the opportunistic politicos and their families it was a pragmatic decision. They wanted a railroad, they needed political support in Washington DC, and the southerners offered a quid pro quo: support for the railroad in exchange for protection of slavery as they traveled through New Mexico. The alliance collapsed when the South seceded from the Union, and the politicos repealed the slave code because it put them in opposition to the Union. From her home in Valencia, New Mexico, Miguel Otero's wife voiced her support for the South, but Miguel Otero offered no opinion.[28] It was not in his interest to do so.

The patrónes' interests superseded both morality and white American party alliances. Hispanos could ally with a party for a single interest, like slavery, but disagree and stand against that party on the next issue. For the white Americans in New Mexico this was difficult to understand. The white Americans thought in terms of two parties and party agendas; in their world, when you endorsed one issue you endorsed the entire platform. In New Mexico, these white American politicians wrote of the intense party divisions they perceived, and it is true that white Americans were embittered with their political enemies. White American politicians, however, vastly overestimated the importance of both themselves and these divisions in New Mexico. The two-party system was a white American construct, and on the biggest issues Nuevomexicano patrónes refused to be bound by their party. The Nuevomexicanos continued to work together, in spite of the divisions among the white Americans in New Mexico. Their allegiance to white American parties was but a thin veneer.

The local patrónes had their own agenda, which had nothing to do with white party politics, and it can best be summed up in one simple phrase: no taxes, no Texas. The politicos refused to implement taxes because they believed that the United States should fund the local government. From their perspective, the local government was a tool to promote their interests and to provide them with economic security. For the local patrónes, economic security included repelling potential Apache, Comanche, and Navajo attacks and keeping the vecinos under heel. In addition, the local patrónes wanted to secure their territorial integrity, which meant repudiating the Texans, who suffered under the delusion that New Mexico was somehow part of Texas. Nuevomexicanos also wanted to keep Texans out of New Mexico, which local white American officials wanted as well.[29] The politicos composed and passed laws and regulations to facilitate their interests, but they were not about to pay for them.

For the politicos, once their bond with the vecinos was severed it was in their best interests to work with the white American courts to punish criminals, and to accomplish this they ultimately supported the colonial-style punishments laid out in the Kearny Code. In part, the local patrónes backed the code because the laws dealing with crime and punishment were drawn from the Mexican and American military legal traditions. They empowered the white American judges and juries to treat vecinos like colonized people, just as the old Spanish colonizers had done. As we have seen, many among the local patrónes preferred the corporal punishments of the Spanish period to the fines, exiles, public labor, forced labor in the mines, and service at the presidio that marked the Mexican period.[30] In 1850, the politicos made their position clear at their first meeting of the territorial legislature. Ralph Emerson Twitchell noted, "The people of New Mexico, as soon as power was given to them, adopted the code and laws prescribed by the military governor."[31]

In the 1850s, the politicos went further and passed laws that expanded on the crime and punishment section in the Kearny Code, and these additional laws illuminated the interests of the local patrónes. During the second session, the politicos passed laws that regulated gambling in the territory.[32] The politicos sought to fund their government with regulatory taxes, and they targeted gambling because it was a lucrative business. They taxed gaming in New Mexico, which they perceived was an alternative to property taxes. The politicos also realized that white American gambling was a problem in Santa Fe County. White American soldiers frequented gambling halls, where they drank, sought women of the night, and committed violent crimes when they failed. Thus the politicos and their white American allies regulated gaming in order to raise capital and curb violence.

They also established high fees for gambling licenses, which amounted to $600 for a six-month license.[33] The politicos also outlawed several games, including monte, faro, ten pins, dice, and roulette, and they assigned large fines to soldiers who broke that law.[34] The politicos established such high fees for licenses that the vecinos, who ran smaller gaming halls, were either pushed out of business or forced underground. Between March and June of 1851, eleven vecinos and two white Americans were arrested for illegal gaming, and their cumulative fines amounted to $275.[35] After June, there were only two more cases of illegal gaming in Santa Fe County; the politicos succeeded in boosting tax dollars and the vecino gambling halls were out of business.[36]

From 1852 to 1853, the politicos in the legislature again targeted white American settlers when they passed laws during the third session against vagrancy, carrying small arms into settlements, and running fandangos[37]; during the fifth session in 1855–1856, they added new crimes that included cursing in the plaza, slander in the church, cohabitation out of wedlock, enticing minors, and prostituting minors.[38] The politicos primarily targeted white American settlers with these laws as well. One law, "Against Persons Who Disturb Good

CHAPTER FIVE

Order," targeted people who appeared drunk "Within the plaza or streets (and), use, in a loud voice, scandalous or obscene language" and sentenced them to jail and a fine.[39] Additionally, the politicos passed a law that targeted white Christian ministers who slandered the Catholic Church:

> Whereas, various ministers of the gospel are frequently committing grave slanders against particular persons in temples and chapels, losing sight of charity and evangelical meekness, and profaning those sacred places, which are dedicated exclusively to the worship of the Supreme Being; therefore. . . . If in the future any minister of the gospel of any denomination whatever, or any other person, shall, by word or in any other manner, slander any other person or persons within any temple, upon conviction . . . (they will pay) any sum not exceeding fifty dollars, nor less than twenty-five dollars.[40]

The politicos knew that the Catholic churches were the only places that qualified as sacred under this definition, because only they could afford to use their chapels exclusively for worship.[41] Thus their law only protected the Catholic Church from slander. During the same session, the politicos also passed an act "Requiring and Authorizing Judges of Probate and Justices of the Peace to Punish Depraved Persons in Cases Herein Prescribed."[42] These included more white American crimes, such as cohabitation out of wedlock with Hispano females, enticing female Hispano minors, and prostituting female Hispano minors. More specifically, they targeted white American settlers who preyed on Hispano women and young girls. Section 2 concerned women and dictated that persons living out of wedlock needed to either marry or separate and pay a fine of $80; a second offense carried a one-year jail sentence.[43] Section 5 targeted white Americans who seduced, enticed, or carried away female minors from their families. "Such persons who shall so do, or shall have them in their possession for evil purposes" were fined between $80 and $100 and sentenced to between eight months and a year in jail.[44] Finally, section 6 targeted "Any father, or mother, or guardian, who shall surrender up in bad faith, any women under their charge," and they received the same punishment as those in violation of section 5.[45] The politicos passed these laws to block white American males from invading their daughters, which they perceived as enough of a problem by 1855 to warrant legislation.

The politicos authorized the probate judges to prosecute these "depraved persons," which was significant because probate judges in New Mexico were often Nuevomexicanos. By doing so, the politicos took a major step toward reclaiming at least some of the power from federally appointed white American judges. In 1853, the politicos confronted a new challenge: The U.S. government appointed new judges to the territorial courts in New Mexico.[46] Shortly afterward, the politicos composed a petition intended for the president of the United States. They protested the appointment of white American judges from outside the territory and asked the president to replace them with native New Mexicans:

> Petition of the Legislative Assembly of New Mexico Territory for the President of the United States[47]
>
> We representatives respectfully submit that the administration of justice in this territory is an extreme embarrassment, for the District Court Judges don't understand the language of the land. We lament this difficulty, which has arisen because the male and female litigants in the courts are natives of the Territory and understand only the Spanish language; the witnesses and jury don't speak other languages either.
>
> The judges are incapable of understanding the different sides of affairs from those testifying, and the jurors are incapable of understanding the instructions from the judges except through the medium of the interpreters, of which very few in the Territory can truly understand and interpret the traditional language anywhere near perfectly—due to its idiomatic particularities—and consequently much illegal evidence reaches the jury and so the judge is able to win out over the existing evidence and the jury, who are often ignorant of his instructions because of the stupidity and incompetence of the interpreters, and it is in this manner that the administration of justice is as embarrassing as it is imperfect.
>
> The judges themselves, named by the United States, are generally indifferent and when family or personal interests require their attention—and on many occasions when they are needed in court—they are absent from the territory for months at a time.
>
> We representatives respectfully petition that in the future the judges for this territory be men who know the language of this land and who can understand both the testimonies of the witnesses and the jurors. We respectfully and humbly request that you appoint from the residents of our Territory and secure the removal of the current judges from their duties.
>
> We representatives do not wish to condemn and provoke the judges of the territory and we especially don't have any motives against your Excellency, but we do not believe that the current system is in the best interests of the territory and the administration of justice. We would like all future appointed judges for this territory to be persons competent with the language of the territory.[48]

It appears this letter exists only in draft form, and it is not known whether it was completed and mailed to the president of the United States.[49] It is misplaced and free floating in the archives; at some point it was tucked between numerous bills that were passed during the 1853 legislative session. It is unlikely this letter was ever circulated. If it had been, it would have sparked quite a controversy among the judges.

The politicos introduced troubling problems that highlighted a real cultural gap. The new judges struggled with the language, their interpreters did not know the local dialect, and the judges and interpreters confused the jury with garbled instructions. The longtime American residents who filled the initial judgeships knew the language, but the American judges appointed by the federal government had difficulties with the local Spanish dialect in New Mexico, if they knew Spanish at all. The interpreters who accompanied these judges did speak Spanish, but were not familiar with the local dialect.[50] The politicos described the problems this caused. A judge could not communicate clearly without an interpreter, and the interpreter did not understand the local dialect. To make matters worse, their awkward messages to the jury caused great confusion.

The politicos accused the white American judges of trying to "win out over the existing evidence and the jury, who are often ignorant of his instructions because of the stupidity and incompetence of the interpreters."[51] In New Mexico the judge's guidance had a major bearing on the verdict because they established the parameters of what a jury could decide. The appointed judges wielded more power in the Santa Fe County courtroom because their case summaries confused the Spanish-speaking jurors. Hispano jurors took their duty seriously, and they must have assumed it was their duty to convict when there was doubt. The politicos were concerned by these problems, but they were likely far more bothered by the fact that the federal government appointed foreigners to judgeships in the territory. In response, they empowered the probate judges to prosecute "depraved persons." By 1858, they authorized probate courts to hear criminal court cases, except murder.[52] They decreed that the courts should be made up of the probate judge, plus two associate judges to be appointed by the governor, subject to the approval of the legislature.[53]

The decline in the Nuevomexicano population in Santa Fe County impacted larceny rates, but it did not change the patrónes approach to the punishment. The large number of Nuevomexicanos who left Santa Fe County between 1850 and 1860 coincided with a one-third decline in the total number of indictments issued against Nuevomexicanos from 1855 to 1860.[54] Still, the politicos increased the punishment for larceny in all forms. They decreed that burglars should receive an increased number of lashes, from thirty-nine to fifty, and increased jail sentences from two to five years.[55] They also rewrote the larceny laws and instituted thirty to sixty lashes for those convicted of stealing more than ten dollars in goods, along with a jail term of one to two years.[56] They dictated that those who committed petty larceny, meaning those who stole less than ten dollars in goods, should receive fifteen lashes for their actions, but no jail time.[57] Before the 1858 law, the white American judges and juries gave lashes to vecinos for all forms of larceny, and this was often illegal. In 1858, the politicos legalized their punishments instead of protesting what the white American judges had done. Ironically by the time the politicos fully endorsed lashes, the white judges were already moving away from corporal punishment and toward longer jail terms and larger fines.

The politicos dominated the New Mexican territorial legislature and continued to prosper in the territorial period, but for the vecinos the application of justice remained unequal. The politicos confirmed and redefined the Kearny Code, and they increased the punishments that vecinos faced for petty crimes. At the same time, they remained silent while white American judges and territorial juries meted out guilty verdicts and punishments along ethnic lines in the early years. During this time, they convicted vecinos at higher percentages than they did white immigrant settlers. These judges and white jurors passed lighter sentences against whites, while the vecinos and their peers received colonial-style punishments and extensive jail sentences. The local patrónes used their political power to defend their personal interests, but they turned a blind eye to the manner in which white American judges and territorial juries victimized the vecinos. For that, there would be long-term consequences.

WHITE FEDERAL JUDGES, TERRITORIAL JURIES, AND CONVICTION RATES

The federally appointed judges became dominant figures in the territory. But Nuevomexicano jurors assisted in doling out harsh punishments for vecinos. Since most jurors stemmed from the fringes of large landholding families, they carried their own prejudices into the courtroom. For Nuevomexicano jurors, class constituted a major factor in their prejudicial viewpoints, since most of them came from the upper to middle landholding classes. Nuevomexicano jurors loathed the pobres, whom they also viewed as *Indios barbaros*. When their prejudices combined with that of white American judges and territorial jurors, their motivations combined into a desire to keep vecinos under heel. Together they convicted vecino prisoners at rates similar to those that blacks faced in the courts and slave courts of the Deep South, where fear of rebellion was rampant.[58]

The first white judges were appointed by Kearny because they knew

Spanish and many were business partners with the local patrónes; these judges were convinced that the vecinos needed to be controlled through the territorial courts. During the Mexican period, the alcaldes used punishment to repair the damage a criminal did to society and to deter potential criminals from repeating their crimes.[59] White American judges, however, believed that the Chimayo Rebellion of 1837 and the Taos Campaign of 1847 were revolts that would have been prevented if the alcaldes had been harder on the vecinos, genízaros, and Puebloans. They blamed lax laws for vecino unrest in New Mexico, and they were determined to see vecino criminals brought to justice. As a result, the early territorial judges used their power and influence over the juries to ensure that the vecinos were convicted of their crimes.

The white American judges demonstrated their power when they gave instructions to the jury; they recounted crimes in a leading way and dictated the verdicts and punishments that jurors could hand down. From 1847 to 1853, they gave verbal instructions to the jury, but after 1853 they wrote out detailed instructions for the jury. By 1853 the early judges, like Joab Houghton, were replaced by the federally appointed judges in the district courts like Theodore Wheaton, J. J. Davenport, and the notorious Kirby Benedict.[60] The local patrónes opposed the overreach of centralist power and resented that the federal government appointed judges from outside the territory. As a way to reassert their authority over the courst, the politicos pushed through a law in the legislature that decreed the new white American judges must write down their instructions to the jury. They also suspected that the white American judges were purposefully misleading Hispano jurors in order to secure guilty verdicts. To again rein in the federally appointed judges, the politicos decreed, "The judges shall give their instructions to the jury in writing only, and such instructions thus given shall be filed with the papers in the case."[61]

After these laws passed in 1853, the federally appointed judges recorded their instructions to the jury, and many of these documents were preserved in the case files; they reveal the extent to which judges influenced jurors.[62] In 1856, a vecino named Eligio Gutierrez was accused of assaulting Monico Gonzales with a knife. According to Gonzalez, he stabbed Gutierrez in self-defense. Gutierrez maintained that Gonzalez stabbed him without provocation. Judge Wheaton believed Gonzalez and offered the jurors two options in this case: either guilty of assault with intent to kill or guilty of assault and battery, thereby excluding not guilty by reason of self-defense. Moreover, Judge Wheaton's opinion was revealed in his instructions to the jury for assault with intent to kill. He wrote that if the jury believed Gonzalez meant to kill they must find him guilty.[63] His instructions for assault and battery contended that if Eligio "used more violence in his defense than was necessary" they must find him guilty of assault and battery.[64] The jury ruled as Wheaton argued and they convicted Gonzalez of assault and battery.[65]

The patrónes also sought to more heavily influence jury selection. In 1846, the Kearny Code originally established property and citizenship qualifications for jurors, and in 1850s the politicos passed laws that secured property qualifications, and this was done to disempower the poorest vecinos. As a result, Nuevomexicano jurors mostly came from the families of the local patrónes, especially those who were primarily farmers and artisans. They were middling classes, kin to patrónes. They harbored the same prejudices against the vecinos, genízaros, and Puebloans as did the local patrónes, who kept servants and abused vecinos with little restraint. In 1857 the politicos passed a law that made the selection qualifications even more stringent. They decreed jurors must be landholders and heads of households to qualify for selection.[66] Over time, the local patrónes used jury appointments as a form of patronage to reward their kin; Nuevomexicanos often wanted to serve because jurors were paid for their service.[67]

From 1847 to 1860, Hispano jurors and grand jurors only judged Hispano defendants as a general rule, while white American jurors judged both Hispano and white American defendants. Hispano and white jurors showed no mercy to vecino prisoners but more sympathy for white criminals, who in fact proved to be a far rowdier lot. From 1847 to 1860, white American judges and the territorial juries convicted 74 percent of all Nuevomexicano defendants who went to trial in the Santa Fe District Court (figure 5.2).[68]

From 1847 to 1853, white American judges and territorial juries convicted three out of every four Hispano defendants; this ratio increased after 1855, during which four of every five vecino defendants were convicted in the Santa Fe County District Courts (figure 5.3).

White defendants fared better, at least early on. Only 58 percent of white Americans who entered the courtroom were found guilty of their crimes, while the jury declared the remaining 42 percent of white American perpetrators not guilty from 1846 to 1854.[69] That changed dramatically after 1855, and for at least the next six years 76 percent of whites that went to trial were found guilty, which was roughly equal to the overall vecino experience (figure 5.4). There were several reasons for this change: It was partially due to the efforts of the politicos, partially to the types of crimes whites were convicted of, and partially to the simple fact that whites in Santa Fe tired of the disorder immigrant whites brought.

■ Guilty, 74%
■ Not Guilty, 26%

Figure 5.2. Total vecino *known trial conviction by percent in Santa Fe County for all crime, by percentage 1846–1860. These numbers only include those who reached trial. In addition to the 206 guilty verdicts and the 62 not guilty verdicts, a total of 86 cases were dismissed. Many of the dismissed cases concerned landholding Nuevomexicanos caught up in various commerce violations.*

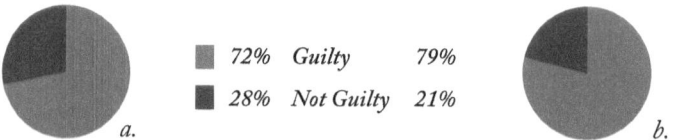

Figure 5.3a. Vecino *Trial conviction percentages for homicide, larceny, assault, and other crimes, 1846–1854.* Source: New Mexico State Records Center and Archives, "Records of the United States Territorial and New Mexico District Courts for Santa Fe County, 1846–1854," box 1–2.

Figure 5.3b. Vecino *Trial conviction percentages for homicide, larceny, assault, and other crimes, 1855–1860.* Source: New Mexico State Records Center and Archives, "Records of the United States Territorial and New Mexico District Courts for Santa Fe County 1855–1860," box 2–3.

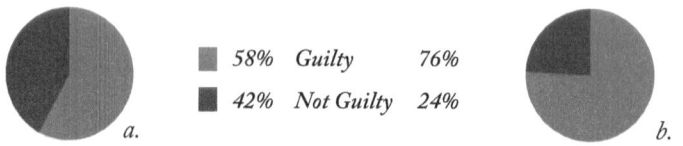

Figure 5.4a. White trial conviction percentages for homicide, larceny, assault, and other crimes, by period, 1846–1854. Source: New Mexico State Records Center and Archives, "Records of the United States Territorial and New Mexico District Courts for Santa Fe County, 1846–1854," box 1–2.

Figure 5.4b. White trial conviction percentages for homicide, larceny, assault, and other crimes, 1855–1860. Source: New Mexico State Records Center and Archives, "Records of the United States Territorial and New Mexico District Courts for Santa Fe County 1855–1860," box 2–3.

Santa Fe County, Vecino Only (1846–1860)	77%
Chatham County, Georgia, Black Only (1866–1879)	77%
Greene County, Georgia, Black Only (1866–1870)	80%
South Carolina, Black Only (1851–1860)	68%
Virginia Slave Trials (1786–1865)	57%
St. Andrews Slave Courts, Jamaica (1746–1882)	76%

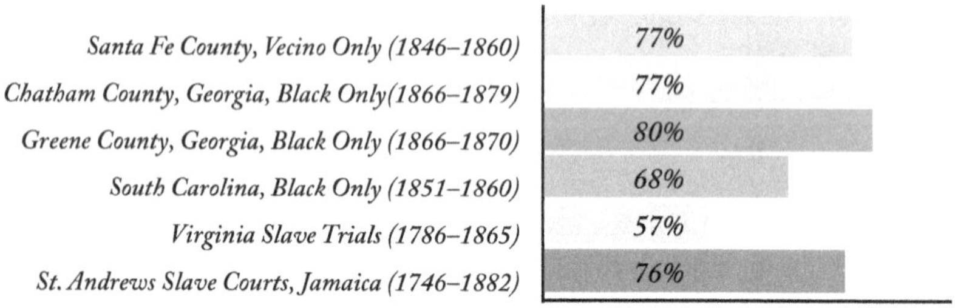

Figure 5.5. Conviction by percentage, vecinos *in Santa Fe County vs. Chatham County, GA (black Only), Greene County, GA (black Only), South Carolina (black Only), and the slave courts in Virginia and Colonial Jamaica.* Source: New Mexico State Records Center and Archives, "Records of the United States Territorial and New Mexico District Courts for Santa Fe County 1847–1951," Box 1–3, 1847–1853; Ayers, Vengeance and Justice, 323; Schwarz, Twice Condemned, 50; Hindus, "Black Justice Under white Law," 590; Paton, "Crimes and the Bodies of Slaves in Eighteenth-Century Jamaica," 932–33.

Even still, white American settlers fared better than their vecino counterparts in every statistical category.[70]

To truly understand the inherent racial biases in conviction rates in Santa Fe County, we must look more closely at types of crimes for which vecinos were prosecuted by the courts. For vecinos the crimes of larceny, assault, and homicide most often resulted in convictions, while the courts dismissed most commerce violations. The conviction percentage among vecinos increased from 72 percent from 1846 to 1854 to 86 percent from 1855 to 1860. Yet the removal of commerce violations among whites dropped the conviction percentage from 58 percent to 51 percent for that same period.

The vecino conviction rates in Santa Fe County were deplorable. To put them in context, statistically they were comparable to the rates at which blacks were convicted in both regular courts and the slave courts in the Deep South and the slave courts in colonial Jamaica (figure 5.5). The white American judges and territorial jurors convicted the vecinos in 77 percent of the cases they heard from 1846 to 1860, which was higher than the Virginia Slave Trials (1786–1865, 57 percent) and the South Carolina conviction rates for slaves and free blacks (1851–1860, 68 percent).[71]

Everyday white men enjoyed a privilege normally reserved for patrónes, and this was in part based on their knowledge of the insufficiencies built into the American legal system. The story of John Gorman, the poor marksman later stabbed in the heart by Preston Beck Jr., illustrates how Americans were able to use their knowledge of the legal system to their advantage. First, in October of 1854, Gorman became so angry with a carpenter from the Quartermaster's Department named William Goodfellow that he pulled out his gun and started shooting in Goodfellow's general direction. Gorman fired five shots at Goodfellow, and all of them missed their mark.[72] In December of 1854, John Gorman became angry once more, and this time he opened fire at Jose Gaveldon. As before, he shot and missed, but this time he chased down his target, tackled him to the ground, and pistol-whipped Gaveldon.[73] In March of 1855, the two cases were heard only three days apart, and John Gorman was found guilty of assault and fined heavily for his actions. He must have been a much better shoemaker than shot, because he had enough resources to appeal his convictions. He had the cases transferred to Taos and Rio Arriba Counties respectively, where, thanks to the inability of witnesses to travel, both convictions were ultimately overturned for lack of evidence.[74]

But it wasn't just that Americans understood how to manipulate the legal system. When Americans failed to manipulate the legal system, the white American judges and jurors in Santa Fe County were there to assist them. First, white judges provided white territorial jurors with different instructions than they did Nuevomexicano jurors; white jurors had more leeway to acquit white defendants

CHAPTER FIVE

than Nuevomexicano jurors were given to acquit vecino defendants. In addition, these white judges sometimes behaved in ways that favored white American defendants. This was the case when Judge Grafton Baker tried Oliver P. Anderson for murder in a Santa Fe County Court.[75] Not much is known about Anderson except that he had recently arrived in New Mexico. According to the court records, Anderson attacked a young vecino boy named Joseph Garcia without provocation. One witness account noted that Anderson beat Garcia senseless, then pulled out his revolver and shot him in the head.[76] The attack outraged the vecino community, and the local authorities arrested Anderson and placed him in the Santa Fe County jail.

Anderson hired an attorney, who petitioned to have the case dismissed on September 4, 1851, but Judge Grafton Baker rejected his appeal and ordered Anderson remanded until trial.[77] It is possible that Baker rejected the motion to dismiss in the name of justice, but it is more likely that Baker feared that the vecinos may riot if Anderson was somehow acquitted so soon after his crime. On March 17, 1852, Anderson's trial finally commenced. A full six months had passed since he was charged, which was time enough for the vecinos to cool down. The judges usually tried cases within six weeks of an arrest, which made this an unusually long delay in the Santa Fe County court system. Anderson favored the delay as he and his attorney calculated that Judge Grafton Baker was more likely to convict him than other judges. Anderson and his unnamed attorney filed extensions until Judge Baker was away.

And that's when Judge Horace Mower stepped in to help. He first selected twenty-four white American settlers to serve on a new jury, then he reopened the investigation, and he oversaw a jury that ultimately acquitted Anderson of all charges. Judge Mower formed this jury and ordered it to determine the validity of the charges against Oliver P. Anderson, which a grand jury had already done.[78] Judge Mower's move was an act of unprecedented judicial discretion in Santa Fe County; outside of cases that involved soldiers, there is no evidence of a jury being formed in this manner within the criminal dockets, the court docket books, or the district court records. On March 22, 1852, the all-white American jury returned the verdict of not guilty. Anderson was released from custody and exonerated of all charges.[79] Anderson executed Joseph Garcia and the evidence was overwhelming, but Judge Mower and the white American jurors allowed him to go unpunished because Garcia was a vecino.[80]

The Santa Fe County courts functioned as tool of racial domination—especially in the early years—one that placed the state in opposition to local vecinos. Ironically, white Americans continued to cry foul: In December of 1853 the editor of the *Santa Fe Weekly Gazette* wrote, "We hear much complaint, and we fear there is some truth in it, that even after a man is arrested and bound over for a crime there is no certainty of his being convicted, if guilty."[81] It is difficult to imagine higher conviction rates, especially among vecinos, but white settlers incessantly complained. No matter how high conviction rates went, white settlers continued to call for more convictions and harsher punishments.

Racialized Punishment

The white territorial judges and juries sentenced vecinos to corporal punishment during the early period to accentuate the differences between themselves as colonizers and the vecinos as the colonized, and they kept the practice of lashing and servitude alive through 1860.[82] They used lashes, indentured servitude, jail, and fines as their four basic punishments in Santa Fe County, but they sentenced prisoners along ethnic lines. Even as poor and violent whites became a larger problem after 1854, corporal punishment and servitude remained the burden of the vecino. The patrónes ignored both the plight of the vecinos and the lenient punishments against white Americans perpetrators. In doing so, the patrónes endorsed a white privilege that they too ultimately benefited from.[83]

The New Mexico territorial courts used indentured servitude as a punishment against poor vecinos and Indigenous peoples from 1846 to 1860. This was in keeping with the Spanish and English traditions. They had used indentured servitude as a form of punishment, and subsequently Mexico and the United States followed suit. In Spanish New Mexico, fledgling patrónes pressed vecinos, genízaros, and Puebloans into debt peonage.[84] By the nineteenth century, the Nuevomexicano patrónes were actively conducting slave raids against the Navajo, Ute, and Apache nations. The patrónes took captives to punish nomadic nations such as the Navajo. Between 1804 and 1845, the patrónes captured 317 Navajo women and children, all of whom were pressed into servitude.[85] During the Mexican period, the alcaldes sentenced vecinos to public labor, forced labor in the mines, and service at the presidio.[86] The local patrónes benefited fiscally from these sentences, and to further bolster their numbers they secured their peons by pushing them hopelessly into debt.

The Kearny Code legalized servitude as a punishment in New Mexico, and during the next thirteen years politicos passed numerous laws that reinforced both sentencing prisoners to servitude and the right to keep servants indebted.[87] This also happened in other parts of the United States and in the borderlands.[88] For example, the California legislature legalized selling the people of the California Nations into indentured servitude, and as a result the California judges opened markets in several counties that resembled the old slave markets of the South. This Vagrancy Act of California was in reality a labor grab that applied exclusively to Indigenous Californians. The act stated that any unemployed Native peoples "found loitering and strolling about, or frequenting public places

CHAPTER FIVE

where liquors are sold, begging, or leading an immoral or profligate course of life shall be liable to be arrested on the complaint of any resident citizen."[89] They permitted the justice of the peace to hire out prisoners to the highest bidder for up to four months. In San Diego, the justice of the peace leased out California peoples—who were jailed or convicted—to labor gangs that worked on the ranches.[90] Miroslava Chávez-García writes, "In Los Angeles, where they had a similar city ordinance, California Indians were sold to the highest bidder, akin to a slave market, according to Horace Bell, a contemporary resident."[91]

In New Mexico, the groundwork for servitude as punishment was laid in the Kearny Code. Article III, section 14 stated, "If such convict shall not discharge and satisfy the fine and costs it shall be lawful for the sheriff of the county in which the convict may be imprisoned, if the circuit judge of that county shall so direct, to bind such convict to labor for any term, not exceeding five years, to any person who will pay such fine and costs."[92] From 1847 to 1860, territorial judges handed down this punishment and the local patrónes utilized the opportunity at least eight times to increase their number of household servants. Proportionally, however, the state sold a minuscule number of servants at auction, especially when compared to the servants already indebted to the local patrónes. In 1850, the local patrónes held 242 servants in bondage in Santa Fe County: 28 were born in Mexico, 20 were Indigenous, and the other 194 were New Mexican–born vecinos.[93] Still, the patrónes in New Mexico camouflaged indentured servitude as an alternative to prison. Like in California, the sheriff took his prisoners to a central location and auctioned them off to the highest bidder.[94]

Althought American judges and territorial juries rarely sentenced vecinos to indentured servitude, when they did it was a public event. As noted in chapter 2, the career criminal Jose Sena was among those to be punished with indentured servitude. U.S. Marshal John Jones sold him at a public auction, and in his notes to Judge Grafton Baker he wrote, "I certify that I have this 14th day of Feb 1853, sold the written the named Jose Sena at public auction, after having given due notice."[95] Only two weeks before, Grafton Baker—who had replaced the recently deceased judge Rufus Beach—ordered Jose Sena sold into indentured servitude. Judge Baker found Sena guilty of larceny and threatening two Hispano women; as punishment he was fined $1,000. Baker fined him an amount no vecino could satisfy, and by doing so he pushed Sena into servitude. Marshal Jones noted that he told Sena he would be sold to pay the fee, but that Sena—like so many vecinos before and after him—said nothing. Marshal Jones stood next to Jose Sena in front of the Governors Palace, where the local patrónes gathered to bid for the convicted vecino. Jones wrote, "He objected not ... and Miguel E. Pino did bid him off for the Sum of $61—and that was the highest and best bid offered for him the said Jose Sena."[96] Marshal Jones sold Jose Sena into servitude for the term of what was meant to be five years, that quickly and that cheaply. Baker's punishment meant that Sena was legally bound to Miguel E. Pino, one of the most prominent patrónes in modern memory, a statesman, and eventual Civil War colonel in the First Regiment, New Mexican Volunteers, of the Union Army.[97]

Over the next fourteen months, Marshall John Jones sold three more vecinos into servitude as punishment, all of them for the crime of larceny.[98] That same month Luis Ribera was arrested for stealing a carpenter's square from the French baker Louis Dorrance. Ribera was found guilty and sentenced to a fine of $25. Ribera was a poor vecino, so he was unable to pay; as a result, Judge Grafton Baker pushed Ribera into servitude. On Valentine's Day of 1853—from the porch of the Palace of the Governors—Marshal John Jones sold Luis Ribera to a five-year term indenture for only $25. The highest bidder, ironically, was the very Marshal John Jones who auctioned Ribera off.[99]

A similar fate awaited Guadalupe the Navajo—a servant to the fifty-seven-year-old wealthy patrón and farmer Antonio Maria Ortiz—who was convicted of stealing a large sum of currency from his estate. According the court records, Guadalupe stole a massive amount of gold and silver coins, which were valued at a total of $826. Guadalupe was charged for the actual crime, but she was not alone. Antonio Aragon stood accused of being her coconspirator, but the jury found insufficient proof of his involvement.[100] She was also sold on the plaza, though it's not clear to whom. The only thing that is certain is that she was no longer a servant in the house of Antonio Maria Ortiz in 1860.[101] During that same period a fourteen-year-old boy named Tomas Ceballes also ran afoul of the law. Ceballes committed the pettiest of offenses when he falsely obtained two pieces of wool valued at $3.50 from Miliana Castillo. The young boy was fined $50 for his crime, which of course he could not pay and was thus pressed into servitude.[102]

Not more than a month later, Dolores Sena and Jesus Rael plotted to steal a firearm from a twenty-year-old blacksmith named Ramon Baca. Their plan was simple enough: Dolores Sena approached Ramon Baca in a grocery store and asked to see his gun, and when Baca handed him the firearm, Sena passed it to the much faster Jesus Rael, who ran away with it. A second crime was committed when Ramon Baca confronted Dolores Sena, who responded by grabbing a butcher's knife from the store. Sena grazed Baca, who wisely took flight and escaped with only a minor injury.[103] Both Sena and Rael were charged with robbery, but only Dolores Sena was found guilty, and he was sentenced to thirty-nine lashes for his crime. This was made worse by his conviction for assault, for which he was sentenced to a five-dollar fine. Alas, even that was more than the vecino could pay, so after he was lashed in the plaza he was then sold into indentured servitude for the term of five years.[104]

Servitude continued to be a form of punishment after 1855. While a

CHAPTER FIVE

minimum of five vecinos were pressed into servitude during the early period, at least an additional three met the same fate after 1855. On January 5, 1857, Manuel Baca (alias "Bacacitos") stole a pistol from a twenty-seven-year-old cook named John W. Gerhart, who had recently arrived from Europe.[105] Bacacitos was convicted and received a fine for his actions, but it was the charge for receiving goods under false pretenses that got him into big trouble. Like young Tomas Ceballes four years before, Manuel Baca was convicted of his offense and sentenced a fine that he could not satisfy. Unable to come up with five dollars, the vecino took the now familiar walk to the plaza and was sold off to the highest bidder.[106] The same fate awaited Mauricio Silva, who was convicted of both larceny and obtaining money under false pretenses in the amount of $84; he was left in jail for three months, but since he could not pay his court fees—how could he do so while confined?—he was also sold into servitude.[107]

The use of servitude as punishment severely altered and likely ruined the lives of those sold in the plaza, but the white American judges and territorial juries sentenced many more vecinos to lashes, and they started doing so early on. When the Americans arrived in 1846, they reinstituted corporal punishment against robbers, burglars, and those who committed perjury in New Mexico; in total, twenty-three vecinos were sentenced to lashes in Santa Fe County between 1847 and 1853.[108] With corporal punishment codified, white American judges stretched the law so that the jurors were free to sentence vecinos to lashes for all manners of crime. They even prescribed lashes for petty larceny, even though the law was reserved for individuals convicted of burglary and stealing livestock.[109] As previously noted, the Kearny Code called for thirty-nine lashes, but in 1857 the politicos increased that number to fifty and raised jail sentences from two years to five.[110] They also legalized lashes for petty larceny and grand larceny, and decreed fifteen lashes for petty larceny and thirty to sixty lashes, and one to two years in jail, for those convicted of stealing more than ten dollars in goods.[111] Indeed, the patrónes supported the use of state violence against everyday Nuevomexicanos.[112]

The white American judges and territorial juries sentenced both vecinos and white Americans to jail as well, but vecinos were more likely to be jailed and served longer sentences than Americans on average. From 1846 to 1860 one out of every two vecinos—and three out of every five vecinos who committed larceny, assault, or homicide—were sentenced to jail, while among whites one out of every three defendants were sent to jail between 1846 and 1860 regardless of the crimes they committed.[113] Additionally, American judges and territorial jurors sentenced vecinos to an average of thirteen months in jail, while white Americans from 1847 to 1854 were sentenced to six months on average. In 1850, they sentenced Charles Porter to two months in jail when he stole two gold rings ($20), clothes ($25), and a black silk ($25); that same year, they sentenced

Jose Francoso to one year for stealing a watch and some tools and Jose Benito Gonzales to three years for stealing a fork and two pounds of candles.[114]

The politicos in the territorial legislature were also responsible for the high percentage of fines that both Nuevomexicanos and white settlers paid; in addition to the gambling licenses they required, the politicos also mandated licenses for alcohol distributors.[115] The politicos likely targeted gambling and selling alcohol because they were popular and profitable businesses. The probate judge Tomás Ortíz alone enforced the law, and it is known that he collected $750.50 in fines and added it to the local treasury.[116] Here it is prudent to recall that Judge Tomás Ortíz was entangled with Diego Archuleta as coconspirators, who plotted together against Governor Bent during the Taos Campaign, but he was a member of the powerful Ortíz clan and through his connections he was exonerated and reinstalled to his judgeship.[117] Judge Ortíz prosecuted both Nuevomexicanos and white Americans settlers with equal vigor. He collected $375 from Nuevomexicanos and $375.50 from white Americans in Santa Fe County.[118] The Nuevomexicano defendants were often small-time merchants and owners of poor gambling houses, while the white American defendants included many longtime residents and prominent businessmen. In 1851, Judge Ortíz had James Josiah Webb arrested for illegal gaming, found him guilty, and fined him $50. In 1852, Judge Ortíz ordered William Messervy and James Josiah Webb arrested for failure to obtain a license. Judge Ortíz did not care that Messervy and Webb were among the powerful white Americans in New Mexico.[119] He issued fines against everyone, including fourteen Nuevomexicanos and thirteen white Americans.

White American judges and juries also passed down fines for assault and battery, perjury, and larceny, and they did so along ethnic lines. They fined sixty-six Hispanos but only thirteen white Americans.[120] In 1848, a white American judge convicted the vecino Antonio Tafoya of assault and battery against Maria Candalera Gonzalez and fined him $50. Alcalde J. O. Smith demonstrated his power in the courtroom. He found Tafoya guilty and fined him $50 even though there was a hung jury.[121] In 1851, Alcalde Joseph Johnston and his jury ruled that the vecino Gregorio Ortega assaulted Jose Ochoa and fined him $20; they ruled that Ortega was guilty of stoning Ochoa in a fight that escalated into assault and battery.[122] In 1851, Alcalde Johnston also convicted Aniceito Abeytia of perjury and fined him $50; specifically, they found him guilty of "willful and corrupt misleading and swearing at the Sheriff."[123] This was the only case of perjury that resulted in a fine in the early period. The white judges issued fines for larceny in three cases, two of which featured female defendants. In 1849, Alcalde Smith ruled that Maria Pacheco stole six yards of material, and she escaped with a fine of $10; in 1850, Alcalde Johnston convicted Martin Delores of stealing a pair of earrings and a breast pin, and she was fined $25.[124] That same year Felipe Basques was convicted of stealing one pair of pants, which normally resulted in lashes; instead he was fined $25. For the white American judges this sentence was an anomaly, so it is possible that they were merciful to Basques because he was very young; it's also possible that this sentence was used to entrap him in servitude, but the case file is incomplete.

The territorial authorities were determined to secure their holdings—a cause the local patrónes were most supportive of—and they punished vecino larceny more harshly than any other crime. When larceny is removed from the punishment data, corporal punishments, incarcerations, and servitude all but vanish: 97 percent of those sentenced to crimes other than larceny received either fines or jail (figure 5.6a and 5.6b). The white judges and territorial jurors gave lashes to crimes outside of larceny in only two cases. In 1849, they convicted an unknown vecino for perjury and he received sixty-five lashes in the plaza.[125] That same year, they convicted Santos Sandoval of forgery and sentenced him to twenty-five lashes and one month in jail; he presented a forged document to the U.S. Army for the release of shoes, which meant he committed a form of larceny.[126]

No case illustrates white immunity to the lash better than New Mexico vs. Louis Dorrance. In August of 1859, Dorrance was indicted for stealing a calf from Francisco Ortis y Salazar, who testified that he witnessed the deed. Ortis y Salazar's account was confirmed by his brother-in-law, Jesus Sena y Baca, who also testified that he witnessed Dorrance taking the calf.[127] Louis Dorrance, a forty-six-year-old French-born baker and longtime resident of Santa Fe, retained Spruce M. Baird as his attorney. Baird shrewdly filed for continuances numerous times, on the grounds that Dorrance was unable to coordinate the scheduled court dates with the schedules of his two witnesses. Baird assured Judge Kirby Benedict that the two witnesses, Justin Lippie and Antonio Phiffner, could definitively prove his client's innocence. The problem was that both Lippie and Phiffner were only available to testify in certain hours of the morning. If the hour was too early, Lippie and Phiffner would still be too hung over to testify, whereas if the hour was too late in the morning, Lippie and Phiffner would be far too drunk to testify.[128] It was quite the conundrum, one that led to numerous delays.

By March, a full seven months after Louis Dorrance was charged, Judge Benedict grew tired of Baird's charade, and on March 8, 1860, the trial commenced. The jury that day was a mix of American settlers and Nuevomexicano landholders—something that would have been unthinkable a few years before—and both they and the judge were certain the defendant was guilty.[129] Indeed, Louis Dorrance was found guilty of stealing a calf and sentenced to thirty lashes, which was the minimum prescribed by the territorial legislature.[130]

Baird immediately drew up an appeal to Gov. Abraham Rencher and had it signed by numerous prominent members of the white community in Santa Fe. In it, Baird claimed that the trial had been unfair because Francisco Ortis y Salazar was on the grand jury, and because the only witness besides Ortis y Salazar was his brother-in-law. He also claimed that Ortis y Salazar was a "known criminal," though it should be noted that Ortis y Salazar was never indicted for a crime.[131] Baird next argued that the trial was unfair because both of Dorrance's witnesses—whom he assured the governor would have proven his client's innocence—were now missing and could not be found. Baird assured the governor—and this is a new one—that although the calf was found at his residence, the witnesses did not see Dorrance possessing the calf, and even if they had it would not matter because Dorrance in fact purchased the calf late that night without knowing that it was stolen. Baird concluded by pleading that Governor Rencher have mercy on Louis Dorrance, "on account of his age and his past good character."[132]

In response, Governor Rencher inscribed this passage on the appeal:

> In this case I have great consideration for the age and past good conduct and character of Louis Dorrance. That he was not better prepared for his trial, or more successfully defended, was more his own fault than that of the court or jury. The purchase of the calf from an unknown person, at an unseemly hour, did not constitute the crime of larceny, but it was certainly improper, and unexplained by proper testimony, would justly create strong suspicions. I therefore consent to pardon Louis Dorrance, but upon the condition that he pay to Francisco Ortis y Salazar fifteen dollars for his calf, which it is admitted Louis Dorrance purchased of another person and converted to his own use.[133]

Gov. Abraham Rencher pardoned due to sentiment rather than sound reason. The petition to pardon was poorly argued and might be best described as Baird desperately arguing everything that came to mind, but in truth it was not at all convincing. Even Governor Rencher seemed to recognize what the judge and jury clearly found: that Louis Dorrance was guilty of this crime. Perhaps the most ironic argument, and one that Rencher embraced for the purposes of his pardon, was that because Dorrance was forty-six he was simply too old to be lashed. That

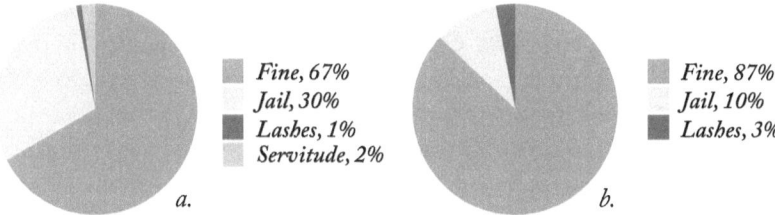

Figure 5.6a. Vecino *punishments (without larceny), 1846–1860.*

Figure 5.6b. White *punishments (without larceny), 1846–1860.*

information would have been useful for the seventy-year-old Pedro Sandoval, who it should be recalled was whipped twenty times and left bleeding and bound to the flag pole in the plaza as an example to other Nuevomexicanos.[134] But Rencher based his pardon on sentimentality, and he left unsaid what was likely the true reason for the pardon: it would be untoward to lash a white person in Santa Fe County. This was the one case where a territorial judge enforced the law on a white settler, but the governor pardoned him.[135]

Meanwhile, white American judges and territorial jurors punished criminals in a manner that affected the lives of everyday vecinos; they victimized vecinos for petty crimes but allowed white Americans to escape severe punishment. Individuals like Jose Seguro—who stole one pair of pantaloons and a blanket from the powerful Albino Chacón—were arrested, convicted, and then marched out to the plaza. Sheriff E. L. Vaughn wrote, "Seguro is to receive six months jail and no less than thirty-nine lashes with cowhide to his bare back."[136] Thus Seguro and his accomplice—the aforementioned and ever-unlucky Jose Francoso—each received this vicious punishment in a plaza full of onlookers.[137] Meanwhile, Charles Porter was found guilty of stealing two gold rings ($20), clothes ($25), and a roll of black silk ($25). The recently arrived Porter was sentenced to two months in the Santa Fe County jail and nothing more.[138]

Capital Punishment and the Lynch Mob

From 1847 to 1853, the death penalty in Santa Fe County was statistically insignificant for two reasons. First, Nuevomexicano jurors did not believe in capital punishment. Second, white American judges and jurors hesitated to hang fellow white Americans, at least those who were not from Texas. Among Nuevomexicanos there was no tradition of capital punishment; from 1827 to 1846, not a single person was condemned to capital punishment in all of New Mexico. The white Americans called for capital punishment in newspapers and in the letters they wrote to their friends, families, and political allies, but until 1860 white American judges and jurors refused to sentence white Americans to capital punishment. The judges and jurors heard at least fifteen cases in the Santa Fe County District Court in which the perpetrator was clearly guilty of first-degree murder, but they only sentenced one of them to capital punishment. In fact, white Americans lynched as many accused murderers as they legally put to death in Santa Fe County; they lynched the Texan who they thought committed homicide in Santa Fe County, which was the exact number they legally hanged. The whites in Santa Fe County proved very much to be all talk. They refused to sentence defendants who committed first-degree murder to capital punishment, yet they continued to complain that murderers were going unpunished in Santa Fe County.[139]

From 1827 to 1846, Nuevomexicano alcaldes heard nineteen homicide cases and did not execute a single person. The alcaldes, however, discussed capital punishment in two cases. As previously noted, in 1834, Manuel Gallego murdered his wife María Espíritu Santo Ruival. According to the records, Gallego confessed to his crime and explained to the alcalde that he strangled his wife with a sinewy cord because she always argued with him.[140] The prosecution maintained that Gallego was a scoundrel by nature and that he murdered his wife without remorse.[141] The defense agreed that Gallego was guilty and that he should be punished. At the same time, the defensor maintained that capital punishment should not be invoked because Gallego was clearly remorseful; he noted that Gallego stayed with the body of his dead wife all night, which proved his remorse. Interestingly, María's brother Antonio Ruival came forward and argued that Gallego should be forgiven for his transgression, but María's mother believed that Gallego should be banished from New Mexico. Neither thought he should die for his crime.

The prosecution and the defense were at an impasse and alcalde Juan Madrid decided to seek outside help, so he forwarded the case to a legal advisor in Chihuahua. Alcalde Madrid waited one year, but there was no response from Chihuahua. Alcalde Juan Gallego y Martínez succeeded Alcalde Madrid and decided to resend the case to Chihuahua; later, he followed up with another letter in which he asked for closure on the case.[142] If Alcalde Martínez received a response, that record is now lost, but we know that Gallego was not executed for his crime. The alcaldes in the Mexican period were obsessed with protocol, and it is extremely unlikely that Gallego would be executed without a massive paper trail.[143] The alcaldes held Gallego in jail, which was probably the only punishment he ever received; there is a good chance Gallego was sitting in jail when the Chimayó Rebellion broke out. Similarly, in 1846 the alcaldes heard the case against Juan Antonio Chaves and although that verdict did not survive either, it is certain that Chaves did not receive capital punishment.

The New Mexican alcaldes could have sentenced Gallego and Chaves to death, but capital punishment was not part of Nuevomexicano culture. In the end, they left both Gallego and Chaves in jail, which was a terrible punishment in and of itself. The alcaldes avoided carrying out capital punishment within the community, even when the laws called for it. The alcaldes likely had Chaves in jail when Kearny marched into Santa Fe. After the Americans came, Nuevomexicano jurors displayed the same aversion to capital punishment that the alcaldes had before them. The Nuevomexicano jurors heard at least one case that called for capital punishment in the early period—the double murder committed by Ignacio Tapia—but they ruled that he was insane and sent him home with his family.[144] They heard at least seven more after 1855, but they never passed a sentence for capital punishment.

CHAPTER FIVE

White American judges and territorial jurors also rarely sentenced convicted persons to capital punishment in New Mexico, and as a result the capital punishment rates in New Mexico were significantly lower than in California. In the years before the railroad, capital punishment in New Mexico was statistically nonexistent. But Howard W. Allen and Jerome M. Clubb, who situated New Mexico into the mountain regions, noted that from 1846 to 1855 the capital punishment rate was .68 per 100,000 (9), which was one-sixth that of the Pacific region at 4.19 per 100,000 (73).[145] In California, capital punishment occurred along ethnic lines: from 1850 to 1900, white American judges only executed white Americans when they killed other white Americans, but they commuted sentences to life in prison for white Americans who killed nonwhites.[146]

In New Mexico, that rarely happened because—as is clear by now—white American judges and jurors rarely convicted other white Americans; white privilege was central to their actions and since they didn't convict, sentencing was rendered moot. From 1847 to 1877, the white American judges and territorial jurors sentenced a total of four men to death in all of New Mexico, of which two were Hispano and two were white Americans; they sentenced two white Americans to death in Santa Fe County, one Nuevomexicano in Taos, and one Nuevomexicano in San Miguel.[147] From 1847 to 1853, Hispano jurors heard one clear case of first-degree murder among the Hispano population, and they found that defendant insane. During the same period, white jurors heard six white American clear-cut homicide cases, all of which ended with execution-style gunshots to the head, yet they convicted only one defendant, and he was sentenced to capital punishment.[148]

From our full period of study, 1846 to 1860, only two white defendants were sentenced to capital punishment; they were Andrew Jackson Simms and the aforementioned Thaddeus Rogers. In 1849, Simms became the first person legally hanged in Santa Fe County.[149] Little is known about Simms, but it is likely that he was yet another recently arrived white American settler, who may not have even been within the boundaries of Santa Fe County when he committed his murder.[150] Simms was an extranjero—perhaps even from Texas—and the white American judge and all-white American jury quickly convicted him and sentenced him to death.[151] According to the indictment, Simms assaulted a man named Jackson Johnson and gave him a thorough beating. Afterward, Simms pulled out his pistol, placed it to Johnson's right temple, and fired a shot that instantly killed the victim.[152] Simms's homicide was similar to the murders of both Maria Antonia Lenoia and the young vecino named Joseph Garcia; the sole difference is that Simms's victim was white.[153] Judge Theodore Wheaton's instructions to Sheriff C. H. Merritt dictated that Simms be "Hanged by the neck till he be Dead! Dead! Dead!" but did not dictate Simms be hanged immediately.[154]

Uniquely, the sentence called for a six-month period of incarceration, after which Simms was legally hanged.[155] If the judge was waiting for a pardon, it never came.

Throughout the nineteenth century and beyond, white Americans have been central advocates of capital punishment; in the territory they contended it was a sentence that should be used more frequently in New Mexico, but despite their complaints it rarely was, and this was true in other parts of the United States. Even white American judges and jurors in places like Chatham County, Georgia, rarely sentenced convicted persons to capital punishment during Reconstruction: only 3 percent of blacks and 2 percent of whites were sentenced to death by hanging.[156] In Santa Fe County, white American judges and jurors sentenced eleven men to death by hanging, but only three of these occurred before 1895.[157]

These American judges and juries failed to condemn perpetrators in obvious homicide cases, such as the case of Henry Wheeler.[158] In late October of 1849, the recently arrived Missourian merchant Henry Wheeler shot and murdered Capt. Alexander Papin of the United States Army.[159] Missourians, like Texans, also had a well-deserved reputation for both being uncouth and resorting to violence. In this case Wheeler was an ambitious white man from Missouri who tried to forge relationships with local powers as he sought land and wealth. A few weeks earlier, Wheeler and Papin, both new to Santa Fe, had a disagreement that turned to blows. Afterward, Wheeler posted slanderous proclamations about Papin—who was also from Missouri—on bulletin boards and buildings around town.[160] When Captain Papin saw the proclamation on the side of the "Makers, Austin, and Dalton" store, he tore it down and entered the store, cursing Wheeler as a rascal. Wheeler also entered the store and Papin confronted him, demanding to know whether it was his signature on the document. Wheeler said that it was, and Papin raised a yardstick and struck Wheeler, who in turn drew his pistol and shot Captain Papin in his right temple.[161]

The all-white American jury was presented with a solid case that included several eyewitnesses, but even still Henry Wheeler escaped capital punishment. The jury's verdict is missing, but Henry Wheeler was listed as a prisoner in the Santa Fe County jail several months after his case was heard.[162] The turnaround for trials in Santa Fe County was fast. In the previously discussed case against Andrew Jackson Simms, the court convicted him quickly, though the judge stalled his execution.[163] Wheeler was still sitting in the Santa Fe County jail in 1850 even though he was clearly guilty. It is possible that the jury decided that Wheeler killed in self-defense, because he was not sentenced to death.[164]

Even still, Americans blamed Hispano jurors for not convicting criminals, despite the high conviction rates and harsh punishments that vecinos endured. When Gillion Scallion and his friend Stephenson came to Santa Fe County they entered a society that was predisposed to violence. Scallion severely wounded

CHAPTER FIVE

Judge Hugh N. Smith, and the lynch mob hanged him for it. There was no public remorse in the wake of Scallion's death, even after everyone learned that Judge Smith survived. Instead, an eyewitness—and a rather insincere person—recounted the lynching for his readers in the *Santa Fe Weekly Gazette*:

> Another reason that had its effect in producing the closing scene in this sad affair, is the fact that many murders have been committed in this Territory within the last two or three years, some of them of the most unprovoked character, and the guilty parties have invariably escaped without punishment; some from the insufficiency of the jails, and others from being acquitted by jurors when the proof was most positive against them, and others from being permitted to escape without even an arrest.[165]

The white Americans' negative perception of justice in New Mexico was both inaccurate and ironic. They voiced their displeasure with the entire legal system, though it is likely that the white American settlers were dissatisfied because homicides went unpunished. Of the vecinos whose homicide cases were heard by the Santa Fe District Court, 57 percent (three of every five) were found guilty from 1846 to 1860 (figure 5.7a).[166] By contrast, only 21 percent (one of every five) of whites that committed homicide and ended up in court were found guilty (figure 5.7b). With control of both the judges and juries, white settlers had only themselves to blame when white perpetrators left the courtroom as free men.

American settlers committed twenty-five homicides in Santa Fe County during the territorial period, but only two guilty verdicts were returned, a third likely returned, and a fourth was pronounced against Gillion Scallion by a rogue jury. Additionally, there were at least eleven cases where defendents were either found not guilty or their cases were dismissed; if the remaining eleven ever saw the inside of the courtroom, there no records to reveal their fates.[167] The American judges and jurors were statistically responsible for all the not guilty verdicts in homicide cases, but those who criticized in the surviving written records blamed Nuevomexicanos. As a result of their skewed perceptions, the white American settlers responded with mob violence on at least three occasions.

Between 1846 and 1860, white American lynch mobs killed three men in Santa Fe County. Two were transients from Texas and the third a vecino who awaited his trail for murder. Through the *Santa Fe Weekly Gazette*, we learn that white American settlers lynched another Texan in Santa Fe County before Gillion Scallion. On June 14, 1851, a lone Texan entered the Exchange Hotel, took a glass of brandy, and commenced firing his pistol at random.[168] The unknown Texan discharged his weapon four times before he was tackled and shackled, but he had already shot one person in the arm and an unknown lawyer in the abdomen. The sheriff asked the Texan for his motive, and the Texan said that "a friend of his from Texas was killed in Santa Fe, and all the inhabitants of the place were cut-throats, robbers, and murderers."[169] The lynch mob arrived at the jail later that night, took the Texan, and hung him in back of the Exchange Hotel.

In 1853, as previously noted, a white American lynch mob captured Gillion Scallion, who had shot Judge Smith. This time the lynch mob behaved more formally: They called together a lynch court, appointed a judge, and feigned an objective trial against Scallion. The mob took pains to follow legal protocol, which meant there were white American officials and well-known white American citizens present. For them, the illusion of justice was important. They were mindful of how the affair would be perceived; one of them wrote about it in the *Santa Fe Weekly Gazette*.[170] Their actions were illegal but they could not be prevented. The public officials—who were likely in the Exchange Hotel and perhaps a little drunk themselves—wasted no time and facilitated a guilty verdict. Although local officials went through the motions to ensure that justice was done, the mob acted quickly to ensure the insolent Texan was punished; it is likely there were also Nuevomexicanos there, and they were no doubt pleased to see a Texan swing from a tree.[171]

It is significant that the first two lynch mobs targeted Texans. Their actions demonstrated that lynch mob violence in New Mexico was part of a larger dispute between Texans and the white American settlers in New Mexico. During the Mexican period, Texans represented a direct threat to Nuevomexicano and white American sovereignty; during the American period, Texans continued to threaten to annex parts of New Mexico, including Santa Fe County. The white American settlers perceived crime by Texans as an attack on their community. To them, Texans were outsiders and illegitimate strangers who wronged the community. They responded with community violence against the Texans. For them, lynch mob violence was a political statement in Santa Fe County.

From 1847 to 1923, there were only two other lynchings in Santa Fe County, Matias Ribera was lynched in 1857 and another person was lynched in 1880.[172] In greater New Mexico, white American lynch mobs committed 151 illegal lynchings between 1847 and 1923. Comparatively, the residents of Santa Fe County were

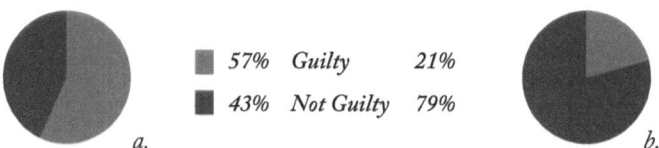

Figure 5.7a. Known homicide verdicts, 1846–1860, vecino.

Figure 5.7b. Known homicide verdicts, 1846–1860, white.

not prone to mob justice. They were, however, prone to lynching Texans. The white American settlers feared that the Texans meant to invade and rob them of their chance for success, which was something vecinos also fretted over. It seemed that everyone in New Mexico supported lynching Texans as part of an interstate rivalry, even if Hispanos did not actively participate.[173] Like those in the military—and whites more broadly—the white Americans who lynched the two Texans never faced charges, even though everyone in town knew precisely who they were.

The Americans in Santa Fe County resented the Texans because they were arrogant, violent, and disrespectful foreigners who came to Santa Fe to make a quick dollar; they never saw the irony that they too were arrogant, violent, and disrespectful foreigners who invaded Santa Fe to make their fortunes. The white American judges and jurors issued lashes and servitude along racial lines and allowed many white murderers to go free, even when they slayed Nuevomexicano women and children. Still, these Americans were outraged when Ignacio Tapia was found not guilty for the July 4, 1853, attack on white American settlers at the Exchange Hotel.[174] From the bizarre perspective of the white American, they were always the victims.

What they really wanted was more sentences like the one Joab Houghton bellowed at Don Antonio Maria Trujillo in March of 1847. Trujillo was one of many prominent Hispanos involved in the plot that claimed the life of Gov. Charles Bent at Taos. The white American judges allowed the other local patrónes who planned the rebellion to go free, but they charged Trujillo with treason. The evidence consisted of letters Trujillo had written that called for Nuevomexicanos to rise up against the Americans and "Shake off this yoke of a foreign government."[175] Trujillo had written patriotic letters that he hoped would inspire Mexican pride, but instead he was convicted of treason. Trujillo was seventy-five years old when Judge Houghton presented the following verdict:

> Your age and grey hairs have excited the sympathy of both the court and jury. Yet ... It would appear that old age has not bought you wisdom, nor purity, nor honesty of heart; while holding out the hand of friendship to those whom circumstances have brought to rule over you, you have nourished bitterness and hatred in your soul. For such foul crimes an enlightened and liberal jury ... find you guilty of treason ... sentence ... you be taken thence to the place of execution and there be hanged by the neck till you are dead! dead! dead! And may the almighty God have mercy on your soul."[176]

Donaciano Vigil petitioned Washington DC on behalf of Trujillo, and he made the case that treason could not be committed because New Mexico was not yet part of the United States.[177] Trujillo was pardoned. After all, Trujillo was still a local patrón, and Nuevomexicanos of means were never hanged. At least fifteen other conspirators were hanged for treason in trials stemming from the Taos Campign of 1847. All of them were either Pueblos or vecinos.[178]

Conclusion

New Mexico resembled a colonized society in some ways and a racist southern society in others. The presence of the local patrónes in places like Santa Fe County differentiated the territory from other parts of the United States. The patrónes were complex historical actors who simultaneously resisted and adapted to US political and cultural infringement, especially in the legal system. The patrónes focused on profits. They passed laws that demonstrated their power and furthered their agendas, but by and large they left white American judges and territorial jurors to their work. White American settlers, for their part, bemoaned the failed justice system and called for capital punishment. Yet they refused to convict their fellow white Americans. Their failure to punish murderers fueled their misconceptions of lawlessness: from 1847 to 1860, they convicted only three white perpetrators out of the twenty-five whites they indicted for homicide in Santa Fe County. Of the three they convicted, two were sentenced to capital punishment.[179]

The inequitable state of the New Mexican legal system is evident in the case of Thaddeus Rogers. Rogers faced a mixed jury that included local patrónes, so clearly his antics caught everyone's attention. After an extensive trial and appeals process, Thaddeus Rogers was finally to be held accountable for his incredibly violent behavior on September 14, 1860. Yet even in that moment—when a cold-blooded murderer stood ready to feed white hunger for executions—his white privilege showed. That privilege became clear in the days leading up to and immediately after his execution. The *Gazette* provides insight into what was happening within the white community: The *Gazette* ran a column on September 15, 1859, romanticizing both the life and execution of Rogers. The *Gazette* reported, "During his confinement in jail, after the sentence of death was passed upon him, he insisted that he committed the deed in self-defense and that his conviction was brought about by wrongful testifying, and to this he adhered up to the hour of his death."[180] The *Gazette* then venerated Rogers, writing, "In the trying scenes of yesterday he is said to have exhibited an extraordinary degree of calm."[181] There was no mention of either Marcelino Valdez, or Euligio Gonzalez, or Marcelino Savalas, the three men who Rogers had shot in the head. Instead, they waxed poetic:

> At the gallows he calmly gave directions as the mode of procedure; bade his acquaintances farewell, warning them against the intemperate use of intoxicating liquors; joined by Reverend S. Gorman,

who administered his religious consolation in his dying moments, in prayer; requested Sheriff Baca to fasten his hands behind his (back), furnishing his own pocket handkerchief for the purpose; said he had lived like a man and was not now afraid to die.

At 12 o'clock precisely, the wagon moved, the table upon which he stood went over, and the spirit departed to another and it is hoped, a better world.[182]

It was the conclusion of the column, however, that was the most egregious affront to Rogers's victims and their families, for the despite insuperable evidence that Thaddeus M. Rogers was guilty, the *Gazette* concluded by stoking the fire of reasonable doubt. After celebrating the good order and decorum of the crowd, which in truth had gathered to enjoy the spectacle of an execution, the *Gazette* closed, "Thus ended the life of a fellow creature, in regard to the merits of whose punishment there exists in the minds of the public a variety of opinions."[183] Like many in the white community in Santa Fe County, Rogers was privileged in life, and so too was he privileged in death.

The inequality was not lost on everyday vecinos. Seventy years later—and in the rarest of historical moments in Nuevo Mexico—a vecino named Isidoro Miranda spoke for his people as he stood at the gallows awaiting his execution. During and after sentencing, so many vecinos stood silent when asked by their colonizers if they had anything to say about the heinous punishments that were to befall them. At last, Isidoro Miranda addressed a crowd of bustling spectators that anxiously awaited the spectacle of his death: "In New Mexico there is no justice for the poor man. He is led like a helpless lamb through the courts and to his punishment. This is an injustice you are doing now."[184] It seems nothing had changed.

EPILOGUE

ADDRESS OF THE LEGISLATIVE ASSEMBLY OF NEW MEXICO.

MANIFESTO OF

The Council and House of Representatives to the Inhabitants of the Territory of New Mexico.

FELLOW CITIZENS:

... The enemy is Texas and the Texans.... They threaten you with ruin and vengeance.... They come to subsist upon our property and industry.... We must not forget that they are our ancient enemies. Twenty years ago they came with intents like they now come. Then they were overcome, and the integrity of our soil vindicated. In 1849, they strove to set up their power over our people, and sent their agents among our people, to carry out their schemes, but our people stood firm, and the General Government silenced Texas pretension.

Now is the day to feel the tinglings of our ancient, and unconquerable Castillian blood, that our ancestors brought to this land. The fire-sparks are deathless in every drop.- Now is the day for the flame, that shall conquer and consume. The remains of our intrepid and glorious ancestors, slept in no grave, that did not entomb a hero. Their pride and honor could endure no invader ...

Facundo Pino, President of the Council
J. M. Gallegos, Speaker of the House
[T] N.M. Jan. 29, 1862[1]

In 1862, the Nuevomexicanos faced a familiar adversary, and when the Texans returned to New Mexico under the banner of the Confederate flag the Nuevomexicano patrónes gathered their men and volunteered to fight for the Union. They were threatened by the Confederate army, which was made up of Gen. Henry H. Sibley and a force of nearly three thousand Texans. General Sibley believed the New Mexicans would welcome their arrival and issued a proclamation that encouraged the military patrónes to "drop at once the arms which degrade you into tools of tyrants, renounce their service, and array yourselves under the colors of justice and freedom!"[2] Among Union commanders there was concern that the Nuevomexicanos would waver in their commitment to the Union, but their fears—and the Confederate's optimism—demonstrated how little the whites

EPILOGUE

understood Nuevomexicanos.³ The local patrónes were determined to repel the Texans; according to Gov. Henry Connelly thirty-five hundred Nuevomexicanos volunteered for service.⁴ Governor Connelly claimed there was not a disloyal Hispano in the territory and that the Nuevomexicanos would never consent to be ruled by Texans.⁵ He exaggerated, but was not far from the truth.

The Hispano soldiers and volunteers who served in the Union army were a who's who among the local patrónes, and when they were properly supported, they conducted themselves well. Among them were Cols. Miguel E. Pino, Nicolas Pino, and José Guadalupe Gallegos; Lt. Cols. José Francisco Chávez, Manuel Chaves, Diego Archuleta, and Francisco Perea; and Capts. Rafael Chacón, Román Baca, and Rafael Ortiz y Chávez. Their family members rounded out the leadership and their ranks were filled with the remains of their vecino allies and servants. Among the patrónes, Captain Chacón—who we recall was beaten by Armijo as a child—was joined by his cousins, the Velarde brothers; Lt. Col. Manuel Chaves served with his brother Román Baca and his cousin, Lt. Col. José Francisco Chávez; and both the Pino brothers, Miguel E. Pino and Nicolas Pino, assumed leadership roles in the defense of New Mexico.⁶ The local patrónes were pragmatic in their service: they charged when their numbers were superior and fled to fight another day when they were outnumbered. The white commanders for the Union accused the Nuevomexicanos of cowardice when things went awry, but these charges proved unfounded. When the commanders failed at the Battle of Valverde, they blamed the Nuevomexicanos, but in truth the Hispanos fought bravely and the Union army was only defeated because of an inept field leadership.⁷

The local patrónes were not the pawns of the Union, and those who volunteered did so on their own terms. Rafael Chacón embodied the New Mexican patrónes that served in the Union army. In 1861, Captain Chacón was stationed at Fort Union and under his charge was a bilingual first lieutenant named A. P. Damours. According to Chacón, Damours continuously insulted the Nuevomexicanos while at the dinner table, and he soon tired of the act. Chacón was infuriated when his cousins told him that Damours was also speaking against his authority behind his back. He noted that when Damours began to assail the Mexican people at dinner that next evening, he warned him, "Until now I have suffered and allowed you to talk of my race, but from now and henceforth I will not allow you to return to denigrating them in my presence."⁸ Chacón gave Damours another warning, and when Damours started again Chacón grabbed a board that was leaned up against the wall and struck him so violently that the board splintered. Rafael Chacón grabbed another and gave chase through the camp, and the white officers looked on in shock as he wielded his board and smacked Damours at every opportunity.⁹

Later that year, Rafael Chacón and the Union forces stopped for the night at Algodones; again, Chacón's patrón nature manifested in front of the Americans. Chacón explained that some of the vecinos started drinking and became drunk. He noted that the American officers retired to their tents, in fear of a rebellion. "I took out my sword and began to hit the drunken soldiers with blows with the flat of it. My cousins, the Velardes, and the rest of my soldiers . . . put themselves on alert . . . but everything calmed down."[10] Chacón noted that from that point forward the American officers treated him with the utmost respect. In both instances Rafael Chacón behaved as Manuel Armijo and Manuel Chaves would have—he used violence and the threat of violence to intimidate his adversaries—and in the process he demonstrated that his caudillo ways were well-suited for military command.

The local patrónes would never have surrendered their autonomy to the Texans; if they and the Union failed to defeat the Confederates in battle, a revolt among the people surely would have followed. The Nuevomexicanos were already falling into the familiar pattern of passive resistance that marked the Chimayo Rebellion and the Taos Campaign. In 1862, Col. Nicolas Pino of the Second Regiment, New Mexico Militia, prepared to engage the Confederate forces near Albuquerque. Colonel Pino, like Manuel Armijo in 1846, parlayed with the Confederate commander and postured for battle, but like Armijo he was severely outnumbered and surrendered to save the town from bloodshed.[11] Although the Nueomexicano militias surrendered there and elsewhere, the patrónes and vecinos continued to withhold supplies and harass the Confederates. In October of 1861, Confederate Lieutenant Colonel Baylor wrote that the "Mexican population are decidedly Northern in sentiment, and avail themselves of the first opportunity to rob us or join the enemy."[12] Later, a Confederate committee of officers from the campaign wrote to the Confederate War Department:

> It had been erroneously supposed also that the citizens of New Mexico would greet us as benefactors and flock to our standard upon our approach. On the contrary, however, we found that there was not a friend to our cause in the territory, with a very few honorable exceptions. Everything needed for the consumption of our command had been destroyed by the enemy or concealed by the citizens. The troops of the command were sent out some twenty miles from Albuquerque to a bleak, sterile cannon in the mountains, where the most part remained.[13]

The Hispanos did not have the strength to repel the Texans without full Union support, which they did not have at Albuquerque, so they adhered to the dictum "Time and patience, patience and time." On April 1, 1862, the Confederates also marched into Santa Fe unopposed. They discovered that "there were no supplies at Santa Fe—that everything fit for consumption had been destroyed by

EPILOGUE

the enemy or concealed by the citizens upon our approach."[14] Now threatened, the local patrónes and the vecinos worked once more in concert to prevent the Confederates from foraging, and this left them solely dependent on their supply trains. Near Santa Fe, the Union defeated the Confederates at the Battle of Glorieta Pass, but the real defeat came when the Union destroyed the Confederate supply trains. It was Manuel Chaves, the local patrón who years before had defied Bishop Jean Baptiste Lamy, who guided the unit of Colorado volunteers that destroyed the Confederate supplies.[15] His actions eliminated the Confederate supply trains and forced the Texans to withdraw.

In this study I have sought to illuminate how everyday Nuevomexicanos experienced the process of territorialization in New Mexico. My hope is that my reliance on quantitative methods will ultimately contribute to how we look at the borderlands. Data matter. They reveal trends and anomalies that we as humans might otherwise not perceive. In this book, the data allowed me to shift away from a dependence on writings left by white chroniclers, officers, and politicians. Instead, I let the data guide this narrative. In terms of the wealthy Nuevomexicano landholders, the data reveal three trends: first, that they dominated the economy in Santa Fe County; second, that wealth was increasingly concentrated in select families and that the local patrónes benefited from the process of territorialization; and third, that the Nuevomexicanos dominated the legislature and exercised tremendous influence as politicos through their legislative actions.

The data show that the powerful New Mexican patrónes-turned-politicos were not victims, but rather the victimizers who pushed the vecinos from their lands. They were the descendants of Mexican patrónes, prominent political leaders, wealthy merchants, and regional military icons in New Mexico. The New Mexican families that bore the Chaves, Archuleta, Armijo, Ortiz, Otero, Pino, and Vigil surnames have been labeled *ricos* or elites, but they were also capitalists and caudillos.[16] Individuals like Donaciano Vigil and Diego Archuleta ingrained themselves into the political machine.[17] They refused taxes and stood against Texas. Merchants like Manuel Otero amassed massive fortunes through trade.[18] Military figures like Manuel Chaves and Rafael Chacón gained acclaim for their prowess in arms.[19] By 1862, the local patrónes were entrenched into New Mexican society at all levels. It was no surprise that when the Hispano legislature called for war against the Texans, the local patrónes organized and funded units and pressed their vecinos into service.

Although some patrónes resisted, such as Don Albino Chacón, most were pragmatic in the way they viewed the American invasion.[20] They regarded the Americans as potential trading partners who could augment their holdings. At the same time, white authorities viewed the local patrónes as necessary allies. They feared rebellion and they needed the local patrónes to be pacified so they could keep the vecinos at bay. By recognizing the partnership between the local patrónes and the white settlers, we move away from the narrative of Nuevomexicano victimization and toward one of vecino oppression. In this top-down society, the Hispano bastion remained secure.

This was the backdrop for everyday vecinos, and through both crime and census data, the world of the vecino comes into focus. The data also reveal the challenges faced by vecinos and how they endured the process of territorialization. After 1846, the local patrónes and the white colonizers victimized the vecinos and pushed the vecinos deeper into poverty. During the Mexican period, the vecinos were beaten by ill-tempered patrónes; after 1846, drunken and racist Anglos and ill-tempered patrónes beat them. The vecinos were accustomed to subsistence living, but they faced more abuses and worse poverty during the American territorial period. They lost access to public lands, became victims of white violence, and were lashed and sold into servitude by the white judges. They were condemned by juries made up of the extended family of their patrónes. They were convicted at rates that rivaled slave courts and were subjected to racialized punishments.

Many vecinos resisted by departing from Santa Fe County, but others stayed and endured.[21] Others still violently lashed out in their frustration. Economic security no doubt played a part in their decision. Vecinos were accustomed to a hard life and they depended on the local patrónes to represent them, which was ultimately to their detriment. In spite of everything they suffered, the vecinos remained passive in their resistance to the patrónes and in times of trouble they sided with those they knew best. They remained ever-suspicious of white motives because they were part of a parochial culture that viewed whites as outsiders. When the Texans came the vecinos stood with their patrónes, just as they had in 1836 and 1847, when the Mexicans and Americans invaded respectively. They denied the Texans supplies, spied, stole, and served in the militias. Though we do not know much beyond their names, the crimes they committed, and the punishments they endured, we know for certain that they proved more loyal to the local patrónes than the patrónes were to them.

As a whole, Nuevomexicanos maintained their power through 1862; they endured fifteen years of American colonization, and in times of trouble the vecinos banded together with the local patrónes and supported whatever steps they deemed necessary to preserve their order. The key for the patrónes remained their vast kinship networks, which were built on generations of business partnerships, marriages, and alliances. The local vecino population accepted that these networks were necessary until it no longer benefited them to do so. But for the New Mexican patrónes it was not enough to dominate the region and monopolize its sparse resources; the landholding class wanted to expand their opportunities and increase their wealth beyond the local economy.[22] They made pragmatic decisions that reflected their agendas. They befriended whites they seldom trusted, and even dealt with the Confederates to gain support for the railroad. For the local patrónes, it was always about business, and indeed they made great capitalists.[23]

EPILOGUE

In this project, I have sought to amplify the voices of everyday Nuevomexicanos and to dampen the white American voices that dominate many parts of our New Mexican scholarship. To hear Nuevomexicano voices, I first used numbers, and I have focused on the stories the data tell, rather than those narrative frameworks left by white settlers. I have sought to allow the numbers to define what was important in this narrative; only afterward did I draw connections between the numbers and the existing historiography. These data reveal that the Hispanos were more powerful than American chroniclers were either willing or able to perceive. They also reveal that the local patrónes were more culpable in the process of territorialization than Nuevomexicanos could have imagined. Through quantitative analysis, it became clear that the American chroniclers demonstrated a propensity to overblow American power and importance. Whether by ignorance or deceit, Americans with pens and presses seldom inked true words. For the most part, the patrónes' words were reflected in their deeds, dealings, laws, and late life memories. The stories of the vecinos—whose lives I have sought to foreground—survived in numbers and court cases alone.

APPENDIX

ADDRESS OF THE LEGISLATIVE ASSEMBLY OF NEW MEXICO.

MANIFESTO OF

The Council and House of Representatives to the Inhabitants of the Territory of New Mexico.

FELLOW CITIZENS:

Being at the close of the present session of your Legislative Assembly, and knowing from this Capital, the danger that threatens you, we have thought it well, to address you this

MANIFESTO

That the savage tribe of Indians should be your enemies, and plunder and murder, is not a thing new or unexpected. Such has been their habits, since our brave ancestors first possessed the Valley of the Rio Grande. But we have now another enemy less excusable than the barbarians, because he has grown in the midst of civilization, and enlightenment.

Without any fault or even offense of yours, your honor and property, your families and children are now in peril, by an enemy you have not injured, and whose invasion of the peace, security, and integrity of your soil and homes, you have not provoked.

The enemy is Texas and the Texans. With their hostile armed regiments, rebels to the Government of the United States, to whose protection and flag, our good faith, our duties, our confidence, interests and hopes turn and belong, they have come upon us, in violation of every principle of right, of justice and friendship. They threaten you with ruin and vengeance.- They strive to cover the iniquity of their marauding inroad, under the pretense, that they are under the authority of a new arrangement they call a Confederacy, but in truth is a rebel organization. But this pretense cannot deceive. They come to subsist upon our property and industry. They are without money or credit.

They come to destroy the Government under which we have lived, prospered, and been happy, and whose protection and care we need. They come to turn from their places, those in offices and authority among you, and to erect by military despotism alone, a power to oppress, to harass, and to crush you. You are free and unmolested in your religion, and they who are in violation of everything held sacred by our religion pretend to come to protect our religion already protected.

They pretend to relieve you from the expenses of Government, when they have no Government, that can bring into our Territory one dollar of money or credit.

To even eat for a day, they must take and plunder your cattle, your sheep, your wheat, corn and beans. They must plunder from our people, all their living. Could they succeed in their infamous and iniquitous attempts, they have no way of subsisting, but upon the substance of our people. A lawless body of men, banded together, hoping to kill or conquer us, would then be established among us, and our shame, injuries and suffering, we will not attempt to describe.

May a just and avenging God, not withdraw his arm from us, and leave our people to the insults, wrongs, dishonors, cruelties and oppression, that these Texan invaders will inflict, the moment they shall have the power! We must not forget that they are our ancient enemies. Twenty years ago they came with intents like they now come. Then they were overcome, and the integrity of our soil vindicated. In 1849, they strove to set up their power over our people, and sent their agents among our people, to carry out their schemes, but our people stood firm, and the General Government silenced Texas pretension.

Taking advantage of the troubles of the United States, they have now come hoping to succeed. Their long smothered vengeance against our Territory and people, they now seek to gratify.

We are a free people and our fathers abhorred negro slaves and slavery.- Our enemies found their rebellion upon pretenses touching the negro, negro slaves and slavery. They have set up their rebel organization upon those elements, and boast in the face of a Christian world, of their skill and wisdom in building upon such foundations.

We have condemned, and put slavery from among our laws. It is not congenial with our history, our feelings and interests. The marauders come to destroy our enactments, and force upon us by the cannon and rifle, slave institutions, against our will, protests and tastes.

We have no interests to promote, by being drawn within the destinies of the rebels and rebellion. All in that direction is danger and ruin. Listen not to their agents or emissaries, whether sent for mischief, of shall be found as traitors, living among us. In the midst of our wrongs and dangers, neutrality is without excuse. He that is not for us, is for the rebels and rebellion, and his sympathies favor the invaders.- The Texans may circulate their seditious papers and proclamations, by traitors to us among our people. Be not deceived by these pretensions. Put far from you, the language and sentiments of treason.- Touch not the poison. A serpent's fang is in it. Expose your loyalty to no suspicions. Look to the Government for reward for your services. Forfeit no claim by giving any favor to the enemy. Trust the justice and generosity of the Government. We are well assured, that we will be relieved from the assessment, placed upon us. The matter is brought to the attention of Congress. We have no doubt of liberality being extended to us. Could our enemies gain advantages and even battles, they could not long profit by their success. But success cannot crown so iniquitous, so unholy a cause. Success is impossible where there is not the treachery, the cowardice, weakness or folly, that condemned to undying infamy, the conduct, the affairs and surrender of Fort Fillmore. The time has fully come to wipe out that shame.- The army feels it, the people and the whole government feel it. The means of your complete success, in driving the enemy from our limits, are in our hands, large columns of well armed, well disciplined, and well prepared United States of American troops, are ready for the fight. These are commanded by officers, who should know the whole art of war. It is their education and profession. We would recoil from even the approach of the thought, that they have not the spirit, courage, conduct, skill and judgment, that they must lead the elements under their command, to victory and glory. May they and their troops, win fame that shall dazzle with its brightness, and honor that shall endure as the mountains. With out native soldier, and volunteers, our pride, our solicitude and sympathies, are too deep for expression. Side by side they are, with the veteran regular soldiers. They live at a time and are actors in the scenes when they may win wreaths of glory and renown, for themselves, their children, and their children's children's generations.- We know they have spirit and courage,- Let us trust to their love of country, justice and honor.

In one sense, the period and event upon us, is fortunate. The enemy is accustomed to sneer at our valor, and depreciate our force and capacity. Never did time, present to outraged men, a fairer field in which to save a country, punish an enemy, and make a name, that invaders shall ever dread, that now surrounds us. Now is the day to feel the tinglings of our ancient, and unconquerable Castillian blood, that our ancestors brought to this land. The fire-sparks are deathless in every drop.- Now is the day for the flame, that shall conquer and consume. The remains of our intrepid and glorious ancestors, slept in no grave, that did not entomb a hero. Their pride and honor could endure no invader. To violate the truth, and to commit cowardice, and their high souls scorned and abhorred.- Now is the day to show ourselves worthy of our ancestors. Now is the day in which we can make a bright name, that shall shine throughout the union and through time. Let not the veteran Regular surpass you in daring. Emulate the boldest daring he has the spirit to attempt. Let him who commands know no fear like defeat, no dishonor like flying from the face of the invader, and then the Indian marauders can be exterminated. If the invader gets a foothold further within the country, there are many modes of depriving him of any profit by his advance, more than the plunder he will gather. This people will never consent to his rule, his military, his slave despotism. The brave and just from neighboring sections will come to our aid. Already reinforcements of Regiments are organized to march to our assistance. They are coming with strong arms and hearts, and will join in driving off all enemies. The Texans will be driven from our soil. Let no one despair. Our troops are ready and eager to win their laurels and security.

APPENDIX

Let every Mexican in the Territory rally to the brave in the field; your fathers, sons and brothers. Let no discouragement or alarm disturb you. Your deliverance from enemies is at hand. Be true, be faithful, and be courageous; then your native land will be full of songs, in honor of your glorious deeds, and New Mexico blaze with fame, and her sons and daughters glow with pride when wheresoever they may travel hereafter through the Union or other lands, they shall find how great the benefit and distinction will be, in being known as sons and daughters of New Mexico.
—Fecundo Pino, President of the Council
—J. M. Gallegos, Speaker of the House [T] N.M. Jan. 29, 1862[1]

NOTES

Preface

1. This interaction occurred in 2008, while I was still gathering data for what became this project. The names of both individuals have been omitted to protect the identities and privacy of those involved.
2. Kate Parker Horigan, "Signs of the Vanished: Commemoration in Contexts of Precarity," *Journal of Folklore Research* 58, no. 3 (September–December 2021), 37–39.
3. Carmella Padilla, "Archi-Story: Building the National Hispanic Cultural Center," *El Palacio: Arts, History, & Culture of the Southwest* (Fall 2021), accessed December 5, 2021, https://www.elpalacio.org/2021/08/archi-story/.
4. Waldo Alarid, *Santa Fe Shadows Whisper: The History of the Moya and Alarid Families* (Pueblo, CO: El Escritorio Books, 1997), 68; Fray Angélico Chávez, *The Origins of New Mexico Families* (Santa Fe: Historical Society of New Mexico, 1954), 122–23.
5. "Behind the Bars," *St. John's Herald and Apache News*, August 27, 1814, accessed December 5, 2021, https://azmemory.azlibrary.gov/digital/collection/sn95060582/id/2497/.
6. This is meant as a quip, and something of a curtain call to the beloved Silva's Saloon, a community bar founded by Felix Silva, a one-time bootlegger who, by policy, welcomed anyone to his establishment, even when it was illegal to do so. Accessed December 5, 2021, https://www.huffpost.com/entry/silvas-saloon-new-mexico_b_4010413.
7. My mother is from the Saldivar and Flores families, who have been in Bexar since at least to the nineteenth century.
8. I share my lineage here because my fellow Nuevomexicanos will want to know precisely who I am and how I fit into the genealogical landscape of New Mexico.

Introduction

1. Marc Simmons, *The Little Lion of the Southwest: A Life of Manuel Antonio Chaves* (Chicago: Sage Books, Swallow Press, 1973), 117–20.
2. Simmons, *The Little Lion of the Southwest*, 120.
3. There is evidence that this incident did indeed occur. See Fray Angélico Chávez and Thomas E. Chávez, *Wake for a Fat Vicar: Father Juan Felipe Ortiz, Archbishop Lamy, and the New Mexican Catholic Church in the Middle of the Nineteenth Century* (Albuquerque: LPD Press, 2004), 151.
4. Simmons, *The Little Lion of the Southwest*, 117–120. Also see Nancie L. González, *The Spanish-Americans of New Mexico: A Heritage of Pride* (Albuquerque: University of New Mexico Press, 1969); Manuel G. Gonzales, *The Hispanic Elite of the Southwest* (El Paso: Texas Western Press, University of Texas at El Paso, 1989); Jacqueline Dorgan Meketa, *Legacy of Honor: The Life of Rafael Chacón, a Nineteenth Century New Mexican* (Albuquerque: University of New Mexico Press, 1986); Lynn I. Perrigo, *Hispanos: Historic Leaders in New Mexico* (Santa Fe: Sunstone Press, 1985); Maurillo E. Vigil, *Los Patrones: Profiles of Hispanic Leaders in New Mexican History* (Washington, DC: University Press of America, Inc., 1980).
5. For Fray Angélico Chávez's account of this event, see Chávez, *Wake for a Fat Vicar*, 151.
6. Susan Calafate Boyle, *Los Capitalistas: Hispano Merchants and the Santa Fe Trade* (Albuquerque: University of New Mexico Press, 1997).
7. By Hispanos I mean those with varying degrees of Hispanic and Indigenous (primarily Pueblo) ancestry who have been living in New Mexico for at least a generation, as opposed to the Indigenous peoples of New Mexico with exclusively Indigenous ancestry, or recently arrived

immigrants. I am aware that Nuevomexicanos was the term these people used to describe themselves, and I do utilize that term in this book as well. Whichever I use, my intention is to highlight the rich multiethnic relationships that made New Mexico different from other regions of the Latino West.
8. Under both Mexican and United States stewardship, a small stream of Europeans also immigrated to New Mexico. Their experiences will also be analyzed as part of this project.
9. My intent is to convey that the patrónes embraced a specific type of capitalism, not to suggest that they were not already capitalists. See Boyle, *Los Capitalistas*, chaps. 5–7.
10. Here I am indebted to Ross Frank, who helped bridge the gap between his vecino world and my world of patrónes and vecinos. It was through our discussions that the period of socioeconomic change became clear, and this helped me make sense of the quantitative divergence I saw in the data from this period. For more on vecinos in the eighteenth century, see Ross Frank, *From Settler to Citizen: New Mexican Economic Development and the Creation of Vecino Society, 1750–1820* (Berkeley: University of California Press, 2007), 1–7.
11. The term "vecino" is a legal one that was originally translated to mean "citizen." For quantitative purposes, I include those indebted in servitude in this definition, both because they make up a very small statistical proportion of Nuevomexicano society, and because outside the home they faced similar pressures as everyday vecinos.
12. 1850 Federal Census, Santa Fe County, New Mexico Territory; 1860 Federal Census, Santa Fe County, New Mexico Territory.
13. Gary LaFree, *Losing Legitimacy: Street Crime and the Decline of Social Institutions in America* (Boulder, CO: Westview Press, 1998), 6–7, 100–104.
14. LaFree, *Losing Legitimacy*, 100–104; Randolph Roth, *American Homicide* (Cambridge, MA: Belknap Press of Harvard University Press, 2009), 450–51.
15. Roth, *American Homicide*, 17–18.
16. Roth, *American Homicide*, 18.
17. Roth, *American Homicide*, xiii.
18. Roth, *American Homicide*, 2–10; Clare V. McKanna Jr., *Race and Homicide in Nineteenth-Century California* (Reno: University of Nevada Press, 2002), 103–5; Randolph Roth, "Homicide Rates in the 19th Century West," in Criminal Justice Research Center, Historical Violence Database, https://cjrc.osu.edu/research/interdisciplinary/hvd/homicide-rates-american-west.
19. Michael J. Alarid, "Beyond Banditry: The Significance of Everyday Larceny in New Mexican Social History, 1837–1865," *Western Historical Quarterly* 50, issue 2 (Summer 2019): 113–36.
20. Alarid, "Beyond Banditry," 113–15.
21. It is important to note that the local patrónes benefited when Spain enacted the Bourbon Reforms, which exempted Nuevomexicanos from taxes, and this tax cut was aimed to spur industry in New Mexico. Following independence from Spain, Mexico loosened trade regulations and New Mexicans branched out, trading sheep in the south and west and other goods to the north, east, and south. Ramón Gutiérrez, *When Jesus Came, the Corn Mothers Went Away: Marriage, Sexuality, and Power in New Mexico, 1500–1846* (Stanford, CA: Stanford University Press, 1991), 300–305. For the Bourbon Reforms in Mexico, see William B. Taylor, *Magistrates of the Sacred: Priests and Parishioners in Eighteenth-Century Mexico* (Stanford, CA: Stanford University Press, 1996), 13–14.
22. Frank, *From Settler to Citizen*, xiv.
23. Though there may be others, sociologist Thomas D. Hall is the only scholar I have located who has associated caudillismo with New Mexico. Hall links the New Mexican patrónes to caudillismo, but does so only thrice, more often using the term "elites" to describe large landholding New Mexicans. See Thomas D. Hall, *Social Change in the Southwest, 1350–1880* (Lawrence: University Press of Kansas, 1989), 184, 191, 213.
24. Andrés Reséndez, *Changing National Identities at the Frontier: Texas and New Mexico, 1800–1850* (Cambridge: Press Syndicate of the University of Cambridge, 2005), 244–45.

25. David J. Weber, *The Mexican Frontier, 1821–1846: The American Southwest Under Mexico* (Albuquerque: University of New Mexico Press, 1982), 267–69.
26. Boyle, *Los Capitalistas*, chaps. 5–7.
27. See Vigil, *Los Patrones*; Gonzales, *The Hispanic Elite of the Southwest*; Perrigo, *Hispanos*.
28. After his anointment in Santa Fe, Bishop Jean Baptiste Lamy set out on a campaign to remove what he viewed as the corruption within the church, but in actuality he targeted the Hispano padres. Of the various types of colonization that New Mexicans experienced, the ecclesiastical was the only one that displaced Hispano landholders from power. See Chávez, *Wake for a Fat Vicar*; Fray Angélico Chávez, *But Time and Chance: The Story of Padre Martinez of Taos, 1793–1867* (Santa Fe: Sunstone Press, 1981).
29. Weber, *The Mexican Frontier*, 103–111.
30. Brian DeLay, *War of a Thousand Deserts: Indian Raids and the U.S. Mexican War* (New Haven, CT: Yale University Press, 2008), 13–14.
31. John Lynch, *Caudillos in Spanish American, 1800–1850* (Oxford: Clarendon Press, 1992), 5.
32. For an overview of New Mexican trade with Native Americans, see Weber, *The Mexican Frontier*, 95–103.
33. The practice of trading firearms with Natives was forbidden by officials in Chihuahua, whose traders were being harassed by armed Natives. See Weber, *The Mexican Frontier*, 97.
34. Boyle, *Los Capitalistas*, 28–29.
35. Boyle, *Los Capitalistas*, 35–36.
36. The value of these guías, a document that authorized transportation of goods and that acted as both passports and packing lists, is presumably for 1843. See Boyle, *Los Capitalistas*, 43
37. John O. Baxter, *Los Carneradas: Sheep Trade in New Mexico, 1700–1860* (Albuquerque: University of New Mexico Press, 1987), 106–7.
38. Vigil, *Los Patrones*, 37.
39. Hugh M. Hamill, ed., *Caudillos* (Norman: University of Oklahoma Press, 1992), 35. Hugh Hamill writes, "The men whom caudillos call upon first will naturally be their relatives, because the ties of blood are the surest and the strongest."
40. Hall, *Social Change in the Southwest*, 217.
41. William A. Keleher, *Turmoil in New Mexico, 1846–1868* (Santa Fe: Rydal Press, 1952), 118 note 25.
42. Lynch, *Caudillos in Spanish America*, 3.
43. Rio Arriba meaning upriver, Rio Abajo meaning downriver. Janet Lecompte notes that though Santa Fe was technically part of the Rio Arriba, it was in reality neutral. See Janet Lecompte, *Rebellion in Rio Arriba, 1837* (Albuquerque: University of New Mexico Press, 1985), 4.
44. Lecompte, *Rebellion in Rio Arriba*, 4–5.
45. Weber, *The Mexican Frontier*, 210.
46. Boyle, *Los Capitalistas*, xii–xv.
47. New Mexico State Records Center and Archives, *Mexican Archives of New Mexico, 1821–1846* (Santa Fe: New Mexico State Records Center and Archives, 1969) (hereafter *MANM*).
48. Roth, *American Homicide*, 7.
49. *MANM*; New Mexico State Records Center and Archives, *Records of the United States Territorial and New Mexico District Courts for Santa Fe County 1847–1951*, box 1–3.
50. 1850 Federal Census, Santa Fe County, New Mexico Territory; 1860 Federal Census, Santa Fe County, New Mexico Territory.
51. For this data, see table 3.4 in chapter 3.
52. LaFree, *Losing Legitimacy*, 3.
53. Omar S. Valerio-Jiménez notes similar behavior in his study of the Rio Grande borderlands, where Tejanos acted pragmatically in their choices. See Omar S. Valerio-Jiménez, *River of Hope: Forging Identity and Nation in the Rio Grande Borderlands* (Durham, NC: Duke University Press, 2013), 1–3.

CHAPTER ONE

1. Martinez was the author of the 1844 "Exposition of the Affairs in New Mexico," which outlined a plan to pacify local Indigenous peoples nations by encouraging them to settle and adopt farming as a way of subsistence. Martínez criticized the practice of granting land to American businessmen, and New Mexican landholders were infuriated by this idea because they were partnered with the foreign merchants who were receiving these land grants. Martínez's plan was not revolutionary, but rather it was a continuation of the Spanish policy of pacification and acculturation. See Fray Angélico Chávez, *But Time and Chance: The Story of Padre Martinez of Taos, 1793–1867* (Santa Fe: Sunstone Press, 1981), 66; Ramón Gutiérrez, *When Jesus Came, the Corn Mothers Went Away: Marriage, Sexuality, and Power in New Mexico, 1500–1846* (Stanford, CA: Stanford University Press, 1991), 300–301.
2. Chávez, *But Time and Chance*, 67.
3. The Palacio Nacional is now the Palace of the Governors.
4. Vigil ignores the use of intimidation by Armijo, writing, "Governor Armijo nominated Diego Archuleta instead, and Archuleta was thus selected delegate." See Maurillo E. Vigil, *Los Patrónes: Profiles of Hispanic Leaders in New Mexican History* (Washington, DC: University Press of America, Inc., 1980), 9.
5. Vigil, *Los Patrónes*, 15.
6. Pedro Sanchez, *Memorias Sobre La Vida Del Presbitero Don Antonio Jose Martinez: Original Spanish text with English translation by Ray John de Aragon* (Santa Fe: The Lightning Tree—Jean Lyon Publishing, 1978), 58–59.
7. Marc Simmons, *The Little Lion of the Southwest: A Life of Manuel Antonio Chaves* (Chicago: Sage Books, Swallow Press, 1973), 117–20.
8. Chávez, *But Time and Chance*, 67–68.
9. The Bourbon Reforms were applied differently in New Mexico, especially in regard to taxes. For the Bourbon Reforms in Mexico, see William B. Taylor, *Magistrates of the Sacred: Priests and Parishioners in Eighteenth-Century Mexico* (Palo Alto, CA: Stanford University Press, 1996), 13–14. For the Bourbon Reforms in New Mexico, see Thomas D. Hall, *Social Change in the Southwest, 1350–1880* (Lawrence: University Press of Kansas, 1989), 134–66.
10. Hall, *Social Change in the Southwest*, 154.
11. Hall, *Social Change in the Southwest*, 151–55.
12. Hall, *Social Change in the Southwest*, 159.
13. Hall, *Social Change in the Southwest*, 155.
14. Susan Calafate Boyle, *Los Capitalistas: Hispano Merchants and the Santa Fe Trade* (Albuquerque: University of New Mexico Press, 1997), 9.
15. Boyle, *Los Capitalistas*, 9–10.
16. Andrés Reséndez, *Changing National Identities at the Frontier: Texas and New Mexico, 1800–1850* (Cambridge: Press Syndicate of the University of Cambridge, 2005), 257.
17. Jean Jaques Rousseau, *Political Writings* (Madison: University of Wisconsin Press, 1986), 3–7.
18. William H. Wroth, "Taos Rebellion: 1847," accessed June 7, 2012, http://www.newmexicohistory.org/filedetails.php?fileID=515. Moved and accessed December 11, 2021: https://www.facebook.com/FreeTaosPueblo/posts/taos-rebellion-1847by-william-h-wrothin-the-summer-of-1846-general-stephen-watts/497340946971220/. Wroth writes, "The rebellion has been depicted, both in accounts written at the time and even in more recent works, as the plotting of 'barbarous' Indians and the poorer class of uneducated Hispanos, but in fact resentment against the American invaders and the consequent loss of sovereignty was shared by all classes."
19. Gutiérrez, *When Jesus Came, the Corn Mothers Went Away*, 337.
20. Hall, *Social Change in the Southwest*, 151.
21. Hall, *Social Change in the Southwest*, 159.
22. Michael P. Costeloe, *The Central Republic in Mexico, 1835–1846: Hombres de Bien in the Age of Santa Anna* (New York: Cambridge University Press, 1993), 8.
23. Gutiérrez, *When Jesus Came, the Corn Mothers Went Away*, 323–24.
24. H. Bailey Carroll and J. Townsana Haggard, *Three New Mexico Chronicles: The Exposición of Don*

Pedro Bautista Pino 1812; the Ojeada of Lic. Antonio Barreiro 1832; and the Additions by Don José Augustín Escudero, 1849 (Albuquerque: The Quivira Society, 1942).
25. Hall, *Social Change in the Southwest*, 146.
26. Politically, Mexico as a whole was unstable: When Santa Anna left office in 1844, Gen. Valentin Canalizo advised the general-in-chief of the Army of the North, along with northern commandants, to adopt a policy of acculturation, domesticating Indigenous people. In short, patrónes needed to either negotiate for peace or defend themselves and their people at their own expense. See Ward Allen Minge, "Frontier Problems in New Mexico Preceding the Mexican War, 1840–1846" (PhD diss., University of New Mexico, 1965), 203.
27. Mexican federal officials seldom made good on pledges of economic aid, leaving Nuevomexicanos to fend for themselves. Officials in Chihuahua partially paid at first, but ultimately they ignored Santa Anna's 1841 decree for New Mexico's monthly stipend, while those from the customs house in Mazatlán never sent a single peso. The New Mexican government received little of what was promised and continued to rely on local financing. See Minge, "Frontier Problems in New Mexico," 106–7, and David J. Weber, *The Mexican Frontier, 1821–1846: The American Southwest Under Mexico* (Albuquerque: University of New Mexico Press, 1982), 267–68.
28. Ralph Emerson Twitchell, *Old Santa Fe: A Magazine of History, Archeology, Geneaology, and Biography*, vol. 1, 1913–1914 (Santa Fe: Old Santa Fe Press, 1914), 266 note 242.
29. Hall, *Social Change in the Southwest*, 155–56.
30. Daniel Tyler, "Gringo Views of Manuel Armijo," *New Mexico Historical Review* XLV (1970): 1.
31. Simmons, *The Little Lion of the Southwest*, 52–67.
32. Albino Chacón, "An Account of the Chimayó Rebellion, 1837," in Janet Lecompte, *Rebellion in Rio Arriba, 1837* (Albuquerque: University of New Mexico Press, 1985), 17.
33. Chacón, "An Account of the Chimayó Rebellion, 1837," 18.
34. Gutiérrez, *When Jesus Came, the Corn Mothers Went Away*, 303.
35. Boyle, *Los Capitalistas*, 11.
36. Gutiérrez, *When Jesus Came, the Corn Mothers Went Away*, 298.
37. Hall, *Social Change in the Southwest*, 137.
38. Taylor, *Magistrates of the Sacred*, 13–14.
39. Gutiérrez, *When Jesus Came, the Corn Mothers Went Away*, 298.
40. Gutiérrez, *When Jesus Came, the Corn Mothers Went Away*, 303–5.
41. Gutiérrez, *When Jesus Came, the Corn Mothers Went Away*, 304.
42. Pekka Hämäläinen, *The Comanche Empire* (New Haven, CT: Yale University Press, 2008), 108–12.
43. Hall, *Social Change in the Southwest*, 144–45.
44. Boyle, *Los Capitalistas*, 10.
45. Gutiérrez, *When Jesus Came, the Corn Mothers Went Away*, 303–5.
46. Boyle, *Los Capitalistas*, 11–12.
47. Hall, *Social Change in the Southwest*, 146.
48. Gutiérrez, *When Jesus Came, the Corn Mothers Went Away*, 323.
49. These numbers omit individuals in the censuses who are listed as without an occupation. The data from 1790 and 1827 comes from a table created by Gutiérrez; the data from 1850 comes from the 1850 census and only includes Hispanos in Santa Fe County. Gutiérrez used the 1790 census and the 1827 statistics contained in *Three New Mexico Chronicles*. I have modified my data to conform to Gutiérrez's data set. This included combining professions that I would normally separate, such as servants and laborers. While I use the term "artisans" in my data sets, Gutiérrez favors the term "craftsmen." For the purpose of this comparative table, I consider these labels to be interchangeable. In addition, I leave those without occupations unlisted in this table. See Gutiérrez, *When Jesus Came, the Corn Mothers Went Away*, 322; Carroll and Haggard, *Three New Mexico Chronicles*, 88; 1850 Federal Census, Santa Fe County, New Mexico Territory.
50. Alicia V. Tjarks, "Demographic, Ethnic, and Occupational Structure of New Mexico, 1790," *The Americas* 35, no. 1 (July 1978): 68.
51. Charles Powers, "The Role of Sticking Points in Pareto's Theory of Social Systems," in *Vilfredo*

Pareto: Beyond Disciplinary Boundaries, ed. Joseph V. Femia and Alasdair J. Marshall (New York: Routledge, 2016), 68.
52. James Lang, *Conquest and Commerce: Spain and England in the Americas* (New York: Academic Press, 1975).
53. Michael P. Carroll, *The Penitente Brotherhood: Patriarchy and Hispano-Catholicism in New Mexico* (Baltimore: Johns Hopkins University Press, 2002), 40.
54. Taylor, *Magistrates of the Sacred*, 25.
55. Gutiérrez, *When Jesus Came, the Corn Mothers Went Away*, 306–11.
56. Gutiérrez, *When Jesus Came, the Corn Mothers Went Away*, 311.
57. Chihuahua was established as part of an effort to push the northern boundary beyond Zacatecas. Zacatecas had produced massive amounts of silver, and residents petitioned to move north in search of more wealth. It is telling that in the early years of Chihuahua's history there was an emphasis on mining and on the founding of haciendas. From the beginning, Chihuahua's purpose was to provide wealth to the mother country. See Florence C. Lister and Robert H. Lister, *Chihuahua: Storehouse of Storms* (Albuquerque: University of New Mexico Press, 1966), 18–20.
58. Gutiérrez, *When Jesus Came, the Corn Mothers Went Away*, 298; Costeloe, *The Central Republic in Mexico*, 8.
59. Hall, *Social Change in the Southwest*, 154.
60. Costeloe, *The Central Republic in Mexico*, 86.
61. Boyle, *Los Capitalistas*, 29.
62. Josiah Gregg, *Commerce of the Prairies: A Selection* (Indianapolis, IN: Bobbs-Merrill Company, Inc., 1970), 167–70.
63. Boyle, *Los Capitalistas*, ix.
64. Hall, *Social Change in the Southwest*, 154; Max L. Moorhead, *New Mexico's Royal Road: Trade and Travel on the Chihuahua Trail* (Norman: University of Oklahoma Press, 1958), 65.
65. Hall, *Social Change in the Southwest*, 154–55.
66. Minge, "Frontier Problems in New Mexico," 356–58.
67. Boyle, *Los Capitalistas*, 56.
68. Boyle, *Los Capitalistas*, 55.
69. Weber, *The Mexican Frontier*, 152.
70. Gregg, *Commerce of the Prairies*, 45.
71. Boyle, *Los Capitalistas*, 51.
72. Richard L. Wilson, *Short Ravelings from a Long Yarn or Camp and March Sketches from the Santa Fe Trail* (Santa Ana: Fine Arts Press, 1936), 140, quoted in Tyler, "Gringo Views of Manuel Armijo," 35.
73. The same can likely be said of nearly every New Mexican caudillo, but because of Armijo's popularity he is the most often cited transgressor.
74. Hall, *Social Change in the Southwest*, 155.
75. Weber, *The Mexican Frontier*, 153.
76. Minge, "Frontier Problems in New Mexico," 239.
77. Boyle, *Los Capitalistas*, 51, 209.
78. David Lavender, *Bent's Fort* (Garden City, NY: Doubleday & Company, Inc., 1954), 68–71.
79. The exclamation point was added by Lavender and is intended to add emphasis to James Baird's seemingly misguided sense of Mexican identity. One must remember, however, that racial categories were much more fluid in the early nineteenth century. What Baird meant in identifying himself as Mexican likely had more to do with citizenship than race. See Lavender, *Bent's Fort*, 68.
80. This is a good example of a New Mexican citizen reporting contraband in exchange for a share of the value seized by the Mexican government.
81. Lavender, *Bent's Fort*, 70.
82. Lavender, *Bent's Fort*, 70–71.
83. Weber, *The Mexican Frontier*, 152.

84. Andrés Reséndez, *Changing National Identities at the Frontier: Texas and New Mexico, 1800–1850* (Cambridge: Press Syndicate of the University of Cambridge, 2005), 171–72.
85. Janet Lecompte, *Rebellion in Rio Arriba, 1837* (Albuquerque: University of New Mexico Press, 1985), 16–19.
86. It is likely that Santa Anna was more frustrated by the instability and constant revolutions that were the result of deep-seated regional divisions. See Costeloe, *The Central Republic in Mexico*, 23.
87. Mexico experienced problems similar to those the United States experienced under the Articles of Confederation: a powerless central government that neither collected wealth nor made policy on behalf of the nation. But where the United States used political guile to change from the Articles of Confederation to the U.S. Constitution, the Mexican centralists used force to end the constitution of 1824.
88. Reséndez, *Changing National Identities at the Frontier*, 176.
89. Upon assuming dictatorial powers, Santa Anna promptly annulled Gómez Farías's reforms and abolished the constitution of 1824. The authoritarian principles that underlay Santa Anna's rule were subsequently codified in the constitution of 1836, also known as the Siete Leyes (Seven Laws). Under the constitution of 1836, Mexico became a centralist regime in which power was concentrated in the president and his immediate subordinates. The states of the former federal republic were refashioned as military districts administered by regional patrónes appointed by the president, and property qualifications were decreed for congressional officeholders and voters.
90. Weber, *The Mexican Frontier*, 243.
91. Weber, *The Mexican Frontier*, 170–73.
92. Stephen L. Hardin, *Texian Illiad: A Military History of the Texas Revolution* (Austin: University of Texas Press, 1994), 6–8.
93. Weber, *The Mexican Frontier*, 180.
94. Weber, *The Mexican Frontier*, 128–29.
95. Hardin, 208–17.
96. Wilfrid Hardy Callcott, *Santa Anna: The Story of an Enigma Who Once Was Mexico* (Norman: University of Oklahoma Press, 1936), 108.
97. Gutiérrez, *When Jesus Came, the Corn Mothers Went Away*, 334–35.
98. Thomas E. Chávez, *Manuel Alvarez, 1794–1856: A Southwestern Biography* (Niwot: University Press of Colorado, 1990), 22.
99. Lecompte, *Rebellion in Rio Arriba*, 6.
100. Hall, *Social Change in the Southwest*, 190–91.
101. Weber, *The Mexican Frontier*, 262.
102. Reséndez, *Changing National Identities at the Frontier*, 167–68.
103. The most popular interpretation of the Chimayo Rebellion is written by Lecompte, who conducted the most thorough research on the rebellion. Lecompte argues that the Chimayo Rebellion was perpetuated by the lower classes, meaning the vecinos. Unfortunately Lecompte's research undermines her own argument. When I reviewed the documents critically, instead of reading them all as truthful, it became clear that many of the accounts she cited and took as truth contained mistruths and propaganda.
104. Hall, *Social Change in the Southwest*, 191.
105. Benjamin M. Read, *Illustrated History of New Mexico* (New York: Arno Press, 1976), 373–74.
106. Albino Chacón, "An Account of the Chimayó Rebellion, 1837," contained in Lecompte, *Rebellion in Rio Arriba*, 95.
107. Donaciano Vigil, "Assembly Address of Donaciano Vigil to the Departmental Assembly of New Mexico, June 22, 1846," in Lecompte, *Rebellion in Rio Arriba*, 86.
108. Joseph P. Sánchez, "It Happened in Old Santa Fe, the Death of Governor Albino Pérez, 1835–1837," in *All Trails Lead to Santa Fe: An Anthology Commemorating the 400th Anniversary of the Founding of Santa Fe, New Mexico in 1610*, ed. Orlando Romero (Santa Fe: Sunstone Press, 2010), 272.

109. Sánchez, "It Happened in Old Santa Fe," 271–72.
110. The duties of the subcomisario include raising funds for both the government and the troops stationed in New Mexico. See Lecompte, *Rebellion in Rio Arriba*, 12.
111. Sánchez, "It Happened in Old Santa Fe," 272.
112. Manuel Armijo to Governor Pérez, April 12, 1837, New Mexico State Records Center and Archives, *Mexican Archives of New Mexico*, roll 23, frames 341–42.
113. Lecompte, *Rebellion in Rio Arriba*, 12.
114. Sánchez, "It Happened in Old Santa Fe," 272. Another example of Armijo retiring due to a sudden illness occurred in 1844, when Native attacks were running rampant and Mexico City was about to replace Manuel Armijo with Gen. Mariano Martínez. Armijo pre-emptively turned the government over to his ally Mariano Chávez. See Minge, "Frontier Problems in New Mexico," 159.
115. This is a highly controversial contention, one that I do not make lightly. But it is based on a thorough review of every known surviving scrap of paper related to the Chimayo Rebellion. A central source in informing my argument is the work of Janet Lecompte, specifically the documents she transcribed and published in *Rebellion in the Rio Arriba, 1837*. One of the most compelling pieces of evidence is in Lecompte's appendix, specifically "Assembly Address of Donaciano Vigil to the Departmental Assembly of New Mexico, June 22, 1846." Therein, Donaciano Vigil clearly recounts the hatred that the local patrónes felt toward both Albino Perez and the centralist movement. He also recounts important and long-overlooked details of the rebellion. But this is but one of many pieces of evidence, all of which point to the local patrónes playing an important role in inciting the Chimayo Rebellion. See "Assembly Address of Donaciano Vigil to the Departmental Assembly of New Mexico, June 22, 1846."
116. Lecompte, *Rebellion in Rio Arriba*, 17–18.
117. L. B. Prince, Note of Conversation with Aniceto Abeytia, July 19, 1909, Mauro Montoya Collection (AC 152), box 1, folder 10-B.
118. Read, *Illustrated History of New Mexico*, 378–80.
119. Read, *Illustrated History of New Mexico*, 378–80.
120. Read, *Illustrated History of New Mexico*, 373–74. See chapter IV note "*" for a detailed account of these rumors regarding unjust taxes.
121. Read, *Illustrated History of New Mexico*, 373. See chapter IV note "*" for details.
122. Read, *Illustrated History of New Mexico*, 373. See chapter IV note "*" for details.
123. Read, *Illustrated History of New Mexico*, 373–74. See chapter IV note "*" for a details.
124. Sánchez, "It Happened in Old Santa Fe," 273.
125. Lecompte, *Rebellion in Rio Arriba*, 18; Read, *Illustrated History of New Mexico*, 373–74. See chapter see chapter IV note "*" for details.
126. Donaciano Vigil, "Assembly Address of Donaciano Vigil to the Departmental Assembly of New Mexico, June 22, 1846," in Lecompte, *Rebellion in Rio Arriba*, 87.
127. Marc Simmons, *Yesterday in Santa Fe: Episodes in a Turbulent History* (Santa Fe: Sunstone Press, 2007), 38.
128. Simmons, *Yesterday in Santa Fe*, 38.
129. Sánchez, "It Happened in Old Santa Fe," 273.
130. William H. Wroth, "The 1837 Rebellion of Rio Arriba," accessed June 7, 2012, http://www.newmexicohistory.org/filedetails.php?fileID=318.
131. Lecompte, *Rebellion in Rio Arriba*, 19–20.
132. Read, Benjamin M. (Benjamin Maurice) Papers relating to the history of New Mexico, 1634-1921, box 7, folder 16, State Records Center and Archives (SRCA), Santa Fe, NM.
133. Weber, *The Mexican Frontier*, 261–63.
134. The identity of Don A. Antonito Chávez remains a mystery—he is not mentioned again in any known record—but it is curious that a Chávez and his militia prevented Pérez from fleeing to the Rio Abajo. Pérez must have viewed Chávez as an ally because he sought asylum from him, but was rebuffed. It is also curious that Don A. Antonito Chávez, whom Don Albino Chacón labeled an insurrectionist, did not eliminate Governor Pérez and his absconding political allies.

Instead, Chávez and his men funneled Governor Pérez back to Santa Fe, as one might do in a hunt. Don A. Antonito Chávez was most likely a patrón from the Rio Abajo: he was associated with the title Don by Don Albino Chacón, he blocked the road to the Rio Abajo, and he forced Governor Pérez back to Santa Fe. It is likely that Chávez did not wish to have the governor's blood on his hands, but when he decided to block Pérez's escape from the vengeful rebels, he ensured Governor Pérez's death. See Jacqueline Dorgan Meketa, *Legacy of Honor: The Life of Rafael Chacón, a Nineteenth Century New Mexican* (Albuquerque: University of New Mexico Press, 1986), 31.

135. Charles Blumner, Letter to Germany, March 18, 1841, Charles Blumner Letters (AC 231), Angélico Chávez Library, Palace of the Governors, Santa Fe, translated from German with the assistance of Tomas Jaehn.
136. Read, *Illustrated History of New Mexico*, 373–74. See chapter IV note "*" for a details. Read was the most prominent scholar to accuse Armijo of fomenting the Chimayo Rebellion.
137. What survived are a few oral histories, the assembly speech by Donaciano Vigil, an account likely penned by Albino Chacón, and several letters and reports by either Armijo or peripheral parties. See Reséndez, *Changing National Identities at the Frontier*, 189 note 60.
138. L. B. Prince, Note of Conversation with Aniceto Abeytia, July 19, 1909, Mauro Montoya Collection (AC 152), box 1, folder 10-B.
139. L. B. Prince, Note of Conversation with Aniceto Abeytia, July 19, 1909, Mauro Montoya Collection (AC 152), box 1, folder 10-B.
140. L. B. Prince, Note of Conversation with Aniceto Abeytia, July 19, 1909, Mauro Montoya Collection (AC 152), box 1, folder 10-B.
141. It is possible that scholars ignored Abeytia's account because he was only eight years old when the rebellion occurred. In addition, Prince did not interview him until late in his life. It is also likely that his version of the story was informed by what he heard from others. But Armijo was a central figure in New Mexican society. Children and adults alike knew him and talked about him. He was something of a folk figure. Even if Abeytia's account is buttressed by what he heard from adults and from community memory, it provides a valuable window into the 1837 rebellion.
142. Read, *Illustrated History of New Mexico*, 378–80.
143. L. B. Prince, Note of Conversation with Aniceto Abeytia, July 19, 1909, Mauro Montoya Collection (AC 152), box 1, folder 10-B.
144. Read, *Illustrated History of New Mexico*, 378–80.
145. Read, *Illustrated History of New Mexico*, 378–80.
146. Weber, *The Mexican Frontier*, 263.
147. John O. Baxter, *Los Carneradas: Sheep Trade in New Mexico, 1700–1860* (Albuquerque: University of New Mexico Press, 1987), 105–6.
148. Baxter, *Los Carneradas*, 104.
149. Hall, *Social Change in the Southwest*, 191.
150. Read, *Illustrated History of New Mexico*, 385.
151. Ralph Emerson Twitchell, *Old Santa Fe: A Magazine of History, Archaeology, Genealogy, and Biography, Volume II* (Santa Fe: Old Santa Fe Press, 1915), 35.
152. Weber, *The Mexican Frontier*, 264.
153. Marc Simmons, *Albuquerque: A Narrative History* (Albuquerque: University of New Mexico Press, 1982), 135.
154. Lecompte, *Rebellion in Rio Arriba*, 102.
155. Donaciano Vigil, "Assembly Address of Donaciano Vigil to the Departmental Assembly of New Mexico, June 22, 1846," in Lecompte, *Rebellion in Rio Arriba*, 88–89.
156. Donaciano Vigil Collection, 1727–1877, Santa Fe: New Mexico State Records Center and Archives, OCLC# 37800720.
157. In 1838, Donaciano Vigil was brought before the court to answer for his involvement in the 1837 rebellion. His political rivals brought the charges against Vigil, and although there was much to question in Vigil's actions, the case was ultimately dismissed. See New Mexico State

Records Center and Archives, *Mexican Archives of New Mexico, 1821–1846* (Santa Fe: New Mexico State Records Center and Archives, 1969) (hereafter *MANM*), roll #25, frame #507.
158. Hall, *Social Change in the Southwest*, 191.
159. Samuel Sisneros, "She Was Our Mother: New Mexico's Change of National Sovereignty and Juan Bautista Vigil y Alarid, The Last Governor of New Mexico," in *All Trails Lead to Santa Fe: An Anthology Commemorating the 400th Anniversary of the Founding of Santa Fe, New Mexico in 1610*, ed. Orlando Romero (Santa Fe: Sunstone Press, 2010), 296–97.
160. George B. Anderson, *History of New Mexico, Its Resources and People, Volume I* (Los Angeles: Pacific States Publishing Company, 1907), 59; Tyler, "Gringo Views of Manuel Armijo," 23.
161. Hamill, *Caudillos*, 11.

CHAPTER TWO

1. Thomas J. Steele, S.J., *Archbishop Lamy: In His Own Words* (Albuquerque: LPD Press, 2000), 10. Historians have not been able to determine the ethnicity of the assailant. Moreover, the assailant is not identified in any way by the *Santa Fe Weekly Gazette*. But considering the demographics of Santa Fe County in 1865, and the animosity that existed between Lamy and many Hispanos, it's more likely that he was Hispano.
2. *Santa Fe Weekly Gazette*, December 30, 1865.
3. Paul Horgan, *Lamy of Santa Fe: His Life and Times* (New York: Noonday Press, 1975), 323.
4. Horgan, *Lamy of Santa Fe*, 323.
5. Csvhistory.org/orgsite/18651899.aspx, accessed April 24, 2011.
6. New Mexico State Records Center and Archives, "Records of the United States Territorial and New Mexico District Courts for Santa Fe County 1847–1951," box 1–3 (hereafter TRNMSF, District Court Records), "New Mexico v. Juan Lucero," December 15, 1852; "New Mexico v. Antonio Lucero," December 20, 1850; TRNMSF, Santa Fe County Criminal Court Docket Book (1847–1858), 93. These two case files are fragmentary, but some details did survive. The records for Juan Lucero indicate that he was found not guilty, but how that decision was reached is not clear. The records of Antonio Lucero are more complete, specifically because the case was continued until 1853 and found its way into the criminal court docket books. Antonio Lucero's case was finally heard on September 19, 1853, a long wait for what turned out to be a short hearing; Lamy sent a legal representative to the court, who informed the judge that he did not wish to press charges against the defendant. The case was dismissed, and Antonio Lucero went free. It is quite possible that Lamy declined to press charges against Juan Lucero as well, which would be in keeping with his religious views, and that the not guilty verdict was mistakenly filed in his folder.
7. The Hispano share of the overall property value in Santa Fe County increased from 36 percent in 1850 to 52 percent in 1860, and this trend can be seen in the vast majority of other New Mexican counties. In terms of Hispano property value owned in Santa Fe County, in 1850 Hispanos owned a total of $308,110 in property; by 1860, that number nearly doubled to reach $571,090, an increase of $262,980. Property distribution, however, remained uneven within the Hispano communities. Among property-owning-age Hispano males (twenty-one or over), only 46 percent owned property. This means 54 percent of the Hispano population was without property, and 90 percent of these were listed as either laborers or servants in the 1850 census. Even within the property-owning class, the majority owned very little, which further highlights the uneven distribution of wealth. Younger land-owning Hispanos tended to be poorer, while the majority of the wealth remained concentrated in the hands of Hispanos over the age of fifty-one.
8. Lovalerie King, *Race, Theft, and Ethics: Property Matters in African American Literature* (Baton Rouge: Louisiana State University Press, 2007), 1–5.

9. James C. Scott, *Weapons of the Weak: Everyday Forms of Peasant Resistance* (New Haven, CT: Yale University Press, 1985), 267.
10. Gary LaFree, *Losing Legitimacy: Street Crime and the Decline of Social Institutions in America* (Boulder, CO: Westview Press, 1998), 3.
11. LaFree, *Losing Legitimacy*, 6. While LaFree illuminates the symbiotic relationship between failing social institutions and the rise in street crime, he stops short of concluding that the African Americans whom institutions failed were justified in their crimes.
12. See Jerome Hall, *Theft, Law, and Society* (Indianapolis, IN: Bobbs-Merrill Company, 1952); Michael E. Tigar, "The Right of Property and the Law of Theft," 62 *Texas Law Review* 1443–75 (1984); George P. Fletcher, "The Metamorphosis of Larceny," *Harvard Law Review* 89, no. 3 (Jan. 1976), 469–530.
13. Tigar, "The Right of Property and the Law of Theft," 1444–45.
14. Tigar, "The Right of Property and the Law of Theft," 1457.
15. See Felipe Gonzales, *Política: Nuevomexicanos and American Political Incorporation, 1821–1910* (Lincoln: University of Nebraska Press, 2016), 3, and Laura E. Gómez, "Race, Colonialism, and Criminal Law: Mexicans and the American Criminal Justice System in Territorial New Mexico," *Law and Society Review* 34, no. 4 (2000): 1192–93, for the role that politics played in the power-sharing model that defined New Mexico after the US-Mexican War.
16. David Weber, *Foreigners in Their Native Land: Historical Roots of the Mexican Americans* (Albuquerque: University of New Mexico Press, 2003), 97–98.
17. Miguel A. Otero, *Report of the Governor of New Mexico to the Secretary of the Interior* (Washington, DC: Government Printing Office, 1901), 48.
18. Weber, *Foreigners in Their Native Land*, 97.
19. Roger D. Launius, *Alexander William Doniphan: Portrait of a Missouri Moderate* (Columbia: University of Missouri Press, 1997), 114.
20. Launius, *Alexander William Doniphan*, 114; Joseph G. Dawson III, *Doniphan's Epic March: The 1st Missouri Volunteers in the Mexican War* (Lawrence: University of Kansas Press, 1999), 85.
21. Benjamin M. Read, *Illustrated History of New Mexico* (New York: Arno Press, 1976), 439.
22. New Mexico State Records Center and Archives, New Mexico Secretary of State Collection: Laws of New Mexico, Serial #4863, 58–85; Ramón Gutiérrez, *When Jesus Came, the Corn Mothers Went Away: Marriage, Sexuality, and Power in New Mexico, 1500–1846* (Stanford, CA: Stanford University Press, 1991), 191.
23. Launius, *Alexander William Doniphan*, 115.
24. Ralph Emerson Twitchell, *The Leading Facts of New Mexican History* (Santa Fe: Sunstone Press, 2007 [1911]), 272.
25. Larry D. Ball, *United States Marshals of the New Mexico and Arizona Territories, 1846–1912* (Albuquerque: University of New Mexico Press, 1978), 21.
26. Ball, *United States Marshals of the New Mexico and Arizona Territories*, 24.
27. 1850 Federal Census, Santa Fe County, New Mexico Territory.
28. Fray Angélico Chávez and Thomas E. Chávez, *Wake for a Fat Vicar: Father Juan Felipe Ortiz, Archbishop Lamy, and the New Mexican Catholic Church in the Middle of the Nineteenth Century* (Albuquerque: LPD Press, 2004), 76–77.
29. Launius, *Alexander William Doniphan*, 116.
30. Josiah Gregg, *Commerce of the Prairies: A Selection* (Indianapolis, IN: Bobbs-Merrill Company, 1970), 74–75.
31. Jill Mocho, *Murder and Justice in Frontier New Mexico 1821–1846* (Albuquerque: University of New Mexico Press, 1997), 13.
32. Mocho, *Murder and Justice in Frontier New Mexico*, 7–10.
33. Mocho, *Murder and Justice in Frontier New Mexico*, 12–14.
34. In homicide cases specifically, cases were often sent to Chihuahua for legal advice, where

they could take numerous months to be returned. Often they returned without definitive answers and instead contained more questions. This is especially true in cases where alcaldes sought capital punishment, a sentence that was not carried out in New Mexico until after the American government began grafting their legal policies onto the pre-existing Mexican laws and practices; see Mocho, *Murder and Justice in Frontier New Mexico*, 17.
35. Mocho, *Murder and Justice in Frontier New Mexico*, 16.
36. See chapter 1.
37. Robert J. Torrez, "Crime and Punishment in Colonial New Mexico," *New Mexico Bar Journal* (2000), 23, accessed June 14, 2012, http://www.nmbar.org/AboutSBNM/Committees/Historical/Crime_and_Punishment_In%20Colonial_New_Mexico.pdf.
38. Charles R. Cutter, *The Legal Culture of Northern New Spain* (Albuquerque: University of New Mexico Press, 1995), 133.
39. TRNMSF, District Court Records, boxes 1–3, most of the criminal files therein contain arrest warrants and a description of the crime, but little more.
40. TRNMSF, District Court Records, "New Mexico v. Christian Mild," August 27, 1847. Between 1846 and 1860, there is one exception to this rule: a homicide case that involved the murder of an American soldier at a local fandango (dance). On that occasion, the judge teamed up with the military and followed a process similar to the one utilized by the alcaldes in the Mexican period. The case demonstrated continuity between the Mexican and American territorial judicial apparatuses, but only because the military was involved. This was an anomaly.
41. 1850 Federal Census, Santa Fe County, New Mexico Territory.
42. Thomas D. Hall, *Social Change in the Southwest, 1350–1880* (Lawrence: University Press of Kansas, 1989), 217.
43. David Lavender, *Bent's Fort* (Garden City, NY: Doubleday & Company, Inc., 1954), 173.
44. In 1838, Donaciano Vigil was brought before the court to answer for his involvement in the 1837 rebellion. His political rivals brought the charges against Vigil, and although there was much to question in Vigil's actions, the case was ultimately dismissed. See New Mexico State Records Center and Archives, *Mexican Archives of New Mexico, 1821–1846* (Santa Fe: New Mexico State Records Center and Archives, 1969) (hereafter *MANM*), roll #25, frame #507.
45. Donaciano Vigil was favorably portrayed by his contemporaries, but it is difficult to ignore his willingness to switch allegiances. It has been argued that Vigil was merely dedicated to public representation, no matter the flag, but there are strong signs of intrigue surrounding his activities during the Chimayo Rebellion. See Maurillo E. Vigil, *Los Patrones: Profiles of Hispanic Leaders in New Mexican History* (Washington, DC: University Press of America, Inc., 1980), 20–31.
46. Twitchell, *The Leading Facts of New Mexican History*, 248–49.
47. Twitchell, *The Leading Facts of New Mexican History*, 249.
48. Read, *Illustrated History of New Mexico*, 455.
49. Howard Roberts Lamar, *The Far Southwest, 1846–1912: A Territorial History* (New Haven, CT: Yale University Press, 1966, reprint, New York: W. W. Norton and Co., 1970), 71; Read, *Illustrated History of New Mexico*, 455.
50. Read, *Illustrated History of New Mexico*, 453–54.
51. It is difficult to determine how long West and Quinn had been in New Mexico, but it is likely that both were among the recently arrived Anglos who allied themselves with the local landholders. All that is known is that West held the position of U.S. district attorney from 1851 to 1853, while Quinn was a lawyer and speculator. Lamar, *The Far Southwest*, 70–72.
52. Hall, *Social Change in the Southwest*, 216–17.
53. Lamar, *The Far Southwest*, 71–73.
54. Lamar, *The Far Southwest*, 79–80.
55. William A. Keleher, *Turmoil in New Mexico, 1846–1868* (Santa Fe: Rydal Press, 1952), 118 note 25.
56. The dictum "I obey but do not comply" was repeated in New Mexico out of necessity in colonial times, and the tradition of ignoring laws for the local good endured among New Mexicans.

Although the phrase does not appear in the Territorial Records between 1847 and 1853, Judge Tomás Ortiz repeatedly evokes the tradition in several decisions, some of which will be explored in this chapter. Also See John L. Kessell, *Spain and the Southwest: A Narrative of Colonial New Mexico, Arizona, Texas, and California* (Norman: University of Oklahoma Press, 2002), 99.

57. Lamy was critical of the New Mexican padres and what he characterized as their excesses and abuses. Fray Angélico Chávez convincingly argued that Lamy's persecution of Mexican-trained clergy was fueled by a deep-seated anti-Hispano sentiment. Numerous historians continue to celebrate Lamy, and their books have received nearly every major prize imaginable. Today, a tall bronze statue stands in front of the St. Francis Cathedral Basilica to honor Lamy, but many native New Mexicans take a dim view of his legacy. See Fray Angélico Chávez, *But Time and Chance: The Story of Padre Martínez of Taos, 1793–1867* (Santa Fe: Sunstone Press, 1981); Chávez and Chávez, *Wake for a Fat Vicar.*
58. Even Manuel Chaves eventually conceded to the church, ultimately choosing to compromise with the church authorities. Church officials were threatened, intimidated, and harassed, but rarely assaulted. It is unlikely that the perpetrator who wounded two priests was a caudillo, not least because a caudillo would never have agreed to work for the hated Lamy. See Chávez and Chávez, *Wake for a Fat Vicar*, 151.
59. Steele, *Archbishop Lamy*, 127, Sermon of Archbishop Lamy, Third Sunday of Lent, March 14, 1852, Santa Fe, New Mexico, is the earliest surviving sermon written in Spanish by Lamy.
60. Horgan, *Lamy of Santa Fe*, 416.
61. *Santa Fe Weekly Gazette*, January 8, 1853, 2.
62. Chávez and Chávez, *Wake for a Fat Vicar*, 141.
63. Chávez and Chávez, *Wake for a Fat Vicar*, 91–92.
64. Chávez and Chávez, *Wake for a Fat Vicar*, 92.
65. Chávez contends that Martínez and Lamy were friendly at first, but that after one year a dispute between Martínez and Machebeuf turned Lamy against him. Chávez, *But Time and Chance*, 100.
66. Chávez and Chávez, *Wake for a Fat Vicar*, 17.
67. Chávez and Chávez, *Wake for a Fat Vicar*, 140.
68. Fray Angélico Chávez, *Très Macho—He Said: Padre Gallegos of Albuquerque, New Mexico's First Congressman* (Santa Fe: William Gannon, 1985), 43–44.
69. Chávez, *Très Macho—He Said*, 50.
70. William H. Wroth, "Lamy, Jean Baptiste," accessed June 11, 2012, http://www.newmexicohistory.org/filedetails.php?fileID=501.
71. Chávez, *But Time and Chance*, 137.
72. Chávez, *But Time and Chance*, 147.
73. Chávez and Chávez, *Wake for a Fat Vicar*, 118–23.
74. *Santa Fe Weekly Gazette*, January 8, 1853, 2.
75. Roxanne Dunbar Ortiz, *Roots of Resistance: Land Tenure in New Mexico, 1680–1980* (Los Angeles: Chicano Studies Research Center Publications, 1980), 7.
76. Ortiz, *Roots of Resistance*, 5.
77. See chapter 1.
78. Gutiérrez, *When Jesus Came, the Corn Mothers Went Away*, 323–24.
79. "Treaty of Guadalupe Hidalgo; February 2, 1848," accessed June 7, 2012, http://avalon.law.yale.edu/19th_century/guadhida.asp.
80. Ortiz, *Roots of Resistance*, 8–9.
81. Ortiz, *Roots of Resistance*, 8.
82. It is difficult to explain why historians have not analyzed the data in the 1850 census before drawing their conclusions, but the myth that New Mexicans were displaced is commonly accepted. It might be due to the source material that historians continue to rely on: Anglo accounts, early history books written by Anglos, and nativists seeking to amplify the tragic components of the American conquest.
83. There is a good deal of confusion regarding the 1850 and 1860 censuses because property values

versus personal wealth are not clearly defined. The most intelligent assessment of these censuses comes from Tomas Jaehn, who explains that while the property values listed in the census never match the property records, there is a discernible pattern that suggests that the proportions between properties are consistent. The census numbers in 1850 are property values only, while 1860 offers both property values and wealth. See Tomas Jaehn, *Germans in the Southwest: 1850–1920* (Albuquerque: University of New Mexico Press, 2005), 40, 167 note 46.

84. Hubert Howe Bancroft, *The Works of Hubert Howe Bancroft, Volume XVII: History of Arizona and New Mexico, 1530–1888* (San Francisco: The History Company, Publishers, 1889), 645.
85. This fact is likely what misled scholars of New Mexico into believing that the occupation of New Mexico resulted in dispossession.
86. The territorial government was particularly powerful in Santa Fe County and local Anglo settlers worked hard to make sure their power was not compromised. As Hall notes, as long as New Mexico was a territory, Anglos would continue to control how the government spent wealth. This positioned them to bargain with the more numerous New Mexican caudillos, who wanted federal contracts. See Hall, *Social Change in the Southwest*, 215–17.
87. These data were combed from the complete United States Census data for Santa Fe County. Presumably, real estate includes only property, but it is possible that it may include wealth also.
88. Other services includes shoemakers, hat makers, tailors, silversmiths, and tobacco rollers, to name a few.
89. Interestingly, when the Hispano real estate ($308,110) is compared with the Anglo real estate ($482,186), minus what the military seized from the Mexican government ($173,750), the total worth of real estate ($308,436) is only $326 more than what the Hispanos owned in 1850 in Santa Fe County.
90. 1850 Federal Census, Santa Fe County, New Mexico Territory.
91. Paul Foos, *A Short, Offhand, Killing Affair: Soldiers and Social Conflict during the Mexican-American War* (Chapel Hill: University of North Carolina Press, 2002). Paul Foos offers the best and most comprehensive look at the racism that drove the US-Mexican War. The United States worked hard to demonize the Mexican people during the US-Mexican War, depicting them as uncivilized, corrupted by Native American intermarriage, and capable of wretched acts of barbarism and murder.
92. Foos, *A Short, Offhand, Killing Affair*, 8.
93. Foos, *A Short, Offhand, Killing Affair*, 113.
94. Although Anglo settlers faced the same system, they received different punishments than did the vecinos. See chapter 4.
95. White settlers owned 56 percent of all property in Santa Fe County in 1850, but 36 percent was in the hands of the government and government officials. This included community property that the U.S. government had seized. See 1850 Federal Census, Santa Fe County, New Mexico Territory.
96. Robert V. Hine and Jack Mack Faragher, *The American West: A New Interpretive History* (New Haven, CT: Yale University Press, 2000), 216.
97. Tigar, "The Right of Property and the Law of Theft," 1457.
98. Emily E. Keita, "The New Mexico Fandango," *Wagontracks* 19, no. 3 (May 2005): 1–13.
99. James A. Bennett's accounts portray the two very different types of fandango. The first account is of a traditional fandango in San Miguel del Bado, and the second is a commodified fandango in Santa Fe. Though Bennett does not situate them in this fashion and fails to perceive this distinction between the two fandangos, it becomes clear to the modern reader that what separates the two fandangos he documents is the presence of alcohol, Americans, and fees that partygoers needed to pay. See Clinton Brook and Frank Reeve, *Forts and Forays: James A. Bennett, a Dragoon in New Mexico, 1850–56* (Albuquerque: University of New Mexico Press, 1948), 15, 20.
100. New Mexico State Records Center and Archives, New Mexico Secretary of State Collection, Laws of New Mexico, Serial # 4863, 1851–54.
101. In the nineteenth century the United States Indian Service (USIS) was the closest thing to a social welfare program that there was in the United States. They were charged with overseeing

the assimilation of Native Americans into American society, but instead they utilized their resources to systematically remove Natives from their land. The atrocities their leaders perpetuated are a blight on the history of the United States, and Hispanos were fortunate to avoid such help assimilating into American society. The atrocities they committed have been well documented, most recently by Cathleen D. Cahill, *Federal Fathers and Mothers: A Social History of the United States Indian Service, 1869–1933*, First Peoples: New Directions in Indigenous Studies (Chapel Hill: University of North Carolina Press, 2013).

102. The increase in larceny from the Mexican period into the American period was dramatic, and the records for Santa Fe during the Mexican period are remarkably complete. In fact, they provide far greater detail than the records from the American territorial period. In other parts of New Mexico, the records are fragmentary for all crimes, but officials in Santa Fe took their record keeping very seriously.
103. 1860 Federal Census, Santa Fe County, New Mexico Territory.
104. It is difficult to track the exact movements of those who left Santa Fe County. According to the 1860 census, there were 655 individuals living outside of New Mexico territory who listed New Mexico as their birthplace. Among these it is equally difficult to tell which were Hispano, because Hispanos intermarried with American settlers. Regardless, the majority of those who left Santa Fe County appear to have stayed within the territory. Some of these were part of the repatriation efforts that Samuel Sisneros has documented, which saw four thousand Hispanos from the entirety of the territory depart and repatriate as Mexican citizens; together they founded the towns of Mesilla, San Ignacio, and Guadalupe. Sadly, those living in Mesilla saw their repatriation efforts thwarted when they were reincorporated into New Mexico territory as a result of the Gadsden Purchase of 1853. See 1850 Federal Census, Santa Fe County, New Mexico Territory; Samuel E. Sisneros, "'She Was Our Mother,' New Mexico's Change of National Sovereignty and Juan Bautista Vigil y Alarid, The Last Mexican Governor of New Mexico," in *All Trails Lead to Santa Fe: An Anthology Commemorating the 400th Anniversary of the Founding of Santa Fe, New Mexico in 1610*, ed. Orlando Romero (Santa Fe: Sunstone Press, 2010), 289.
105. TRNMSF, District Court Records, "New Mexico v. Jose Francoso," March 3, 1848.
106. TRNMSF, District Court Records, "New Mexico v. Jose Seguro," March 3, 1848; "New Mexico v. Jose Francoso," March 3, 1848.
107. TRNMSF, District Court Records, "New Mexico v. Eugenio Ortiz," June 28, 1849.
108. TRNMSF, District Court Records, "New Mexico v. Rafael Sandobal," August 3, 1853; "New Mexico v. Justo Gonzalez," June 29, 1848.
109. TRNMSF, District Court Records, "New Mexico v. Calistro Garcia," July 19, 1848.
110. TRNMSF, District Court Records, "New Mexico v. Jose Antonio Martin," January 30, 1852.
111. TRNMSF, District Court Records, "New Mexico v. Francisco Griego, Manuel Salvador, & Justo Sandoval," March 15, 1847.
112. The legal definition of petty larceny evolved over time in Santa Fe County, and I maintain that it did so because, as Tigar has argued, the primary purpose of larceny law was to secure the holdings of the wealthier class and subjugate the lower class. The authors of the Kearny Code initially set the line for petty larceny at anything below $10 in value, but that law proved nonsensical. For example, Tomas Perea was accused of stealing a used blanket valued at $20 by owner Richard Owens, which under the Kearny Code constituted grand larceny. This meant that Perea's crime was technically in the same category as that of Samuel Rino, who stole a trunk full of money. An analysis of the court documents reveals that prosecutors valued items traditionally associated with petty larceny as, by the standard of the Kearny Code, worthy of the label grand larceny, for which the punishment was often more severe: a blanket was worth between $4 and $20, a coat was valued at $5, a necklace at $40, a robe at $3.37, shoes were valued at anywhere from $2 to $8 per pair, and mules were valued at $100 to $120. In these same documents, a single sheep is valued at a mere $2. In short, the numbers simply didn't add up. The Third Legislative Assembly of New Mexico Territory recognized that this line was flawed, and in 1853 they redrew the line for petty larceny from $10 to $100, which was far closer to the line

of $50 that existed in neighboring California. This remained the line until the Seventh Legislative Assembly of New Mexico Territory met in 1857–1858. This legislature was determined to crack down on the recurring larceny problem, and they intentionally manipulated larceny laws to better protect their property. They reinstituted $10 as the limit for petty larceny, but dictated that the punishment for petty larceny (less than $10) should be reduced to fifteen lashes and no jail time. In short, the line for petty versus grand larceny, as it was drawn, redrawn, then redrawn yet again, was artificial, and those who moved that line were more concerned with their own interests than any rational interpretation of petty versus grand larceny. For this reason, in this chapter I have chosen to follow the line set forth by the legislature in 1853, meaning I have categorized petty larceny as anything valued at less than $100. See New Mexico State Records Center and Archives, New Mexico Secretary of State Collection: Laws of New Mexico, Serial # 4863, 59, Kearny Code; TRNMSF, District Court Records, "New Mexico v. Tomas Perea," June 27, 1850; *Laws of the Territory of New Mexico, Passed by the Third Legislative Assembly, in the City of Santa Fe, at a Session Begun on the Fifth Day of December, A.D. 1853* (Santa Fe: J. L. Collins & W. W. H. Davis, 1854); New Mexico State Records Center and Archives, New Mexico Secretary of State Collection, Laws of New Mexico, Serial #4869, Laws of the Seventh Session, 1857–1858, chapter IX, section 14.

113. TRNMSF, District Court Records, "New Mexico v. Jesus Garcia, Justo Gonzalez, & Manuel Pena," June 28, 1849.
114. The crime is curious because Jose Arce does not appear in the 1850 census and only the matriarch from the Arce family is a resident of Santa Fe County in 1850. She was born in Mexico, but had $1,000 in property in Santa Fe County. The most famous individual with this surname was Jose Antonio Arce, who was the governor of Chihuahua during the Mexican period. The fact that Jose Arce possessed $609 means he was likely related to him, which means he was also likely a merchant from Chihuahua.
115. TRNMSF, District Court Records, "New Mexico v. Jesus Francoso," November 6, 1851; "New Mexico v. Felipe Santiago," August 12, 1850.
116. TRNMSF, District Court Records, "New Mexico v. Jose Tenorio," November 19, 1850; TRNMSF, District Court Records, "New Mexico v. Eugenio Ortiz," June 28, 1849.
117. TRNMSF, District Court Records, "New Mexico v. Jose Maria Sanchez," July 5, 1850.
118. TRNMSF, District Court Records, "New Mexico v. Jose Montoya and Jose Francoso," February 9, 1850; Lavender, *Bent's Fort*, 18–19.
119. TRNMSF, District Court Records, "New Mexico v. Jose Montoya and Jose Francoso," February 9, 1850; Lavender, *Bent's Fort*, 18–19.
120. 1850 Federal Census, Santa Fe County, New Mexico Territory.
121. TRNMSF, District Court Records, "New Mexico v. Jose Francoso," March 3, 1848.
122. The verdict for this case does not survive, but somehow Francoso made bail at $150. See TRNMSF, District Court Records, "New Mexico v. Jose Francoso," June 27, 1849.
123. TRNMSF, District Court Records, "New Mexico v. Jose Francoso," November 14, 1849.
124. Jose Francisco was never indicted for a violent crime, which suggests that he was unlikely to be robbing at gunpoint. See TRNMSF, District Court Records, "New Mexico v. Jose Montoya and Jose Francoso," February 9, 1850.
125. TRNMSF, District Court Records, "New Mexico v. Jose Francoso," September 25, 1856.
126. 1850 Federal Census, Santa Fe County, New Mexico Territory.
127. TRNMSF, District Court Records, "New Mexico v. Jose Sena," March 12, 1847.
128. New Mexico State Records Center and Archives, New Mexico Secretary of State Collection, Laws of New Mexico, Serial #4869, Laws of the Seventh Session, 1857–1858, chapter IX, section 13.
129. Gutiérrez, *When Jesus Came, the Corn Mothers Went Away*, 191.
130. New Mexico State Records Center and Archives, New Mexico Secretary of State Collection: Laws of New Mexico, Serial # 4863, 59, Kearny Code.
131. TRNMSF, District Court Records.
132. New Mexico State Records Center and Archives, New Mexico Secretary of State Collection,

Laws of New Mexico, Serial #4869, Laws of the Seventh Session, 1857–1858, chapter IX, section 13.
133. New Mexico State Records Center and Archives, New Mexico Secretary of State Collection, Laws of New Mexico, Serial #4869, Laws of the Seventh Session, 1857–1858, chapter IX, section 14.
134. TRNMSF, District Court Records, "New Mexico v. Jose Sena," January 6, 1853.
135. 1860 Federal Census, Santa Fe County, New Mexico Territory.
136. Although the records don't exist detailing this crime, the 1850 census shows only one Maria Martin in the same household as a person named Maria Cepreana, and they are listed as living with Jose Maria Martin, a thirty-seven-year-old farmer in Bernalillo County. See 1850 Federal Census, Santa Fe County, New Mexico Territory
137. TRNMSF, District Court Records, "New Mexico v. Jose Sena," January 18, 1853.
138. In addition to legalizing public lashings, the Kearny Code also allowed for indentured servitude as a punishment. The code was written by the American military, so it is not surprising that the punishments therein mirror the harsh punishments usually used in military courts. But the addition of indentured servitude as a punishment is different, and it provides insight into how the authors of the Kearny Code viewed New Mexican vecinos. Article III, section 14 allowed that if a person was unable to pay their fine, they may be bound to labor for up to ten years. Kearny Code, 66–67.
139. The only existing evidence documenting this practice are the on small scraps of paper scribbled in the hand of Marshal Jones. See TRNMSF, District Court Records, "New Mexico v. Jose Sena (1853), New Mexico v. Luis Rivera (1853), New Mexico v. Guadalupe the Navajo (1853)," box 2-3.
140. The 1850 U.S. Census data for Santa Fe County reveals that there were 253 servants: 28 were born in Mexico, 20 Native Americans, 9 African, 2 European, and 194 New Mexican vecinos. Servitude was a major issue in the territory, as it was throughout the United States. Like slavery, many Hispano and Mexicano servants were born into servitude and passed on by local caudillos.
141. TRNMSF, District Court Records, "New Mexico v. Jose Sena," June 13, 1853.
142. The New Mexico sociopolitical structure made indebted servitude a permanent institution, not unlike slavery. Though New Mexicans called their institution indebted peonage, there was little difference between peons in New Mexico and slaves in the American South.
143. Foos, *A Short, Offhand, Killing Affair*, 113–16.
144. See, for example, Rebecca McDowell Craver, *The Impact of Intimacy: Mexican-Anglo Intermarriage in New Mexico, 1821–1846* (El Paso: Texas Western Press, 1982); Claire V. McKanna, *Race and Homicide in Nineteenth Century California* (Reno: University of Nevada Press, 2002). There were 6,912 Hispanos in Santa Fe and 773 whites (which includes Europeans) in 1850. Many whites had been in Santa Fe since the Mexican period, and they were often married to the daughters of New Mexico's landholding class. Familial ties tethered their loyalty to one another, and they did not waver in the face of newly arrived soldiers, federally appointed officials, and most of all white *adventurers*. These officials, many of them early traders, were bound by marriage to the Hispano families, even naming their children Hispanicized names like Juan and Jose. This (combined with the small numbers in which whites came) prevented white settlers from behaving as they did in California, where in many places they simply overran the population with numbers, pushed Californios and Natives from their own land, and often murdered those who resisted.
145. For data on New Mexico and California homicide rates, see Michael J. Alarid, "They Came From the East: Importing Homicide, Violence, and Misconceptions of Soft Justice into Early Santa Fe, New Mexico, 1847–1853" in Orlando Romero, ed., *All Trails Lead to Santa Fe: An Anthology Commemorating the 400th Anniversary of the Founding of Santa Fe, New Mexico in 1610* (Santa Fe: Sunstone Press, 2010), 301–3; and McKanna, *Race and Homicide in Nineteenth Century California*, 103–5. There simply has not been enough work on larceny in other regions to mathematically contextualize vecino and white larceny in Santa Fe County. In the case of homicide, however, much has been done to demonstrate that homicide is lower among

established populations, and I am convinced we will ultimately see that the same applies to crime more broadly. Whites in California made up the vast majority: they multiplied from 8,000 in 1846, to 92,597 in 1850, to 379,942 in 1860; meanwhile, the population of Californios was roughly 7,500. Where they were the majority, and where they fared well fiscally, whites committed homicide at dramatically lower rates: between 1849 and 1865, whites in California killed at the rate of 52 per 100,000; meanwhile, whites in Santa Fe County, where whites were a decided minority, they killed at the rate of 222 per 100,000 from 1847 to 1853. The inverse was true for Hispanics: empowered Hispanos in Santa Fe killed at the rate of 23 per 100,000, while destabilized Californios killed at the rate of 161 per 100,000.

146. Lavender, *Bent's Fort*, 276.
147. TRNMSF, District Court Records, "New Mexico v. Charles Robbinsdean," May 21, 1849.
148. 1850 Federal Census, Santa Fe County, New Mexico Territory; 1860 Federal Census, Santa Fe County, New Mexico Territory. There were few whites who stayed in the territory, and the overwhelming majority of those who remained were still without prospects in 1860.
149. Hall, *Social Change in the Southwest*, 216–17.
150. See Mocho, *Murder and Justice in Frontier New Mexico*.
151. These cases in Santa Fe County took place in military court.
152. *MANM*, utilizing the available microfilm edition of the *MANM*, I have transcribed the surviving criminal court cases into a data set. Of these thirty-four from other towns, twenty are records of violent crimes, suggesting that perhaps cases involving violence were more likely to have surviving documentation while those for petty larceny were dealt with locally.
153. There are three plausible and intermingling explanations to account for this dearth of regional documentation: (1) documenting lesser cases, such as petty larceny, in more rural areas of New Mexico was not a priority; (2) many alcaldes in some rural areas were not literate; (3) the case files for the majority of nonviolent crimes simply never made it back to Santa Fe. Some combination of these contributing factors likely accounts for the paucity of criminal records throughout the more rural areas, but though they make it challenging to analyze crime in other parts of New Mexico, the same cannot be said for the villa of Santa Fe. Cutter notes that during the Spanish period, petty larceny did not mandate record keeping and was often dealt with swiftly, without documentation. Jill Mocho writes, "It seems safe to assume that most local justices, although they had no legal education, were generally literate men, respected by their communities as competent and fair arbitrators." See Cutter, *The Legal Culture of Northern New Spain*, 9; Mocho, *Murder and Justice in Frontier New Mexico*, 8.
154. In total, there are references in criminal court records, the writings of Manuel Alvarez, and the letters of Charles Blumner, that suggest a total of nineteen homicides in New Mexico between 1838 and 1846. See Charles Blumner Collection, Letters (AC 231). Angélico Chávez History Library, Palace of the Governors, Santa Fe, NM; Thomas E. Chávez, *Manuel Alvarez, 1794–1856: A Southwestern Biography* (Niwot: University Press of Colorado, 1990), 100–101.
155. It is difficult to distinguish Anglo soldiers from Anglo settlers in the Santa Fe County District Court Records, but it is telling that in the 1850 census four American soldiers are in the Santa Fe County Jail for burglary. Their case files are not in the district court records.
156. TRNMSF, District Court Records, "New Mexico v. Henry Potter and Samuel Rino," February 27, 1850.
157. 1850 Federal Census, Santa Fe County, New Mexico Territory.
158. TRNMSF, District Court Records, "New Mexico v. Henry Potter and Samuel Rino," February 27, 1850.
159. TRNMSF, District Court Records, "New Mexico v. Heinrich Boze," March 3, 1849.
160. Article III, section 1 of the Kearny Code was the only law that empowered judges to pass punishments of this length. It dictated that perjury was punishable by five to ten years of imprisonment. It is also possible, however, that a combination of crimes took place, such as committing larceny and also illegally selling alcohol to non-Pueblo Natives. Boze must have done more than the surviving records suggest, because the maximum penalty for larceny was capped at two years. See Kearny Code, 59–67.

161. 1850 Federal Census, Santa Fe County, New Mexico Territory.
162. TRNMSF, District Court Records, "New Mexico v. John Cline," January 7, 1849.
163. 1850 United States Census, Santa Fe County.
164. TRNMSF, District Court Records, "New Mexico v William Goodfellow," May 25, 1850.
165. Records do not exist in the Santa Fe District Court Records for eight of the fourteen Anglo prisoners who were locked up for larceny and burglary in the Santa Fe County jail in 1850. This means that Anglos committed larceny at higher rates than are noted in table 2.3.
166. TRNMSF, District Court Records, "New Mexico v. William Guiser," October 24, 1849.
167. TRNMSF, District Court Records, "New Mexico v. Thomas Stone," May 10, 1850.
168. TRNMSF, District Court Records, "New Mexico v. Levon," March 1, 1849.
169. TRNMSF, District Court Records, "New Mexico v. Thomas Stone," May 10, 1850.
170. By 1860, the percentage of whites in Santa Fe County had fallen from 10 percent of the county population (803) to 6 percent (511). Those that remained were either those who were already part of the community or those who filled the needs of the town, such as lawyers, craftsmen, and laborers. By 1860, white larceny dramatically decreased, with seldom more than five occurring per annum after 1855. See 1850 Federal Census, Santa Fe County, New Mexico Territory; 1860 Federal Census, Santa Fe County, New Mexico Territory; TRNMSF, 1847–1860.
171. Hall, *Social Change in the Southwest*, 217.
172. Although all Hispanos and Anglos are considered when calculating rates, the names of wealthier segments of the population do not appear in the criminal court records, which is proof that crime was more often among vecinos and poor Anglo settlers.

CHAPTER THREE

1. *Santa Fe Weekly Gazette*, November 19, 1853, 2. The article contained here was written by an eyewitness, who was present throughout the affair.
2. Randolph Roth, *American Homicide* (Cambridge, MA: Belknap Press of Harvard University Press, 2009), 360.
3. The homicide rate for the Hispano community was 23.3 per 100,000 per year, which is a relatively low rate when compared to other western counties. The Anglo settler homicide rate was 166.3 per 100,000 per year, making them seven times as likely to commit homicide. New Mexico State Records Center and Archives, *Records of the United States Territorial and New Mexico District Courts for Santa Fe County 1847–1951* (hereafter TRNMSF).
4. The overall homicide rate in Santa Fe from 1847 to 1853, including both Anglo settlers and Hispanos, was 42 per 100,000 per year, nearly double the rate of 23.3 per 100,000 per year within the older Hispano community. TRNMSF.
5. Roth, *American Homicide*, 354–55.
6. New Mexico State Records Center and Archives, *Records of the United States Territorial and New Mexico District Courts for Santa Fe County 1847–1953*, collection 1974-033, II box 1–3.
7. Randolph Roth, "Homicide Rates in the Nineteenth-Century West: Tables, July 2010 Version," Historical Violence Database, Criminal Justice Research Center, Ohio State University, 2010; TRNMSF, collection 1974-033, II.
8. TRNMSF, box 1–3; Roth, "Homicide Rates in the Nineteenth-Century West."
9. Donald Walker, "Hispanics in San Joaquin County, 1850–1930," *San Joaquin Historian* XV, no. 1 (2001): 3.
10. My interpretation of the homicide data in Santa Fe County is the basis of this chapter. I am aware that homicide is not monocausal. There is, however, an irrefutable historical correlation between homicide rates and how people feel about their government. My arguments, therefore, are based on those correlations, as well as other long-standing theories about why people commit homicide. To be clear, there are other variables that also correlate with homicide in different historical moments. For example, after the Civil War, homicide rates in counties that

were renamed in honor of Union heroes declined across the board. Roth postulates that this is due to a rise in patriotism in those counties. But in terms of homicide rates over time, the level of faith people have in their institutions correlates more directly than any other known variable, including poverty and the proliferation of guns.

11. Roth notes that low homicide rates correlate with three variables: political stability, legitimate government, and legitimate status hierarchies. At least two of these variables were present in Santa Fe County, from 1846 to 1854. See: https://cjrc.osu.edu/sites/cjrc.osu.edu/files/grant-proposal-and-bibliography.pdf, 2.
12. As Roth argued, "Nothing suppresses homicide within a social group more powerfully than a sense of connectedness that extends beyond the bounds of family and neighborhood and forges a strong bond among people who share race, ethnicity, religion, or nationality." See Roth, *American Homicide*, 22.
13. Hubert Howe Bancroft, *The Works of Hubert Howe Bancroft, Volume XVII: History of Arizona and New Mexico, 1530–1888* (San Francisco: The History Company, Publishers, 1889), 642.
14. Stephen S. Birdsall and John Florin, "Regional Landscapes of the United States: Southwest Border Area," Outline of American Geography, November 1988.
15. Sumner moved many of his soldiers in an effort to curb crime in Santa Fe County, but this failed because the white American and European soldiers still traveled to Santa Fe during their off days. The army moved its headquarters back to Santa Fe in 1852 but left the majority of the soldiers at Fort Union; as a result, they were not counted in the 1860 census, even though they continued to commit crimes in Santa Fe County. See "The Founding of Fort Union," Fort Union National Monument, Historical Handbook Number 35, 1962.
16. 1850 Federal Census, Santa Fe County, New Mexico Territory; 1860 Federal Census, Santa Fe County, New Mexico Territory.
17. Felipe Gonzales, *Política: Nuevomexicanos and American Political Incorporation, 1821–1910* (Lincoln: University of Nebraska Press, 2016), 2–3.
18. Andrés Reséndez, *Changing National Identities at the Frontier: Texas and New Mexico, 1800–1850* (Cambridge: Press Syndicate of the University of Cambridge, 2005), 255–56.
19. Roth, *American Homicide*, 360–61.
20. Clare V. McKanna Jr., *Race and Homicide in Nineteenth-Century California* (Reno: University of Nevada Press, 2002).
21. Roth, *American Homicide*, 360.
22. See Roth, *American Homicide*, 360, McKanna, *Race and Homicide in Nineteenth-Century California*, 74.
23. Randolph Roth, "American Homicide Supplemental Volume: American Homicides," Historical Violence Database, Criminal Justice Research Center, Ohio State University, May 2010, table 34.
24. 1850 Federal Census, Santa Fe County, New Mexico Territory; 1860 Federal Census, Santa Fe County, New Mexico Territory.
25. This was a condition of the Compromise of 1850 contained in section 5.
26. Bancroft, *The Works of Hubert Howe Bancroft*, 634–37.
27. Alvin R. Sunseri, *Seeds of Discord: New Mexico in the Aftermath of the American Conquest, 1846–1861* (Chicago: Nelson-Hall, 1979), 126–27.
28. William G. Ritch, *New Mexico Blue Book, 1882* (Albuquerque: University of New Mexico Press, 1968), 99–107.
29. Fray Angélico Chávez, *Très Macho—He Said: Padre Gallegos of Albuquerque, New Mexico's First Congressman* (Santa Fe: William Gannon, 1985), 66–69.
30. Fray Angelico Chávez and Thomas E. Chávez, *Wake for a Fat Vicar: Father Juan Felipe Ortiz, Archbishop Lamy, and the New Mexican Catholic Church in the Middle of the Nineteenth Century* (Albuquerque: LPD Press, 2004), 127, 194–95.
31. Chávez, *Très Macho—He Said*, 77.
32. Bancroft, *The Works of Hubert Howe Bancroft*, 637.
33. Sunseri, *Seeds of Discord*, 128.

34. Sunseri, *Seeds of Discord*, 127–28.
35. Bancroft, *The Works of Hubert Howe Bancroft*, 637.
36. Sunseri, *Seeds of Discord*, 128.
37. Letters From the Secretary of The Territory of New Mexico, 32nd Congress, 1st Session, Miscellaneous, No. 4, 1851, 15 (hereafter Letters).
38. Letters, 16.
39. Letters, 16–17.
40. Sunseri, *Seeds of Discord*, 130.
41. Letters, 32.
42. Letters, 32, 65.
43. New Mexico State Records Center and Archives, New Mexico Secretary of State Collection, Laws of New Mexico, Serial # 4863, 1851–54.
44. New Mexico State Records Center and Archives, New Mexico Secretary of State Collection, Laws of New Mexico, Serial # 4863, 1851–54.
45. Mocho found records for only eleven homicides throughout the twenty-five-year Mexican period. There are additional references to another eight homicides, all taking place outside of Santa Fe, but if these ever reached the court no documentation remains. Though Mocho concedes there are likely missing records, the dearth of New Mexico homicides during the Mexican period reveals a society far less prone to violence before American settlement.
46. Josiah Gregg, *Commerce of the Prairies: A Selection* (Indianapolis, IN: Bobbs-Merrill Company, Inc., 1970), 76.
47. The other five case files contain sparse details and do not reveal the weapon used by the perpetrators. TRNMSF.
48. Roth, *American Homicide*, 5.
49. The Exchange Hotel, once known as the Inn at the End of the Trail or La Fonda, was purchased in 1847 by Anglo settlers. The building was not altered until it was purchased again in the twentieth century by a corporation that demolished it and built the new Hotel La Fonda, which remains at the original site on the plaza.
50. West Gilbreath, *Death on the Gallows: The Story of Legal Hangings in New Mexico 1847–1923* (Silver City, NM: High Lonesome Books, 2002), 215.
51. The Texans marched toward Santa Fe in 1841 with the intention of fomenting a rebellion, but after they lost their way they submitted to the forces of New Mexico and were marched back to Mexico City. Most of the Texans died on the march, and animosity between the two parties never subsided. Anglo Settlers and Hispanos alike despised the Texans and were always fearful of another potential Texas invasion. See: Chávez and Chávez, *Wake for a Fat Vicar*, 56–58.
52. *Santa Fe Weekly Gazette*, November 19, 1853, 2, Stephenson offered his gun as collateral.
53. *Santa Fe Weekly Gazette*, November 19, 1853, 2.
54. *Santa Fe Weekly Gazette*, November 19, 1853, 2.
55. *Santa Fe Weekly Gazette*, November 19, 1853, 2.
56. This was obviously anything but impartial. In fact all available sources, which include the conversations related, the language of the trial, and the decision to condemn without the authority of the alcaldes made it overwhelmingly clear that the lynch mob was made up primarily of whites, with a smattering of curious observers from the old New Mexican community. This was a kangaroo court indeed!
57. *Santa Fe Weekly Gazette*, November 19, 1853, 2.
58. Gilbreath uncovered evidence of 155 lynchings in the New Mexico territory between 1851 and 1893. Another Texan, whose name remains unknown, was also lynched on June 14, 1851, in Santa Fe. See Gilbreath, *Death on the Gallows*, 215.
59. Court records connect the following citizens to Jesus Maria Baca y Sena. They include Ignacio Tapia, Andres Tapia, Felix Tapia, Candido Ortiz, Clemente Ortiz, Jesus Silva, Poleto Olivas, Jose Zaccarillos, Rufugio Villalobas, Delores Sena, Jesus Romero, Jesus Maria Baca, Jose Baca, Fernando Sandoval, Pablo Duran, Juan Duro, and Mauricio Arce.

60. Samuel E. Sisneros, "She Was Our Mother: New Mexico's Change of National Sovereignty," in *All Trails Lead to Santa Fe: An Anthology Commemorating the 400th Anniversary of the Founding of Santa Fe, New Mexico in 1610*, ed. Orlando Romero (Santa Fe: Sunstone Press, 2010), 279–80; *Santa Fe Weekly Gazette*, July 9, 1853, 2.
61. *Santa Fe Weekly Gazette*, July 9, 1853, 2.
62. District Court Records, Court Docket Book, 1850–53.
63. *Santa Fe Weekly Gazette*, July 9, 1853, 2. The *Gazette* also names John Tuley as defense attorney and Justice Reed as presiding judge.
64. *Santa Fe Weekly Gazette*, July 16, 1853, 2.
65. *Santa Fe Weekly Gazette*, July 16, 1853, 2.
66. *Santa Fe Weekly Gazette*, July 16, 1853, 2.
67. The use of females as victims has long been a rhetorical tool utilized to inspire outrage, especially against people from different ethnic groups. *Santa Fe Weekly Gazette*, July 16, 1853, 2.
68. *Santa Fe Weekly Gazette*, July 16, 1853, 2.
69. TRNMSF, District Court Records, "New Mexico v. Ignacio Tapia," June 1, 1853.
70. There is no mention of Tapia or his alleged conspirators in this comprehensive study of legal hangings. There is also no mention of Tapia and his fellow rebels in the list of known lynchings in New Mexico. See Gilbreath, *Death on the Gallows*, 134–47, 215–19.
71. I have included this homicide as a Hispano homicide, one of two that involved a gun. I suspect that John Finnegan was killed by friendly fire from a fellow Anglo, but since Tapia was accused I have counted it as committed by him.
72. Leo E. Olive, "Fort Union and the Frontier Army in the Southwest: A Historical Research, Fort Union National Monument, Fort Union, New Mexico" (Santa Fe: Southwest Cultural Resources Center Professional Paper #41 Division of History, 1993), chap. 9, accessed May 5, 2011, http://www.nps.gov/history/history/online_books/foun/chap9.htm.
73. TRNMSF, District Court Records, box 1–3; all jury lists in the twelve Anglo homicide cases are made up exclusively of Anglo jurors.
74. Jill Mocho, *Murder and Justice in Frontier New Mexico, 1821–1846* (Albuquerque: University of New Mexico Press, 1997), 24–25.
75. Mocho, *Murder and Justice in Frontier New Mexico*, 26.
76. Mocho, *Murder and Justice in Frontier New Mexico*, 51–53.
77. Mocho, *Murder and Justice in Frontier New Mexico*, 54.
78. Alcalde Trinidad Barceló refused to believe that Chaves had killed his wife in retaliation, but Chaves repeated the story. This enraged the alcalde, who protested his reasoning and contended that being struck by a rock was not sufficient grounds to murder one's spouse. The defensor Cabesa de Baca argued that the murder was not premeditated, but was in fact a spontaneous action provoked by the argument between Chaves and his wife. The defensor called for leniency because Chaves was Puebloan and thus was raised with a different value system that permitted murder in the form of defense. Unfortunately, the case file ends before a resolution is found, but Chaves was likely sitting in jail as the Americans approached Santa Fe. See Mocho, *Murder and Justice in Frontier New Mexico*, 57–58.
79. TRNMSF, District Court Records, "New Mexico v. Pablo Rael," 1848.
80. Rael is listed as nonworking, and the writing in the far column of the census page declares him "insane," having "killed his wife and sister." The family is listed as having $60 worth of land. 1850 United States Census, Santa Fe County, 26.
81. TRNMSF, District Court Records, "New Mexico v. Manuel Sandoval," 1849.
82. In the 1850 United States Census, Santa Fe County, Santa Fe City, 85, Sandoval is listed as in jail, convicted of the crime of manslaughter.
83. TRNMSF, District Court Records, "New Mexico v. James C. Brady," 1848.
84. TRNMSF, District Court Records, "New Mexico v. James C. Brady," Indictment by John Tulles, 1, 1848.
85. TRNMSF, District Court Records, "New Mexico v. James C. Brady," Indictment by Hugh N. Smith, 1, 1848.

86. TRNMSF, District Court Records, "New Mexico v. James C. Brady," Notes of Attorney Allen Clark, 1–2, 1848.
87. TRNMSF, District Court Records, "New Mexico v. James C. Brady," Jury List, 1, 1848; of the twelve jury members listed, only two, John Abell and Charles Giddings, remained in the territory until 1850.
88. TRNMSF, District Court Records, "New Mexico v. O.P. Anderson," Indictment by Alcalde J. Smith, 1852.
89. Sunseri was mistaken about the fate of the homicide and the name of the perpetrator, whom he called W. C. Anderson. Sunseri got the story from the *Missouri Republican*, which reported the details inaccurately. Sunseri, *Seeds of Discord*, 101.
90. TRNMSF, District Court Records, "New Mexico v. O.P. Anderson," Indictment by unknown Author, 1852.
91. TRNMSF, District Court Records, Court Docket Book, 1850–53, 20, 28–29.
92. TRNMSF, District Court Records, Court Docket Book, 1850–53, 16.
93. Made only eight years removed from Mexican rule, the depiction in figure 3.8 mirrors fandangos in Santa Fe, which were filled with peoples of all classes and ethnic origins. As in the picture, Santa Fe fandangos featured ornately decorated rooms with crucifixes, pictures of saints, and damsels waltzing with men of all backgrounds. The depiction here is of a more humble fandango, very common in the countryside, but ornate fandangos with champagne and fine foods were held at wealthier homes and within the Palace of the Governors. The fandango remained an important part of Santa Fe culture after American settlers arrived, though they became increasingly violent when whiskey-drinking Americans participated. Hispanos had used the fandango to transcend cultural and class barriers; wealthy Nuevomexicanas could be seen waltzing with poor farmers, Native Americans with Nuevomexicanas, and wealthy elites with poor vecinas. As more settlers arrived, American participation increased and the function of the fandango as a social bonding institution was permanently altered into an event directed toward entertainment. See C. Castro, J. Campillo, L. Auda, and G. Rodriguez "Mexico y Sus Alrededores" (Alicante: Miguel de Cervantes Virtual Library, 2006); Casimiro Castro y J. Campillo "Trajes Mexicanos: A Fandango" (1855), XXIX; Emily E. Keita, "The New Mexico Fandango," *Wagontracks* 19, issue no. 3 (May 2005): 1–13. Hyslop documents numerous accounts of traditional fandangos by early travelers from the United States. See Stephen G. Hyslop, *Bound for Santa Fe: The Road to New Mexico and the American Conquest, 1806–1848* (Norman: University of Oklahoma Press, 2002), 268.
94. Bennett's account portrays these two fandangos as being diametrically opposed, the first account of a traditional fandango in San Miguel del Bado and the second a commodified fandango in Santa Fe. Though Bennett does not situate them in this fashion and fails to perceive this distinction between the two fandangos he documents, it becomes clear to the modern reader that what separates the two fandangos he documents is the presence of alcohol and Americans. Clinton Brook and Frank Reeve, *Forts and Forays: James A. Bennett, a Dragoon in New Mexico, 1850–56* (Albuquerque: University of New Mexico Press, 1948), 15, 20.
95. New Mexico State Records Center and Archives, *Mexican Archives of New Mexico, 1821–1846* (Santa Fe: New Mexico State Records Center and Archives, 1969) (hereafter *MANM*), roll 5, frame 1016.
96. Mocho, *Murder and Justice in Frontier New Mexico*, 76.
97. Mocho, *Murder and Justice in Frontier New Mexico*, 78–79.
98. Mocho, *Murder and Justice in Frontier New Mexico*, 81.
99. Mocho, *Murder and Justice in Frontier New Mexico*, 82. The defensor was the person selected to defend the accused, much like a public defender, but not formally schooled in law.
100. Mocho, *Murder and Justice in Frontier New Mexico*, 83.
101. For a quick reference guide to crime committed by Mexican soldiers, see the finding aid for the microfilm edition of the *MANM*, housed in the New Mexico State Records Center and Archive. See *MANM*.

102. In actuality, soldiers proved to be a great deal of trouble for the Hispano people and arguably caused more problems than their protection was worth. From incidents of burglary, to assaults on the local population, to homicides, Mexican soldiers committed as many crimes as recently arrived Anglo settlers. Of the 164 surviving criminal court cases from the Mexican period, 29 involved Anglo settlers while 27 involved Mexican soldiers. See *MANM*.
103. *MANM*, roll 33, frame 979.
104. Mocho, *Murder and Justice in Frontier New Mexico*, 87.
105. The presence of items for sale, including spirituous beverages, is a clear sign that this was not a fandango given by a local patrón, but instead one organized by poorer members of the community who often sold items to offset the cost of throwing such a party.
106. Mocho, *Murder and Justice in Frontier New Mexico*, 91.
107. Mocho, *Murder and Justice in Frontier New Mexico*, 90.
108. Mocho, *Murder and Justice in Frontier New Mexico*, 92–93.
109. Charles R. Cutter, *The Legal Culture of Northern New Spain* (Albuquerque: University of New Mexico Press, 1995).
110. Mocho, *Murder and Justice in Frontier New Mexico*, 95.
111. TRNMSF, boxes 1–3.
112. TRNMSF, District Court Records, "New Mexico v. Christian Mild," Inquest by Sheriff E. L. Vaughn, 1853.
113. Alcaldes would not have used a jury.
114. Traditionally, drinking was kept to a minimum, but white American soldiers, settlers, and European settlers were more given to excess at these soirées. Keita, "The New Mexico Fandango."
115. The German population in the American Southwest was small and Jaehn's book is the definitive book on their activities in New Mexico. Though the case happens before Jaehn's study begins and is therefore omitted from his work, the inquest of Sheriff E. L. Vaughn clearly identifies Christian Mild as a German immigrant. Although Mild was German, I include him with other white settlers for the purpose of this study. See Tomas Jaehn, *Germans in the Southwest: 1850–1920* (Albuquerque: University of New Mexico Press, 2005), 31.
116. Traditional fandangos were held by wealthy Hispanos at the cost of the host, who used the occasion to better relations between his person and the other classes of citizens. Everyone was invited who wished to attend without cost, and all were welcome to the event. See Keita, "The New Mexico Fandango," 3.
117. TRNMSF, District Court Records, "New Mexico v. Christian Mild," Inquest by Sheriff E. L. Vaughn, 1–2, 1853.
118. TRNMSF, District Court Records, "New Mexico v. Christian Mild," Inquest by Sheriff E. L. Vaughn, 1–9, 1853.
119. TRNMSF, District Court Records, "New Mexico v. Christian Mild," Indictment by Hugh N. Smith, 1–2, 1853.
120. TRNMSF, District Court Records, "New Mexico v. Christian Mild," Inquest by Sheriff E. L. Vaughn, 1–2, 1853.
121. TRNMSF, District Court Records, "New Mexico v. Christian Mild," Inquest by Sheriff E. L. Vaughn, 2, 1853.
122. TRNMSF, District Court Records, "New Mexico v. Christian Mild," Inquest by Sheriff E. L. Vaughn, 2, 1853.
123. TRNMSF, District Court Records, "New Mexico v. Christian Mild," Inquest by Sheriff E. L. Vaughn, 2, 1853.
124. TRNMSF, District Court Records, "New Mexico v. Christian Mild," Inquest by Sheriff E. L. Vaughn, 2–3, 1853.
125. TRNMSF, District Court Records, "New Mexico v. Christian Mild," Inquest by Sheriff E. L. Vaughn, 3, 9, 1853.
126. TRNMSF, District Court Records, "New Mexico v. Christian Mild," Inquest by Sheriff E. L. Vaughn, 10, 1853.

127. TRNMSF, District Court Records, "New Mexico v. Christian Mild," Inquest by Sheriff E. L. Vaughn, 3, 1853.
128. TRNMSF, District Court Records, "New Mexico v. Christian Mild," Inquest by Sheriff E. L. Vaughn, 4, 1853.
129. TRNMSF, District Court Records, "New Mexico v. Christian Mild," Inquest by Sheriff E. L. Vaughn, 1–10, 1853.
130. TRNMSF, District Court Records, "New Mexico v. Christian Mild," Inquest by Sheriff E. L. Vaughn, 5, 1853.
131. TRNMSF, District Court Records, boxes 1–3. Commencing in late 1848, Hispanos are listed in the jury lists and witnesses in the majority of cases, including those that do not involve Hispano litigants.
132. Sunseri, *Seeds of Discord*, 129.
133. There were six Anglos who served in the House and one who served in the Council. Hugh N. Smith served in the Council and he was a longtime resident of Santa Fe. Merrill Amhurst, Theodore Wheaton, Robert T. Brent, Palmer J. Pilans, William C. Skinner, and Spruce M. Baird all served in the House.
134. McKanna, *Race and Homicide in Nineteenth-Century California*, 56.
135. McKanna, *Race and Homicide in Nineteenth-Century California*, 75.
136. Roth, *American Homicide*, 18.
137. Paul Foos, *A Short, Offhand, Killing Affair: Soldiers and Social Conflict during the Mexican-American War* (Chapel Hill: University of North Carolina Press, 2002), 151–54.

CHAPTER FOUR

1. 1850 United States Federal Census, Santa Fe County, New Mexico Territory.
2. *Santa Fe Weekly Gazette*, November 1, 1856, 2.
3. New Mexico State Records Center and Archives, "Records of the United States Territorial and New Mexico District Courts for Santa Fe County 1847–1951" (hereafter TRNMSF), collection 1974-033, II, "New Mexico v. Francisco Martin," November Term, 1856.
4. *Santa Fe Weekly Gazette*, November 1, 1856, 2.
5. Mocho found records for only eleven homicides committed by Nuevomexicanos throughout the entire twenty-five-year Mexican period (1820–1846). There are additional references to another eight homicides, all taking place outside of Santa Fe, but if these ever reached the court, no documentation remains. Though Mocho concedes there are likely missing records, the dearth of New Mexico homicides during the Mexican period reveals a society far less prone to violence before American settlement. Jill Mocho, *Murder and Justice in Frontier New Mexico 1821–1846* (Albuquerque: University of New Mexico Press, 1997).
6. As LaFree and Roth show, increases in homicide historically correlate with how people feel about their government, meaning if it protects their interests or not. This is not to say that the rise of homicide is monocausal. Instead, I am arguing that vecinos lost their recourse to resolve problems peacefully when they lost faith in their system of government. Gary LaFree, *Losing Legitimacy: Street Crime and the Decline of Social Institutions in America* (Boulder, CO: Westview Press, 1998); Randolph Roth, *American Homicide* (Cambridge, MA: Belknap Press of Harvard University Press, 2009).
7. Jean Jaques Rousseau, *Political Writings* (Madison: University of Wisconsin Press, 1986), 3–7.
8. Between 1847 and 1855, vecinos committed a total of twelve homicides. In 1856–1856 vecinos committed fifteen homicides. TRNMSF, collection 1974-033, II, 1847–1860.
9. TRNMSF, collection 1974-033, II, 1847–1860.
10. This move to combine crimes to make a logical category is similar to what the sociologist Gary LaFree did in his landmark book *Losing Legitimacy*. Lafree combined homicide, assault, and larceny into the category he called street crime, and this was done to understand crime in post–World War II America more broadly. In this instance, I have combined only homicide

and assault, creating the category of "violent crime," and I have done so because prior to 1856 assaults often unintentionally became homicides. Combining assault and homicide here reveals much about how violence in Santa Fe County was actually trending upward for much of the early period. See LaFree, *Losing Legitimacy*; TRNMSF, collection 1974-033, II, 1847–1860.
11. See Chapter 3.
12. As we can see in figure 4.2, 1850 marked the first sizable wave in violent crime (256.71 per 100,000). That number dropped, but was then eclipsed in 1854, when the rate of violent crime reached 292.83 per 100,000. From 1854 to 1857, the upward trend continued to 366.03 per 100,000, to 485.93 per 100,000, and finally to the apex of 511.51 per 100,000. For our purposes, though, the trend is more important than the actual rates, and what is truly revealed here is that *something* was building in Santa Fe County within the Nuevomexicano community, and it ultimately manifested in the form of violence. Still, the rates in this instance have no equivalents outside of this study, because the statistical category of "violent crime" has been created specifically for this study, but it most closely resembles Gary LaFree's category of "street crime." As a result, we cannot yet contextualize these rates and situate them within broader trends elsewhere. Regardless, what really matters is the gradual trend that emerges through this category, so it is my hope that others may also find this category useful and might implement this same category in future studies. See TRNMSF, collection 1974-033, II, 1847–1860.
13. From 1847 to 1850, the white homicide rate was 161.71 per 100,000 compared to 29.17 per 100,000 in the Hispano community; from 1851 to 1855, white homicide was 141.24 per 100,000 versus the Nuevomexicano rate of 34.16 per 100,000; from 1856 to 1857, the Hispano historical moment that saw Nuevomexicano community homicide reach the epic high of 179.03 per 100,000, white homicide was *still* higher at 233.65 per 100,000; and even from 1858 to 1860, as the Nuevomexicano rate declined to 75.44 per 100,000, white homicide reached an all-time high for this period of study of 652.32 per 100,000 in Santa Fe County. TRNMSF, collection 1974-033, II, 1847–1860.
14. There was a slight rise in the number of fatal knifings among whites. In one instance Daniel Chastain had a terrible problem with James H. Houston, who plunged his knife into the right side of Chastain's stomach during their quarrel in 1859. Houston drove his full six-inch blade into Chastain, creating a gaping hole that could not mend; Chastain suffered three full days before finally succumbing to his wound. Still, the gun remained the weapon of choice. TRNMSF, collection 1974-033, II, "New Mexico v. James H. Houston," August 7, 1859.
15. From 1851 to 1855, white assault dropped to 194.05 per 100,000 versus the Nuevomexicano rate, which stayed consistent at 122.52 per 100,000; from 1855 to 1857, Hispano assault climbed to its highest rate, nearly tripling to 323.96 per 100,000, yet white assault roughly tripled and skyrocketed to 623.05 per 100,000; and once again from 1858 to 1860, as the Nuevomexicano assault rate dropped to 253.73 per 100,000, white assault ballooned to an all-time high of 717.55 per 100,000 in Santa Fe County. TRNMSF, collection 1974-033, II, 1847–1860.
16. There were three periods of extreme white settler violence. Two of these three periods were followed by precipitous declines in white violent crime, which illuminates the volatile nature of both the white community and recently arrived white settlers. Whites were anywhere from three to six times more likely than Nuevomexicanos to commit violent crime in the worst years, and it is telling that the risk of being a victim of a violent crime was higher among Nuevomexicanos in only three of the fourteen years covered in this study (1848, 1851, and 1855).
17. This was the same Jesus Maria Sena y Baca who got into trouble with the Americans on July 4, 1853, at the Exchange Hotel. He was among the group that opened fire on the Exchange Hotel that day and was named in the indictment. Sena y Baca, however, was part of the ruling class, so his charges were quickly dismissed, while the others were left to answer for the crime. See TRNMSF, collection 1974-033, II, "New Mexico v. Vicente Garcia, Juan Garcia, Manuel Garcia, and Pablo Delgado," June term, 1855.
18. 1850 United States Federal Census, Santa Fe County, New Mexico Territory; 1860 United States Federal Census, Santa Fe County, New Mexico Territory.
19. Felix Garcia was a wealthy merchant, and his son Vicente Garcia was an emerging merchant

worth $6,000 by 1860. Juan Garcia was a tailor and Manuel Garcia was a silversmith.
20. Pablo Delgado was the son of a well-known and wealthy merchant, Manuel Delgado, and was himself worth $5,000 by 1860. Susan Calafate Boyle, *Los Capitalistas: Hispano Merchants and the Santa Fe Trade* (Albuquerque: University of New Mexico Press, 1997), 70–71. 1860 United States Federal Census, Santa Fe County, New Mexico Territory.
21. TRNMSF, collection 1974-033, II, "New Mexico v. Jesus Sena y Baca," June term, 1855.
22. TRNMSF, collection 1974-033, II, "New Mexico v. Vicente Garcia, Juan Garcia, Manuel Garcia, and Pablo Delgado," June term, 1855.
23. 1850 United States Federal Census, Santa Fe County, New Mexico Territory; 1860 United States Federal Census, Santa Fe County, New Mexico Territory. It's noteworthy that these specific numbers only include property changes. While the 1860 census listed both property and wealth, the 1850 census only asked for property value. Therefore, I have left out the $447,760 in wealth that Nuevomexicanos reported in 1860 that no doubt also represented a massive increase in assets from 1850.
24. TRNMSF, collection 1974-033, II, "New Mexico v. Vicente Garcia, Juan Garcia, Manuel Garcia, and Pablo Delgado," June term, 1855.
25. Sena y Baca adamantly denied that he drew his gun at all, much less that he fired at Juan Garcia. He maintained that the Garcia brothers and Delgado conspired and lied to cover up the fact that they gave him a second beating when they saw him get up after the first. But the evidence did not support his claim. Court records indicated that Sena y Baca's sidearm contained only five live rounds; one of the shell casings was missing its projectile. TRNMSF, collection 1974-033, II, "New Mexico v. Jesus Sena y Baca," June term, 1855.
26. TRNMSF, collection 1974-033, II, "New Mexico v. Jesus Sena y Baca," June term, 1855.
27. Pierre Bourdieu, *Outline of a Theory of Practice*, in Bruce B. Lawrence and Aisha Karim, *On Violence: A Reader* (Durham, NC: Duke University Press, 2007), 193.
28. Lawrence and Karim, *On Violence*, 193–94.
29. Lawrence and Karim, *On Violence*, 195.
30. Hispano landholders ages fifteen to twenty, twenty-six to thirty, and thirty-one to forty in 1850 saw the most dramatic increases in upper value by 1860; their landholdings increasing fourteen times, twenty-four times, and two times respectively. That equated to an increase in mean landholding for these same age groups from nine times, to eight times, to seven times per person respectively.
31. The distribution of assets data, not included in this table, are similar to that of land: the vast majority of the holdings were concentrated in the hands of the large landholding families. Specifically, the number of those with land (814) and those with assets (831) is nearly identical, with seventeen more who own assets than those who own land (table 4.2). The only noticeable differences when comparing land and assets is in the value: The total value of land held by Nuevomexicano males fifteen and older ($427,400) is higher than the value of the assets owned ($393,026). This difference can be seen in higher mean value of land per person compared to the mean value of assets per person, most dramatically in the land value held by those aged thirty-six to forty ($414) versus the mean value of their assets ($245), a difference of $169 per person. In short, property remained the biggest source of wealth in New Mexico, but the value of assets was not far behind.
32. https://www.marketwatch.com/story/its-been-almost-a-100-years-since-the-americas-1-had-so-much-wealth-2019-02-11.
33. 1860 United States Federal Census, Santa Fe County, New Mexico Territory.
34. TRNMSF, collection 1972-011, I, Santa Fe County Docket Book, 1847–1858, 341–43, 374–75, 398.
35. TRNMSF, collection 1972–011, I, Santa Fe County Docket Book, 1847–1858, 398.
36. TRNMSF, collection 1974-033, II, "New Mexico v. Jesus Maria Baca y Salazar," June 2, 1855.
37. TRNMSF, collection 1972-011, I, Santa Fe County Docket Book, 1847–1858, 331.
38. TRNMSF, collection 1974-033, II, "New Mexico v. Jesus Maria Baca y Salazar," June 4, 1855.

39. New Mexico Contested Election: Papers and Testimony in the Case of Miguel A. Otero, Contesting the Seat of Jose M. Gallegos, Delegate from the Territory of New Mexico, H.R. Misc. Doc. No. 15, 34th Cong., 1st Sess. (1856), 32. There is a great deal of confusion as to the timeline of Sena y Baca's ascension to the office of sheriff, but on December 26, 1855, both Sheriff Jesus Maria Baca y Salazar and Deputy Jesus Maria Sena y Baca signed and certified a document sent by Judge Davenport regarding a contested election.
40. Larry D. Ball, *The United States Marshals of the New Mexico and Arizona Territories, 1846–1912* (Albuquerque: University of New Mexico Press, 1978), 24.
41. TRNMSF, collection 1974-033, II, "New Mexico v. Ignacio Tapia, Andres Tapia, Candido Ortiz, Jesus Maria Sena y Baca, Jesus Silva, Jose Zaccarillos, Clemente Ortiz, Rufugio Villalobas, and Jose Baca," October 9, 1856.
42. TRNMSF, collection 1974-033, II, "New Mexico v. Ignacio Tapia," March 1, 1850.
43. TRNMSF, collection 1974-033, II, "New Mexico v. Ignacio Sena," November 17, 1850.
44. TRNMSF, collection 1974-033, II, "New Mexico v. Ignacio Tapia, Delores Sena," February 20, 1852.
45. TRNMSF, collection 1974-033, II, "New Mexico v. Jesus Romero, Pablo Duran, Jesus Maria Sena y Baca, Fernando Sandoval, and Felix Tapia," April 9, 1853.
46. TRNMSF, collection 1972-011, I, Santa Fe County Docket Book, 1847–1858, 60–64; TRNMSF, collection 1972-011, I, Santa Ana County Docket Book, 1846–1856, 48.
47. TRNMSF, collection 1974-033, II, "New Mexico v. Ignacio Tapia," June 21, 1853.
48. TRNMSF, collection 1974-033, II, "New Mexico v. Pablo Duran," June 22, 1853.
49. TRNMSF, collection 1974-033, II, "New Mexico v. Andres Tapia," July 5, 1853; TRNMSF, collection 1974-033, II, "New Mexico v. Jesus Silva," July 21, 1853.
50. TRNMSF, collection 1972-011, I, Santa Fe County Docket Book, 1847–1858, 115.
51. TRNMSF, collection 1974-033, II, "New Mexico v. William Rowan," September 1, 1855.
52. TRNMSF, collection 1974-033, II, "New Mexico v. Peter Moran," August 1, 1856.
53. TRNMSF, collection 1974-033, II, "New Mexico v. Christobal Santiago," August 21, 1857. This was the one small exception. Christobal Santiago attacked and beat up Andres Tapia, who kept finding himself on the wrong end of numerous assaults.
54. TRNMSF, collection 1974-033, II, "New Mexico v. Jesus Maria Sena y Baca, John H. Mink, Jose Revera," July 25, 1859.
55. TRNMSF, collection 1974-033, II, "New Mexico v. Jose Gregorio Revera," July 25, 1859.
56. TRNMSF, collection 1974-033, II, "New Mexico v. Ignacio Tapia," July 6, 1859.
57. TRNMSF, collection 1972-011, I, Santa Fe County Docket Book, 1859–1863, 119.
58. Roth, *American Homicide*, 254–55. At their worst, these numbers were small when compared to homicide more broadly, a rate somewhere between 0.4 and 1.7 per hundred thousand, but as Roth notes, this was new and these numbers added up over time.
59. Roth, *American Homicide*, 251–52.
60. Roth, *American Homicide*, 253.
61. TRNMSF, collection 1974-033, II, "New Mexico v. William Hovey," May 15, 1857.
62. Roth, *American Homicide*, 256.
63. TRNMSF, collection 1974-033, II, "New Mexico v. William Hovey," May 15, 1857.
64. TRNMSF, collection 1974-033, II, "New Mexico v. William Hovey," May 15, 1857.
65. Yale University, The Avalon Project: *Documents in Law, History, and Diplomacy*, "New Mexico—Laws for the Government of the Territory of New Mexico, September 22, 1846, https://avalon.law.yale.edu/19th_century/kearney.asp.

    Section 3 of "The Practice of Law in Criminal Cases" in the Kearny Code reads, "If the offense be an assault, battery or affray, or gaming, or the disturbance of a religious congregation, the prisoner shall be taken before some alcalde, and punished in a summary manner; the trial of all such offenses shall be by a jury of twelve competent men, who if they find the defendant guilty, shall assess the fine to be paid by him, which shall be not less than one dollar, nor more than fifty dollars."
66. TRNMSF, collection 1974-033, II, "New Mexico v. William McLaughlin," August 26, 1858.
67. TRNMSF, collection 1974-033, II, "New Mexico v. Private Smith (Company B, 7th Infantry)," August 16, 1860.

68. TRNMSF, collection 1974-033, II, "New Mexico v. Private Smith (Company B, 7th Infantry)," August 16, 1860; TRNMSF, collection 1972-011, I, Santa Fe County Docket Book, 1847–1858, 218–19. The loose case files indicate what the jury actually found; there is no mention of the disagreement between the judge and jury in the Santa Fe County Docket Book.
69. TRNMSF, collection 1974-033, II, "New Mexico v. Candido Ortiz," October 6, 1856.
70. TRNMSF, collection 1974-033, II, "New Mexico v. Antonio Rodriguez," September 6, 1856.
71. TRNMSF, collection 1974-033, II, "New Mexico v. Antonio Rodriguez," September 6, 1856; TRNMSF, collection 1972-011, I, Santa Fe County Docket Book, 1847–1858, 378. The case files indicate that there was conflict between what the jury found and what verdict Judge Davenport could legally deliver; the docket book does not indicate any such disagreement and sets this fine at only twelve dollars. Perhaps Judge Davenport fined him less than $50 because he knew that Rodriguez couldn't pay more. Had he fined Rodriguez the maximum allowed, there's little doubt he would have spent a substantial amount of time in jail. Judge Davenport many not have wanted that, as the jail in Santa Fe County was almost always at capacity. It's also very possible that Judge Davenport, like many men in his time, considered Juana Maria Lovato to be Rodriguez's property and believed that what happened in the home was not the concern of the courts. Since Judge Davenport did not record his reasoning, we are left only to our speculation and reasoning for why Antonio Rodriguez was barely punished for nearly killing his partner.
72. 1860 United States Federal Census, Santa Fe County, New Mexico Territory.
73. TRNMSF, collection 1974-033, II, "New Mexico v. Thaddeus M. Rogers," February 28, 1857.
74. TRNMSF, collection 1974-033, II, "New Mexico v. Thaddeus M. Rogers," March 1, 1857.
75. TRNMSF, collection 1974-033, II, "New Mexico v. Thaddeus M. Rogers," February 28, 1857; TRNMSF, collection 1974-033, II, "New Mexico v. Thaddeus M. Rogers," March 1, 1857; TRNMSF, collection 1972-011, I, Santa Fe County Docket Book, 1847–1858, 583.
76. TRNMSF, collection 1974-033, II, "New Mexico v. Benito Borrego," December 24, 1855.
77. TRNMSF, collection 1974-033, II, "New Mexico v. Benito Borrego," December 24, 1855; Vicente Garcia, the victim's brother, and several others testified against Borrego. Vicente Garcia signed a sworn statement, which read in part, "Benito Borrego attacked and gave a mortal wound to Sinaco Garcia. . . . Borrego did unlawfully and of his malice aforethought kill and murder the said Sinaco Garcia." If the defense had witnesses, they were not listed in the case file.
78. TRNMSF, collection 1974-033, II, "New Mexico v. Benito Borrego," December 24, 1855.
79. 1860 United States Federal Census, Santa Fe County, New Mexico Territory.
80. TRNMSF, collection 1974-033, II, "New Mexico v. Benito Borrego," December 24, 1855.
81. TRNMSF, collection 1974-033, II, "New Mexico v. Benito Borrego," December 24, 1855.
82. TRNMSF, collection 1974-033, II, "New Mexico v. Benito Borrego," December 24, 1855.
83. TRNMSF, collection 1974-033, II, "New Mexico v. Benito Borrego," December 24, 1855.
84. TRNMSF, collection 1974-033, II, "New Mexico v. Benito Borrego," December 24, 1855.
85. TRNMSF, collection 1974-033, II, "New Mexico v. Benito Borrego," December 24, 1855.
86. TRNMSF, collection 1974-033, II, "New Mexico v. Benito Borrego," December 24, 1855.
87. Randolph Roth, "Homicide Rates in the Nineteenth-Century West: Tables, July 2010 Version," Historical Violence Database, Criminal Justice Research Center, Ohio State University, 2010; TRNMSF, collection 1974-033, II, 1847–1860.
88. See chapter 3.
89. TRNMSF, collection 1974-033, II, "New Mexico v. Jose Zacharias," March 22, 1856; *Santa Fe Weekly Gazette*, February 9, 1856, 2.
90. 1850 United States Federal Census, Santa Fe County, New Mexico Territory.
91. TRNMSF, collection 1974-033, II, "New Mexico v. Estevan Tenorio," September 14, 1856.
92. TRNMSF, collection 1974-033, II, "New Mexico v. Estevan Tenorio," September 14, 1856.
93. 1850 United States Federal Census, Santa Fe County, New Mexico Territory; 1860 United States Federal Census, Santa Fe County, New Mexico Territory.
94. *Santa Fe Weekly Gazette*, December 12, 1857, 2.
95. *Santa Fe Weekly Gazette*, March 20, 1858, 2.

96. TRNMSF, collection 1974-033, II, "New Mexico v. Jose Euligio Rena," December 14, 1857.
97. 1860 United States Federal Census, Santa Fe County, New Mexico Territory.
98. 1850 United States Federal Census, Santa Fe County, New Mexico Territory; 1860 United States Federal Census, Santa Fe County, New Mexico Territory.
99. TRNMSF, collection 1974-033, II, "New Mexico v. Antonio Padilla," March 15, 1858.
100. TRNMSF, collection 1974-033, II, "New Mexico v. Antonio Padilla," March 5, 1858.
101. TRNMSF, collection 1974-033, II, "New Mexico v. Antonio Padilla," March 5, 1858; TRNMSF, collection 1974-033, II, "New Mexico v. Antonio Padilla," March 15, 1858.
102. 1860 United States Federal Census, Santa Fe County, New Mexico Territory.
103. 1860 United States Federal Census, Santa Fe County, New Mexico Territory.
104. TRNMSF, collection 1974-033, II, "New Mexico v. Francisco Quintana," June 1, 1858.
105. TRNMSF, collection 1974-033, II, "New Mexico v. Francisco Quintana," June 1, 1858.
106. TRNMSF, collection 1974-033, II, "New Mexico v. Ramon Gonzalez y Moya," September 8, 1859.
107. TRNMSF, collection 1974-033, II, "New Mexico v. Francisco Trujillo," April 4, 1860.
108. TRNMSF, collection 1974-033, II, "New Mexico v. Rafael Rodriguez," May 16, 1857.
109. TRNMSF, collection 1972-011, I, Santa Fe County District Court Journal, 1859–1863, 80–81.
110. TRNMSF, collection 1974-033, II, "New Mexico v. Estefanio Prada," August 24, 1859.
111. TRNMSF, collection 1972-011, I, Santa Fe County District Court Journal, 1859–1863, 80–81; 1860 United States Federal Census, Santa Fe County, New Mexico Territory.
112. TRNMSF, collection 1974-033, II, "New Mexico v. Estefanio Prada," August 24, 1859.
113. TRNMSF, collection 1974-033, II, "New Mexico v. Estefanio Prada," August 24, 1859. The court did not record Ashurst's precise words, but Judge Kirby Benedict addressed them in his jury instructions.
114. TRNMSF, collection 1974-033, II, "New Mexico v. Estefanio Prada," August 24, 1859. The jury instructions stand out in this case. Benedict influenced the jury and was not impartial in his presentation to the jury members.
115. TRNMSF, collection 1972-011, I, Santa Fe County District Court Journal, 1859–1863, 97.
116. 1860 United States Federal Census, Santa Fe County, New Mexico Territory.
117. TRNMSF, collection 1972-011, I, Santa Fe County District Court Journal, 1859–1863, 98.
118. *Santa Fe Weekly Gazette*, March 14, 1857, 2.
119. *Santa Fe Weekly Gazette*, March 14, 1857, 2.
120. *Santa Fe Weekly Gazette*, March 14, 1857, 2.
121. TRNMSF, collection 1974-033, II, "New Mexico v. Matias Ribera," July 7, 1856.
122. *Santa Fe Weekly Gazette*, March 14, 1857, 2.
123. *Santa Fe Weekly Gazette*, March 14, 1857, 2. The *Gazette* identified the officer as one Lieutenant Clitz.
124. TRNMSF, collection 1972-011, I, Santa Fe County Docket Book, 1847–1858, 566–67.
125. TRNMSF, collection 1972-011, I, Santa Fe County Docket Book, 1847–1858, 547.
126. *Santa Fe Weekly Gazette*, March 27, 1857, 2; 1850 United States Federal Census, Santa Fe County, New Mexico Territory. Preston Beck Jr. was listed in the 1850 census with $10,000 in property.
127. 1850 United States Federal Census, Santa Fe County, New Mexico Territory. John Gorman was listed in the 1850 Census without property.
128. TRNMSF, collection 1974-033, II, "New Mexico v. John Gorman," March 24, 1855; TRNMSF, collection 1974-033, II, "New Mexico v. John Gorman," March 27, 1855.
129. 1850 United States Federal Census, Santa Fe County, New Mexico Territory.
130. *Santa Fe Weekly Gazette*, March 27, 1858, 2.
131. *Santa Fe Weekly Gazette*, March 27, 1858, 2.
132. *Santa Fe Weekly Gazette*, March 27, 1858, 2.
133. *Santa Fe Weekly Gazette*, April 3, 1858, 2.
134. 1860 United States Federal Census, Santa Fe County, New Mexico Territory.
135. TRNMSF, collection 1974-033, II, "New Mexico v. Henry Elam," June 6, 1860.
136. TRNMSF, collection 1974-033, II, "New Mexico v. Henry Elam," June 6, 1860.

137. TRNMSF, collection 1972-011, I, Santa Fe County District Court Journal, 1859–1863, 205.
138. TRNMSF, collection 1974-033, II, "New Mexico v. Thaddeus M. Rogers," December 25, 1859. The complete investigation is recounted in great deal in the jury instructions that are contained within this case file.
139. 1860 United States Federal Census, Santa Fe County, New Mexico Territory.
140. TRNMSF, collection 1974-033, II, "New Mexico v. Thaddeus M. Rogers," December 25, 1859.
141. TRNMSF, collection 1974-033, II, "New Mexico v. Thaddeus M. Rogers," December 25, 1859.
142. TRNMSF, collection 1974-033, II, "New Mexico v. Thaddeus M. Rogers," December 25, 1859.
143. TRNMSF, collection 1974-033, II, "New Mexico v. Thaddeus M. Rogers," December 25, 1859. Their detailed testimony is contained in the jury instructions, which are extensive.
144. TRNMSF, collection 1974-033, II, "New Mexico v. Thaddeus M. Rogers," December 25, 1859.
145. *Santa Fe Weekly Gazette*, September 15, 1860, 2.

CHAPTER FIVE

1. New Mexico State Records Center and Archives, "Records of the United States Territorial and New Mexico District Courts for Santa Fe County 1847–1951," (hereafter TRNMSF), Collection 1972-011, I, Santa Fe County District Court Journal, 1846–1858, 548–49.
2. Michel Foucault, *Discipline and Punish: The Birth of the Prison* (New York: Vintage Books, 1995), 8.
3. For legal histories, see Jerome Hall, *Theft, Law, and Society* (Indianapolis: Bobbs-Merrill Company, 1952); Michael E. Tigar, "The Right of Property and the Law of Theft," 62 *Texas Law Review* 1443–75 (1984); George P. Fletcher, "The Metamorphosis of Larceny," *Harvard Law Review* 89, no. 3 (Jan. 1976), 469–530. For more contemporary accounts, see Michelle Alexander, *The New Jim Crow: Mass Incarceration in the Age of Colorblindness* (New York: The New Press, 2012); Matthew Clair, *Privilege and Punishment: How Race and Class Matter in Criminal Court* (Princeton, NJ: Princeton University Press, 2020). For a comprehensive survey of the origins of Western Law, see Bruce B. Lawrence and Aisha Karim, *On Violence: A Reader* (Durham, NC: Duke University Press, 2007).
4. TRNMSF, Collection 1974-033, II, "New Mexico vs. Louis Dorrance," August 3, 1859. Although three white settlers were sentenced to lashes, only two actually received them. Louis Dorrance was found guilty of stealing a calf and sentenced to lashes, but Gov. Abraham Rencher stepped in and pardoned him on the condition he pay the local strongman from whom he stole the calf fifty dollars, the value of the calf.
5. TRNMSF, Collection 1974-033, II, 1846–1860; TRNMSF, Collection 1972-011, I, Santa Fe County District Court Journal, 1846–1858, 548–49; TRNMSF, Collection 1972-011, I, Santa Fe County District Court Journal, 1859–1863, 548–49.
6. TRNMSF, District Court Records, "New Mexico v. Henry Potter and Samuel Rino," February 27, 1850.
7. In nineteenth-century Natal, for example, whites treated natives with blend of "paternalism, fear and contempt." Stephen Peté and Annie Devenish noted, "On the one hand, flogging was regarded as a form of punishment that the 'childlike Native' could understand. On the other hand, it was seen as a powerful deterrent, justified by the brutal nature of the 'savages' to whom it was applied." The colonizers in Natal also "believed that any black challenge to white authority or civilisation needed to be dealt with swiftly and severely, in order to prevent it from developing into open rebellion." See Stephen Peté and Annie Devenish, "Flogging, Fear and Food: Punishment and Race in Colonial Nata," *Journal of Southern African Studies* 31, no. 1 (March 2005): 3, 9.
8. Felipe Gonzales helped correct the misconception that Nuevomexicanos in the legislature were mere tools of the Americans. That argument was advanced by early scholars, including Loomis Morton Ganaway, who wrote, "From 1846 until 1855, native New Mexicans were generally under the political domination of Anglo American-Americans, many of whom had not been in the territory a

decade." See Felipe Gonzales, *Politica: Nuevomexicanos and American Political Incorporation, 1821–1910* (Lincoln: University of Nebraska Press, 2016), 8–9; Loomis Morton Ganaway, *New Mexico and the Sectional Controversy, 1846–1861* (Albuquerque: University of New Mexico Press, 1944), 60.

9. For example, when the white Americans tried to empower judges to marry, the politicos adjourned. See chapter 3.
10. Robert W. Larson, *New Mexico's Quest for Statehood, 1846–1912* (Albuquerque: University of New Mexico Press, 1968), 32–33.
11. Larson, *New Mexico's Quest for Statehood*, 33.
12. Felipe Gonzales credits Joab Houghton with breaking the stalemate. See Gonzales, *Politica*, 218.
13. Lawrence R. Murphy argued that the governor's veto power and ability to appoint officials rendered the Hispano legislature powerless in New Mexico. James S. Calhoun, for example, manipulated elections during the first session, excluded the Pueblo people from the polls, and encouraged white Americans to illegally vote. In 1851, William G. Kephart wrote, "Add to this enormous amount of power (the veto) the fact that almost all the appointed power for the territory is vested in the Executive, and that all the Indian agents are subject to his instructions . . . and then tell me if I am mistaken that our Executive is clothed with the powers of a dictator." The voting returns that survived from this period, however, along with the results of these elections, indicate that American attempts to manipulate elections were for naught. See Lawrence R. Murphy, *Antislavery in the Southwest: William G. Kephart's Mission to New Mexico, 1850–53* (El Paso: Texas Western Press, 1978), 18–20.
14. Alvin R. Sunseri, *Seeds of Discord: New Mexico in the Aftermath of the American Conquest, 1846–1861* (Chicago: Nelson-Hall, 1979), 129.
15. Sunseri, *Seeds of Discord*, 130.
16. Larry D. Ball, *The United States Marshals of the New Mexico and Arizona Territories, 1846–1912* (Albuquerque: University of New Mexico Press, 1978), 26.
17. Gonzales, *Politica*, 21.
18. Gonzales, *Politica*, app. 1.
19. Gonzales, *Politica*, 22–23, app. 1.
20. Sunseri, *Seeds of Discord*, 115–17.
21. Sunseri, *Seeds of Discord*, 116.
22. Sunseri, *Seeds of Discord*, 116.
23. Larson, *New Mexico's Quest for Statehood*, 64.
24. Sunseri, *Seeds of Discord*, 117.
25. Ganaway, *New Mexico and the Sectional Controversy*, 66–68.
26. Ganaway, *New Mexico and the Sectional Controversy*, 68–69.
27. Ganaway, *New Mexico and the Sectional Controversy*, 80.
28. Ganaway, *New Mexico and the Sectional Controversy*, 90.
29. Larson, *New Mexico's Quest for Statehood*, 47–51.
30. Jill Mocho, *Murder and Justice in Frontier New Mexico 1821–1846* (Albuquerque: University of New Mexico Press, 1997), 18.
31. Ralph Emerson Twitchell, *The Bench and the Bar During the American Occupation, A.D. 1846–1850* (Santa Fe: New Mexican Printing Company, 1912 [1891]), 9.
32. New Mexico State Records Center and Archives, New Mexico Secretary of State Collection, Laws of New Mexico, Serial #4863, Laws of the Second Session, 1852, 285.
33. New Mexico State Records Center and Archives, New Mexico Secretary of State Collection, Laws of New Mexico, Serial #4863, Laws of the Second Session, 1852, 285.
34. By 1853, monte and faro were being played at the licensed gambling hall in the Exchange Hotel. This part of the law lasted a short time, but the licensing fees endured.
35. TRNMSF, District Court Records, box 2, 1851.
36. TRNMSF, District Court Records, box 1–3, 1847–53.
37. See chapter 2; New Mexico State Records Center and Archives, New Mexico Secretary of State Collection, Laws of New Mexico, Serial # 4863, 1851–54.

38. New Mexico State Records Center and Archives, New Mexico Secretary of State Collection, Laws of New Mexico, Serial #4866, Laws of the Fifth Session, 1855–1856.
39. New Mexico State Records Center and Archives, New Mexico Secretary of State Collection, Laws of New Mexico, Serial #4866, Laws of the Fifth Session, 1855–1856, 26–28.
40. New Mexico State Records Center and Archives, New Mexico Secretary of State Collection, Laws of New Mexico, Serial #4866, Laws of the Fifth Session, 1855–1856, 28.
41. Murphy, *Antislavery in the Southwest*, 18–20.
42. New Mexico State Records Center and Archives, New Mexico Secretary of State Collection, Laws of New Mexico, Serial #4866, Laws of the Fifth Session, 1855–1856, 90–92.
43. New Mexico State Records Center and Archives, New Mexico Secretary of State Collection, Laws of New Mexico, Serial #4866, Laws of the Fifth Session, 1855–1856, 90.
44. New Mexico State Records Center and Archives, New Mexico Secretary of State Collection, Laws of New Mexico, Serial #4866, Laws of the Fifth Session, 1855–1856, 92.
45. New Mexico State Records Center and Archives, New Mexico Secretary of State Collection, Laws of New Mexico, Serial #4866, Laws of the Fifth Session, 1855–1856, 92.
46. Twitchell, *The Bench and the Bar During the American Occupation*, 10.
47. New Mexico State Records Center and Archives, New Mexico Secretary of State Records, Serial # 7417, G-xxx Legislature—Laws, Originals, 1848–1860 (hereafter NMSSR).
48. Portions of this letter are no longer legible; this appears to have been an early draft of a letter that was never completed. Where the language is extremely awkward, I have taken the liberties to modernize the structure and word selection. Translated from Spanish to English by the author. See NMSSR.
49. It was likely written between 1853 and 1854. Because the document has no true proper place, and because one needs special permission to see this collection, it is unlikely that it moved from its current file folder. As a precaution, however, the author has taken a personal copy for his own records and created a digital copy.
50. The early folklorist Aurelio M. Espinosa was a pioneer of early linguistic studies in New Mexico. Espinosa maintained that the Spanish dialect in New Mexico was an old Castilian variety, while others contend that New Mexican Spanish has been strongly influenced by Pueblo and later American English interaction. See Aurelio Espinosa, *The Folklore of Spain in the American Southwest: Traditional Spanish Folk Literature in Northern New Mexico and Southern Colorado*, ed. J. Manuel Espinosa (Norman: University of Oklahoma Press, 1986), 18.
51. NMSSR.
52. New Mexico State Records Center and Archives, New Mexico Secretary of State Collection, Laws of New Mexico, Serial #4869, Laws of the Seventh Session, 1857–1858.
53. New Mexico State Records Center and Archives, New Mexico Secretary of State Collection, Laws of New Mexico, Serial #4869, Laws of the Seventh Session, 1857–1858, chapter IX.
54. TRNMSF, collection 1974-033, II, 1846–1860; TRNMSF, collection 1972-011, I, Santa Fe County District Court Journal, 1846–1858, 548–49; TRNMSF, collection 1972-011, I, Santa Fe County District Court Journal, 1859–1863.
55. New Mexico State Records Center and Archives, New Mexico Secretary of State Collection, Laws of New Mexico, Serial #4869, Laws of the Seventh Session, 1857–1858, chapter IX, section 13.
56. New Mexico State Records Center and Archives, New Mexico Secretary of State Collection, Laws of New Mexico, Serial #4869, Laws of the Seventh Session, 1857–1858, chapter IX, section 14.
57. New Mexico State Records Center and Archives, New Mexico Secretary of State Collection, Laws of New Mexico, Serial #4869, Laws of the Seventh Session, 1857–1858, chapter IX, section 15.
58. Diana Paton, "Crimes and the Bodies of Slaves in Eighteenth-Century Jamaica," *Journal of Social History* 34, no. 4 (Summer 2001): 933.
59. Charles R. Cutter, *The Legal Culture of Northern New Spain* (Albuquerque: University of New Mexico Press, 1995), 133.
60. Lowell C. Green, "Bar Activities," *American Bar Association Journal* 44 (July 1958), 694.

61. New Mexico State Records Center and Archives, New Mexico Secretary of State Collection, Laws of New Mexico, Serial # 4863, Laws of the Third Session, 1852–53, 57.
62. The jury instructions survived for assault and homicide cases, but very few survived for larceny and burglary; TRNMSF, District Court Records, box 4–5, 1854–56.
63. TRNMSF, District Court Records, box 4–5, 1854–1856, "Territory of New Mexico vs. Eligio Gonzalez," September 15, 1856, Judges Instructions to the Jury.
64. TRNMSF, District Court Records, box 4–5, 1854–1856, "Territory of New Mexico vs. Eligio Gonzalez," September 15, 1856, Judges Instructions to the Jury.
65. TRNMSF, District Court Records, box 4–5, 1854–56, "Territory of New Mexico vs. Eligio Gonzalez," September 15, 1856, Jury Verdict.
66. New Mexico State Records Center and Archives, New Mexico Secretary of State Collection, Laws of New Mexico, Serial #4867, Laws of the Sixth Session, 1856–1857, chapter XXVII, section 2.
67. Laura E. Gómez, "Race, Colonialism, and Criminal Law: Mexicans and the American Criminal Justice System in Territorial New Mexico," *Law & Society Review* 34, no. 4 (2000): 1169–70.
68. TRNMSF, District Court Records, box 1–3, 1846–1853; 107 individuals were found guilty, 41 were found not guilty, and 40 were dismissed.
69. TRNMSF, District Court Records, box 1–3, 1847–1853; twenty-eight whites were found guilty, sixteen were found not guilty, and fourteen dismissed.
70. TRNMSF, District Court Records, box 1–3, 1855–60; thirty-one whites were found guilty, ten were found not guilty, and ten dismissed.
71. Phillip J. Schwarz, *Twice Condemned: Slaves and the Criminal Laws of Virginia, 1705–1865* (Baton Rouge: Louisiana State University Press, 1988), 50; Michael S. Hindus, "Black Justice Under White Law: Criminal Prosecutions of Blacks in Antebellum South Carolina," *Journal of American History* 63, no. 3 (Dec. 1976): 590.
72. TRNMSF, collection 1974-033, II, "New Mexico v. John Gorman," March 24, 1855.
73. TRNMSF, collection 1974-033, II, "New Mexico v. John Gorman," March 27, 1855.
74. TRNMT, collection 1974-033, II, "New Mexico v. John Gorman," March 24, 1855.
75. Chapter 3.
76. Sunseri, *Seeds of Discord*, 101.
77. TRNMSF, District Court Records, Court Docket Book, 1850–53, 16.
78. TRNMSF, District Court Records, Court Docket Book, 1850–53, 80.
79. TRNMSF, District Court Records, Court Docket Book, 1850–53, 113.
80. *Santa Fe Weekly Gazette*, December 17, 1853, 2.
81. *Santa Fe Weekly Gazette*, December 17, 1853, 2.
82. Paton, "Crimes and the Bodies of Slaves in Eighteenth-Century Jamaica," 923.
83. Peté and Devenish, "Flogging, Food, and Fear," 3, 5.
84. Ramón Gutiérrez, *When Jesus Came, the Corn Mothers Went Away: Marriage, Sexuality, and Power in New Mexico, 1500–1846* (Stanford, CA: Stanford University Press, 1991), 323.
85. James F. Brooks, *Captives and Cousins: Slavery, Kinship, and Community in the Southwest Borderlands* (Chapel Hill: University of North Carolina Press, 2002), 382.
86. Mocho, *Murder and Justice in Frontier New Mexico*, 18.
87. There was precedent for this punishment in America. In the seventeenth and eighteenth centuries, English courts sentenced prisoners to indentured servitude in the American colonies and they disguised that punishment as an alternative to the gallows. By the nineteenth century, local judges in Delaware *offered* prisoners indentured servitude as a way to repay their debts and avoid prison sentences. However in 1840, the Delaware courts racialized servitude as a punishment and thereafter only blacks were sentenced to servitude. The Delaware legislature pushed black prisoners into servitude with a series of acts. They passed the Servitude Act of 1807, which decreed that blacks convicted of larceny must pay four times restitution and could be bound for

up to eleven years; they passed the 1828 law that determined that blacks were to be indentured if they were a burden to the state; they passed the 1837 law, which dictated that whites who committed assault could be discharged from their obligation to become indentured; and they passed the 1839 law that ruled that whites could be exempted from all obligations of servitude. In 1852 the Delaware legislature passed a law that required all "idle and vagabond free Negroes and mulattos" to be pressed into servitude. Don Jordan and Michael Walsh, *White Cargo: The Forgotten History of Britain's White Slaves in America* (New York: New York University Press, 2008), 249; Robert L. Hayman Jr., "A History of Race in Delaware: 1639–1950," in *Choosing Equality: Essays and Narratives on the Desegregation Experience*, ed. Robert L. Hayman Jr. and Leland Ware (University Park: Pennsylvania State University Press, 2009), 38.

88. During Reconstruction, legislatures in Georgia and places throughout the South implemented the convict lease program to bolster their labor force and utilize black prisoners in overcrowded prisons. Southern courts used black prisoners like the Mexican alcaldes used vecinos: blacks were lent out and labored in fields, swamps, mines, and public works, while vecinos were directly sentenced to public labor, forced labor in the mines, and service at the presidio. During the 1850s, the courts in Greene County sentenced forty-seven blacks to Georgia's convict lease system, but only three were sentenced to jail. Meanwhile, the courts in Chatham County sent 76 percent of convicted blacks to prison, many of whom ended up working on the railroads and in the mines. See Edward L. Ayers, *Vengeance and Justice: Crime and Punishment in the 19th Century American South* (New York: Oxford University Press, 1984), 185–86, 197, 329; Mocho, *Murder and Justice in Frontier New Mexico*, 18.

89. Miroslava Chávez-García, *States of Delinquency: Race and Science in the Making of California's Juvenile Justice System* (Berkeley: University of California Press, 2012), 28.

90. Richard L. Carrico, *Strangers in a Stolen Land: American Indians in San Diego, 1850–1880* (Sacramento: Sierra Oaks Publishing Company, 1987), 32.

91. Chávez-García, *States of Delinquency*, 28.

92. New Mexico State Records Center and Archives, "Secretary of State Collection: Laws of New Mexico," #4863 (hereafter Laws), Kearny Code 67.

93. The 1850 U.S. census data for Santa Fe County reveals that there were 253 servants: 28 were born in Mexico, 20 Native Americans, 9 African, 2 European, and 194 New Mexican vecinos. Servitude was a major issue in the territory, as it was throughout the United States. Like slavery, many Hispano and Mexicano servants were born into servitude and passed on by local caudillos.

94. The only existing evidence documenting this practice are the on small scraps of paper scribbled in the hand of Marshal Jones. See TRNMSF, District Court Records, "New Mexico v. Jose Sena (1853), New Mexico v. Luis Rivera (1853), New Mexico v. Guadalupe the Navajo (1853)," box 2–3.

95. TRNMSF, "New Mexico v. Jose Sena," February 14, 1853.

96. TRNMSF, District Court Records, "New Mexico v. Jose Sena," February 14, 1853.

97. Maurillo E. Vigil, *Los Patrónes: Profiles of Hispanic Leaders in New Mexican History* (Washington, DC: University Press of America, Inc., 1980), 49–51.

98. The New Mexico sociopolitical structure made indebted servitude a permanent institution, much like slavery in the South. Though New Mexicans called their institution indebted peonage, there was little difference between peons in New Mexico and slaves in the American South.

99. TRNMSF, District Court Records, "New Mexico v. Luis Ribera," January 20, 1853.

100. TRNMSF, District Court Records, "New Mexico v. Guadalupe the Navajo and Antonio Aragon," January 5, 1853.

101. 1860 Federal Census, Santa Fe County, New Mexico Territory.

102. TRNMSF, District Court Records, "New Mexico v. Tomas Sevilles (Ceballes)," February 2, 1854.

103. *Santa Fe Weekly Gazette*, April 8, 1854, 2.

104. TRNMSF, District Court Records, "New Mexico v. Dolores Sena," March 29, 1854.
105. TRNMSF, District Court Records, "New Mexico v. Manuel Baca," January 1, 1857; 1860 Federal Census, Santa Fe County, New Mexico Territory.
106. TRNMSF, collection 1972-011, I, Santa Fe County Docket Book, 1847–1858, 777.
107. TRNMSF, District Court Records, "New Mexico v. Mauricio Sylva," August 25, 1858; TRNMSF, collection 1972-011, I, Santa Fe County Docket Book, 1847–1858, 776.
108. Laws, 59.
109. TRNMSF, box 1–3.
110. New Mexico State Records Center and Archives, New Mexico Secretary of State Collection, Laws of New Mexico, Serial #4869, Laws of the Seventh Session, 1857–1858, chapter IX, section 13.
111. New Mexico State Records Center and Archives, New Mexico Secretary of State Collection, Laws of New Mexico, Serial #4869, Laws of the Seventh Session, 1857–1858, chapter IX, section 14.
112. Gutiérrez, *When Jesus Came, the Corn Mothers Went Away*, 191.
113. TRNMSF, collection 1974-033, II, 1847–1860; TRNMSF, collection 1972-011, I, Santa Fe County District Court Journal, 1846–1858; TRNMSF, District Court Records, Court Docket Book, 1850–53.
114. TRNMSF, District Court Records, "New Mexico v. Charles Porter," July 27, 1850; "New Mexico v. Jose Francoso," February 28, 1850; "New Mexico v. Jose Benito Gonzales," February 12, 1850.
115. New Mexico State Records Center and Archives, New Mexico Secretary of State Collection, Laws of New Mexico, Serial #4863, Laws of the Second Session, 1852, 285.
116. TRNMSF, District Court Records, box 1–3, 1847–1853.
117. Andrés Reséndez, *Changing National Identities at the Frontier: Texas and New Mexico, 1800–1850* (Cambridge: Press Syndicate of the University of Cambridge, 2005), 255–56.
118. TRNMSF, District Court Records, box 1–3, 1847–53.
119. James D. Cockcroft, *Encyclopedia of Forms and Precedents, For Pleading and Practice, at Common Law, In Equity, and Under the Various Codes and Practices Acts* (New York: James D. Cockcroft, 1900), 13054.
120. This does not include the fines that were handed down for both commerce violations and for illegal gaming. Among Nuevomexicanos, another fifteen were fined for commerce violations and another sixteen were fined for illegal gaming. Among white defendants, eighteen were fined for commerce violations and another nineteen for illegal gaming.
121. TRNMSF, District Court Records, "New Mexico v. Antonio Tafoya," September 26, 1848.
122. TRNMSF, District Court Records, "New Mexico v. Gregorio Ortega," February 16, 1851.
123. This was the same Aniceito Abeytia who accused Manuel Armijo of fomenting the 1837 rebellion during his 1909 interview with L. B. Prince. It is another indicator that although he denounced Armijo, he remained a loyal Hispano; see chapter 1; TRNMSF, District Court Records, "New Mexico v. Aniceito Abeytia," December 18, 1851.
124. TRNMSF, District Court Records, "New Mexico v. Maria Pacheco," October 23, 1849; "New Mexico v. Delores Martin," June 27, 1850.
125. Richard Smith Elliott et al., *The Mexican War Correspondence of Richard Smith Elliott* (Norman: University of Oklahoma Press, 1997), 157.
126. TRNMSF, District Court Records, "New Mexico v. Santos Sandoval," October 24, 1849.
127. TRNMSF, collection 1974-033, II, "New Mexico vs. Louis Dorrance," March 10, 1860, appeal to Gov. Abraham Rencher for a pardon.
128. TRNMSF, collection 1974-033, II, "New Mexico vs. Louis Dorrance," August 9, 1859, Louis Dorrance signed statement to the court.
129. *Santa Fe County District Court Journal*, 1859–1863, 111–12.
130. *Santa Fe County District Court Journal*, 1859–1863, 112.
131. Francisco Ortis y Salazar only appears once in the following records, and that is as a victim of larceny in this case: TRNMSF, collection 1974-033, II, 1846–1860; TRNMSF, collection 1972-011, I, Santa Fe County District Court Journal, 1846–1858, 548–49; TRNMSF, collection 1972-011, I, Santa Fe County District Court Journal, 1859–1863, 548–49.

132. TRNMSF, collection 1974-033, II, "New Mexico vs. Louis Dorrance," March 10, 1860, appeal to Gov. Abraham Rencher for a pardon.
133. TRNMSF, collection 1974-033, II, "New Mexico vs. Louis Dorrance," March 10, 1860, appeal to Gov. Abraham Rencher for a pardon.
134. TRNMSF, collection 1972-011, I, Santa Fe County District Court Journal, 1846–1858, 548–49.
135. TRNMSF, collection 1974-033, II, "New Mexico vs. Louis Dorrance," August 3, 1859; Santa Fe County District Court Journal, 1859–1863, 138–41.
136. TRNMSF, District Court Records, "New Mexico v. Jose Seguro," March 3, 1848.
137. TRNMSF, District Court Records, "New Mexico v. Jose Francoso," March 3, 1848.
138. TRNMSF, District Court Records, "New Mexico v. Charles Porter," July 27, 1850.
139. TRNMSF, collection 1974-033, II, 1847–1860; TRNMSF, collection 1972-011, I, Santa Fe County District Court Journal, 1846–1858; TRNMSF, District Court Records, Court Docket Book, 1850–1853.
140. Mocho, *Murder and Justice in Frontier New Mexico*, 24.
141. Mocho, *Murder and Justice in Frontier New Mexico*, 26.
142. Mocho, *Murder and Justice in Frontier New Mexico*, 27.
143. Cutter, *The Legal Culture of Northern New Spain*, 138.
144. TRNMSF, District Court Records, "New Mexico v. Ignacio Tapia," June 1, 1853.
145. Howard W. Allen and Jerome M. Clubb, *Race, Class, and the Death Penalty: Capital Punishment in American History* (Albany: State University of New York Press, 2008), 121, 124.
146. Clare V. McKanna Jr., *Race and Homicide in Nineteenth-Century California* (Reno: University of Nevada Press, 2002), 99.
147. West Gilbreath, *Death on the Gallows: The Story of Legal Hangings in New Mexico 1847–1923* (Silver City, NM: High Lonesome Books, 2002), 135, 149, 192.
148. The other five case files contain sparse details and do not reveal the weapon used by the perpetrators. TRNMSF.
149. Robert Tórrez mistakenly concluded that a Hispano jury was responsible for hanging Simms; he even accused Hispanos of sentencing Simms to capital punishment because Simms was a white American settler. But Horace Long was the foreman in the Simms case, and it is unlikely there were any Hispanos in the jury. Tórrez insinuates that New Mexican juries were unwilling to pass the sentence against individuals with Spanish surnames and uses Andrew Jackson Simms as an example of the New Mexican community willing to deal capital punishment against a white American settler. Robert J. Torrez, *Myth of the Hanging Tree: Stories of Crime and Punishment in Territorial New Mexico* (Albuquerque: University of New Mexico Press, 2008), 53.
150. TRNMSF, District Court Records, "Territory v. A. J. Simms," 1849.
151. TRNMSF, District Court Records, "New Mexico v. A. J. Simms," 1849. Simms traveled from Santa Fe to Taos, and there committed the murder. The case was tried in Santa Fe County because it was the residence of Simms.
152. TRNMSF, District Court Records, "New Mexico v. A. J. Simms," indictment dated July 2, 1849.
153. TRNMSF, District Court Records, "New Mexico v. James C. Brady," indictment by John Tulles, 1, 1848; TRNMSF, District Court Records, "New Mexico v. O. P. Anderson," indictment by Alcalde J. Smith, 1852.
154. TRNMSF, District Court Records, "New Mexico v. A. J. Simms, instructions to the Santa Fe County Sheriff, 1849.
155. *Santa Fe New Mexican*, November 28, 1849, 2. The prison sentence was carried out, as Simms is described as being in jail awaiting his execution.
156. Edward L. Ayers, *Vengeance and Justice: Crime and Punishment in the 19th Century American South* (New York: Oxford University Press, 1984), 329.
157. Gilbreath was unaware of the conviction and execution and Andrew Jackson Simms. Gilbreath, *Death on the Gallows*, 148.

158. TRNMSF, District Court Records, "New Mexico v. Henry Wheeler," November 1, 1849.
159. TRNMSF, District Court Records, "New Mexico v. Henry Wheeler," November 1, 1849.
160. 1850 United States Census, Santa Fe County, Santa Fe City, 85.
161. *Santa Fe New Mexican*, November 28, 1849, 2. Two days later Captain Papin was buried with full military honors.
162. 1850 United States Census, Santa Fe County, Santa Fe City, 85. Regulators of the justice system prided themselves on expeditious punishments and two months was longer than citizens normally waited for punishment. The census lists Wheeler as in jail for the crime of murder.
163. Torrez, *Myth of the Hanging Tree*, 25–26.
164. This book contains a good discussion of the abuse of the self-defense plea in the nineteenth-century Southwest. See Larry D. Ball, *Desert Lawmen: The High Sheriffs of New Mexico and Arizona, 1846–1912* (Albuquerque: University of New Mexico Press, 1992), 180–81.
165. *Santa Fe Weekly Gazette*, November 19, 1853, 2.
166. TRNMSF, District Court Records, box 1–3 (1847–1853). Numerous verdicts are missing for the territorial era, especially from homicide cases. This seems to be a byproduct of the manner in which verdicts were delivered, on small strips of torn paper, generally 6 by 8 ½ inches, with the verdict scribbled and signed by the foreman. For all criminal cases, including homicide, assault, and larceny (totaling 422 cases), 191 verdicts are known and 62 percent of these verdicts were returned guilty.
167. Many case files from this era are incomplete, especially for cases that were never prosecuted. Rather than making an assumption that incomplete cases were never prosecuted, this study leaves the possibility open that verdicts were simply lost. Statistically, this is why rates are implemented, rather than using aggregate numbers as foundational data.
168. Clinton Brook and Frank Reeve, *Forts and Forays: James A. Bennett, a Dragoon in New Mexico, 1850–56* (Albuquerque: University of New Mexico Press, 1948), 27.
169. Brook and Reeve, *Forts and Forays*, 27.
170. *Santa Fe Weekly Gazette*, November 19, 1853, 2.
171. Lynching was a gruesome business in Santa Fe County, especially because there were no gallows behind the Exchange Hotel. Scallion was strangled, a process that would have been slow and painful. Normally, a person condemned to hang would have their neck snapped by the quick drop, which supposedly spares the victim from an extended period of pain and thus prevents an execution from being construed as torture. But when the lynch mob came, there was no time for building gallows. Thus, in an age that had supposedly moved beyond violence against the body, the lynch mob in territorial Santa Fe reveled in the justice that slow asphyxiation by strangulation afforded. See Torrez, *Myth of the Hanging Tree*, 42–43; Foucault, *Discipline and Punish*, 7–9.
172. *Santa Fe Weekly Gazette*, March 14, 1857, 2.
173. Gilbreath, *Death on the Gallows*, 215–19.
174. See chapter 3.
175. Gilbreath, *Death on the Gallows*, 149.
176. Gilbreath, *Death on the Gallows*, 150.
177. Thomas E. Chávez, *Manuel Alvarez, 1794–1856: A Southwestern Biography* (Niwot: University Press of Colorado, 1990), 113.
178. Michael McNierney, *Taos 1847: The Revolt in Contemporary Accounts* (Boulder, CO: Johnson Publishing Company, 1980), 83–86.
179. TRNMSF, District Court Records, box 1–3.
180. *Santa Fe Weekly Gazette*, September 15, 1860, 2.
181. *Santa Fe Weekly Gazette*, September 15, 1860, 2.
182. *Santa Fe Weekly Gazette*, September 15, 1860, 2.
183. *Santa Fe Weekly Gazette*, September 15, 1860, 2.
184. Tórrez, *Myth of the Hanging Tree*, 49.

Epilogue

1. Richard Barksdale Harwell, *The Union Reader: As the North Saw the War* (New York: Dover Publications, 1996), 77–82; for a complete transcription, see this book's appendix.
2. Ralph Emerson Twitchell, *The Leading Facts of New Mexican History* (Santa Fe: Sunstone Press, 2007 [1911]), 372–73.
3. Loomis Morton Ganaway, *New Mexico and the Sectional Controversy, 1846–1861* (Albuquerque: University of New Mexico Press, 1944), 90–92.
4. Jacqueline Dorgan Meketa, *Legacy of Honor: The Life of Rafael Chacón, a Nineteenth Century New Mexican* (Albuquerque: University of New Mexico Press, 1986), 126.
5. Robert W. Larson, *New Mexico's Quest for Statehood, 1846–1912* (Albuquerque: University of New Mexico Press, 1968), 85.
6. Meketa, *Legacy of Honor*, 351–54.
7. Meketa, *Legacy of Honor*, 79–82.
8. Meketa, *Legacy of Honor*, 131.
9. Meketa, *Legacy of Honor*, 131.
10. Meketa, *Legacy of Honor*, 133.
11. Ralph Emerson Twitchell, *Old Santa Fe: A Magazine of History, Archaeology, Genealogy, and Biography, Volume III* (Santa Fe: Old Santa Fe Press, 1916), 40–41.
12. Larson, *New Mexico's Quest for Statehood*, 85.
13. John P. Wilson, *When the Texans Came: Missing Records from the Civil War in the Southwest, 1861–1862* (Albuquerque: University of New Mexico Press, 2001), 305.
14. Wilson, *When the Texans Came*, 306.
15. Marc Simmons, *The Little Lion of the Southwest: A Life of Manuel Antonio Chaves* (Chicago: Sage Books, Swallow Press, 1973), 185–86.
16. Manuel G. Gonzales, *The Hispanic Elite of the Southwest* (El Paso: Texas Western Press, University of Texas at El Paso, 1989), 12.
17. David J. Weber, *Arms, Indians, and the Mismanagement of New Mexico: Donaciano Vigil, 1846* (El Paso: Texas Western Press, University of Texas at El Paso, 1986).
18. Susan Calafate Boyle, *Los Capitalistas: Hispano Merchants and the Santa Fe Trade* (Albuquerque: University of New Mexico Press, 1997), 142.
19. Simmons, *The Little Lion of the Southwest*, 1–6.
20. In 1846, Don Albino Chacón refused to retain his appointment as alcalde in Santa Fe County.
21. My great-great grandfather, Matias Alarid, was one of many who was forced to swear allegiance to the United States, and then left the county to avoid further dealings with the incoming American settlers and their new government.
22. Boyle, *Los Capitalistas*, chaps. 5–7.
23. Felipe Gonzales contends that the "Otero Party" genuinely believed in this law, because they wanted to use it to protect their rights to keep servants. I remain skeptical. Felipe Gonzales, *Politica: Nuevomexicanos and American Political Incorporation, 1821–1910* (Lincoln: University of Nebraska Press, 2016), 349.

Appendix

1. Richard Barksdale Harwell, *The Union Reader: As the North Saw the War* (New York: Dover Publications, 1996), 77–82.

REFERENCES

Primary Resources

1850 Federal Census, Santa Fe County, New Mexico Territory.
1860 Federal Census, Santa Fe County, New Mexico Territory.
Blumner, Charles. Letters (AC 231). Angélico Chávez History Library, Palace of the Governors, Santa Fe, NM.
Congressional Globe, United States House of Representatives, 32nd Congress, 1st Session, "Contested Election in New Mexico—Mr. Weightman," March 15, 1853.
Donaciano Vigil Collection, 1727–1877, Santa Fe: New Mexico State Records Center and Archives, OCLC# 37800720.
Letters From the Secretary of the Territory of New Mexico, 32nd Congress, 1st Session, Miscellaneous, No. 4, 1851.
Mauro Montoya Collection of New Mexican Historical Documents, Fray Angelico Chavez History Library, Santa Fe, New Mexico.
The New Mexican, 1849.
New Mexico State Records Center and Archives, "Governors' Office Affiliates, Governors' letter book," Serial #13892, 1853–1862.
New Mexico State Records Center and Archives, *Mexican Archives of New Mexico, 1821–1846*, Santa Fe: New Mexico State Records Center and Archives, 1969.
New Mexico State Records Center and Archives, New Mexico Secretary of State Collection, Laws of New Mexico, Serial # 4863, 1851–1854.
New Mexico State Records Center and Archives, New Mexico Secretary of State Collection, Laws of New Mexico, Serial #4866, 1855–1856.
New Mexico State Records Center and Archives, New Mexico Secretary of State Collection, Laws of New Mexico, Serial #4869, Laws of the Seventh Session, 1857–1858, chapter IX, section 14.
New Mexico State Records Center and Archives, New Mexico Secretary of State Records, Serial # 7417, G-xxx Legislature—Laws, Originals, 1848–1860.
New Mexico State Records Center and Archives, New Mexico Secretary of State Collection, Laws of New Mexico, Serial #4869.
New Mexico State Records Center and Archives, Records of the United States Territorial and New Mexico District Courts for Santa Fe County 1847–1951, box 1–6.
Otero, Miguel A. Report of the Governor of New Mexico to the Secretary of the Interior (Washington, DC: Government Printing Office, 1901).
Read, Benjamin M. (Benjamin Maurice), Benjamin Read Collection, Papers relating to the history of New Mexico, 1634–1921.
Roth, Randolph. "American Homicide Supplemental Volume: American Homicides." Historical Violence Database, Criminal Justice Research Center, Ohio State University, May 2010. https://cjrc.osu.edu/research/interdisciplinary/hvd/ahsv.
Santa Fe Weekly Gazette, 1852–1869.
Yale University. The Avalon Project: *Documents in Law, History, and Diplomacy*. "New Mexico—Laws for the Government of the Territory of New Mexico, September 22, 1846." https://avalon.law.yale.edu/19th_century/kearney.asp.

Secondary Sources

Alarid, Waldo. *Santa Fe Shadows Whisper: A History of the Alarid and Moya Families*. Pueblo, CO: El Escritorio, 1997.
Alexander, Michelle. *The New Jim Crow: Mass Incarceration in the Age of Colorblindness*. New York: The New Press, 2012.

REFERENCES

Allen, Howard W., and Jerome M. Clubb. *Race, Class, and the Death Penalty: Capital Punishment in American History*. Albany: State University of New York Press, 2008.

Anderson, George. *History of New Mexico, Its Resources and People*, Vol. I. Los Angeles: Pacific States Publishing Company, 1907.

Andrien, Kenneth J., and Lyman L. Johnson, eds. *The Political Economy of Spanish America in the Age of Revolution*. Albuquerque: University of New Mexico Press, 1994.

Ayers, Edward L. *Vengeance and Justice: Crime and Punishment in the 19th Century American South*. New York: Oxford University Press, 1984.

Ball, Larry D. *Desert Lawmen: The High Sheriffs of New Mexico and Arizona, 1846–1912*. Albuquerque: University of New Mexico Press, 1992.

Ball, Larry D. *The United States Marshals of the New Mexico and Arizona Territories, 1846–1912*. Albuquerque: University of New Mexico Press, 1978.

Bancroft, Hubert Howe. *The Works of Hubert Howe Bancroft, Volume XVII: History of Arizona and New Mexico, 1530–1888*. San Francisco: The History Company, Publishers, 1889.

Baxter, John O. *Los Carneradas: Sheep Trade in New Mexico, 1700–1860*. Albuquerque: University of New Mexico Press, 1987.

Baxter, John O. *Dividing New Mexico's Waters, 1700–1912*. Albuquerque: University of New Mexico Press, 1997.

Billington, Ray Allen. *The Far Western Frontier, 1830–1860*. New York: Harper and Row, 1956.

Boyle, Susan Calafate. *Los Capitalistas: Hispano Merchants and the Santa Fe Trade*. Albuquerque: University of New Mexico Press, 1997.

Bolton, Charles C. *Poor Whites of the Antebellum South: Tenants and Laborers in Central North Carolina and Northeast Mississippi*. Durham, NC: Duke University Press, 1994.

Bourdieu, Pierre. *Outline of a Theory of Practice*. In Bruce B. Lawrence and Aisha Karim, *On Violence: A Reader*. Durham, NC: Duke University Press, 2007.

Briggs, Charles L., and John R. Van Ness. *Land, Water, and Culture: New Perspectives on Hispanic Land Grants*. Albuquerque: University of New Mexico Press, 1987.

Brook, Clinton, and Frank Reeve. *Forts and Forays: James A. Bennett, a Dragoon in New Mexico, 1850–56*. Albuquerque: University of New Mexico Press, 1948.

Brooks, James F. *Captives and Cousins: Slavery, Kinship, and Community in the Southwest Borderlands*. Chapel Hill: University of North Carolina Press, 2002.

Cahill, Cathleen D. *Federal Fathers and Mothers: A Social History of the United States Indian Service, 1869–1933*, First Peoples: New Directions in Indigenous Studies. Chapel Hill: University of North Carolina Press, 2013.

Callcott, Wilfrid Hardy. *Santa Anna: The Story of an Enigma Who Once Was Mexico*. Norman: University of Oklahoma Press, 1936.

Carroll, H. Bailey, and J. Townsana Haggard. *Three New Mexico Chronicles: The Exposición of Don Pedro Bautista Pino 1812; the Ojeada of Lic. Antonio Barreiro 1832; and the Additions by Don José Augustín Escudero, 1849*. Albuquerque: The Quivira Society, 1942.

Carlson, Alvar W. *The Spanish-American Homeland: Four Centuries in New Mexico's Rio Arriba*. Baltimore: Johns Hopkins University Press, 1990.

Carrico, Richard L. *Strangers in a Stolen Land: American Indians in San Diego, 1850–1880*. Sacramento, CA: Sierra Oaks Publishing Company, 1987.

Chaput, Donald. *Francois X. Aubry: Trader, Trailmaker and Voyageur in the Southwest*. Glendale, CA: Arthur H. Clark Company, 1975.

Carroll, Michael P. *The Penitente Brotherhood: Patriarchy and Hispano-Catholicism in New Mexico*. Baltimore: Johns Hopkins University Press, 2002.

Chasteen, John Charles. *Heroes on Horseback: A Life and Times of the Last Gaucho Caudillos*. Albuquerque: University of New Mexico Press, 1995.

Chávez, Fray Angélico. *But Time and Chance: The Story of Padre Martinez of Taos, 1793–1867*. Santa Fe: Sunstone Press, 1981.

Chávez, Fray Angélico. *Très Macho—He Said: Padre Gallegos of Albuquerque, New Mexico's First Congressman*. Santa Fe: William Gannon, 1985.

REFERENCES

Chávez, Fray Angélico, and Thomas E. Chávez. *Wake for a Fat Vicar: Father Juan Felipe Ortiz, Archbishop Lamy, and the New Mexican Catholic Church in the Middle of the Nineteenth Century.* Albuquerque: LPD Press, 2004.
Chávez, Thomas E. *Manuel Alvarez, 1794–1856: A Southwestern Biography.* Niwot: University Press of Colorado, 1990.
Chávez-García, Miroslava. *States of Delinquency: Race and Science in the Making of California's Juvenile Justice System.* Berkeley: University of California Press, 2012.
Clair, Matthew. *Privilege and Punishment: How Race and Class Matter in Criminal Court.* Princeton, NJ: Princeton University Press, 2020.
Cook, Mary Straw. *Loretto: The Sisters and Their Santa Fe Chapel.* Santa Fe: Museum of New Mexico Press, 2002.
Costeloe, Michael P. *The Central Republic in Mexico, 1835–1846: Hombres de Bien in the Age of Santa Anna.* New York: Cambridge University Press, 1993.
Craver, Rebecca McDowell. *The Impact of Intimacy: Mexican-Anglo Intermarriage in New Mexico, 1821–1846.* El Paso: Texas Western Press, 1982.
Cockcroft, James D. *Encyclopedia of Forms and Precedents, For Pleading and Practice, at Common Law, In Equity, and Under the Various Codes and Practices Acts.* New York: James D. Cockcroft, 1900.
Crutchfield, James A. *Tragedy at Taos: The Revolt of 1847.* Plano: Republic of Texas Press, 1995.
Cutter, Charles. R. *The Legal Culture of Northern New Spain.* Albuquerque: University of New Mexico Press, 1995.
Davis, William Watts Hart. *El Gringo: New Mexico & Her People.* Santa Fe: Rydal Press, 1938.
DeLay, Brian. *War of a Thousand Deserts: Indian Raids and the U.S. Mexican War.* New Haven, CT: Yale University Press, 2008.
Dawson, Joseph G. III. *Doniphan's Epic March: The 1st Missouri Volunteers in the Mexican War.* Lawrence: University of Kansas Press, 1999.
Drumm, Stella M. *Down the Santa Fe Trail and into Mexico: The Diary of Susan Shelby Magoffin, 1846–1847.* New Haven, CT: Yale University Press, 1965.
Elder, Jane Lenz, and David Weber. *Trading in Santa Fe: John M. Kingsbury's Correspondence with James Josiah Webb, 1853–1861.* Dallas: Southern Methodist University Press, 1996.
Elliott, Richard Smith, and Mark L. Gardner. *The Mexican War Correspondence of Richard Smith Elliott.* Norman: University of Oklahoma Press, 1997.
Ellis, Bruce. *Bishop Lamy's Santa Fe Cathedral: With Records of the Old Spanish Church and Convent Formally on the Site.* Albuquerque: University of New Mexico Press, 1985.
Espinosa, Aurelio. *The Folklore of Spain in the American Southwest: Traditional Spanish Folk Literature in Northern New Mexico and Southern Colorado,* ed. J. Manuel Espinosa. Norman: University of Oklahoma Press, 1986.
Foos, Paul. *A Short, Offhand, Killing Affair: Soldiers and Social Conflict during the Mexican-American War.* Chapel Hill: University of North Carolina Press, 2002.
Foucault, Michel. *Discipline and Punish: The Birth of the Prison.* New York: Vintage Books, 1995.
Frank, Ross. *From Settler to Citizen: New Mexican Economic Development and the Creation of Vecino Society, 1750–1820.* Berkeley: University of California Press, 2007.
Frazer, Robert W. *Forts and Supplies: The Role of the Army in the Economy of the Southwest, 1846–1861.* Albuquerque: University of New Mexico Press, 1983.
Ganaway, Loomis Morton. *New Mexico and the Sectional Controversy, 1846–1861.* Albuquerque: University of New Mexico Press, 1944.
Garfielde, Selucius, and F. A. Snyder. *Compiled Laws of the State of California: Containing all the Acts of the Legislature of a Public and General Nature, Now in Force, Passed at the Sessions of 1850–51–52–53.* Boston: Press of the Franklin Printing House, 1853.
Garrard, Lewis H. *Wah-to-yah and the Taos Trail: Or, Prairie Travel and Scalp Dances with a Look at Los Rancheros.* Cincinnati: H. W. Derby & Co., New York—A. S. Barnes & Co., 1850.
Gilbreath, West. *Death on the Gallows: The Story of Legal Hangings in New Mexico 1847–1923.* Silver City, NM: High Lonesome Books, 2002.

REFERENCES

Gildersleeve, Charles H. *Reports of the Cases Argued and Determined in the Supreme Court of the Territory of New Mexico, From January Term, 1852, to January Term, 1879.* San Francisco: A. L. Bancroft Company, 1881.
Gonzales, Felipe. *Política: Nuevomexicanos and American Political Incorporation, 1821–1910.* Lincoln: University of Nebraska Press, 2016.
Gonzales, Manuel G. *The Hispanic Elite of the Southwest.* El Paso: Texas Western Press, University of Texas at El Paso, 1989.
González, Deena J. *Refusing the Favor: The Spanish-Mexican Women of Santa Fe, 1820–1880.* New York: Oxford University Press, 1999.
González, Nancie L. *The Spanish-Americans of New Mexico: A Heritage of Pride.* Albuquerque: University of New Mexico Press, 1969.
Gregg, Josiah. *Commerce of the Prairies: A Selection.* Indianapolis, IN: Bobbs-Merrill Company, 1970.
Grivas, Theodore. *Military Governments in California, 1846–1850.* Glendale, CA: Arthur H. Clark Company, 1963.
Grodin, Joseph R., Calvin R. Massey, and Richard B. Cunningham. *The California State Constitution: A Reference Guide.* Westport, CT: Greenwood Press, 1993.
Gutiérrez, Ramón. *When Jesus Came, the Corn Mothers Went Away: Marriage, Sexuality, and Power in New Mexico, 1500–1846.* Stanford, CA: Stanford University Press, 1991.
Hall, Jerome. *Theft, Law, and Society.* Indianapolis, IN: Bobbs-Merrill Company, 1952.
Hall, Thomas D. *Social Change in the Southwest, 1350–1880.* Lawrence: University Press of Kansas, 1989.
Hamill, Hugh M., ed. *Caudillos.* Norman: University of Oklahoma Press, 1992.
Hamnett, Brian. *Roots of Insurgency: Mexican Regions, 1750–1824.* New York: Cambridge University Press, 1986.
Hämäläinen, Pekka. *The Comanche Empire.* New Haven, CT: Yale University Press, 2008.
Harwell, Richard Barksdale. *The Union Reader: As the North Saw the War.* New York: Dover Publications, 1996.
Hardin, Stephen L. *Texian Illiad: A Military History of the Texas Revolution.* Austin: University of Texas Press, 1994.
Hine, Robert V., and Jack Mack Faragher. *The American West: A New Interpretive History.* New Haven, CT: Yale University Press, 2000.
Horgan, Paul. *Lamy of Santa Fe: His Life and Times.* New York: The Noonday Press, 1975.
Horn, Calvin. *New Mexico's Troubled Years: The Story of the Early Territorial Governors.* Albuquerque: Horn & Wallace, Publishers, 1963.
Hughes, John T. *Doniphan's Expedition: Containing an Account of the Conquest of New Mexico.* Cincinnati: J. A. & U. P. James, 1847.
Hunt, Aurora. *Kirby Benedict: Frontier Federal Judge.* Glendale, CA: Arthur H. Clark Company, 1961.
Hyslop, Stephen G. *Bound for Santa Fe: The Road to New Mexico and the American Conquest, 1806–1848.* Norman: University of Oklahoma Press, 2002.
Jaehn, Tomas. *Germans in the Southwest: 1850–1920.* Albuquerque: University of New Mexico Press, 2005.
Jones, Oakah. *Los Paisanos: Spanish Settlers on the Northern Frontier of New Spain.* Norman: University of Oklahoma Press, 1979.
Jordan, Don, and Michael Walsh. *White Cargo: The Forgotten History of Britain's White Slaves in America.* New York: New York University Press, 2008.
Jordon, Terry G., Jon T. Kilpinen, and Charles F. Gritzner. *The Mountain West: Interpreting the Folk Landscape.* Baltimore: Johns Hopkins University Press, 1997.
Karnes, Thomas L. *William Gilpin: Western Nationalist.* Austin: University of Texas Press, 1970.
Keleher, William A. *The Fabulous Frontier: Twelve New Mexican Items.* Albuquerque: University of New Mexico Press, 1962.
Keleher, William A. *Turmoil in New Mexico, 1846–1868.* Santa Fe: Rydal Press, 1952.
Kessell, John L. *Spain and the Southwest: A Narrative of Colonial New Mexico, Arizona, Texas, and California.* Norman: University of Oklahoma Press, 2002.

REFERENCES

King, Lovalerie. *Race, Theft, and Ethics: Property Matters in African American Literature.* Baton Rouge: Louisiana State University Press, 2007.
LaFree, Gary. *Losing Legitimacy: Street Crime and the Decline of Social Institutions in America.* Boulder, CO: Westview Press, 1998.
Lamar, Howard Robers. *The Far Southwest, 1846–1912: A Territorial History.* New Haven, CT: Yale University Press, 1966. Reprint, New York, W. W. Norton and Co., 1970.
Lang, James. *Conquest and Commerce: Spain and England in the Americas.* New York: Academic Press, 1975.
Launius, Roger D. *Alexander William Doniphan: Portrait of a Missouri Moderate.* Columbia: University of Missouri Press, 1997.
Larson, Robert W. *New Mexico's Quest for Statehood, 1846–1912.* Albuquerque: University of New Mexico Press, 1968.
Lavender, David. *Bent's Fort.* Garden City, NY: Doubleday & Company, Inc., 1954.
Lawrence, Bruce B., and Aisha Karim. *On Violence: A Reader.* Durham, NC: Duke University Press, 2007.
Lecompte, Janet. *Rebellion in Rio Arriba, 1837.* Albuquerque: University of New Mexico Press, 1985.
Lincoln, George. *Mexican Treacheries and Cruelties: Incidents and Sufferings in the Mexican War.* Boston, New York. Entered according to Act of Congress, 1848.
Lister, Florence C., and Robert H. Lister. *Chihuahua: Storehouse of Storms.* Albuquerque: University of New Mexico Press, 1966.
Loveman, Brian, and Thomas M. Davies. *The Politics of Antipolitics: The Military in Latin America.* Lanham, MD: SR Books, 1997.
Lynch, John. *Caudillos in Spanish American, 1800–1850.* Oxford: Clarendon Press, 1992.
Martínez, Oscar J. *Border People: Life and Society in the U.S.-Mexico Borderlands.* Tucson: University of Arizona Press, 1994.
McKanna, Clare V., Jr. *Race and Homicide in Nineteenth-Century California.* Reno: University of Nevada Press, 2002.
McNierney, Michael. *Taos 1847: The Revolt in Contemporary Accounts.* Boulder, CO: Johnson Publishing Company, 1980.
McCall, Col. Archibald George. *New Mexico in 1850: A Military View.* Edited by Robert W. Frazer. Norman: University of Oklahoma Press, 1968.
McShane, Marilyn, and Frank P. Williams III, ed. *Encyclopedia of American Prisons.* New York: Garland Publishing, 1996.
Meinig, D. W. *Southwest: Three Peoples in Geographic Change, 1600–1970.* New York: Oxford University Press, 1971.
Meketa, Jacqueline Dorgan. *Legacy of Honor: The Life of Rafael Chacón, a Nineteenth Century New Mexican.* Albuquerque: University of New Mexico Press, 1986.
Miller, Darlis A. *Soldiers and Settlers: Military Supply in the Southwest, 1861–1885.* Albuquerque: University of New Mexico Press, 1989.
Mills, C. Wright. *The Power Elite.* Oxford: Oxford University Press, 1956.
Mocho, Jill. *Murder and Justice in Frontier New Mexico 1821–1846.* Albuquerque: University of New Mexico Press, 1997.
Montoya, Maria E. *Translating Property: The Maxwell Land Grant and the Conflict Over Land in the American West, 1840–1900.* Berkeley: University of California Press, 2002.
Moorhead, Max L. *New Mexico's Royal Road: Trade and Travel on the Chihuahua Trail.* Norman: University of Oklahoma Press, 1958.
Murphy, Lawrence R. *Antislavery in the Southwest: William G. Kephart's Mission to New Mexico, 1850–53.* El Paso: Texas Western Press, 1978.
Murphy, Lawrence R. *Frontier Crusader—William F. Arny.* Tucson: University of Arizona Press, 1972.
Ortiz, Roxanne Dunbar. *Roots of Resistance: Land Tenure in New Mexico, 1680–1980.* Los Angeles: Chicano Studies Research Center Publications, 1980.

REFERENCES

Perrigo, Lynn I. *Hispanos: Historic Leaders in New Mexico*. Santa Fe: Sunstone Press, 1985.

Poling-Kempes, Lesley. *Valley of the Shining Stone: The Story of Abiquiu*. Tucson: University of Arizona Press, 1997.

Powers, Karen Vieira. *Andean Journeys: Migration, Ethnogenesis, and the State in Colonial Quito*. Albuquerque: University of New Mexico Press, 1995.

Read, Benjamin M. *Illustrated History of New Mexico*. New York: Arno Press, 1976.

Resendéz, Andrés. *Changing National Identities at the Frontier: Texas and New Mexico, 1800–1850*. Cambridge: Press Syndicate of the University of Cambridge, 2005.

Riley, Glenda, and Richard W. Etulain, eds. *By Grit & Grace: Eleven Women Who Shaped the American West*. Golden, CO: Fulcrum Publishing, 1997.

Ritch, William G. *New Mexico Blue Book, 1882*. Albuquerque: University of New Mexico Press, 1968.

Rodríguez O., Jaime E., and Kathryn Vincent, eds. *Myths, Misdeeds, and Misunderstandings: The Roots of Conflict in U.S. Mexican Relations*. Wilmington, DE: Scholarly Resources Inc., 1997.

Romero, Orlando, ed. *All Trails Lead to Santa Fe: An Anthology Commemorating the 400th Anniversary of the Founding of Santa Fe, New Mexico in 1610*. Santa Fe: Sunstone Press, 2010.

Rosenbaum, Robert J. *Mexicano Resistance in the Southwest: The Sacred Right of Self-Preservation*. Austin: University of Texas Press, 1981.

Roth, Randolph. *American Homicide*. Cambridge, MA: Belknap Press of Harvard University Press, 2009.

Rousseau, Jean Jacques. *Political Writings*. Madison: University of Wisconsin Press, 1986.

Ruxton, George F. *Adventures in Mexico and the Rocky Mountains*. London: John Murray, Albemarle Street, 1847.

Sanchez, Pedro. *Memorias Sobre La Vida Del Presbitero Don Antonio Jose Martinez*. Original Spanish text with English translation by Ray John de Aragon. Santa Fe: The Lightning Tree—Jean Lyon Publishing, 1978.

Schwarz, Phillip J. *Twice Condemned: Slaves and the Criminal Laws of Virginia, 1705–1865*. Baton Rouge: Louisiana State University Press, 1988.

Simmons, Marc. *Albuquerque: A Narrative History*. Albuquerque: University of New Mexico Press, 1982.

Simmons, Marc. *The Little Lion of the Southwest: A Life of Manuel Antonio Chaves*. Chicago: Sage Books, Swallow Press, 1973.

Simmons, Marc. *Ranchers, Ramblers, and Renegades: True Tales of Territorial New Mexico*. Santa Fe: Ancient City Press, 1984.

Simmons, Marc. *Yesterday in Santa Fe: Episodes in a Turbulent History*. Santa Fe: Sunstone Press, 2007.

Spicer, Edmund. *Cycles of Conquest: The Impact of Spain, Mexico, and the United States on the Indians of the Southwest, 1533–1960*. Tucson: University of Arizona Press, 1967.

Starrs, Paul F. *Let the Cowboy Ride: Cattle Ranching in the American West*. Baltimore: Johns Hopkins University Press, 1998.

Steele, Thomas J., S.J. *Archbishop Lamy: In His Own Words*. Albuquerque: LPD Press, 2000.

Stevens, Donald Fithian. *Origins of Instability in Early Republican Mexico*. Durham, NC: Duke University Press, 1991.

Stoddard, Ellwyn R., Richard L. Nostrand, and Jonathan P. West. *Borderlands Sourcebook: A Guide to the Literature on Northern Mexico and the American Southwest*. Norman: University of Oklahoma Press, 1983.

Stratton, Porter. *The Territorial Press of New Mexico, 1834–1912*. Albuquerque: University of New Mexico Press, 1969.

Sunseri, Alvin R. *Seeds of Discord: New Mexico in the Aftermath of the American Conquest, 1846–1861*. Chicago: Nelson-Hall, 1979.

Taylor, Alan. *The Civil War of 1812: American Citizens, British Subjects, Irish Rebels, & Indian Allies*. New York: Alfred A. Knopf, Random House, 2010.

Taylor, William B. *Drinking, Homicide and Rebellion in Colonial Mexican Villages*. Palo Alto, CA: Stanford University Press, 1979.

Taylor, William B. *Magistrates of the Sacred: Priests and Parishioners in Eighteenth-Century Mexico*. Palo Alto, CA: Stanford University Press, 1996.
Thompson, Jerry. *Texas & New Mexico on the Eve of The Civil War: The Mansfield & Johnston Inspections, 1859–1861*. Albuquerque: University of New Mexico Press, 2001.
Torrez, Robert J. *Myth of the Hanging Tree: Stories of Crime and Punishment in Territorial New Mexico*. Albuquerque: University of New Mexico Press, 2008.
Twitchell, Ralph Emerson. *The Bench and the Bar During the American Occupation, A.D. 1846–1850*. Santa Fe: New Mexican Printing Company, 1891, 1912.
Twitchell, Ralph Emerson. *Old Santa Fe: A Magazine of History, Archaeology, Genealogy, and Biography*, vol. I, 1913–1914. Santa Fe: Old Santa Fe Press, 1914.
Twitchell, Ralph Emerson. *The Leading Facts of New Mexican History*, vol. II. Santa Fe: Sunstone Press, 2007 (1911). New edition, Santa Fe: Sunstone Press 2007.
Twitchell, Ralph Emerson. *Old Santa Fe: A Magazine of History, Archaeology, Genealogy, and Biography*, vol. II. Santa Fe: Old Santa Fe Press, 1915.
Twitchell, Ralph Emerson. *Old Santa Fe: A Magazine of History, Archaeology, Genealogy, and Biography*, vol. III. Santa Fe: Old Santa Fe Press, 1916.
Twitchell, Ralph Emerson. *Old Santa Fe: The Story of New Mexico's Ancient Capital*. Facsimile of number 281 of the original 1925 edition. Santa Fe: Sunstone Press, 2007.
Tyler, Daniel. *Sources for New Mexican History, 1821–1848*. Santa Fe: Museum of New Mexico Press, 1984.
Valerio-Jiménez, Omar S. *River of Hope: Forging Identity and Nation in the Rio Grande Borderlands*. Durham, NC: Duke University Press, 2013.
Vigil, Maurillo E. *Los Patrones: Profiles of Hispanic Leaders in New Mexican History*. Washington, DC: University Press of America, Inc., 1980.
Villar, Ernesto de Torre, Moises Gonzalez Navarro, and Stanley Ross. *Historia Documental de Mexico*, vol. II. México Cuidad: Universidad Nacional Autónomo, 1964.
Weber, David J. *Arms, Indians, and the Mismanagement of New Mexico: Donaciano Vigil, 1846*. El Paso: Texas Western Press, University of Texas El Paso, 1986.
Weber, David J. *The Extranjeros: Selected Documents from the Mexican Side of the Santa Fe Trail, 1825–1828*. Santa Fe: Stagecoach Press, 1967.
Weber, David J. *Foreigners in Their Native Land: Historical Roots of the Mexican Americans*. Albuquerque: University of New Mexico Press, 2003.
Weber, David J. *The Mexican Frontier, 1821–1846: The American Southwest Under Mexico*. Albuquerque: University of New Mexico Press, 1982.
Westphall, Victor. *Mercedes Reales: Hispanic Land Grants of the Upper Rio Grande Region*. Albuquerque: University of New Mexico Press, 1983.
Wilson, John Paul. *When the Texans Came: Missing Records from the Civil War in the Southwest, 1861–1862*. Albuquerque: University of New Mexico Press, 2001.
Wilson, Richard. *Short Ravelings from a Long Yarn or Camp and March Sketches from the Santa Fe Trail*. Santa Fe: Fine Arts Press, 1936.

Articles

Alarid, Michael J. "Beyond Banditry: The Significance of Everyday Larceny in New Mexican Social History, 1837–1865." In *Western Historical Quarterly* 50, issue 2 (Summer 2019): 113–36.
Bakken, Gordon Morris. "The Courts, the Legal Profession, and the Development of Law in Early California." *California History* 81, no. 3/4, Taming Elephants: Politics, Government, and Law in Pioneer California (2003): 74–95.
Bakken, Gordon Morris. "Death for Grand Larceny." In *Historic U.S. Court Cases, 1690–1990, An Encyclopedia*, edited by John W. Johnson. New York: Garland Publishing, 1992.
Birdsall, Stephen S., and John Florin. "Regional Landscapes of the United States: Southwest Border

REFERENCES

Area" (Outline of American Geography, November 1988), accessed June 28, 2012: http://www.america.gov/publications/books/outline-of-american-geography.html.

Bowden, J. J. "Town of Cebolleta Grant." New Mexico Office of the State Historian. Accessed March 29, 2011: http://www.newmexicohistory.org/filedetails.php?fileID=24969.

Castro, C., J. Castro, J. Campillo, L. Auda and G. Auda, and G. Rodriguez Rodriguez. "Mexico y Sus Alrededores." Alicante: Miguel de Cervantes Virtual Library, 2006.

"The Founding of Fort Union." Fort Union National Monument, Historical Handbook Number 35, 1962. Accessed June 28, 2012: http://www.cr.nps.gov/history/online_books/hh/35/hh35toc.htm.

Fletcher, George P. "The Metamorphosis of Larceny," *Harvard Law Review* 89, no. 3 (Jan. 1976): 469–530.

Gómez, Laura E. "Off-White in an Age of White Supremacy: Mexican Elites and the Rights of Indians and Blacks in Nineteenth-Century New Mexico." *Chicano-Latino Law Review* 25, no. 9 (2005).

Gómez, Laura E. "Race, Colonialism, and Criminal Law: Mexicans and the American Criminal Justice System in Territorial New Mexico." *Law & Society Review* 34, no. 4 (2000).

Green, Lowell C. "Bar Activities." *American Bar Association Journal* 44 (July 1958).

Hayman, Robert L., Jr. "A History of Race in Delaware: 1639–1950." In *Choosing Equality: Essays and Narratives on the Desegregation Experience*, edited by Robert L. Hayman Jr. and Leland Ware. University Park: Pennsylvania State University Press, 2009.

Hindus, Michael S. "Black Justice Under White Law: Criminal Prosecutions of Blacks in Antebellum South Carolina." *Journal of American History* 63, no. 3 (Dec. 1976): 575–99.

Keita, Emily E. "The New Mexico Fandango." *Wagontracks* 19, no. 3 (May 2005).

McClarey, Donald R. "The First." Accessed July 1, 2012: http://the-american-catholic.com/2009/03/09/the-first/.

Minge, Ward Allen. "Frontier Problems in New Mexico Preceding the Mexican War, 1840–1846." PhD dissertation, University of New Mexico, 1965.

Moore, Waddy W. "Some Aspects of Crime and Punishment on the Arkansas Frontier." *Arkansas Historical Quarterly* 23, no. 1 (Spring 1964).

Olive, Leo E. "Fort Union and the Frontier Army in the Southwest: A Historical Research, Fort Union National Monument, Fort Union, New Mexico." Southwest Cultural Resources Center Professional Paper #41 Division of History, 1993. Accessed May 5, 2011: http://www.nps.gov/history/history/online_books/foun/chap9.htm.

Paton, Diana. "Crimes and the Bodies of Slaves in Eighteenth-Century Jamaica." *Journal of Social History* 34, no. 4 (Summer 2001).

Peté, Stephen, and Annie Devenish. "Flogging, Fear and Food: Punishment and Race in Colonial Natal." *Journal of Southern African Studies* 31, no. 1 (March 2005).

Powers, Charles. "The Role of Sticking Points in Pareto's Theory of Social Systems." In *Vilfredo Pareto: Beyond Disciplinary Boundaries*, edited by Joseph V. Femia and Alasdair J. Marshall. New York: Routledge, 2016.

Roth, Randolph. "Homicide Rates in the Nineteenth-Century West: Tables." Historical Violence Database, Criminal Justice Research Center, Ohio State University. https://cjrc.osu.edu/research/interdisciplinary/hvd/homicide-rates-american-west.

Tigar, Michael E. "The Right of Property and the Law of Theft." 62 *Texas Law Review* 1443–75 (1984).

Tjarks, Alicia V. "Demographic, Ethnic, and Occupational Structure of New Mexico, 1790." *The Americas* 35, no. 1 (July 1978).

Torrez, Robert J. "Crime and Punishment in Colonial New Mexico." *New Mexico Bar Journal* (2000). Accessed June 14, 2012: http://www.nmbar.org/AboutSBNM/Committees/Historical/Crime_and_Punishment_In%20Colonial_New_Mexico.pdf.

Tyler, Daniel. "Gringo Views of Manuel Armijo." *New Mexico Historical Review* XLV, no. 1 (1970).
Walker, Donald. "Hispanics in San Joaquin County, 1850–1930." *San Joaquin Historian* XV, no. 1 (2001): 3.
Wroth, William H. "Lamy, Jean Baptiste" Accessed June 11, 2012: http://www.newmexicohistory.org/filedetails.php?fileID=501.
Wroth, William H. "Taos Rebellion: 1847." Accessed June 7, 2012: http://www.newmexicohistory.org/filedetails.php?fileID=515. Moved and accessed December 11, 2021: https://www.facebook.com/FreeTaosPueblo/posts/taos-rebellion-1847by-william-h-wrothin-the-summer-of-1846-general-stephen-watts/497340946971220/.
Wroth, William H. "The 1837 Rebellion of Rio Arriba." Accessed June 7, 2012: http://www.newmexicohistory.org/filedetails.php?fileID=318.

INDEX

abductions, 118
Abeytia, Aniceito, 38, 40, 42, 157
Abréu, Ramón, 33, 35, 36, 37
Abreu, Santiago, 33, 37
age: Hispanic and Anglo males compared, 63; land distribution by, 59, 60, 62t, 115t
agricultural exports, 21, 55
agriculture, unpredictable nature of, 18
Alarid, Antonio Jose De La Cruz (Cruzito) (author's great grandfather), xv
Alarid, father of author, xvi
Alarid, Jesus Maria, 37
Alarid, Jose Ignacio (author's ancestor), xv
Alarid, Jose Magdaleno (author's grandfather), xv–xvi
Alarid, Juan María, 29
Alarid, Matias, xv, 173, 217n21
Alarid, Waldo, xiv
Alarid family history, xiv–xvi
Alarid House, xiv, xv
Albuquerque, District of, 39
alcaldes: American attitude toward, 50; capital punishment discussed by, 160–61; as civil case arbitrators, 48; crime curbing measures by, 49–50; juries not used by, 104, 202n113; punishment administered by, 147–48; white judge attitude toward, 49
alcohol, 75, 157
Allen, Howard W., 162
Alverez, Thomas, 105
American authorities: Hispano resistance to, xvi, 2; landholding Hispano cooperation with, 12; patrónes relations with, 13, 48, 52, 172, 173
American-born Anglo property holdings, 57, 58
American colonialism, xiv, xv
American conquest: aftermath of, 17; limits in Santa Fe County, 76; Mexico ripe for, 42; property acquired through, 58; tragic components of, 57, 191n82
American empire, 20
American immigrants, instability brought about by, 12
American invaders, Nuevomexicano resistance to, 17, 182n18
American judges, limited documentation of, 50
American legal system, 138–47
American market, 8
American merchants, 19, 26, 42
American military government, resistance to, 88
American Party, 140, 142

American Revolution, xiv–xv
Americans, trade with, 18, 20, 24–25, 26
American settlers, court cases against, 50
American soldiers: homicides involving, 100, 103–4, 106, 108; murder of, 50, 190n40; politics, attempt to enter, 107
American territorial government: land claimed by, 56, 57, 64, 65, 192n95; landholding Nuevomexicanos under, 3, 72; New Mexican participation in, 83; patrón participation in, 7, 76; persons in need not aided by, 65
American territorialization. See territorialization
American territorial period: crime during, 74; homicides during, 81–82; infrastructure during, 114; landholder entrepreneurialism into, 8; landholding Hispano relations with others during, 3; laws during, 77; patrónes during, 9–10; Sante Fe County Hispano population during, 13–14
American traders, 26–27, 37–38
American two-party system, 142
Anderson, Oliver P., 99, 152
Anglo adult males, 63, 64
Anglos, assault by, 85t, 113
Anglos, thefts against, 68
Anglo settlers: controlling violent, 87; crimes committed by, 73; homicide rates, 107, 110, 110t; obstacles to success, 76; occupations of landholding, 58, 58; patrónes, relations with, 47–48
Anglo settlers, new: age breakdown, 61; larceny committed by, 47, 74–76; patrón-American partnership at expense of, 47
Anglo soldiers, crimes committed by, 74, 75, 196n155
Anglo wealth, transient nature of, 58
Angney, William Z., 68
Anton Chico, 107
Apaches: assault by, 85t; conflict with, 7, 13, 114, 142; defense against, 6, 30, 101, 142; displacement of, 8; peace with, 20; routes controlled by, 25; slave raids against, 153; white traders as targets of, 10
Aragon, Antonio, 155
Arce, Jose (victim of theft), 67–68
Arce, Jose Antonio (governor of Chihuahua), 67–68, 194n114
Archdiocese of Baltimore, 7, 47, 53
Archdiocese of Durango, 47, 53, 54
Archuleta, Diego: in Civil War, 170; election of,

229

INDEX

Archuleta, Diego (*continued*)
  15, 139; in House of Representatives, 86–87; as opportunist, 140; in political machine, 172; rise of, 16; Taos Campaign, role in, 157
Archuleta, Juan Andres, 15, 102
Arias, Jesus, 128
Arizona, Mexicanos in, 82
Arkansas River, routes to, 87
armed robbery, 45, 68, 69
Armijo, Manuel: cases sent to, 102; Chacón, Rafael compared to, 171; Chacón, Rafael encounter with, 170; Chimayo Rebellion, role in, 36, 37–38, 42, 43, 157, 214n123; Chimayo Rebellion put down with help of, 34, 38–42; flight to Chihuahua, 42–43; government position, passing over for, 35; as governor, 38, 42; intimidation used by, 15; Mexican government economic problems, weariness over, 30; as New Mexico governor, 18–19; people serving under, 51; Pérez, Albino opposed by, 33–34; rebellions and incursions, fight against, 18; retirement and death, 44; rise of, 16; trade laws and practices by, 27–28; trapping, illegal, crackdown on, 28–29
Articles of Confederation (U.S.), 30, 185n87
Ashurst, Merrill, 128, 129, 133
assault: conviction rates for, 150; fines for, 157; forces driving, 14; Hispanos and Anglos compared, 85t, 111, 122; homicide, correlation with, 5; increase in, 77, 111; increase in those accused of, 7; sheriff involvement in, 116–17; women as victims of, 11
assets, 112, 115, 205n31

Baca, Desiderio, 133
Baca, Manuela, 112, 121
Baca, Manuel "Bacacitos," 123, 124, 156
Baca, Ramon, 155
Baca, Román, 170
Baca del Pino, Ana, 59
Baca y Salazar, Jesus Maria, 116–17, 122, 123, 124, 133
Baca y Sena, Manuela, 59
Baird, James, 28, 29
Baird, Spruce M., 120, 158–59
Baker, Grafton, 71, 99, 152, 154, 155
Bancroft, Hubert Howe, 57, 85, 87
Barceló, Trinidad, 97, 200n78
Basques, Felipe, 157
Battle of Glorieta Pass, xv, 172
Battle of San Jacinto, 31
Battle of Valverde, 170
Baxter, John, 41
Beach, Rufus, 49, 154

Bealty, Andrew S., 69
Beaubien, Charles, 49
beaver, hunting, 28
Beck, Preston, Jr., 131–32, 151
Bell, Horace, 154
Benedict, Kirby, 121, 128–29, 134, 148, 158
Bent, Charles: as governor, 51; legal code creation, role in, 48; ouster of, 83; patrónes rebellion against, 17; plot to kill, 87, 166
Bernalillo (town), xv
Bernalillo County, 107
bishop, crimes against, 45–46
blacks: criminal convictions of, 147, 150, 151; death penalty against, 163; indentured servitude for, 153, 212–13n87, 213n88; theft by, 46
Blackwood, Mary Josephine, 141
Blea, Bernabel, 126–27
Blumner, Charles, 37, 75, 77
Bolt, William H., 104, 105, 106
Borrego, Benito, 123, 124–25
Borrego, Refugio, 124
Bourbon Reforms (1750-1788): centralization and tax collecting emphasized during, 6, 15; church targeted by, 23; landholder benefits from, 16; manufacturing restricted during, 20; New Mexico economic conditions, impact on, 20–21; Spanish colony profits, attempt to boost through, 19
Bourdieu, Pierre, 114
Boyle, Susan, 8, 24
Boze, Henry, 75
Brady, James C., 98, 99, 103
Briggs, Thomas, 68
Burger, Fredrick, 134
burglars, corporal punishment against, 70–71, 146, 156
burglary, 67–68, 74, 136, 196n155
businessmen, 67–68, 74

Cabesa de Baca (defensor), 97, 200n78
Calhoun, James S., 139, 140, 210n13
California: capital punishment in, 161, 162; demographics, 72, 196n145; Hispano migration to, 66–67; homicide risk in, 80; homicides in, 84; petty larceny as defined in, 67, 193–94n112; routes to, 87; U.S. occupation of, 79; white immigration to, 83–84; white settlers in New Mexico compared to those in, 72, 195n144
California Indians, 154
Californios: homicides by, 84, 90, 90t, 107; immigrant overwhelming of, 83–84; statistics, 82; vecinos compared to, 86; white settler relationship with, 80

INDEX

capitalism: American territorialist system centered on, 114; fractures brought about by, 2; inequality arising from, 78; patrón embrace of American, 2, 3, 109; transition into, 56
capitalists, patrónes as, 80
capital punishment, 134, 137, 160–64, 167–68; Mexican and territorialization periods compared, 50, 189–90n34
Castillo, Miliana, 155
Catholic Church, 53
caudillos: Armijo, Manuel actions characteristic of, 41; authority and legitimacy of, 9–10; land acquired by, 13; during Mexican period, 7; patrónes as, 6, 172; power seized by, 17; trade practices by, 27, 184n73
Ceballes, Tomas, 155, 156
censuses, Mexican and US, 4
centralist movement and resistance to, 30–34, 36–37, 42
centralization, 6, 15, 41
Cepreana, Maria, 71
Chacon, Albino: American authority resisted by, 172; Chimayo Rebellion counterrevolution backed by, 41; elected office held by, 86–87; items stolen from, 67, 69, 160; Pérez, Gov. defeat and killing recalled by, 37; son of, 19
Chacon, Rafael, 19, 170–71, 172
Chastain, Daniel, 111, 204n14
Chaves, Antonio Jose, 128
Chaves, Eugenio, 120
Chaves, Juan Antonio, 96, 97, 161
Chaves, Manuel: in Civil War, 170, 172; clergy, relations with, 53; land boundary claimed by, 1–2, 13; landholder violence illustrated through story of, 3, 15; as opportunist, 140; as patrón, 9, 59; thefts against, 67, 68; uncle of, 40
Chávez, A. Antonito, 37
Chávez, Fray Angélico, 2, 52–53, 86
Chávez, José Francisco, 170
Chávez, Mariano, 34, 39, 40, 186n114
Chávez-García, Miroslava, 154
Chihuahua: establishment of, 24, 184n57; journey to, 25; merchants in, 24; Mexican manufacturers and traders, competition in, 31; New Mexico, rivalry with, 19; trade monopoly, breaking of, 18, 25; trade to, 21
Chimayo Rebellion, 1837: aftermath of, 99–100; analysis of, 43–44; documents relating to, destruction of, 38, 42; hierarchical social structure solidified during, 12; imprisonment during time of, 161; narrative, control over, 38, 41, 42; New Mexico government prior to, 51; overview of, 16–17, 34–42; passive resistance in, 171; patrónes spearheading of, 33; Santa Anna actions sparking, 30–31; white

American judge attitude concerning, 148
church, slander prohibited in, 143, 144
Civil War, 80, 131, 169–72, 197–98n10
class and ethnicity, interweaving of, 14
class inequality, 128–29
class interest, theft relationship to, 65
classism, vecino experience of, 6
clergy, crimes against, 45–46, 53, 55, 78
clergy, purge of, 110
Clever, Charles P., 117, 118
Cline, John, 75
Clubb, Jerome M., 162
"Code of the West," 108
cohabitation out of wedlock, 143, 144
colonization, cultures caught within, 2
colonized African societies, New Mexico compared to, 138
Comanche: conflict with, 10, 114, 142; defense against, 6, 30, 142; peace with, 20; routes controlled by, 25; treaties with, 7
Commandancy General of the Interior Provinces of the North, 20
commerce violations, 5, 74, 151, 157, 214n120
commodified fandangos, 99, 100, 103–6
communal lands, vecino loss of access to, 56, 57, 64–65, 66, 76
community homicides, 82, 96–99
Compromise of 1850, 85, 198n25
confession to crime, 103
connectedness, sense of, 81, 198n12
Connelly, Henry, 170
Constitutional Convention, 1850, 139
constitutions of 1824 and 1836, 30
contraband, 26, 27, 29
conviction and conviction rates: class identity impact on, 5; Nuevomexicanos and white Americans compared, 138; vecinos and white Americans compared, 13, 149
convict lease program, 153, 213n88
corporal punishment: abolition of, 50; Kearny Code provisions for, 136; patrón attitudes and American law compared, 48, 143, 147; during territorial period, 70–71, 156
corregimientos, abolition of, 20
craftsmen/artisans, 22, 56
crime: combining categories, 111; Hispanos and whites compared, 66t; quantitative picture of, 4; rise in, 6–7; vecinos and Anglos compared, 64, 72, 78
crime deterrent, Mexican and American systems compared, 71
crime documentation, Mexican and territorialization periods compared, 49, 50
crime rates, calculating, 5
crime rates, factors affecting, 72, 195–96n145

231

INDEX

criminal court records, 4, 10–11
criminals, forces driving, 14
criminals, redemption for, 71
criollos, 20
cultural domination, judicial system as tool of, 137
Cutter, Charles, 50
Cutter, Martha, 121

Damours, A. P., 170
Davenport, J. J., 122, 136, 148
death penalty. See capital punishment
Decree of 1837, 33
defense, patrón role in, 6
defensor, 101, 201n99
Delaware, indentured servitude in, 153, 212–13n87
Delgado, Pablo, 71, 112, 116
Delores, Martin, 157
departmental plan, 30, 32, 36, 37
Diocese of Baltimore, 7, 47, 53
Diocese of Durango, 47, 53, 54
districts, New Mexico divided into, 49
domestic violence, 82, 120–22, 123, 127
dominance and dependence relations, transition to, 114
Dominguez, Matias, 133
Donahue, Joseph, 105
Doniphan, Alexander William, 48
Dorrance, Louis, 136, 155, 158–59, 209n4
Douglass, Frederick, 46
drunkenness, 82, 171
Duran, Pablo, 118–19

ecclesiastical colonialism (term), 2
ecclesiastical colonialization, 7, 52–53, 55, 86, 181n8
economic development, 87
economic institutions, strengthening of, 112
1856, quantifying importance of, 110–12
Elam, William Henry, 132–33
elders, role in household, 59
elections, American attempt to manipulate, 139
Ellis, Joseph D., 118
employers, patrónes as, 47
Espinosa, Aurelio M., 146, 211n50
Esquibel, Juan José, 36
ethnic identity, arrest and conviction based on, 5
ethnicity, comparing crimes by, 5
ethnicity and class, 14
ethnic lines, verdicts and punishments along, 147, 153, 157
Euro Americans, obstacles to success, 76
European immigrants: in Mexican and American periods, 3, 180n8; obstacles to success, 76; property gained by, 57
examination of the body (reconocimiento de heridas), 49
Exchange Hotel: advertisements for, 94; Alarid House subsumed by, xv; demolishing of, 91, 199n49; shootings at, 79, 92, 93, 164, 165
exports, trade relationships versus, 19
extended families, women as heads of, 59

fandangos: homicides at, 82, 99–106; laws against running, 143; Mexican and territorial periods compared, 65; patrón-hosted, decline in, 114; weapons prohibited in, 89
farmers: versus farm ownership, 21–22; patrónes as, 59; property owned by, 57–58; small, 10, 18, 22, 55–56
farms, small, eroding viability of, 23
female minors, laws protecting, 144
females as victims, 94, 200n67
Fiat Justitia (pseudonym), 94, 95
fines, imposition of, 157–58
Finnegan, John, 93, 94, 95–96, 104, 118
firearms: homicides committed with, 90, 111; Native acquisition of, 8; theft of, 67, 68, 70, 72, 74, 155, 156
Fitzsimmons, William, 132
Florence, Sylvester, 75
foreign-born whites: decline in, 73; homicide rate increase driven by, 82; killing of, 93; obstacles to success, 64, 79; occupations of, 61–62; political process, exclusion from, 80–81; property held by, 61. See also white immigrants
forgery, 158
formal institutions, imposition of new, 2
Foucalt, Michel, 136
Franciscans, 23
Francoso, Jose, 67, 68–70, 75, 156, 160
French clergymen, 47

Gadsden Purchase, 1853, 67, 193n104
Gallego, Manuel, 96–97, 160–61
Gallegos, José Guadalupe, 170
Gallegos, Padre José Manuel, 54, 86, 140, 169, 175–78
Gallego y Martínez, Juan, 161
gambling, regulation and taxes on, 143, 157
Ganaway, Loomis Morton, 138, 209–10n8
Garcia, Calistro, 67
Garcia, Felix, 112, 116, 123
Garcia, Jesus (landholder), 136
Garcia, Jesus (vecino), 67–68
Garcia, Joseph, 99, 152, 162
Garcia, Juan, 112, 114, 123
Garcia, Manuel, 112, 123

Garcia, Ramon, 119
Garcia, Sinaco, 123, 124–25
Garcia, Vicente, 112, 116, 123, 124, 207n77
Garcia de Lara, Alférez Manuel, 101–3
Gaveldon, Jose, 151
gender, land distribution by, 59, 60
genízaros (unfree people), 3, 70, 153
Gerhart, John W., 156
German immigrants, 104
Gold Rush, 80, 83–84, 85
Gonsales, Rafael, 98, 100
Gonzales, Felipe, 138, 140, 173, 209n8, 217n23
Gonzales, Jesusa, 121
Gonzales, Jose Angel, 38, 40, 41
Gonzales, Jose Benito, 156
Gonzales, Miguel, 105
Gonzales, Monico, 148
Gonzalez, Euligio, 122, 167
Gonzalez, Justo, 67–68
Gonzalez, Maria Candalera, 157
Gonzalez, Maria Jesus, 127
Gonzalez y Moya, Ramon, 127
Goodfellow, William, 75, 151
Gorman, John, 131–32, 151
government, confidence (or lack) in: assault correlation to, 5; crime correlation to, 123; homicide correlation to, 4–5, 80, 81, 108, 109, 197–98n10, 203n6
government, legitimate, low homicide correlation to, 81, 198n11
government office holders, ethnicity of, 88
grand larceny, 67–68, 71, 74–75
Great Depression, 116
Gregg, Josiah, 26, 90
Griego, Francisco, 67, 131
Griego, Luis, 116, 123
Gruber, George, 129, 130
Guadalupe the Navajo, 155
Guiser, William, 75–76
Gutierrez, Eligio, 148
Gutierrez, Felipe, 133
Gutiérrez, Ramón, 20, 22

Hall, Thomas, 16, 20, 41
Herrera, Maria Angelina, 97
hierarchical social structure (Mexican period), 12
Higgins, Charles, 75
Hirsch, Joseph, 133
Hispano assault, 85t, 113
Hispano communities, property distribution within, 46, 188n7
Hispano community: assault in, 111; stability of early, 12; violence, rise in, 13
Hispano homicide: accusations of, 93–95; Anglo/white homicide compared to, 90–91, 110, 111, 113, 204n13; Californios, 84, 90, 90t, 107; examples of, 100–103; motives for, 107; rates, 107, 110, 110t, 113. See also Nuevomexicano homicides
Hispano jurors, 149, 163
Hispano larceny, 73, 78
Hispano males, 61, 63, 115t
Hispano padres, 47, 53–55, 76, 86
Hispanos: autonomy, 87; in California, 84; clergy, relations with, 52–53; court system and, 77; displacement, myth of, 57; empowerment of, 86; Indigenous People, buffer against, 10; as jurors, 106, 203n131; political representation, 87–88; population, 66–67; power of, 174; property owned by, 14, 57, 58, 58, 59, 60; relations with others during Mexican period, 3; repatriation of, 67, 193n104; Sante Fe County population of, 13–14; term defined, 2, 179–80n7; territorial government offices held by, 86–89; theft against, 68; violent crime by, 111, 113; as witnesses, 106, 203n131
Hispano women, 121–22, 144
historiography, 174
Hoffman, Edward, 49, 98
home rule, 52
homicide: accusations of, 7, 93–95; cases, examples of, 81–82; community, 82, 96–99; convictions for, 150, 165; forces driving, 14; Fourth of July, 93–96, 119, 121; in Hispano community, 13; intentional versus unintentional, 111, 112; Mexican and territorialization periods compared, 50, 189–90n34; during Mexican period, 49; Mexican soldiers involved in, 100, 101–3; premeditated, 82; problem of, 89–91; public, 82, 91–96; punishment for, 160; references to, 74, 196n154; risk, assessing, 4; sheriffs charged with, 117; social, 82, 99–106; theories of, 4–5; unpunished, 99, 152, 164, 167; victims, white versus nonwhite, 162; women as victims of, 11, 82
homicide rates: in early territorial period, 135; factors affecting, 72, 80, 81, 195–96n145, 197–98nn10–12; high, 130–31; Hispanos and Anglos compared, 79–80, 80t, 107, 110t; rise in, 77, 82; Santa Fe County and other places compared, 5, 83, 125; western, 81t, 125t
Hopkins, Thomas H., 119
horses, theft of, 75–76
Hotel La Fonda, xiv, 91, 199n49; hotel, former at site of (see Exchange Hotel)
Houghton, Joab, 49, 139, 148, 166
Houston, James H., 111, 204n14
Hovey, Oliver, 119
Hovey, William, 120–21

INDEX

Huffington, Stephen, 105
ideological norms, new, 114
indentured servitude: blacks and vecinos compared, 153, 213n88; entrapment into, 157–58; legal precedents for, 153, 212–13n87; as permanent institution, 72, 195n142; as punishment, 65, 70, 71–72, 137, 153–56; statistics, 61
Independence, Missouri, route to, 25
Indian Depredations, 101
Indigenous peoples: assimilation of, 65, 192–93n101; buffer against, 10, 20; in California, 84; as captives, 3–4; crime and punishment for, 136; crimes confessed by, 50; in criminal court documents, 11; Hispanos, conflict with, 8; indentured servitude for, 71, 153–54; Mexican policy toward, 18, 183n26; patrón relations with, 7–8; protection from, 23–24; Spanish policy toward, 15, 182n1; term defined, 2, 179–80n7; threats posed by, 24, 25, 175
Indios barbaros, pobres as, 147
Indios de los pueblos, landholder rise impact on, 3
industry, tax cut stimulation of, 6, 180n21
inequality: capitalism and, 78; growing, trends of, 46; in land distribution, 21, 23, 123, 134; Mexican period and current conditions compared, xvi; in United States, 116. See also wealth inequality
infidelity as motive for homicide, 126
infrastructure, funds for, 87
initial proceedings (auto de cabeza), 49
insanity, court ruling of, 96, 97, 161, 162
intendancy system, 20
intermarriage between whites and Hispanos, 72, 80, 195n144

Jackson, Alexander, 141
Jackson, Charles, 76
Jaehn, Tomas, 57, 192n83
jail sentences, 137
Johnson, Jackson, 162
Johnston, Joseph, 49, 157
Jones, John, 68, 69, 72, 154–55
judge-jury interactions, 146
judges. See white American judges
judges and marriage, 139, 210n9
judicial structure, changes in, 48–49
judicial system, Mexican and American compared, 50
juror qualifications, 148–49
jury system, 48, 138
justice, discriminatory implementation of, 123
justice, social control versus, 136

justice system, New Mexican, 49
Kearny, Stephen Watts: governor appointed by, 51; judges appointed by, 49, 147; patrónes importance recognized by, 9, 47–48; Santa Fe, march into, 161; Vigil y Alarid proclamation read to, 43
Kearny Code: criminal punishments covered in, 136, 142–43, 147, 156; impact of, 52; indentured servitude written into, 71, 153, 154; juror qualifications covered in, 148–49; larceny law covered in, 67, 193n112; overview of, 48; patrónes attitude concerning, 50–51, 142–43, 147; patrónes importance recognized by, 9; sentence length covered in, 75, 196n160
King, Lovalerie, 46
kinship networks: as cultural capital, 114; dominance by, 19; importance of, 9; of landholders, 76; positions secured through, 77; as power source, 12, 173
knifings, assaults as, 148
knifings, fatal, 111, 126–27, 204n14

La Bajada Mesa, 10
laborers: crimes committed by, 70; increase in, 22; Mexican population and whites compared, 64; patrónes versus, 134; as prisoners, 75; small farmers forced to become, 21, 55, 56, 110; statistics, 61
labor gangs, 154
labor market, 65
LaFree, Gary, 4, 46, 78, 111, 203–4n10
Lamy, Bishop Jean Baptiste: appointment of, 7, 53; clergy purged by, 110; crimes against, 45–46, 78; as gringo from France, 9; Hispano priests, relations with, 53–55, 86; land dispute, involvement in, 1–2, 172; priests' fees criticized by, 23
land as commodity, 56
land distribution: by age, 59, 60, 62t, 115t; inequality of, 21, 23, 123, 134; during territorialization, 56–59, 57, 61
landholders, Hispano: agricultural commodities exported by, 55; American authorities, cooperation with, 12; American territorialization impact on, 114–15; autonomy of, 3; Bourbon reforms impact on, 16, 23; clerics defeated by, 1–2; as conference attenders, 51–52; corporal punishment, views on, 70–71; decline in, 115; decrease in small, 14; entrepreneuralism of, 8; greed of, 135; as jurors, 96; labor force needed by, 18; land, additional acquired by large, 16, 21; occupational breakdown in Santa Fe County, 21t; opportunities, expanding,

234

173; power wielded by, 1–2; relations between, 117; relations with others, 2–3; resources monopolized by, 8; rise of, 3, 16, 23; role in society, 59; rule justified by, 32; territorialization impact on, 48; vecinos, proportion to, 22; violence used by, 3; women as, 11
landholding Mexican families, interrelations among, 9
landholding Nuevomexicanos: after American conquest, 3, 57, 72; crimes against, 73; as privileged class, 129; wealth sought by, 8
land inequality, increase in, 21, 23, 123, 134
Lang, Private, 129, 130
"language" (term), 124
larceny: conviction rates for, 150; crimes other than, 158, 159; examples of, 45–46; factors contributing to, 14, 46, 67; Hispanos and whites compared, 66t, 73, 73, 78; hypotheses concerning, 5; increase in those accused of, 7; problem of, 65–76; rates, 5, 146; resistance in form of, 46; whites and vecinos compared, 72–73, 158–60; women charged with, 11
larceny law(s): in American territorial period, 47, 48; evolution of, 46, 67, 193–94n112
larceny punishment: corporal punishment, 70, 136; fines, 157; indentured servitude, 72, 154–55; patrón behavior and American law compared, 48; stiffening of, 146–47
Larson, Robert, 141
lashes: as basic punishment, 153; deterrent, ineffectiveness as, 71; ethnic and class dominion through, 137; examples of, 67, 68, 69, 70, 136; increase in punishments through, 156; landholder views on, 71; larceny and other crimes compared, 158; politico attitudes concerning, 65, 146–47; white immunity to, 158–59, 160; of whites outside military, 74–75, 137
Latino communities, class differences within, xiii
Lavender, David, 72
law, unequal application of, 134
law enforcement, 114
lawlessness, misconceptions of, 45, 46, 49, 167
law officers, crimes committed by, 123, 124
laws, power of coercive and punitive, 114
LeCompte, Jan, 32, 33, 34, 185n103
legal institutions, 112
Lenoia, Maria Antonia, 98, 162
Lerragota, Benito, 68
Leyva y Rosas, Padre Jose Francisco, 55
Lippie, Justin, 158
The Little Lion of the Southwest (Simmons), 1
livestock, stealing, 71

Long, Horace, 162, 215n149
Los Ranchos, 107
Louisiana's Livingston Code, 48
Lovato, Felipe, 109, 110, 126
Lovato, Jesus, 121–22
Lovato, Juana Maria, 121–22
lower-class subsistence, 46
Lucero, Antonio, 45
Lucero, Juan, 45
lynchings, 79, 91, 92–93, 160, 163, 164–68

Machebeuf, Joseph P., 23, 53, 54, 86
machismo, 107
Madrid, Juan, 161
Manifest Destiny, 79
manslaughter versus homicide, 91, 91t
Márquez, Andrés, 100, 101
Márquez, José María, 101
marriage, judges and, 139, 210n9
Martin, Francisco, 109, 110, 125, 126
Martin, Henry, 74
Martin, Jesus, 128
Martin, Maria, 71
Martinez, Adela, xiii, 15, 41, 52, 54–55
Martinez, Francisco, 105
Martínez, Mariano, 102, 103
Martínez, Padre Antonio José, 15, 41, 52, 54–55, 86, 140
Martínez de Lejarza, Mariano, 27
Martinez home, xiii–xiv
matrones, children of, 59
McCaren, Thomas, 132
McGuire, Phillip, 70
McKanna, Clare V., 107, 108
McLaughlin, William, 121
mean property, increase in, 115
mentally ill, crimes by, 97–98
mercantile capitalism, 55
merchants, property owned by, 57–58
Mercure, Joseph, 133
Merritt, C. H., 162
Messervy, William, 157
Mexican-Americans, territorial government offices held by, 86
Mexican central government: centralization efforts, resistance to, 16–17, 18; distant settlement defense beyond means of, 18; drift from, 15; economic problems, 30; funding challenges, 24; weakness of, 30, 185n87
Mexican citizenship, 28
Mexican direct rule, transition from, 114
Mexican federal officials, economic aid lacking from, 18, 183n27
Mexican independence: kinship network

Mexican independence (*continued*)
dominance after, 19; local government support lacking after, 23–24; patrón rise after, 6, 15, 26; power vacuum created by, 16; regionalism after, 30
Mexican infrastructure, 23–24, 42
Mexican legal system, 97–98, 103
Mexican officials, relations with others, 3
Mexican Party, 140
Mexican period: crimes in Sante Fe County during, 74; hierarchical social structure during, 12; Hispano relations with others during, 3; homicides during, 81, 99, 101–3, 134–35; inequality of, xvi; laws during, 77; New Mexico justice during, 49; patrónes divisions dating to, 140; patrón-vecino relations during (see patrón-vecino relations: during Mexican period); stories drawing parallels to, 1–2; white settlers during, 73–74
Mexican regionalism, 16
Mexicans, soldier attitudes toward, 62
Mexican soldiers, 74, 99, 100, 101–3
Mexican state, limits of, 16
Mexican-style loyalty, traditional, 71
Mexico: economic conditions, 18; New Mexico relationship with, 23–24; political instability, 18, 183n26; trade regulations loosened by, 6, 180n21; traveling conditions in, 24–25; weakening of, 42
Mild, Christian, 104, 105, 106
military, American: criminal cases, involvement in, 50, 190n40; criminal code written by, 71, 195n138; property belonging to, 57; punishments for crimes, 137
military courts, cases in, 74, 196n151
military courts, punishments used in, 71, 195n138
military power, abuse of, 130
mining sector, 19–20, 24
Miranda, Isidoro, 168
Missourians, 163
Missouri's Organic Acts, 48
Mitchell, A. J., 105
Mocho, Jill, 49
Monterrey County, California, homicides in, 125
Montoya, Felix, 102
Montoya, Jose, 68, 69
Montoya, Pablo, 41, 51
Moran, Peter, 119
Morgan, George, 105
Mower, Horace, 152
Moya, Antonio, 102, 103
Mueller, Christian, 69
Muffin, Thomas, 72
muggings, 45–46, 53, 55

mules, theft of, 75, 76
Muñoz, Pedro, 102
Murphy, Lawrence R., 139, 210n13

Narbona, Antonio, 28
Natal, colonial rule in, 138, 209n7
National Hispanic Cultural Center, xiii
Navajo: conflict with, 7, 13, 114, 142; defense against, 6, 142; displacement of, 8; slave raids against, 153; as slaves, 153, 155
New Mexico government, funding for, 18, 140, 183n27
New Mexico governor: American merchants, relations with, 19, 42; power of, 139, 210n13; taxes, legislature and, 140
New Mexico infrastructure, 87
New Mexico justice, white American criticism of, 49, 164
New Mexico legal code, 48
New Mexico legislative assembly, addresses of, 169, 175–78
New Mexico legislature, 80, 88, 139, 210n13
New Mexico LowRider Art and Cultural Exhibit, xiv
New Mexico regions, 9, 10
New Mexico statehood, 52
New Mexico vs. Louis Dorrance, 158–59
New Spain, economic policy and reforms in, 19–20. See also Bourbon Reforms (1750-1788)
nonviolent crimes, 74, 196n153
Nuevomexicano culture, 76
Nuevomexicano homicides: in early territorial period, 89–90; intentional, 109, 112, 127–28; political stability as factor in low rate of, 107; rates, 108; wave of, 123, 134; white homicides compared to, 79, 99, 111
Nuevomexicano judges, 49
Nuevomexicano jurors, 97, 138, 147, 151, 160, 161
Nuevomexicano legal system, white settler attitude concerning, 98
Nuevomexicano merchants, 25
Nuevomexicano priests, 7, 53
Nuevomexicanos: American view of, 48; Armijo, Manuel, accusations against, 37–38; assault, increase in, 122; assault between males, 118–20; autonomy of, 107; breaking point for, 134; charges against, 93–94; in Civil War, 169–72; community, 80; crimes committed by, 108, 111, 123; criminal conviction rates for, 149; criminal convictions, 138; dispossession of, 65; economic conditions experienced by, 20–21;

farmer-laborer shift for, 18; fines imposed on, 157; formal institutions, new imposed on, 2; as jurors, 149; landholdings of, 8, 57; political domination by, 80–81, 172; population decline, 146; power held by, 77; power struggle involving, xiii; Southwest Hispanos (general) compared to, 82; space reclaimed by, xiv; territorialization as experienced by, 172; traditions, protection of, 139; us-versus-them mentality, 83; violence among, 111; voices of, 173–74; wealth of, 8, 116; white settlers, relations with, 80, 93–94, 95

occupations: of ethnic groups, 11; of Hispanos, 59; individuals without, 21, 22, 57, 61, 89, 183n49; Nuevomexicano and white American defendants compared, 157; in Sante Fe County, 21t, 22t; shift in, 21–22
Ochoa, Jose, 157
O'Clark, Allen, 98
older landholders, wealth and land owned by, 59
opportunism, xvi
Organic Law of 1850, 86
Ortega, Gregorio, 157
Ortis y Salazar, Francisco, 158, 159
Ortiz, Alejandra, 105–6
Ortiz, Antonio Maria, 155
Ortiz, Blas, 126
Ortiz, Candido, 93, 95, 121
Ortiz, Eugenio, 68
Ortiz, Gaspar, 59
Ortiz, Manuel, 67
Ortiz, Padre Juan Felipe, 15, 53, 54, 73, 86
Ortiz, Tomás: fines imposed by, 157; law, custom of ignoring evoked by, 52, 190–91n56; as probate judge, 49, 140; theft from, 67
Ortiz y Alarid, Gaspar, 127
Ortiz y Chávez, Rafael, 170
Otero, Antonio José, 49, 102
Otero, Manuel, 172
Otero, Miguel, 140, 141, 142
Owens, Richard, 67, 131, 193n112
ownership, legitimizing idea of, 46

Pacheco, Maria, 157
Pacheco, Valentine, 126–27
Padilla, Antonio, 126–27
Palace of the Governors, xiv
Papin, Alexander, 163
pardons, granting of, 159–60, 166
partido system, 55, 56
patrón-American business partnership, 46, 47, 80
patrónes: actions, understanding, 14; American authorities, relations with, 13, 48, 52, 172, 173; American legal system, attitude concerning, 50; American merchants, relations with, 31; during American territorial period, 44, 46, 76, 172; Anglo settlers, relations with, 47–48; assets, 112; autonomy of, 17, 18, 50, 83; capital punishment, exemption from, 166; centralist movement opposed by, 30, 33; children of, 59; Chimayo Rebellion, distancing from, 40; Chimayo Rebellion, role in, 34, 35, 37; in Civil War, 170–71; complexity of, 167; contraband allowed by, 27; crimes against, 70, 75; dangers to, 4; divisions among, 140; foreign-born whites, dealings with, 64; jury selection influenced by, 148–49; Kearny Code impact on, 52; land acquisitions for, 18–19, 56, 57, 76–77, 112; land held by, American recognition of, 56; Mexican central government, relations with, 18, 24; outside forces, response to, 2; own interests, action in, 29, 30, 134, 137, 140–43, 147; political representation, 87; power and influence of, 12, 106; property owned by, 58; property taxes opposed by, 88; punishment racial aspects ignored by, 153; railroad advocated by, 141, 142; relations among, 19, 42; resistance by, 16–17; revenge taken by, 93; rise of, 6–10, 15, 17, 19, 21, 26, 55; role in society, 59; servants indebted to, 154–55; smuggling by, 27–28, 156; tax reforms impact on, 35; term defined, 3; territorialization, collaboration in, 174; territorial legislature dominated by, 80; United States Army negotiations with, 47; violence among, 112, 114; white American judges, attitude toward, 148; white criminals not targeting, 72; white settler relations with, 48–49, 70, 76, 107
patrón single-issue focus, 142
patrón-vecino relations: American authority impact on, 5, 6, 106, 108, 114; during American territorialization, 7, 47, 48, 64, 65, 72, 76, 137, 172, 173; Chimayo Rebellion impact on, 34; in Civil War, 171; homicide and, 90; during Mexican period, 5, 6, 15–16, 24, 29, 65, 83, 114; Nuevomexicano political representation as departure from, 86; patrón attitude toward vecinos, 32; patrón power as feature of, 14, 18; rupture, 13, 109–10, 123, 142; social contract, 17, 110; Spanish colonial legacy impact on, 12; vecino thefts, 67
Peacock, George, 67
Pena, Manuel, 67–68
Perea, Francisco, 170
Perea, Tomas, 67, 193n112
Pérez, Albino: appointment of, 31; background,

Pérez, Albino (*continued*)
  30; conflict with, 37; killing of, 34, 37, 38, 42; opponents of, 18, 32–33, 34, 36; patrónes, clash with, 35; people serving under, 51; successor of, 38; tax reforms, 35
perjury, 70, 75, 156, 157, 158
persons indebted in servitude, 3, 180n11
Peters, Louis, 76
petty larceny: American legal focus on, 77; among vecinos, 68; documentation spotty for, 74, 196nn152–53; factors contributing to, 67; legal definition of, 67, 193–94n112; punishment for, 71, 146–47, 156
Phiffner, Antonio, 158
Phillips, William, 132
Pino, Facundo, 112, 169, 175–78
Pino, Juan Estevan, 33, 34, 35
Pino, Miguel E., 72, 86–87, 154, 155, 170
Pino, Nicolas, 170, 171
Pino, Pedro Bautista, 21
Pino de Ortiz, Gertrudis, 59
Plan de Tomé, 38–40, 41
plenario, 50
Poinsett Joel, 31–32
political alliances, 76–77
political factions, 4–5
political institutions, 112
political stability, low homicide rate correlation to, 81, 198n11
politicos (politicians): and American legal system, 138–47; corporal punishment, views on, 70; courts, authority over, 50; fines imposed by, 157; laws passed by, 71, 72; patrónes as, 80, 110, 134, 137, 172; political system dominated by, 138–39, 147; white immigrants targeted by, 89, 90
poor Hispanos: resistance to unequal system of power, 2, 46; white settlers, new compared to, 78. See also vecinos
poor Nuevomexicanos: ethnic and class dominion over, 136–37; relations with others, 2–3; worsening conditions for, 135. See also vecinos
poor villagers, larcenies committed by, 46
population movement, tracking, 111–12
Porter, Charles, 156, 160
position, protection stemming from, 116–17
Potter, Henry, 74–75, 137
power, abuse of, 123
Powers, James, 98
Prada, Estefanio, 128–29
Prada, Francisco, 130
Presidio, soldiers of, xiv–xv
Price, William, 105

priests, 7, 23, 47, 53–55, 76, 86
Prince, L. B., 38
prison, indentured servitude as alternative to, 154
prisoners, lists of, 77
prisoners, occupations of, 75
prison sentences, vecinos and white Americans compared, 156
private property, communal lands conversion into, 46
probate courts, 146
process of investigation (summaria), 49
property crime, increase in, 137
property ownership by occupation, 58
property range, 115
property taxes, 88, 139–40, 143
property value, 46, 57, 188n7, 191–92n83
public defender, 101, 201n99
public homicides, 82, 91–96
public lands, 47, 56, 173
Puebloans: Chimayo Rebellion, role in, 34, 35, 37, 38, 42; conflict with, 13, 17, 25, 114; defense against, 6, 38; displacement of, 8; homicides among, 97; incitement of, 31; indentured servitude for, 153; labor and goods, priest loss of right to collect, 23; priest dealings with, 23; punishments for, 70; in rebellion, 37; treaties with, 7; vote denied to, 139, 210n13
punishments: by ethnicity, 138; Mexican and territorialization periods compared, 50, 65; racialized, 138, 153–60, 173; vecinos and soldiers compared, 64; vecinos and whites compared, 13, 137, 138, 153, 160

Quinn, James, 52
Quintana, Francisco, 127
Quintana, Nicolas, 121

race as construct, 48
race war, 95
racial groups, 4–5
racial lines, convictions and punishments along, 138, 166
racism, 6, 53, 79
Rael, Jesus, 116, 155
Rael, Maria, 97
Rael, Pablo, 97, 98
Rael, Refugia, 97
railroad, 141, 142, 173
rape, 11, 46, 121
Raymond, William, 74
Read, Benjamin, 37
real estate, 115
Reconstruction, 163

INDEX

Reed, Judge, 93, 95, 200n63
regionalism, 24, 30
Rencher, Abraham, 88, 136, 158, 159–60, 209n4
Republicans, 140
resistance, xiii, xiv, xvi, 1–2
Ribera, Jose Gregorio, 119–20
Ribera, Luis, 155
Ribera, Matias, 130, 165
Rino, Samuel, 67, 74–75, 137
Rio Abajo, 9, 10, 32, 140
Rio Arriba: districts in, 49; interests, 140; landholders from, 36; maps, 9; overview of, 10; patrónes from, 34; in rebellion, 40, 41
Ritch, William G., 138
robbers, corporal punishment against, 70, 156
Robbinsdean, Charles, 73
Rodríguez, Antonio, 121–22
Rodríguez, Miguel, 101
Rodriguez, Rafael, 128
Rodríguez, Ramon, 126
Rogers, Thaddeus M., 122, 133–34, 162, 167–68
Roival, Albino, 118
Romero, Elvino, 105
Romero, Jesus, 104–5, 118–19
Romero, Jose Patricio, 105
Roth, Randolph, 4, 120
Rowan, William, 119, 122
Rowe, John, 75
Roybal, Theodorita, 127
Ruival, Antonio, 161
Ruival, María Espíritu Santo, 96–97, 160–61
ruling class, 46, 136
rural areas, criminal records scarce for, 74, 196n153

Sacramento, California, homicide in, 80
Salas, Silvario, 118
Salazar, Damasio, 102
Saldivar, Mary Carmen (Alarid), xvi
Salvador, Manuel, 67
Sanchez, Apolonia, 120–21
Sanchez, Jose Maria, 68
Sandoval, Fernando, 118
Sandoval, Justo, 67
Sandoval, Manuel, 98, 100
Sandoval, Pedro, 136, 137, 159
Sandoval, Santos, 158
San Francisco, homicide in, 80
San Joaquin, California, homicide in, 80
Santa Anna, Antonio Lopez de: American trade restrictions imposed by, 25; Armijo, Manuel compared to, 28, 41; Armijo, Manuel governorship granted by, 42; centralist movement backed by, 30; supporters of, 33; Texas expedition launching and aftermath, 31–32
Santa Barbara, California, homicide in, 80
Santa Cruz de la Cañada, canton of, 39, 40, 41
Santa Cruz de la Cañada municipal council, dissolving of, 36
Santa Fe: Alarid family move from, xv, 173, 217n21; American authority over, 2; American march into, 42; assaults in, 111; during Civil War, 171–72; homicides in, 89–90; Jefe Político in, 35; military occupation of, 99; as state capitol, 10; as trade gateway, 25
Santa Fe County: American conquest aftermath in, 76; Anglo settlers in, 61, 63; crime increase in, 78; crimes during Mexican period, 74; demographics of, 11, 13–14, 72, 82, 84; executions in, 163; Hispanic adult males in, 63; Hispano and white crime compared, 66t; homicides and homicide risk in, 5, 79–80, 81, 90–91, 90t, 107, 111, 130–31; importance of, 10–12; land concentration, increasing in, 115; land inequality in, 23; larceny spike in, 47; lynchings in, 93; migration from, 6, 66–67; migration in and out of, 78; occupational structure in, 21t, 22t; patrónes in, 167; police force, corruption of, 123; property ownership in, 58, 58; real estate ownership in, 57, 57, 60, 62t; representatives from, 88; risk, calculating for, 4; US Army composition in, 64; vecino conviction rates in, 149, 151; vecino migration from, 56, 173; violence in, 111, 204n10; wealth inequality in, 116; white population in, 13–14, 76, 197n170
Santa Fe County Jail, 77, 130
Santa Fe Trail, 8, 15, 16, 26, 27
Santiago, Christobal, 119, 206n53
Santiago, Felipe, 68
Saracino, Francisco, 33, 35
Savalas, Marcelino, 133–34, 167
Scallion, Gillion: guilty verdict against, 164; lynching of, 79, 90, 92–93, 95, 163, 165; sense of entitlement, 91–92; shooting by, 98
Scott, James, 46
Seguro, Jose, 67, 160
self-defense, 128, 132–33, 163, 167
Sena, Dolores, 118, 154–55
Sena, Francisco, 102
Sena, Ignacio, 118
Sena, Jose, 68, 70, 71, 72
Sena, Jose E. (Jose Euligio), 126
Sena, Miguel, 33, 37
Sena y Baca, Jesus, 158
Sena y Baca, Jesus Maria: assault against Garcias, involvement in, 112, 114, 116; cases,

239

INDEX

Sena y Baca, Jesus Maria (*continued*)
  involvement in, 121; friends of, 118; influence of, 124; in law enforcement, 117, 122; noise riot, involvement in, 119; Tapia, Ignacio aided by, 93, 94–95
servants, 22, 56, 61. See also indentured servitude
servitude and slavery compared, 72, 195n140
sheep-trading families, 8
sheriffs, crimes committed by, 116–17, 122, 124, 130
Sibley, Henry H., 169
Siete Leyes, 30–31
Silva, Jesus, 119
Silva, Mauricio, 156
silver and silver mines, 20, 24
Simmons, Marc, 1, 2
Simms, Andrew Jackson, 134, 162, 163
Slave Code Act of 1859, 140, 141–42
slave courts and trials, 150, 151
slavery, 31, 72, 140–42, 195n140, 195n142; indentured servitude compared to, 153–54, 155, 213n98; opposition to, 176
slave stealing from master, 46
small arms (defined), 89
small farmers, 10, 18, 22, 55–56
Smith, Hugh N.: Council office held by, 107, 203n133; as judge, 49, 98; shooting of, 79, 85, 90, 91, 92, 163, 165
Smith, J. O., 157
Smith, Joseph, 67
social change, 46
social control, 65, 136
social histories, 45
social homicides, 82, 99–106
social institutions, decline of, 46
social relations, foundations for disjointed, xvi
social welfare program, 65, 192–93n101
socioeconomic change, 3, 180n10
socioeconomic class identity, calculating arrest and conviction based on, 5
soldiers, American: crimes committed by, 130; entertainment for, 65; killing of, 129–30; vecinos, treatment compared to that of, 64; violent behavior by, 89; vote denied to, 88–89, 139; young whites as, 61–62
South, secession of, 142
Southwest, Mexicanos in, 82, 84
Spanish colonial legacy, 12, 50
Spanish language, official proceedings conducted in, 87, 145, 146
Spanish mercantilism, 16, 23
Spiegelberg, Salaman, 133–34
Spite Houses, xiii–xiv
spousal homicide, 96–97, 120, 160–61

Staab, Adolpheus, 133–34
state-sanctioned violence, 123
state violence, 71, 156
status hierarchies, low homicide correlation to legitimate, 81, 198n11
Stephenson (Texan), 91–92
Stevens, Thaddeus, 141
Stone, Thomas, 76
street crime, 46, 111, 203–4n10
subcomisario, duties of, 33, 186n110
subsistence items, theft of, 65, 67
Sumner, Edwin V., 82–83
Sunseri, Alvin, 86, 87, 88, 140

Tafoya, Altagracia, 127
Tafoya, Antonio, 157
Taos, clergy in, 54–55
Taos Rebellion, 1847: co-conspirators in, 157; criticism of, 51; hierarchical social structure defended during, 12; passive resistance in, 171; territorial legislature sessions held after, 88; treason trials stemming from, 166; white American judge attitude concerning, 148
Tapia, Andres, 93, 95, 118, 119–20
Tapia, Felix, 118
Tapia, Francisco, 118, 119
Tapia, Ignacio, 93, 94, 95, 118, 119, 120, 161
tariffs, 29
taxation power, 139–40
taxes, patrón opposition to, 142, 172
Taylor, William B., 23
teamsters, 95–96, 107, 137, 139
Tejanos, 14, 31, 82, 181n53
Tenorio, Estevan, 126
Tenorio, Jose, 68
territorial autonomy, laws declaring, 88–89
territorialization: capitalist-centered system under, 114; class-based experiences and responses to, 5; definition and overview of, 46–47; homicide risk in early years of, 4; land distribution changes during, 56–59, 57, 61; Nuevomexicano experience of, 172; patrón collaboration in, 174; patrón-vecino relations during, 7; as process, 47–65; turning point in, 112
territorial judges, American, limited documentation of, 50
territorial legislature, 80, 88, 139, 210n13
Texans: homicides and homicide attempts by, 79, 91, 164–65; lynching of, 164–66; Missourians compared to, 163; patrón repudiation of, 142; relations with others, 92; vecino resistance to, 173; war declared against, 169, 175–78

Texas, war declared against, 169, 175–78
Texas expedition of 1836, 31
Texas Incursion, 1841, 17, 83, 176
Texas Law, 48
Texas rebellion, 31
theft, 46, 65. See also burglary; larceny
threats, 71
Tigar, Michael E., 46, 65
tithing, 54
Tórrez, Robert, 162, 215n149
trade: with Americans, 18, 20, 24–25, 26; embargoes, removal of Spanish, 17–18; relationships, 9, 19; restrictions on, 29; sector, 19–20
traditional fandangos, 99–100, 100, 103, 104, 202n116
transcontinental railroad, 141, 142
trapping, illegal, 28–29
treason, 166
Treaty of Guadalupe Hidalgo, 56
Trujillo, Antonio Maria, 166
Trujillo, Francisco, 127
Tuley, John, 93, 200n63
Twitchell, Ralph Emerson, 143

Union army, Hispanos in, 170–71
United States, trade networks into, 25
United States Army, 47, 64
United States conquest of New Mexico, 17, 42–43
United States Indian Service (USIS), 65, 192–93n101
US federal government resources, appeal for, 87–88
US federal territory, New Mexico incorporation into, 46–47
US-Mexican War: patrónes after, 44; propaganda from, 62; veterans of, 62, 68, 72; violence after, 79
Utes, 7, 10, 20, 153
uxoricide, 96–97, 120, 160–61

Vagrancy Act of California, 153–54
vagrancy law, 89, 143
Valdez, Francisco Esteban, 101
Valdez, Juan, 100–101
Valdez, Marcelino, 122, 167
Vaughn, E. L., 104, 105, 160
vecino assaults, 110
vecino crime: factors contributing to, 64–65; increase in, 6–7; property crime, 137; punishment for, 64; tracking, 5; type breakdown, 151; white crime compared to, 78
vecino criminal convictions and conviction rates: and black conviction rates compared, 150, 151; case breakdown, 149; crackdown on vecinos, 148; crime type breakdown, 150; racial bias as factor in, 152–53; and white conviction rates compared, 13, 138, 147, 149
vecino homicide: changing nature of, 125–27; domestic violence, 96–98; ebbs and flows of, 5; homicide among vecinos, 109; increase in, 110; overview of, 107; surge in, 110; and white homicide compared, 81, 82, 106, 108, 110t, 165
vecino larceny: common patterns, 67; crimes other than, 158; increase in, 12, 47, 65–66; types of, 68; white larceny compared to, 73, 74, 75
vecino punishments: and black punishments compared, 153, 213n88; capital punishment, 168; deterrence as aim of, 136; larceny versus other crimes, 158; Mexican and territorialization periods compared, 50; and white punishments compared, 136, 137, 147, 153, 159, 160
vecinos: abuse of, 19, 42; actions, understanding, 14; American territorialization impact on, 12, 46, 47, 55, 64–65, 76, 78, 114–15, 172–73; American view of, 48; Chimayo Rebellion, role in, 34, 35, 37, 38, 42; church, relations with, 23, 52–53, 55; in Civil War, 170, 171; criminal court cases against, 50; definition and overview of, 3–5; farmer-laborer shift for, 16, 18; as farmers, 22; gambling halls, 143; government, attitude toward, 81; as homicide victims, 152; incitement of, 31; increase in, 55–56; indentured servitude for, 71–72; interracial violence by, 86; juries, barriers to serving on, 149; justice application, unequal toward, 147; Kearny Code impact on, 52; as laborers, 8; land, loss of, 13, 56, 57, 64–65, 66, 76, 110; landholders, large, proportion to, 22; as landholders, 61; legal apparatus and, 77; legal processes, cooperation with, 49–50; New Mexico transition as experienced by, 5; patrón-American partnership at expense of, 47; patrón attitude toward, 32; poverty of, 6, 10, 17, 23, 173; punishments for, 13, 70; relations with others, 10–11 (see also patrón-vecino relations); resistance by, 16; resources monopolized by, 8; stories of, 174; violence against, 6; violence by, 135; white American judge crackdown on, 148; white homicides against, 98–99, 102–3; white settler, new status compared to, 78, 111; white settler, relations with, 106; as witnesses, 104–5, 106
Vigil, Antonio, 41

241

INDEX

Vigil, Donaciano: American military government, attempt to depose, 88; Armijo, M. destruction of documents noted by, 38; as New Mexico governor, 51–52; as patrón, 59; in political machine, 172; speeches, 33, 34, 35–36, 41–42, 186n115; Trujillo, A. M., petition on behalf of, 166
Vigil, Maurillo, 8
Vigil y Alarid, Juan Bautista, 33, 35, 42–43
violence: after US-Mexican War, 79; quantitative picture of, 4; random acts of unprovoked, 81–82
"violent conduct" (term), 124
violent crimes: focus on, 45; increase in, 111, 112; records of, 74, 196n152
Virginia Slave Trials, 151
voting, illegal, 107

Ward, Levon, 76
Watts, John, 76
wealth, distribution of, 116, 117
wealth, personal versus property value, 57, 191–92n83
wealth concentration, 14, 59, 172
wealth inequality: increase in, 12, 15–16, 56, 134; larceny spike due to, 47; within property-owning class, 46, 188n7
Webb, James Josiah, 27, 157
Weber, David, 26, 31
Wells, George, 68
West, Elias P., 52
western counties, Santa Fe County compared to other, 82
Western law, 136
Wheaton, Theodore, 148, 162
Wheeler, Henry, 163
white American criminal convictions: crime type breakdown, 150; fines imposed for, 157; low, factors contributing to, 151–52; Nuevomexicano convictions compared to, 138; vecino convictions compared to, 13, 149
white American criminals, laws targeting, 139
white American judges: capital punishment sentencing rare for, 161; corporal punishment, attitude concerning, 147; jail sentences handed down by, 156; jury instructions given by, 148, 151–52; politico opposition to appointment of, 144–45; racism of, 138; selection of first, 147; vecinos, attitude toward, 76, 148; white jurors selected by, 137, 152; white juror work with, 138; white settlers as, 48–49
white American jurors: capital punishment sentencing rare for, 161; racial bias of, 136–37, 147, 149, 152; vecinos, crackdown on, 151; white bias of, 138
white American males, laws targeting, 144
white Americans: capital punishment, views on, 160, 162–63, 167; capital punishment for, 160, 163, 167; Texans compared to other, 166
white crime: persistence of, 82–83; property crime, 137; punishment for, 136; vecino crime compared to, 78
white homicides: and Californio homicide compared, 84, 90, 90t; ebbs and flows of, 5; factors contributing to, 90; and Hispano/Mexicano homicide compared, 90, 90t, 103, 113; motives for, 108; and Nuevomexicano homicide compared, 79, 99, 111; rates, 129; unpunished, 166; and vecino homicide compared, 81, 82, 106, 108, 111, 165; against vecinos, 98–99; verdicts in cases of, 106; within white community, 130–34
white immigrants: alienation of, 81; California and New Mexico compared, 86; land claimed by, 13; Mexicano reactions toward, 83–84; as murderers, 135; Nuevomexicano trade partnerships with, 8; obstacles to success, 76, 106; political representation versus population size, 85; politicos targeting, 89; relations with others, 3, 9; Santa Fe County, departure from, 83; violence by, 81–82. See also foreign-born whites
white jurors, 137, 138, 147, 156
white larceny: decrease in, 76, 197n170; and Hispano larceny compared, 73, 78; types of, 73; vecino larceny compared to, 73, 74, 75
white-Nuevomexicano relations, 169–70
white privilege, 153, 162, 167–68
white punishments: leniency in, 138; and vecino punishments compared, 136, 137, 147, 153, 159, 160
white settlers: American and European, fissures between, 131; assault by, 111, 113, 122; in California, 72, 108, 195n144, 196n145; California and New Mexico compared, 84–85; code of honor among, 108; crimes against, 69, 70; dangers to, 4; demographics of, 11; federal posts held by, 76; homicide among, 11, 103–4; as judges, 48–49; as jurors, 98–99, 104, 106; migration from New Mexico, 73, 196n148; narratives by, 173–74; Nuevomexicanos, relations with, 80, 93–94, 95; pardons granted to, 159–60; patrónes, relations with, 48–49, 70, 76, 107; politico laws targeting, 143–44; politics, attempt to enter, 107; poor Hispanos compared to, 78; population decline, 82–83; population movement, 111–12; poverty

242

impact on, 77–78; property lost by, 57; property owned by, 65, 192n95; relations with others, 3; ruling group attitude toward, 48; territorial government offices held by, 87; vecinos killed by, 96; vecino status compared to, 78, 111; violence among, 11; violence by, 76, 78, 79

white settlers, new: civil disobedience by, 12–13; crimes committed by, 74; homicides and homicide risk elevated by, 80, 91–92, 106; larceny committed by, 72–74; migration from New Mexico, 73; obstacles to success, 90, 108; occupations, 73–74; political power, weak of, 7, 85; relations with others, 14; violence by, 12–13, 85–86, 90

white traders, 3, 10, 74

white trading partners, 7

white violent crime, 111–12, 113

white women, attacks on, 121

widowed matriarchs, 59

Wilson, Richard L., 27

witness testimonies, transcribing, 49

women: attacks on, 11, 120–22, 123; in criminal court documents, 11; as homicide victims, 11, 120, 127; power and influence of, 11; wealth of, 59

women of color, attacks on, 121–22

Woods, Manuel, 74

Young, Ewing, 28–29

young Hispanos, property owned by, 61

Yucatan, rebellions in, 32

Zacatecas, 24, 32, 184n57

Zacharias, Jose, 125

www.ingramcontent.com/pod-product-compliance
Lightning Source LLC
Chambersburg PA
CBHW020944230426
43666CB00005B/164